The Book of Shen

third edition

Mark Tarver

FastPrint
Publishing

http://www.fast-print.net/bookshop

THE BOOK OF SHEN (THIRD EDITION)
Copyright © Mark Tarver 2015

A catalogue record for this book is available from the British Library

ISBN 978-178456-213-7

First Published 2015 by
Fast-Print Publishing of Peterborough, England.

Dedicated to Magdalena Pamesa (1940-2010)

Contents

Part II Working with Types

Appendices

A Conceptual Dependency Table

The following table indicates the immediate dependencies between the chapters of this book. A dependency of chapter *m* on chapter *n* means that chapter *m* cannot be understood without a grasp of the material in chapter *n*.

Chapter	Title	Dependencies
1	Beginnings	
2	Starting Shen	
3	Recursion	2
4	Lists	3
5	Strings	2-4
6	Higher Order Functions	2-4
7	Assignments	2, 3
8	Vectors	2-4
9	I/O	2-5
10	Macros and Packages	2-4
11	Exceptions and Continuations	2-5, 9
12	Non-determinism	2-4
13	Shen-YACC	2-4, 12
14	Lambda Calculus	2-4
15	Kλ	2-4, 10, 11, 14
16	Writing Good Programs	2-4
17	Types	2-9, 11
18	Sequent Calculus	2-4, 12
19	Defining Types	2- 9, 11, 17, 18
20	Proof and Control	2-11, 17-19
21	Abstract, Semi-Abstract and Algebraic Datatypes	2-11, 17-19
22	The SECD Machine	2-9, 11, 14, 15, 17, 18
23	Shen Prolog	2-4, 12, 18
24	The Compilation of Sequent Calculus	2-4, 8, 11, 12, 18, 23
25	System $\mathfrak{J}$	2-9, 11, 12, 14, 18, 23
26	The Correctness of $\mathfrak{J}$	2-9, 11, 12, 14, 18, 22, 24

Preface to the Third Edition

The third edition of this book eliminates the errata identified in the second edition. The chapter on model checking in the second edition has been replaced by a chapter on abstract, semi-abstract and algebraic datatypes. Material on control of the search space in type checking has been brought forward in the text.

Acknowledgements

I'd also like to thank the sponsors of this work and the members of the 2011 committee who helped make Shen possible on all the platforms on which it has appeared. I'd like to single out the following members for special appreciation.

Vasil Diadov; for supporting Shen financially from 2011-2012.

Ramil Farkshatov, not only for his ports to Python and Javascript, but for his important contribution to chapter 9 in arguing successfully for an approach to I/O based on bytes.

Bruno Defarrari for his excellent web work in converting an amateur web site into a professional one.

Willi Riha for long discussions on Shen and for careful proof reading.

David Holdcroft and Rod Burstall, many moons ago, for both hiring me.

And finally Magdalena Pamesa, who did not understand computers, but whose devotion made all this possible.

Mark Tarver
February 2015

1 Beginnings

1.1 Declarative Programming

One of the first skills that every student acquires in learning to program is to use **assignments**. An assignment has the form "let X = X+1", whereby a variable is given a value in a program. In most languages, assignments are foundational; programs cannot be written without them. If we take a language like C or Fortran, and subtract the ability to write assignments, then the result is no longer a viable programming language. These languages are called **imperative**, **procedural** or **non-declarative** languages.

Declarative languages can survive this kind of subtraction. If we take a language like Shen and subtract assignments, then the result is still a viable programming language. In the case of **pure declarative programming languages** like Miranda^{TM}, where there are no assignments, this subtraction leaves the language unchanged. So in a declarative programming language, any computation can be described without the use of an assignment statement. Declarative languages are themselves partitioned into **functional programming languages**, like Shen and Miranda^{TM}, and **logic programming languages**, of which **Prolog** is the most widely used.[1]

This gives an accurate, but shallow characterisation of the procedural/declarative distinction. It does not explain why some programmers have been attracted to the declarative paradigm; as John Hughes (1990) puts it.

It says a lot about what functional programming isn't (it has no assignments....) but not much about what it is. The functional programmer sounds rather like a mediaeval monk, denying himself the pleasures of life in the hope it will make him virtuous. To those more interested in material benefits, these advantages are totally unconvincing.... It is a logical impossibility to make a language more powerful by omitting features, no matter how bad they may be. Clearly this

---

[1] The partition is a little fuzzy; during the '80s several experimental languages explored the connection between logic and functional programming and the result was a series of hybrid languages such as LOGLISP (Robinson and Sibert (1980)) and LIFE (Ait-Kaci and Podelski (1993)) that shared features of both paradigms. Other systems like POPLOG (Sloman (1985)), provide an environment for communicating between programs written in both styles.

characterisation of functional programming is inadequate. We must find something to put in its place - something that not only explains the power of functional programming but also gives a clear indication of what the functional programmer should strive towards.

To begin to meet Hughes' requirements, it is necessary to understand how functional programming originated and how the split between procedural and declarative programming began. We have to return to the beginning of computer science.

1.2 Mathematical Foundations

Computer science theory began with the attempt to make precise the idea of an **algorithm**. The name derives from the ninth-century Persian mathematician Mohammed ibn Musa al-Khowarizmi who described simple procedures for carrying out addition, subtraction, multiplication and division in the new Indian decimal system. The Cambridge English Dictionary defines an algorithm as

a set of mathematical instructions that must be followed in a fixed order, and that, especially if given to a computer, will help to calculate an answer to a mathematical problem

In ordinary speech, an algorithm is sometimes expressed in the native tongue of the speaker. So the rules for subtracting numbers are taught to us using conversation and examples. Conversational vocabulary is often imprecise and frequently rather verbose at the task of describing algorithms. Take this example, of an explanation of how to find square roots using Newton's Method of Approximation (a method studied in chapter 6 of this book).

Take the number you want to find the square root of and take a guess at the square root. If you are happy with your guess, then fine. If you want to have a better approximation than this guess, then take the average of the guess together with the result of dividing the number you want to find the square root of by that guess. That will give you a better guess. Keep on doing this until you have a guess you're happy with.

These instructions might serve their purpose, but they are vague, long-winded and difficult to follow. The example shows very clearly the weakness of relying on English, or any other conversational language, to express algorithms. Though the Cambridge definition is good enough for casual use, it is not formally precise. But not until the twentieth century did mathematicians try to construct a definition of an algorithm that was formally precise.

When they did so, two leading mathematicians, Alan Turing in England and Alonzo Church in America, came up with different answers. However, the answers, though different, later proved equivalent, in the sense that any procedure that could be represented as an algorithm according to Church's answer, could be represented as an algorithm according to Turing's answer. It was rather as if two biologists trying to characterise the species of tigers, had defined them as "the species of which the largest land carnivore native to India are members" and as "the members of the species *Panthera tigris*". In a similar way, the definitions of Church and Turing were different, but they characterised the same group of processes.

The **Church-Turing thesis** is that any adequate definition of an algorithm will prove equivalent in this way to the definitions provided by Church and Turing. Since the idea of "adequate" is not formally precise, the Church-Turing thesis is not mathematically provable. However, in practice other definitions of "algorithm" offered since Church and Turing, by for example, Post (1943), have proved equivalent to Church and Turing's versions in exactly the way that the Church-Turing thesis predicts. So most computer scientists are happy to accept that these definitions of "algorithm" capture what is important for them about this word.

Both Church and Turing realised that trying to characterise algorithms in terms of what could be said in English was a waste of time. Instead, they both invented different formal languages in which algorithms could be more clearly expressed. In addition, both men provided a series of rules for manipulating this formal language in a set manner. An algorithm was defined by both men as a procedure that could be expressed in their chosen language. However, the language that each chose was very different, and the differences were the foundation for the later procedural-declarative split in programming.

Turing's idea was that an algorithm could be represented as a series of instructions that could be executed by a rather simple machine, that later became known as a **Turing Machine** (figure 1.1). A Turing machine consists of three components.

1. An endless stream of tape segmented into an infinite number of adjacent squares. Some of these squares may have symbols on them.

2. A mechanical head that positions itself over a square and which can read the symbol on that square or overwrite it. The head can also move to the square to the left of the square it is currently over or to the square to the right.

3. A program or series of instructions that tell the mechanical head what to do. It is assumed that a Turing machine is always in an internal state. These states are usually identified by the natural numbers 0,1,2, 3.... An instruction has the form

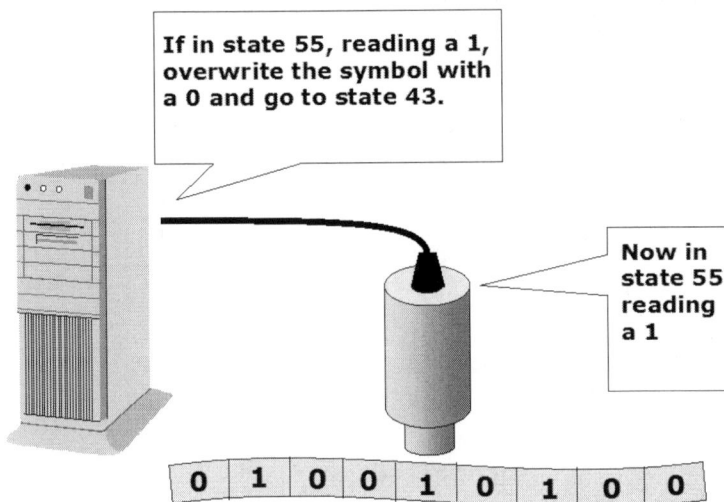

Figure 1.1 A Turing Machine Executing a Program Instruction

If in state n, reading symbol S_j, then execute action A_k and jump to state q_l.

Action A_k could be the action of halting (the computation ends), or of overwriting the scanned symbol by another symbol or of moving to the left adjacent square or the right adjacent square. A program for a Turing machine is a set S of instructions or quadruples $<n, s_j, a_k, q_l>$ such that if $<n, s_j, a_k, q_l> \in$ S and $<n, s_j, a_k', q_l'> \in$ S, then $a_k = a_k'$ and $q_l = q_l'$ (i.e. there are no conflicting instructions about what the machine should doing any given situation). The machine halts when it is reading symbol s_j in state n where for all a_k and for all q_l, $<n, s_j, a_k, q_l> \notin$ S (i.e. the machine has no instructions about what to do when reading symbol s_j in state n).

Turing's machine contains no restrictions on the number of symbols it can read or print, but only two are necessary - conventionally they are 0 and 1. To set a Turing machine running, the machine is started in its lowest state, scanning the leftmost of a series of 0s and 1s; this series represents the input to the machine. The output is what is left on the tape when the machine halts. An algorithm is defined as any terminating procedure that a Turing machine can be programmed to perform.

Turing's approach is easily appreciated by anybody with a simple working knowledge of the architecture of a computer. The states of the Turing machine correspond to the line numbers of a conventional program; the action of jumping to a new state is mirrored in the JUMP of assembly language. The endless tape is just a model of the bounded memory of the computer and the head of the Turing machine becomes the CPU of the digital computer. When World War II began a few years after Turing published his paper on the Turing machine, there was a demand for real computing engines that could tackle the difficult tasks of cracking enemy codes and calculating bomb and shell trajectories. Turing's pencil-and-paper creation provided a blueprint for engineers, and consequently became immensely influential in the design of the modern digital computer.

Across the Atlantic in America, Church had very different ideas. For many years, mathematicians had worked with the idea of a **function**. Put simply, a function is a mathematical object that receives one or more inputs and delivers an output. Algorithms too, receive inputs and deliver an output, so it is natural to consider that algorithms are a subclass of the class of functions. Usually when mathematicians wish to explain the properties of a function, they use equations to do it. Here is an equation that converts Fahrenheit to Centigrade.

$C = 5/9 \times (F - 32)$

We can easily distil a procedure from this equation that reads.

To convert Fahrenheit to Centigrade, subtract 32 from Fahrenheit and multiply by 5/9.

A more complex example comes from Boyle's Law, which relates the pressure of a confined gas to the volume it occupies and its temperature. According to Boyle's Law, if a confined gas is kept at pressure P_1, occupying volume V_1 at temperature T_1, and then the gas has its pressure, volume or temperature changed so that it then has pressure P_2, volume V_2 and temperature T_2, the change will satisfy the equation.

$(P_1 \times V_1) / T_1 = (P_2 \times V_2) / T_2$

So, from Boyle's Law, it is possible to construct a function that given the old temperature of the gas, its pressure and volume, and the new pressure and volume, will produce as output the new temperature. The equation is

$T_2 = (P_2 \times V_2 \times T_1) / (P_1 \times V_1)$

Again, we could easily distil a procedure from this equation. Here is one.

To calculate T_2, first multiply P_1 by V_1 to give a result R. Then multiply P_2 by V_2 by T_1 to give a result S. Then divide S by R.

However, we could also distil this procedure.

To calculate T_2, first multiply P_2 by V_2 by T_1 to give a result S. Then multiply P_1 by V_1 to give a result R. Then divide S by R.

The result is the same whichever procedure we choose. The point about calculations involving Boyle's Law is that they are algorithmic or mechanical, whichever order we choose to do them in, and we should always get the same result. This gives another way of looking at algorithms. *Rather than identify an algorithm with a procedure consisting of a fixed series of steps, we can think of an algorithm as a function that can be characterised in a certain way.* What marks the function as computable is not that the way we compute with it is predetermined (because in the case of Boyle's Law this is not true), but the way in which the function can be described. This insight is the beginning of functional programming.

Nevertheless, things are not so simple. For though all algorithms can be represented as functions, not all functions are algorithms. Consider this function over the natural numbers.

f(n) = 1 if there are n successive 7s in the decimal expansion of π.
    0 otherwise

This describes a function, but not one we can easily use to compute because the decimal expansion of π is infinitely long. If we wanted to compute the value of *f*(1000) we would have to search for 1000 successive 7s in the decimal expansion of π. So far 1000 successive 7s have not been detected in the decimal expansion of π, but this does not mean that they are not there. At best, all we can do is expand π looking for 1000 successive 7s and this may take forever. However the concept of an algorithm requires a terminating procedure that is guaranteed to return a definite answer. Plainly, the function *f* does not define any such procedure. *f* is a **non-computable** function.

Once we begin to look for non-computable functions, they swarm in number. Some are bizarre, for example the function that maps a person to 1 if his maternal grandfather hated boiled eggs is still a function (though a queer one); but obviously there is no algorithm for determining one's ancestors' egg-eating habits. The problem is that ordinary language allows us to concoct functions in a very unrestricted way. If the class of computable functions, to which algorithms correspond, is to be isolated from the broader class of functions as a whole, we need a special language and vocabulary to do it.

This is what Church provided in devising the **lambda calculus**[2] as a notation for describing computable functions. Along with this formalism, Church gave a precise set of rules for reasoning with and for simplifying expressions of this notation. To perform a computation, in Church's terms, was to apply a function to an input, and to derive a value. By formally stating the rules for deriving values, Church defined a model of computability. An algorithm was just a computable function. A computable function was an expression that could be written in the

---

[2] Which we study in chapter 14 of this book

lambda calculus so that when it was supplied an input (again written in lambda calculus), by a fixed and finite series of applications of the rules of lambda calculus, an expression could be derived which could be simplified no further and which represented the solution.

In contrasting the approaches of Turing and Church, it is easy to see why Turing, rather than Church, was immediately influential in shaping the course of computing. Turing provided an actual model of a computing engine. Church's definition of computability gave little clue as to how the lambda calculus was to be implemented. Moreover, some of Church's constructions, like his representation of the natural numbers as lambda expressions, were very convoluted. Here, for example, is Barendregt's representation of 2 in pure lambda calculus.

$$(((\lambda x \, (\lambda y \, (\lambda z \, ((z \, x) \, y)))) \, (\lambda x \, (\lambda y \, y)))$$
$$(((\lambda x \, (\lambda y \, (\lambda z \, ((z \, x) \, y)))) \, (\lambda x \, (\lambda y \, y))) \, (\lambda x \, x)))$$

The example is a little unfair, because functional programming languages do not use pure lambda calculus to represent numbers. However, it is easy to understand why an observer would conclude that Church's definition of computability was of no practical use in computer science. Not until the '60s did computer scientists begin to explore the consequences of applying Church's ideas. In the intervening 20 years, engineers and programmers built their work on the paradigm given by Turing. This was to be fateful in the development of programming as a discipline.

1.3 The American Experience

When World War II ended, America emerged as the richest and most powerful nation on the planet, producing at one point 40% of the world's GDP. Computer engineering gravitated naturally to a country that was rich in émigré scientists and natural resources. Consequently the early years of functional programming belong to America.

These early years are the early years of the American work into **Lisp**. Lisp was the offspring of an intellectual marriage conducted by John McCarthy between Church's work on the lambda calculus and an earlier language called **IPL** (Information Processing Language) that was invented by two American scientists Newell and Simon. Newell and Simon were pioneering the study of automated deduction and needed a flexible language in which to program the computer to simulate human thought. Conventional languages require all information to be predeclared in variables or arrays. What Newell and Simon wanted was a language in which structures could be dynamically built up and broken down in response to the intellectual requirements of the program. They struck upon the idea of using the list as the fundamental data structure on which to organise their procedures.

The basic idea is that, whenever a piece of information is stored in memory, additional information should be stored with it telling where to find the next (associated) piece of information. In this way the entire memory could be organised like a long string of beads, but with the individual beads of the string stored in arbitrary locations. "Nextness" was not determined by physical propinquity but by an address, or pointer, stored with each item, showing where the associated item was located. Then a bead could be added to a string or omitted from a string simply by changing a pair of addresses, without disturbing the rest of the memory.[3]

In fact, the pair consisting of an item of a list and the pointer to the address where the next item is stored is known as a **cons cell pair**. Functional programming languages were to copy IPL in making lists the central data structure in programming. The representation of Newell and Simon using pointers to addresses is the machine basis of the cons representation of a list discussed in chapter 4.

About that time, John McCarthy, then a young mathematician at MIT, was doing preliminary work on a program called 'Advice Taker' that would allow a computer to receive instructions in English. McCarthy knew about IPL and had read Church's work. McCarthy observed that many computable functions could be defined by equations, but only by equations that mentioned that function on both sides of the = sign. One simple example is the function.

$factorial(0) = 1$
$factorial(n) = n \times factorial(n - 1)$ where $n > 0$

These equations are not circular (unlike $factorial(n) = factorial(n)$) because they enable the calculation of a factorial by the calculation of the factorial of the number preceding it. Eventually the simplest case (0) is reached and the computation ends. Such functions are called **recursive** and in McCarthy's new language, recursion was the principal means of defining computable functions. McCarthy also borrowed on use of lists by IPL. But he improved on IPL by adding a reclamation program that allowed the computer to reclaim memory when it was running short, by marking out the symbol structures that the computer no longer needed. This process became known as **garbage collection**.

The resulting language, called **Lisp**[4] (McCarthy 1960), was remarkable. Lisp programs were themselves written as lists of symbols, which meant that Lisp programs could be written which would write Lisp programs. A Lisp program

---

[3] Simon (1991), p 212.

[4] Short for LISt Processing Language.

could even modify itself while it was running, or receive as part of its input some other Lisp program and apply it to another part of its input.[5]

The important advance of Lisp was that it freed the programmer from having to consider the architecture of the computer. By allowing the programmer to define algorithms as functions, and abstracting away from the need to consider allocating or reclaiming memory, Lisp left the programmer free to work on the problems that interested him. To give an analogy, Lisp was transparent as regards the architecture of the machine on which it ran: writing Lisp code was like looking at the problem through a clear window. Writing in a procedural language like assembler requires not only thinking about the problem, but also thinking about the architecture of the underlying machine which is explicit in assembly language. Looking at a problem through assembler is like looking at it through a stained or dirty window, or trying to see to the bottom of a pond on which there is a lot of surface glare and reflection.

So it turned out that the very feature of functional programming that kept Church's ideas in the shadow of Turing's, that is the lack of a specific machine for executing computations, was also its greatest strength! But it was strength purchased at a high price. The structure of a procedural language is dictated by the design of the digital computer, which works by executing a series of commands and shifting data from one address to another. In a programming language like assembler, which reflects the internal architecture of the computer, programs are likely to run quickly. In contrast, a language that ignores the architecture of the machine needs a very sophisticated compiler to relate the language to the computer.

In the early years of Lisp, such sophisticated compilers did not exist. Moreover the garbage collection process was itself expensive, causing the computer to hang for vital seconds while memory was reclaimed. Even the list processing feature, one of the most important ideas to come from computer science, was costly because a lot of the computer's memory was tied up in storing pointers from one address to the next. Functional programming acquired an immediate reputation for inefficiency that confined it to research labs for another 20 years. In the value scales of the '60s, when machines were slow and CPU time was expensive, inefficiency was a serious charge.

By the early '70s, Lisp programmers recognised that the performance lag in Lisp programs was a serious bother, and that the foundation of the problem was the distance of the architecture of the computer from the actual Lisp. Clever compilation was one answer and this was done with versions of Lisp like **MacLisp** (developed for the DEC-10 mainframe); but another was to design the

---

[5] This is called **higher-order programming** and was implicit in Church's lambda calculus; we study this technique in chapter 6.

architecture of the machine around the Lisp language. These machines became famous as the **Lisp machines**.

In the context of their times, the Lisp machines were startlingly innovative, and they introduced many ideas that have since become part of high street computing; such as windows and the mouse (developed for the Xerox Lisp machine). The first serious Lisp machine was **CADR,** which anticipated the personal computer years before the IBM XT.[6] High tech companies like Symbolics and Lisp Machines Incorporated mushroomed around research into Lisp machines and larger companies like Xerox and Texas Instruments also fielded their own Lisp machines.

But Lisp machines were in the end to fail. At the time of writing, no manufacturer is engaged in the production of Lisp machines. Ironically, these machines were to operate to the detriment of the spread of Lisp as a commonly used programming language. By choosing to work on Lisp machines, whose cost confined their use to favoured researchers in well-funded laboratories, the Lisp machine community isolated their work from mainstream computing. Ordinary programmers could not afford to run programs that used 10Mb of memory, when 1Mb was seen as a lot. While Lispers worked in ivory towers, always looking to the future, procedural programmers working in **C** (another product of the '70s) concentrated on developing programs that ran on shoebox machines. By directing their efforts to standard computer architecture, the procedural programmers established a near unchallengeable dominance on conventional machines.

Stimulated by the investment of billions of dollars that the Lisp machine vendors did not have, these shoeboxes were eventually to surpass the performance of the dedicated Lisp machine. By 1990, conventional workstations running efficient Lisp compilers could equal the performance of Lisp machines. By 1996, the humble PC could rival the performance of the workstation. Lisp machine vendors went bankrupt.

Lisp itself survived and in 1984 Lisp was standardised into **Common Lisp**. This had the advantage of providing a common language standard for Lisp implementers to work with, and one that was largely downwards compatible with several existing Lisp dialects. The disadvantages were that the resulting language was very large and many of the bad features of Lisp, that McCarthy himself later acknowledged were in the language, were frozen in the Common Lisp language definition. Across the Atlantic, British computer scientists like David Turner were finding fault with Lisp and British computer science was making its own contribution to the history of functional programming.

---

[6] At the top of CADR's microcode listing was a quote from the rock opera *Tommy* "Here comes a man to bring you a machine all of your own".

1.4 The British Experience

One of the earliest workers in functional programming this side of the Atlantic was Peter Landin who in 1964 published a paper describing a method for mechanically evaluating lambda calculus expressions on a computer. The design, called the **SECD machine** (short for Stack-Environment-Control-Dump), examined in chapter 21, influenced many later compilation strategies, including the **Functional Abstract Machine** (Cardelli, 1983) that was used to compile Standard ML.

Lisp was designed as a functional language that supported a model of computation called **eager evaluation**. In eager evaluation, all the inputs to a function are first evaluated before the function is set to work computing the final answer. Sometimes this is not a sensible strategy; a simple example is the problem of computing $f(factorial(100))$, where f is defined as $f(n) = 0$. Since f always returns 0, no matter what the input, computing the value of $factorial(100)$ is a waste of time. In an eager language like Lisp, $factorial(100)$ would be computed, but in a language that uses **lazy evaluation** it might not. The defining characteristic of lazy evaluation is *procrastination* - only evaluate when you have to. **SASL**, developed by David Turner (1976, 1979), was a functional programming language that was driven by lazy evaluation.

Automated deduction had already provided an important input into functional programming through Newell and Simon's work on IPL. In 1979, it provided another. In that year Milner, Gordon and Wadsworth published their work with the **Edinburgh LCF** marking an important development in both functional programming and automated reasoning. In 1976, Milner had published a paper describing how functional programs could be proved free of type errors in a way that was entirely mechanical. A type error is an error that arises when a function is applied to an input that it cannot compute (the multiplication of two strings is an example).

To accomplish this, Milner used the **unification algorithm,** studied here in chapter 22, and developed for automated reasoning by Robinson in 1965. Using Milner's algorithm (called the $\mathcal{W}$ algorithm), a proof that a program was free from type errors could be executed by a computer. This was an important advance in the production of reliable software and in their 1979 publication, Milner, Gordon and Wadsworth introduced the first functional programming language to incorporate this new technology - the Edinburgh MetaLanguage or **Edinburgh ML**. Since Edinburgh ML, nearly every new functional programming language has incorporated some form of type checking and these languages form the class of what is called **statically typed languages**. .

Edinburgh ML became upgraded and standardised as **Standard ML**. An important addition to the upgraded version was **pattern matching**, which was an old idea that went back as far as **SNOBOL** that was invented in Bell Labs in

1962. SNOBOL was a text processing language that allowed the programmer to isolate pieces of text by searching for patterns. Since all functional languages exploit the use of lists, it is much easier to use patterns to isolate the needed elements than to write functions which search for them. The use of **pattern-directed programming** is common in functional programming today and is used throughout this book.

The '80s in Britain were a very fertile time for the implementation of new models for compiling functional languages. This area is rather outside the ambit of this book, but we shall mention David Turner's (1979) paper, which suggested that **combinatory logic** could be used to implement functional languages as an alternative to lambda calculus. In many ways, combinators are even simpler than lambda calculus. Following Turner, scientists experimented with new models for compiling functional programming languages; **combinators, supercombinators, graph reduction**, and **dataflow machines** were researched in this decade. The result was that the performance gap between functional and procedural languages was narrowed in that decade.

But while implementers of functional languages poured their efforts into building better compilers and new functional programming languages such as Haskell, procedural programming proceeded to capitalise on its lead by expanding into new application areas. An important step in the spread of the procedural paradigm was the invention of the language **C** by Dennis Ritchie and Ken Thompson in 1973. Ritchie and Thompson were working in Bell labs on the first release of the **UNIX** operating system and they needed a fast, portable programming language that was close to assembler but not tied to specific machines. They designed C - a functional programmer's bad dream. Riddled with assignments, and clinging close to the architecture of the computer, C programs run extremely quickly. The success of the UNIX operating system allowed C to spread to nearly every computer, and its good performance meant that programmers took it up as the language of choice when writing CPU-intensive programs for machines of limited power.

The success of the procedural paradigm at a time when machines were too slow to support the functional approach, left computing with a culture that is recognisably procedural. UNIX and **Windows** are built on the foundations of C, and the shell languages that support these systems are recognisably procedural. The **X-windows** system is likewise C-based and the paradigms for building graphical user interfaces are based on procedural languages like **Visual Basic**. **Java** has emerged as a leading language for building Internet applications, and its antecedents are C and **C++.** The 21st century programmer expects access to graphical interface builders, numerical packages, debugging tools, Internet capability, electronic mail, multi-user capability, sound and graphics to be within reach inside his chosen medium. At the end of the twentieth century, functional languages, for all their mathematical sophistication, still presented the user with a cursor and a command line that was recognisably '70s in style.

Luckily in the first decade of the twenty-first century, much ground was made up outside of academia. The creation of **Python** (van Rossum, 1990) provided a language which, if not purely functional, had a core and approach that was recognisably functional and a syntax that was more immediately appealing than Lisp. In contrast to Lisp and other functional languages, Python has a well-supported library with a large and active commercial community and a great deal of support amongst service providers.

In 2007, Rich Hickey introduced **Clojure** which was viewed by many as an overdue modernisation of Lisp. Clojure offered tight integration of a Lisp-like language to **Java** and Java libraries and compilation into the **Java Virtual Machine.** In addition, Hickey developed fast vector manipulation algorithms and provision for multiprocessing which made Clojure a hit for many users. Consequently many programmers rediscovered the power of Lisp through working with Clojure.

The result is that functional programming has experienced something of a renaissance in the opening years of the twenty-first century and the future of the discipline looks bright. It is fairly certain, as the new multiprocessor machines come into common usage, that the clean computational model of functional programming will offer one of the best ways of utilising this power without becoming trapped in the complexities of assignments.

1.5 The Forerunners of Shen: SEQUEL

The history of Shen began in 1989, when I was working as a research assistant at the LFCS in Edinburgh. At that time, I worked in Lisp, and to improve my productivity, I wrote a 700 line Lisp program which translated pattern-directed functional code into reasonably efficient Lisp.

While cycling in the Lake district in the spring of 1990, I had the insight that since type checking was inherently deductive in nature, the type discipline of a language could be specified as a series of deduction rules. Using the techniques of high-performance theorem-proving, these rules could be compiled down into an efficient type checker. The type-discipline would be free from the procedural baggage of low-level encoding and presented in a form that was clear, concise, and accessible to experimentation and extension by researchers in type theory. This was a bold conception that seemed eminently reasonable, but which in fact took a further 15 years of development to realise completely.

The prototype development was the language SEQUEL (**SEQUE**nt processing **L**anguage), written in Lisp and introduced publicly in 1992 and to the International Joint Conference on Artificial Intelligence in 1993. SEQUEL anticipated many of the features of Shen, in particular the use of Gentzen's sequent notation to formulate the type rules. SEQUEL actually contained the type theory for a substantial portion of Common Lisp (over 300 Common Lisp system functions were represented in SEQUEL) necessitating a sizeable source code program of more than 23,000 lines. SEQUEL was not only designed to support type secure Common Lisp programming, it was also supposed to support direct encoding of theorem-provers by giving the user the power to enter logic rules in sequent notation to the SEQUEL system.

SEQUEL sustained Andrew Adams's (1994) reimplementation INDUCT of the Boyer-Moore theorem-prover. His M.Sc. project was written in 6,000 lines of SEQUEL, and generated nearly 30,000 lines of Common Lisp, and gained him a distinction. In 1993, state-of-the-art was a SPARC II, so power was limited. Loading and type checking INDUCT took several minutes.

SEQUEL was a compromise of the ideals of deductive typing for several reasons.

1. The sequent compiler was inefficient.
2. Since SEQUEL was heavily configured to support Common Lisp, the language was not consistent with lambda calculus (since Common Lisp does not support lambda calculus features like currying and partial applications).
3. SEQUEL inherited case-insensitivity from Common Lisp and the use of the empty list NIL to mean false.
4. SEQUEL lacked a formal semantics.
5. SEQUEL also lacked a proof of type correctness.

Over ten years and two countries all these problems were eliminated.

Until 1996, SEQUEL stayed in operation with minor amendments. Most of my creative time from 1993-1996 was spent writing poetry. SEQUEL continued to support final year projects, but late 1996, I returned to computer science research.

1.6 The Forerunners of Shen: Qi

The first modest change was to introduce case-sensitivity and the use of proper booleans in place of T and NIL. Large parts of the implementation were rewritten, reducing the source code by several thousand lines. In 1998 overloading in SEQUEL was dropped and the entire list of function types was placed on a hash table. This was in a sense a move away from Lisp and towards a cleaner model and a smaller language. The plus was the elimination of 10,000 lines of code.

In late 1997, I applied for three years unpaid leave from my job as a lecturer in order to concentrate on finishing this work. One year was granted, and from 1998 to 1999 a lot of work was expended in providing the new language with a formal type theory. After a false start, the current type theory was evolved in 1999 and the semantics was developed between 1999 and 2000.

During that same period, a lot of work was done in testing whether deductive typing was really a practical option. Early results were not encouraging, 30 line programs could take as many seconds to type check. The goals of deductive typing - complete declarative specification and a type checking procedure that was conceptually distinct from the rules that drove it - meant that performance-enhancing hardwired hacks were not allowed. Eventually a technology was developed and the performance benchmarks showed that a 166MHz Pentium under CLisp could just about run the system. At the time of writing, 3.8 GHz machines are on sale, which will no doubt make these old challenges into programming molehills.[7]

The implementation went through two complete rewrites. The first rewrite was very thoroughgoing and introduced partial applications and currying into the language, making it lambda calculus consistent.

At this time I was deeply involved in Taoism, and feeling the need for a name for the new implementation called it *Qi* – the name for the life-force in Taoism.

In 2001 a robust version of a compiler-compiler (first devised by my colleague Dr Gyuri Lajos) was built and used to encode some of the complex parsing routines needed in Qi. This was the compiler-compiler **Qi-YACC** which was later used in Qi.

In 2002 I left the UK for America bearing Qi 1.4 with me. Qi 1.4 was used to build almost the whole of Qi 2.0 which was a clean rebuild of the whole system. Qi 2.0 was never released however, because of an improvement to the type checking algorithm $\mathcal{T}$ used in Qi 1.4.

In 2003, I developed the experimental algorithm $\mathcal{T}*$ and type checking gained a factor of 7 speedup over 1.4. In late 2003 I put the finishing touches on a correctness proof for the type theory and $\mathcal{T}$ and $\mathcal{T}*$. In 2003 Qi won me the Promising Inventor Award from the State University of New York. Carl Shapiro, currently of Google, attended my functional programming class at Stony Brook that same year. He was to exert a significant influence on development of Qi.

In 2004, Qi 2.0 was revised to work with $\mathcal{T}*$ and the result was Qi 3.2. After some more debugging and revisions, Qi 4.0 emerged. Carl's interest in SEQUEL made me revisit my old work. In 2005 I constructed a new model for compiling Horn clauses called the **Abstract Unification Machine**. The AUM compiles

---

[7] It is worth noticing though, that a 166MHz Pentium is about the slowest machine that could feasibly run Qi 1.4 and that this machine appeared about 1997. Therefore the goals of deductive typing that were formulated in my 1990 paper were about seven years short of having the technology they needed to work.

Prolog into virtual machine instructions for a functional language. AUM technology gave 100 KLIPS under CLisp and 400 KLIPS under the faster CMU Lisp and quadrupled the speed of the type checker. The beta version, Qi 5.0, used prototype AUM technology. Qi 6.1, which used the AUM, again improved performance.

Qi 6.1 was also the first version of Qi to use the **preclude** and **include** commands for managing large type theories. Qi 6.1 was released in April 2005, along with the web publication of *Functional Programming in Qi* and at the same time as the creation of **Lambda Associates**. At 6,500 lines of machine-generated Lisp, Qi 6.1 was three times smaller than the SEQUEL of 1993 and was placed online in April 2005.

The appearance of Qi was swiftly followed by a serious illness that laid me up for 2006 and most of 2007. Following a partial recovery in 2008, a factorising version of the Qi compiler was introduced which made Qi competitive with the fastest hand-compiled Lisp code.[8] The revised language, Qi II, corresponding to the text *Functional Programming in Qi* was released in 2008.

1.7 Shen

The chain of events that precipitated Shen began with an invitation to address the European Conference on Lisp in Milan in 2009. The invitation came about because the invited speaker, Kent Pitman, had been himself taken ill with cancer which meant, understandably, that he had to withdraw. I was invited to take his place.

Ironically I was ill too and at first declined, since I was healing at that time. But the organiser was frantic and I finally accepted. My address proposed a language like Qi but based on a primitive instruction set that was so small that it could be translated onto almost any platform. Qi had been implemented in Common Lisp, which has over 700 system functions. But of that large number, Qi only used 118 system functions in its implementation.

I estimated that Qi could be implemented in an even smaller instruction set of less than 50 primitive functions, and that they should be so carefully chosen as to be easily implemented and widely portable. This instruction set defined a very simple Lisp, closer in spirit to Lisp 1.5, the original Lisp from which the gargantuan Common Lisp descended. This micro-Lisp was later to be called **Kλ**.

This idea was the subject of my talk at the conference, but it was ignored since my criticisms of Common Lisp were not well received. Feeling I was wasting my time, I left computer science in 2009 and journeyed to India. Shen therefore

---

[8] www.lambdassociates.org/studies/study10.htm

remained a dream until my partner Dr Pamesa called me back and asked that I complete the work. She died before this was done.

In 2010 an appeal was launched to fund this research and happily it succeeded. Armed with some means of subsistence, I returned to designing and building the new implementation during 2011. Eventually what emerged in September 2011 was a clean, portable language under a $free license, implemented in 43 primitive Kλ instructions running initially under Common Lisp. The new language was named *Shen*, the highest form of energy in Taoism and the Chinese for *spirit*.

Shen introduced quite a number of features not found in Qi; including string and vector handling through pattern matching, the capacity to read streams from non-text files through an 8 bit reader and an advanced and powerful macro system. Designed for portability, Shen was slower than Qi which was optimised for Lisp, but vindicated itself rapidly and within 18 months Shen had been ported to Common Lisp, Scheme, Clojure, Javascript, Java, Python, JVM and Ruby. During this process Kλ acquired three more primitives.

The first edition of this book was written during the first part of 2012 and was a fairly hasty rehash of *Functional Programming in Qi*, adapted to meet the needs of the new language standard. The resulting text was accurate, but rather improvised during a period when I was in and out of clinics.

Following an improvement in 2013, I decided to rewrite the text to cover more carefully the details of Shen and to impart more flow and depth to the treatment of the language. The more leisured approach and the value of being able to see the results of the early work into Shen allowed me make additions and improvement to the work. The second edition was published in 2014.

In September 2014, Aditya Siram gave a talk on Shen at StrangeLoop which led to a general interest in Shen and a demand for the language to be placed under open source. I started an appeal for the open source community to pay for Shen under a BSD license and eventually money was raised and Shen went under BSD in February 2015.

Later that same year, I revised two chapters in the second edition, focusing on the practical techniques for controlling type checking and the relation between Shen and languages like SML. These changes eventually made their way into the third edition, which is the one you are reading.

Further Reading

A discussion of the Turing machine and its properties is found in Boolos, Burgess and Jeffrey (2002). The lambda calculus is discussed in chapter 16 of this book, and references can be found at the end of that chapter. McCarthy (1960) describes the genesis of Lisp. Backus (1978), in his famous Turing award lecture, argues for the declarative paradigm, criticising imperative languages as "fat and weak". Turner (1982) develops the case for functional programming. Gabriel (1990) has an interesting discussion about why declarative programming (in the shape of Lisp) has not displaced the procedural paradigm. Introductions to functional programming and functional programming theory can be found in Bird and Wadler (1998) and Field and Harrison (1988). Introductions to Lisp are provided in Winston and Horn (1989) and Schapiro (1986). Abelson's and Sussmann (1996) is an excellent introduction to functional programming in Scheme - a dialect of Lisp. Shrobe (1988) is a good review of the history of the Lisp machines just before their demise. Wikstrom (1987) and Paulson (1996) introduce SML. An overview of Miranda^{TM} is given in Turner (1990) and Thompson (1995) is a book length introduction to Miranda^{TM}. **Haskell** from the University of Glasgow is a recent and popular addition to the functional programming family, Thompson (1999) is a good introduction.

Tarver (1990) reviews some of the earliest thoughts that led to SEQUEL. Tarver (1993) was an early principal publication of this approach and Tarver (2008) describes Qi.

Web Sites

The life and work of Alan Turing is beautifully presented in a web site dedicated to that purpose; Andrew Hodges' The Alan Turing Home Page (http://www.turing.org.uk/turing/) contains a wealth of information. The University of Arizona (http://www.math.arizona.edu/~dsl/tmachine.htm) provides links to several sites containing downloadable software and applets for simulating Turing machines. http://cm.bell-labs.com/cm/cs/who/dmr/chist.html offers an account of the development of C. The Association of Lisp Users (http://www.lisp.org/table/contents.htm) provides an extensive web site for Internet sources on Lisp including links to original papers on the history of Lisp. New Jersey SML offers a free high-performance ML (http://www.smlnj.org/). http://www.haskell.org is the web address for all things Haskell.

www.lambdassociates.org was the web site for Qi and the site is now archived on the Shen language web site. A 2008 address explaining Qi was recorded as an audio file http://www.lambdassociates.org/blog/l21.wmv. My 2009 address in Italy was postwritten and appears in Appendix D and this explains the motivation for Shen.

Part I

The Core Language

2 Starting Shen

2.1 Starting Up

If Shen has been configured according to the installation instructions, then the top level looks similar to figure 2.1

```
Shen, copyright (C) 2010-2015 Mark Tarver
www.shenlanguage.org, version 17.3
running under Common Lisp, implementation: CLisp 2.49
port 1.8 ported by Mark Tarver

(0-)
```

Figure 2.1 The Shen top level

The italicised portions may vary according to release and platform. The figure shows the Common Lisp implementation of Shen 17.3; should you be using another platform or a different version, the italicised text may be different.

The integer prompt shows that you are in the **read-evaluate-print loop**. Functional programming languages interact with the user at this level. The purpose of this loop is to receive the expressions that you enter, to evaluate them, and to print a response.[9] These expressions can be of various kinds. The simplest expressions that Shen evaluates are the **self-evaluating expressions** that evaluate to themselves. There are four kinds of self-evaluating expression.

---

[9] The symbol ^ within any input, followed by carriage return, will abort the current line input.

1. **Numbers:** this includes integers (-3, 78, 45), floating point numbers (2.89, -0.7) and e-numbers (12.6e14).

2. **Symbols**: this includes any unbroken series of symbols (except booleans, numbers, and strings) such as Mynameisjack, catch22.

3. **Booleans**: true and false.

4. **Strings**: a string is any series of symbols enclosed between a pair of double quotes such as "my name is jack", "catch 22". Notice that strings permit spaces whereas symbols do not.

An expression is evaluated by typing it to the Shen top level and hitting the return key. Figure 2.2 shows some self-evaluating expressions entered to Shen.

```
(0-) 9
9

(1-) "foobar"
"foobar"

(2-) hello
hello
```

Figure 2.2 Some self-evaluating expressions typed to the top level

Every time an expression is evaluated, the Shen top prompt reappears with an integer in parentheses which is the input number.

2.2 Applying Functions

Since typing self-evaluating expressions is not an exciting pastime, we will consider how to apply functions to inputs in Shen. There are three principal ways of writing functional expressions.

1. **Infix**; where the sign for the function comes between the bound variables. This is the usual practice in arithmetic where we write "2 – 1"; the minus sign comes between the "2" and the "1".

2. **Prefix**; the sign comes before the bound variables. So in prefix "2 – 1" would be written "- 2 1".

3. **Postfix**; the sign comes after the bound variables. So in postfix "2 – 1" would be written "2 1 –".

Shen functions are usually written in prefix form.[10] To apply a function f to inputs $x_1,...,x_n$, we enter $(f\ x_1,..,x_n)$ (figure 2.3).

```
(0-) (+ 1 2)
3

(1-) (+ (* 3 4) (+ 1 1))
14
```

Figure 2.3 Some simple applications typed to the top level

There are several ways of evaluating expressions in functional programming languages; one widely used model is **applicative order evaluation**, which is the one Shen usually uses. The evaluation procedure of applicative order evaluation is to first evaluate, from left to right, $x_1,..,x_n$ before applying f to the results of this evaluation.

Thus in figure 2.3, Shen first evaluates (* 3 4) to 12 and then (+ 1 1) to 2 before adding the two together. The result 14 is the **normal form** of the expression (+ (* 3 4) (+ 1 1)); that is, the result produced when the evaluation has completed itself without any error being raised. The **arity** of a function is the number of inputs it is designed to receive. In the case of * and + this is 2, and these are referred to as **2-place** functions. A function like + that is built in to Shen is a **system function**.

2.3 Repeating Evaluations

Typing ! followed by an integer n will repeat the input whose input number is n. !! repeats the last input. ! followed by a symbol s will repeat the last input $(f\ x_1,..,x_n)$ where s is a prefix of f (figure 2.4).

```
(0-) (+ 5.6 9.0)
14.6

(1-) !+
(+ 5.6 9.0)
14.6

(2-) !!
(+ 5.6 9.0)
14.6
```

Figure 2.4 Using ! to repeat evaluations

---

[10] However functions can be written to Shen in infix form using macros (see chapter 11).

The % command will print (without evaluating) every previous expression whose prefix matches what follows %. % on its own will print off all functional expressions typed to the top level since the session began. Where *n* is a natural number, *%n* will print off the *n*th expression typed to the top level since logging in to Shen.

```
(3-) %+
0. (+ 5.6 9.0)
1. (+ 5.6 9.0)
2. (+ 5.6 9.0)
```

Figure 2.5 Using % to print past inputs

2.4 Strict and Non-Strict Evaluation

All computer languages have some provision for detecting conditions operating within the program and then diverting the control of the program depending on whether these conditions are realised. The classic example is the conditional expression *if ... then ... else ...* which in one form or another is found in every computer language. Use of conditional expressions requires the use of **boolean expressions**, where a boolean expression is one that evaluates to either true or false. The *if ... then .. else ...* construction is found in Shen as a 3-place function if that receives

1. A boolean expression X.
2. An expression Y whose normal form is returned if X evaluates to true.
3. An expression Z whose normal form is returned if X evaluates to false.

Though this is all quite simple, it is important to know that conditional expressions are not evaluated using applicative order evaluation. The reason why is easily brought out by example. The 2-place function = returns true if the normal forms of its two inputs are the same, and false if are they are different. Suppose we evaluate (if (= 1 0) (* 3 4) 3) by applicative order evaluation.

(if (= 1 0) (* 3 4) 3)
⇒ (if false (* 3 4) 3)
⇒ (if false 12 3)
⇒ 3

The reduction of (* 3 4) to 12 in the penultimate step is quite unnecessary, because the result of evaluating (if false (* 3 4) 3) cannot depend on the evaluation of (* 3 4). A better evaluation strategy evaluates (= 1 0) to its normal form, and then evaluates the appropriate expression.

This latter form of evaluation is an example of **non-strict evaluation.** A strict evaluation strategy requires that every input to a function to be evaluated before the function is applied to the results. In a non-strict evaluation strategy, it is possible to return a normal form from an expression x even when there is a subexpression of x that has no normal form. The expression (if (= 1 0) (+ a a) no) evaluates to no in Shen, though the evaluation of (+ a a) will raise an error.

The cases function allows the concise expression of nested 'if's; for instance the expression

(if a b (if c d e))

can be written as

(cases a b
       c d
       true e)

If no cases apply an error is raised.

if is one of the 46 **primitive functions** of Kλ from which Shen is built (all the rest being definable in terms of the 46) and we shall point out these functions as we proceed.

2.5 Boolean Operations

A **boolean operation** is a function that receives booleans as inputs, and returns a boolean as a result. The function and is a boolean operation which on receiving boolean inputs X and Y, returns true if the normal forms of X and Y are true and returns false otherwise (figure 2.10).

```
(0-) (and (= 1 1) (= 2 2))
true

(1-) (and (= 1 2) (= 2 2))
false

(2-) (and true 4)
error: 4 is not a boolean
```

Figure 2.6 Using and

Again and expressions are not evaluated by applicative order evaluation. In the second input in figure 2.6, since (= 1 2) is evaluated to false, the value of (= 2 2) is immaterial. and is a **polyadic** function (i.e. it can receive a variable number of inputs) so that (and true true ..... false) is a legitimate construction.

The polyadic function or receives boolean inputs and returns true if at least one evaluates to true, and returns false otherwise. For similar reasons, applicative order evaluation is suspended here too.

```
(3-) (or (= 1 0) (= 2 2))
true

(4-) (or (= 1 0) (= 2 1))
false
```

Figure 2.7 Using or

and and or are also primitive. not returns true if its input evaluates to false and false if its input evaluates to true.

```
(6-) (not (= 1 1))
false

(7-) (not (= 1 2))
true
```

Figure 2.8 Using not

All other Shen function applications are evaluated by applicative order evaluation, which is a strict evaluation strategy.

2.6 Defining New Functions

Equational specifications are a simple way to begin to understand how functions are defined in Shen. For instance, the equation *return-b*$(a) = b$ defines a function *return-b* that receives a and returns b. The domain of *return-b* is the set $\{a\}$ and the range of *return-b* is the set $\{b\}$. Both the range and the domain are finite in size. If we want to add new elements to the domain and range then we add new equations. Often a function can be represented to Shen in the manner of a series of equations. The syntax is slightly different from the one used by mathematicians. First, the = is replaced by a -> and the bracket (is placed before the function symbol, so the first equation would appear more as:-

(return-b a) -> b

Second, all those equations that relate to the same function are grouped in brackets.

((return-b a) -> b
 (return-b c) -> b)

Third, since all the equations bracketed together must relate to the same function, it is tedious to keep typing the name of this function for each such equation. The name of the function is instead given at the top of its definition (figure 2.9). The entries a -> b and c -> b are **rewrite rules** within the Shen function definition (we shall see shortly that they differ a little from equations).

Entering the definition of return-b causes Shen to compile it into its **environment**. The environment can be considered to be a set of function names and their associated definitions. Once the definition of a function has been entered to the Shen environment, Shen will allow the use of this function in evaluation.

```
(15-) (define return-b
        a -> b
        c -> b)
return-b

(16-) (return-b c)
b

(17-) (return-b d)
error: partial function return-b
Track return-b ?  (y/n) n
```

Figure 2.9 Defining and using a simple function in Shen

Supplying an input for which there is no covering rule generates an error message. A function which is not defined for all its inputs is called a **partial function**. And here Shen signals that return-b is partial, accompanied by an offer to track the function which we refuse for now.[11]

But, suppose we want to say that *whatever* the input, return-b will return b. Since the domain of the function is now infinite in size, we cannot produce an equation for every possible input. Mathematicians use variables like x to cope with cases like this. In Shen, a variable is any symbol beginning with an uppercase letter. Using variables, one equation can state that whatever the input, return-b will return b. If we remedy the definition of return-b then Shen overwrites the old definition.

```
(19-) (define return-b
        X -> b)
return-b

(20-) (return-b d)
b
```

Figure 2.10 Overwriting an older definition

---

[11] In the next chapter we see how to gainfully accept this offer.

2.7 Equations and Priority Rewrite Systems

Equational specifications are a useful way of getting to grips with the task of defining functions. But there are significant differences between a set of equations and a series of rewrite rules in a Shen function definition. Consider the following equations.

$$f(a) = b$$
$$f(a) = c$$

Entering this directly into Shen produces the following definition.

```
(define f
  a -> b
  a -> c)
```

Evaluating (f a) produces b and never c. The second rewrite rule a -> c behaves as if it did not exist; the reason being that Shen tries rewrite rules from top to bottom. First a -> b is used and then a -> c. As soon as a -> b is tried with the input a, of course b is returned. The second rewrite rule is irrelevant and is **starved** by the first rule. This feature, of ordering rewrite rules so that some are tried in preference to others, is a characterising feature of **priority rewrite systems**. If we wanted to show that (f a) was identical to c, we could easily do this using the equations above, but in Shen (= (f a) c) would evaluate to false. We could amend the definition of f to allow (= (f a) c) to be true as follows.

```
(define f
  a -> c
  b -> c)
```

The amended definition now gives (f a) and c the same normal form. Nevertheless, the price for achieving this is that we have abandoned a simple transcription of the original equations. The problem of fairly transcribing a set of equations into rewrite rules has been intensively studied and it is known that there is no decision procedure for deriving a fair representation of an arbitrary set of equations.[12]

Equations are, in a sense, more powerful and less controlled than rewrite rules. However, the same sensitivity to ordering gives Shen capacities that a purely equational specification does not have. For example, suppose we want to define a function identical that returns true given two inputs with the same normal form,

---

[12] Meaning by "fair", a set R of rewrite rules, so that $a = b$ follows from the equations when and only when both a and b have unique normal forms a' and b' under R, such that a' and b' are syntactically identical. There is a semi-decision procedure, the **Knuth-Bendix procedure** (see Further Reading), which, when it terminates, will deliver a fair set of rewrite rules from a set of equations.

and returns false otherwise. Using our equational specification approach, we write:-

$$identical(x,\ x) = true$$

This is fine for the positive case. x has been used twice indicating that the two inputs must be the same for true to be returned. But what of the negative case? We cannot write

$$identical(x,\ y) = false$$

This says that for *all* x and y, $identical(x,\ y) = false$. If we want express this function using equations, we have to expand our vocabulary and allow ourselves to use **conditional equations**.

$$identical(x,\ x) = true$$
$$identical(x,\ y) = false\ if\ x \neq y$$

Shen's priority ordering allows identical to be defined in terms of rewrite rules.

```
(define identical
  X X -> true
  X Y -> false)
```

Since the rule X X -> true is tried first, any identical inputs must return true. If the second rule is tried, it can only be because the first rule failed, in which case the output must be false.

Another significant difference between rewrite rules and equations is that rewrite rules, unlike equations, must obey the **variable occurrence restriction**. The variable occurrence restriction requires that a variable that appears on the right-hand side of a rule must appear on the left-hand side. So the equation f(X,Y) = g(X) cannot be oriented into the rewrite rule (g X) -> (f X Y). Shen definitions that violate this restriction produce a free variable error (figure 2.11).

```
(0-) (define g
       X -> (f X Y))
error: the following variables are free in g: Y
```

Figure 2.11 A function that violates the variable occurrence condition

Since free variables often result from clerical errors, Shen raises an error. If we want Shen to accept the free variable we use protect (figure 2.12).

```
(0-) (define g
       X -> (f X (protect Y)))
g

(1-) (define f
       A B -> B)
f
```

Figure 2.12 Protecting free variables

Here for all values of X, (g X) will evaluate to the variable Y.

2.8 A Bible Studies Program

A mid-western millionaire has commissioned a project to build an intelligent question-and-answer program for material from the Bible. Part of the task is to encode the genealogies in the Book of Genesis; the relevant verses are as follows.

... Adam ... begat a son ... called ... Seth: .... and all the days that Adam lived were nine hundred and thirty years: and he died. And Seth ... begat Enos: ...and all the days of Seth were nine hundred and twelve years: and he died. And Enos ... begat Ca-i'nan: .... and all the days of Enos were nine hundred and five years: and he died. And Ca-i'nan ... begat Mahal'aleel: ... and all the days of Ca-i'nan were nine hundred and ten years: and he died. And Mahal'aleel ... begat Jared: ... and all the days of Mahal'aleel were eight hundred ninety and five years: and he died. And Jared ... begat Enoch: and Jared lived after he begat Enoch eight hundred years, and begat sons and daughters:... and all the days of Jared were nine hundred sixty and two years: and he died. And Enoch ... begat Methu'selah: and all the days of Enoch were three hundred sixty and five years: and Enoch walked with God: and he was not; for God took him. And Methu'selah ... begat Lamech: ... and all the days of Methu'selah were nine hundred sixty and nine years: and he died. And Lamech ... begat a son: and he called his name Noah, saying, This same shall comfort us concerning our work and toil of our hands, because of the ground which the LORD hath cursed. And ... all the days of Lamech were seven hundred seventy and seven years: and he died.

King James Bible, Genesis, Chapter 5 verses 3-31

Much of this information can be captured in two functions begat and lived given on the next page. begat says who begat who and lived how long they lived. Since the names are capitalised, to avoid confusion with variables, we use strings for names.

The code introduces comments. A single line comment begins with a \\ and is deemed to continue until a new line begins. A multiline comment begins with * and continues until *\. Here are two examples.

\\ This is a single line comment
* This is a multiline comment which can go on and on and on and on and on and on and on until terminated by *\

First the lived function.

```
(define lived
  \\ the ages of the patriarchs!
  "Adam" -> 930
  "Seth" -> 912
  "Enos" -> 905
  "Ca-i'nan" -> 910
  "Mahal'aleel" -> 895
  "Jared" -> 962
  "Enoch" -> 365
  "Methu'selah" -> 969
  "Lamech" -> 777)
```

The begetting part is more potentially more difficult because begat is not a function but a relation, that is, begat does not map a person to one unique person unless the person has only one offspring.[13] Luckily the Bible only traces the direct line.

```
(define begat
  "Adam" -> "Seth"
  "Seth" -> "Enos"
  "Enos" -> "Ca-i'nan"
  "Ca-i'nan" -> "Mahal'aleel"
  "Mahal'aleel" -> "Jared"
  "Jared" -> "Enoch"
  "Enoch" -> "Methu'selah"
  "Methu'selah" -> "Lamech")
```

Rather than typing this into the top level, it is more logical to enter it into a file "bible.shen" and save the file; the function load loads the file.

```
(0-) (load "bible.shen")
lived
begat
run time: 0.02635635635s
loaded

(1-) (begat "Enoch")
"Methu'selah"

(2-) (lived (begat "Adam"))
912
```

Figure 2.18 Loading and running the Bible program

---

[13] In chapter 4 we will be able to solve this by grouping objects into lists. Logic programming, studied in chapter 22, deals with relations directly.

All operations involving reading and writing to files, including loading files, are conducted relative to the **home directory** which by default is the directory in which Shen is situated. The command (load "myfile") will load a file from the directory in which Shen is located.

The function cd changes this home directory to allow files to be read from elsewhere without the user having to enter the full pathname. cd takes a string argument indicating the pathname; if the string is empty ("") then the home directory defaults again to the directory in which Shen is situated. The directory pathname may be **absolute** or **relative** where the pathname is interpreted relative to the directory in which Shen is situated.[14]   Figure 2.19 shows a session with cd using first an absolute pathname under Windows 7, and then a relative pathname, and ends with resetting the home directory back to the default.

```
(5-) (cd "C:/Users/Mark Tarver/Documents/CS/Languages/Bible")
"C:/Users/Mark Tarver/Documents/CS/Languages/Bible/"

(6-) (load "bible.shen") \\ load a file in the above directory
lived
begat
run time: 0.04680030047893524 secs
loaded

(7-) (cd "") \\ change the directory to the home directory
""
```

Figure 2.19 Changing the home directory

Exercise 2

1. Write a *single* expression that does the following. It waits for the user to type in a number followed by carriage return; and then another number followed by another carriage return; and then prints The sum of the two is X where the place of X is taken by the sum of the two numbers entered.

2. The Centigrade to Fahrenheit conversion is given by the equation $x\text{F}° = (9/5 \times x) + 32\text{C}°$. Write a function cent-to-fahr that calculates the equivalent Fahrenheit from the Centigrade. Write the inverse function fahr-to-cent that calculates the equivalent Centigrade from the Fahrenheit.

3. An **and-gate** is an electronic device that receives two electrical signals that are either high (1) or low (0) and outputs a high (1) signal if and only if both inputs are 1 and outputs 0 otherwise. An **or-gate** is an electronic device that receives two electrical signals that are either high (1) or low (0), outputs a 1 signal if and only if at least one input is 1, and outputs 0 otherwise. An **inverter** is an electronic device that receives an electrical signal that is either high (1) or low (0) and outputs a 1 signal if and only if

---

[14] The behaviour of cd is partly dependent on platform and the operating system .

the input is 0 and outputs 0 otherwise. Write down the Shen definitions of and-gate, or-gate and inverter as functions.

4. Using your answers to question 3, represent the following circuit as a 2-place function so that when 1 is sent down wire A and 1 down wire B, the function produces "Bulb A is lit" and "Bulb B is lit". Can you simplify this circuit? If so how would you reflect this simplification in your function definition?

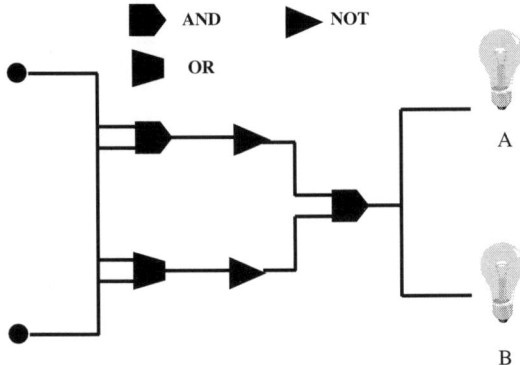

5. In neural nets, a neuron is a device that receives a number of numerical inputs $i_1,...i_n$ each of which it multiplies the corresponding weight $w_1,...,w_n$. If the sum of $(w_1 \times i_1)$ $+ ... (w_n \times i_n)$ is greater than a threshold K then the neurone produces a 1 and if the sum is less than K it produces a 0. Design a function that simulates a neurone designed to receive inputs i_1 and i_2, multiplies them by w_1 and w_2 respectively, and produces an output 0 or 1 depending on K. Your encoding should allow the user to fix the values of w_1 w_2 and K.

6. During the Vietnam War, an American pilot jumped from his downed B-52 from a height of 60,000 feet. Encode the formula $d = \frac{1}{2} at^2$, where d = distance travelled, a = acceleration and t = time elapsed, into a function and calculate the distance the pilot fell in 10 seconds. You can take a to be 30 ft/sec^2.

7. *The speed of light is 186,282 miles per second. The nearest star outside our solar system is *Proxima Centauri* which is 4.243 light years away. How long would the following objects take to travel to that star from earth?

    a.   A jumbo jet, travelling at 550 mph.
    b.   An Apollo rocket travelling at 23,000 mph.
    c.   The Voyager probe travelling at 50,000 mph.

    Your program should allow the traveller to fix his destination distance in light years and enter the speed in miles per hour.

10. Build a currency converter in Shen. Your currency converter will convert dollars, pounds and yen. To help you get started, here is the 2008 exchange scale for all these currencies into Euros.

    1 US Dollar = 0.84104 Euro
    1 British Pound = 1.43266 Euro
    1 Japanese Yen = 0.007725 Euro

Your converter will receive any positive quantity of money in any of the above currencies and convert it into the target currency chosen by the user. Your program will allow the conversion rates to be reset, but only after password authorisation has been given to the system.

Further Reading

O'Donnell (1985) (pp 20-29, 90-97) gives a detailed study of the design and implementation of a programming language based on equations. The Knuth-Bendix procedure is a classic method for transforming arbitrary sets of equations into rewrite rules and is described in Knuth and Bendix (1970). The original account is not very readable and Bundy (1983) and Duffy (1991) provide more readable introductions. Plaisted (1993) gives a nice overview on the field of rewriting. There are regular conferences, devoted specifically to rewrite systems, published in the LNCS series, amongst which a paper by Baeten and Bergstra (1986) details the properties of priority rewrite systems. There has been a lot of discussion in functional programming circles about the advisability of using priority rewriting in the definition of functions. Priority rewriting leads to shorter and simpler programs, but it also separates the definition from its equational representation because these rules can overlap and then prioritising must be used to determine which rule is actually used. In mathematics, changing the order of the equations does not affect what is stated. Order insensitivity is also useful in implementing parallel functional programming languages, since each rule can be tested independently. Jorrand (1987) is a study of FP2; an experimental parallel functional programming language based on term rewriting. Wadler in Peyton-Jones (1987), chapter 5, gives a useful discussion of the conditions under which a set of rewrite rules is order-insensitive.

Web Sites

The Lawrence Livermore National Laboratory (http://www.llnl.gov/sisal/) ran the SISAL project, whose goal is "to develop high-performance functional compilers and runtime systems to simplify the process of writing scientific programs on parallel supercomputers and to help programmers develop functional scientific applications." The result was the SISAL functional programming language available through Sourceforge http://sisal.sourceforge.net that is available for UNIX and Windows. pLisp designed by Thomas Maher (http://www.techno.net/pcl/tm/plisp/) is an experimental implementation of parallel functional programming for a Lisp-like language. IEEE's Parascope site (http://computer.org/parascope/) is the best place for links to the world of parallel computing.

Stand-alone implementations of the Knuth-Bendix completion procedure are very difficult to find; generally the procedure is embedded as proper part of larger systems designed to handle equational problems. The theorem prover OTTER (http://www-unix.mcs.anl.gov/AR/otter/) contains a Knuth-Bendix completion procedure as does MIT's Larch system (http://www.sds.lcs.mit.edu/Larch/index.html).

3 Recursion

3.1 Of Numbers

Numbers in Shen are either integers (...-3,-2,-1,0,1,2,3, ...) or floating point numbers (48.6464, -6776.5) or e numbers (4.5e3, 1.84e-4, 34e20). .9 and .67 etc. are acceptable shorthands for 0.9 and 0.67. Shen automatically recognises the cancellation of repeated subtraction when parsing, so --9 is parsed as 9.

All floating point numbers are treated and parsed as expressing sums of products; thus 434.78 is parsed as

$$434.78 = (10^2 \times 4) + (10^1 \times 3) + (10^0 \times 4) + (10^{-1} \times 7) + (10^{-2} \times 8)$$

e numbers are similarly parsed as products

$$1.84e\text{-}4 = 1.84 \times 10^{-4}$$

The precision of the computation depends very much on the platform. By preference Shen uses **double precision arithmetic** which means that the memory assigned to represent a number spans 64 bits on a modern 32 bit computer. This is the recommended IEEE standard for representing floating point numbers. Any Shen implementation running under Common Lisp, Javascript, Clojure or Scheme will meet this standard. This gives accuracy to around fifteen places. By default Shen gives the most accurate representation of any numerical computation, and the computation can introduce inaccuracies in the least significant place.[15]

An interesting question concerns the comparison of floats and integers - is (= 1 1.0) true or not? If as in Shen, we treat the decimal notation as shorthand for a sum, then the answer is 'yes'; i.e. $1.0 = (1 \times 10^0) + (0 \times 10^{-1}) = 1$

---

[15] However the representation returned by a computation may vary according to platform. Under Common Lisp, Shen computes 56565e34 to 565650000000000000000000000000000000000, whereas under Javascript it is printed as 5.6564999999999995e+38. The standard maths library contains a rounding function for those who are bothered by extraneous digits.

Therefore if = represents identity then (= 1 1.0) is true.   This is the verdict Shen returns.

```
(0-) (= 1 1.0)
true
```

This verdict opens up the differences between languages in their treatment of numbers and reaches down into the philosophy of mathematics. In Prolog 1 = 1.0 is false. In ML the comparison is meaningless (returns an error) because 1.0 and 1 belong to different types - *real* and *int*.

Strictly this is wrong. Computing has fogged the issues here and committed the traditional error of confusing *use* and *mention* in its treatment of integers and floats, in other words, between *numbers* and the signs (*numerals*) we use to represent them.   The number 11 can be represented in various ways; as 11 in decimal, B in hexadecimal, XI in Roman numerals and so on.

We should not confuse the identity of two numbers with the identity of their representation. If we want to say that 1.0 is not an integer and 1 is, we commit an error, because 1.0 = 1; unless we mean by "integer" an expression which is applied to the numeral itself i.e. "1.0". In which case the expression "integer" is predicated of something which is a numeral, in computing terms, it is a string test. In Shen, the integer? test is taken as predicating of numbers and 1.0 is treated as an integer.

However there are often pragmatic grounds for distinguishing numbers as distinct that traditional mathematics has regarded as identical.   In computing it is sometimes *convenient* to treat these alternative representations as different in kind. A case in point are the rational numbers, treated since Pythagoras as a ratio of two whole numbers 1/3, 5/8 etc. Every schoolboy is taught to replace 2/1 by 2 in his calculations and 2/1 and 2 are regarded as the same number.

However finite floating point numbers cannot, with complete accuracy, capture a rational; 1/3 is not 0.3 or even 0.333333 but 0.3 repeated. Hence there is a case for retaining rational numbers as a special type.[16] If we introduce rational numbers as objects composed of two elements it is awkward to maintain that 2/1 = 2 because computationally they are utterly different objects.   So some languages either omit the rationals or regard them as distinct in all cases from integers. However the degree to these distinctions are enforced in computing varies according to platform.[17]

---

[16] Shen lacks them but in chapter 8 we show how to construct them.

[17] The nature and identity of numbers is an old philosophical question over which men have argued for centuries. Regarding the identity of 1.0 and 1, we have kept the traditional view that floating point numbers are simply a representation of numbers of which integers are a special case. The view that 1,

Our excursion into the foundation of number theory being done for now; we will now look at how numerical computation is performed in Shen. In Shen there are four basic numerical operations.

1. Addition +
2. Subtraction -
3. Multiplication *
4. Division /

Both addition and multiplication are **polyadic operations** in Shen, meaning that these operators can take any number of inputs or **arguments** as they are called in functional parlance. The polyadicity arises from the fact that both these functions are associative so that (+ X (+ Y Z)) and (+ (+ X Y) Z) are equivalent. Hence the Shen reader treats the internal bracketing as unwanted hair and accepts (+ X Y Z). Shen division is true division and not integer division so that (/ 5 2) will produce 2.5 and not 2. All these functions are members of a set of 46 **primitive functions** from which Shen is assembled.

In addition there are four numerical relations which are also primitive.

1. Greater than >
2. Less than <
3. Greater than or equal to >=
4. Less than or equal to <=

The generic equality relation = will operate between numbers. The function number? will return true for all and only numbers and both of these are primitive. Shen accepts zero-place functions so that we can define constants like π as follows

---

1/1 and 1.0 are alternative representations of the same number was probably characteristic of mathematics until the early C20; the change in perspective came through two historical sources; the first in mathematical logic and the second in computing.

The basis in mathematical logic lies in Bertrand Russell's reductionist analysis of numbers whereby a number tower is built from the natural numbers (which are themselves reduced to cardinal numbers) consisting of more and more complex set theoretical constructions. In Russell's analysis, rational numbers are quite distinct entities from natural numbers and if you want to compare them, you cannot do so through an equality relation but have to do so through constructing an equivalence relation of the appropriate kind.

Hence 2/1 is not the same object as 2 in Russellian mathematics (though it is in traditional maths) because preserving this identity introduced awkward special cases. However, it is important to note that Russell *completely disavowed* that he was trying to analyse the meaning of mathematical assertions in his work on logical atomism. Rather he was attempting to reconstruct mathematics by providing a mapping from conventional maths into Russellian arithmetic. As in computing, mathematical logic followed the line of convenience.

```
(6-) (define pi
   -> 3.14159)
pi

(7-) (+ (pi) 1)
4.14159
```

Figure 3.1 Defining π as a zero place function

3.2 Recursion and the Factorial Function

The factorial of a natural number n is the result of multiplying n by the all the positive integers less than n. By convention *factorial*(0) = 1. We start writing a series of equations to define factorial (figure 3.2).

$$factorial(0) = 1$$
$$factorial(1) = 1 \times 1 = 1$$
$$factorial(2) = 2 \times 1 = 2$$
$$factorial(3) = 3 \times 2 \times 1 = 6$$
$$factorial(4) = 4 \times 3 \times 2 \times 1 = 24$$
$$....$$

Figure 3.2 Part of an infinite series of equations for the factorial function

The problem is that there are an infinite number of such equations. Can we somehow reduce this infinite set of equations to something finite and of a manageable size?

We can through the device of **recursion**. If we examine these equations, they all fit a common pattern. Above 0, the factorial of any integer is the result of multiplying that integer by the factorial of the integer one less than it.

$$factorial(0) = 1$$
$$factorial(1) = 1 \times factorial(0) = 1 \times 1 = 1$$
$$factorial(2) = 2 \times factorial(1) = 2 \times 1 = 2$$
$$factorial(3) = 3 \times factorial(2) = 3 \times 2 = 6$$
$$factorial(4) = 4 \times factorial(3) = 4 \times 6 = 24$$
$$........$$

Figure 3.3 Isolating the pattern within the equations in 3.1

This allows us to use two equations in place of the infinite list we started with (figure 3.4). The second equation includes the proviso that $x \neq 0$.

$$factorial(0) = 1$$
$$\text{where } x \neq 0, factorial(x) = x \times factorial(x - 1)$$

Figure 3.4 The equations that define the factorial function

In representing these equations in Shen, we take advantage of the fact that Shen tries rewrite rules in the order in which they appear in a function definition. If the first and second equations become the first and second rewrite rules in the definition of factorial, the ordering guarantees that Shen tries the second rule only when the input is not equal to 0. Hence the two equations can be combined into one definition without having to explicitly say that $x \neq 0$ (figure 3.5).

```
(define factorial
  0 -> 1
  X -> (* X (factorial (- X 1)))))
```

Figure 3.5 The factorial function in Shen

Entering this function to Shen shows it to work.

```
(59-) (factorial 6)
720
```

The calculation of the factorial of any natural number > 0 depends on calculating the factorial of the integer one less than it. Thus, the Shen factorial function calls itself $n+1$ times for any natural number n and having reached zero, executes all the deferred multiplications.

3.3 Forms of Recursion

The equational definition of *factorial* in figure 3.3 shows the typical anatomy of a recursive function. The first equation - *factorial*(0) = 1 - gives the **base case** of the recursive definition; this provides a point where the function ceases to call itself. The base case corresponds to a condition within a procedural loop that causes the loop to be exited.

The second equation - where $x \neq 0$, *factorial*(x) = x × *factorial*(x - 1) - corresponds to the **recursive case** where the function calls itself. The recursive case corresponds to the condition within a loop that causes the loop to be repeated. In the example there is one base case and one recursive case, though in other , definitions there can be several of each.

Once the base case 0 is reached, the computation does not cease since the recursive outputs of factorial have to be multiplied to give the answer. We can rewrite our definition of *factorial* so that the answer is returned on reaching the base case (figure 3.6).

```
(define factorial
  X -> (factorialh X 1))

(define factorialh
  0 Accum -> Accum
  X Accum -> (factorialh (- X 1) (* X Accum)))
```

Figure 3.6 A tail recursive definition of factorial

Our new definition of *factorial* passes its input X to an **auxiliary** or **help function** factorialh that helps to define *factorial*. The definition of factorialh contains an extra input (an **accumulator**) Accum, which totals the value calculated for factorial. When the base case 0 is reached, returning the accumulator gives the correct answer.

The two different versions of *factorial* are almost identical, and yet they display different patterns of computation. In the first version, the necessary multiplications are postponed till the end of the recursion. Carrying out this process requires that the computer remember the multiplications to be performed later. The length of the chain of operations, and hence the amount of information needed to keep account of the computation, grows in linear proportion to the value n of *factorial*(n). Such a recursion is called **linear recursion**.

In the second kind of recursion, **tail recursion**, the necessary multiplications are performed during the recursion, and the memory used to keep track of the computation is virtually constant. The difference becomes significant if the chain of deferred calculations made by linear recursion becomes larger than the available memory set aside to store them. In that case the computer may raise an error.[18] For this reason functional programmers generally write computationally intensive recursive functions to be tail recursive.

Addition is another example of a recursive arithmetic function. The problem is to recursively define an addition function *plus* over natural numbers, using only operations which add 1 to or subtract 1 from a number. To begin we write a series of equations giving specific inputs to *plus* and the corresponding results.

$$plus(x, 0) = x$$
$$plus(x, 1) = 1 + plus(x, 0)$$
$$plus(x, 2) = 1 + plus(x, 1)$$
$$plus(x, 3) = 1 + plus(x, 2)$$

Figure 3.7 Part of an infinite series of equations for addition

Apart from the first equation (the model for the base case), all the other equations have the form

$$plus(x, y) = 1 + plus(x, (y - 1)).$$

Using the equations $plus(x, 0) = x$ and $plus(x, y) = 1 + plus(x, (y - 1))$, we define a recursive function plus in Shen (figure 3.8).

---

[18] The distinction between tail and linear recursion is built into many optimising compilers in functional programming languages though not all (e.g. Python). The limit at which linear recursion fails due to memory overflow depends on the size of the **call stack**, which is the area of memeory devoted to storing these deferred computations.

```
(define plus
  X 0 -> X
  X Y -> (+ 1 (plus X (- Y 1)))))
```

Figure 3.8 The plus function in Shen

This definition is linear recursive; we leave the tail recursive version as an exercise for the reader.

The Fibonacci function over the natural numbers is defined through the equations in figure 3.9.

$$fib(0) = 0$$
$$fib(1) = 1$$
$$\text{if } x > 1, \text{ then } fib(x) = fib(x-1) + fib(x-2)$$

Figure 3.9 The equations defining the Fibonacci function

The transcription into Shen is easy (figure 3.10).

```
(define fib
  0 -> 0
  1 -> 1
  X -> (+ (fib (- X 1)) (fib (- X 2)))))
```

Figure 3.10 The Fibonacci function in Shen

One point of note is that fib is invoked twice in the recursion. Recursive functions that call themselves more than once in one recursive call are called **tree recursive** functions, since the computation branches at such a call into two or more calls to the same function.

1 is odd and not even. For any natural number x, which is greater than 1, x is even if its predecessor is odd and odd if its predecessor is even. This definition is used in figure 3.11 to create a program that recognises odd and even numbers. The odd? function calls even and the even? function calls odd? Functions which are defined in terms of each other are **mutually recursive**.

```
(define even?
  1 -> false
  X -> (odd? (- X 1)))
```

```
(define odd?
  1 -> true
  X -> (even? (- X 1)))
```

Figure 3.11 A mutual recursion between even? and odd?

3.4 Tracing Function Calls

These different patterns of execution can be traced through the Shen tracking package. The package allows us to trace the input to any user-defined function and the corresponding output. When a function f is tracked, each time f is called, the inputs to f are printed and so is the normal form of the output f returns. untrack untracks a function. Figure 3.12 shows a trace of the factorial function.

```
(62-) (track factorial)
factorial

(63-) (factorial 3)
  <1> Input to factorial
  3 ==>
    <2> Input to factorial
    2 ==>
      <3> Input to factorial
      1 ==>
        <4> Input to factorial
        0 ==>
        <4> Output of factorial
        ==> 1
      <3> Output of factorial
      ==> 1
    <2> Output of factorial
    ==> 2
  <1> Output of factorial
==> 6

(64-) (untrack factorial)
```

Figure 3.12 Using the Shen trace program

(step +) typed to the top level will cause the tracking package to pause after each Inputs to ... and wait for a keystroke from the user. Typing ^ (abort) at this point will abort the computation. The trace package query is triggered whenever a function f is called with an input for which there is no rule in the definition of f to determine how that input is to be treated.

3.5 Guards

A prime number is a whole number > 1, divisible only by itself and 1 to give another whole number. Our task is to construct a prime number detector which returns true if X is a prime number and false otherwise.

One way to construct such a detector is to start with 2 and try to divide 2 into x. If the result is a whole number > 1, then x is not prime. If the result is not a whole number then we repeat the test, incrementing 2 to 3. We continue, and if we have incremented the divisor to a number greater than the integer square root of x; then we know we have found a prime. This algorithm requires a function that:

(a) holds the number x,
(b) holds the integer square root of x and ..
(c) holds the divisor that is initially set to 2.

Call this function *prime-h?*. We define the function *prime?* in terms of *prime-h?* (and *prime-h* itself) in four equations (figure 3.13).[19]

$prime?(x) = prime\text{-}h?(x, isqrt(x), 2)$
$prime\text{-}h?(x, max, div) = false$ if x / div is an integer and $1 < div \le max$
$prime\text{-}h?(x, max, div) = true$ if $div > max$
$prime\text{-}h?(x, max, div) = y$ if x / div is not an integer
                                       and $max \ge div$
                                       and $prime\text{-}h?(x, max, (1 + div)) = y$

Figure 3.13 Defining a prime detector in equations

The definition of *prime?* is easy - merely a transcription of the equation. The definition of *prime-h?* is trickier. The equations have conditions attached to them that must be represented. Shen represents these conditions by **guards**. A guard is a functional expression that evaluates to true or false, which is placed after the rule and preceded by the keyword where, and which must evaluate to true for the rule to apply (figure 3.14).

```
(define prime?
  X -> (prime-h? X (isqrt X) 2))

(define isqrt
  X -> (isqrt-help X 1))

(define isqrt-help
  X Y -> Y                          where (= (* Y Y) X)
  X Y -> (- Y 1)                    where (> (* Y Y) X)
  X Y -> (isqrt-help X (+ Y 1)))

(define prime-h?
  X Max Div -> true    where (> Div Max)
  X Max Div -> false   where (and (integer? (/ X Div))
                                  (< 1 Div)  (<= Div Max))
  X Max Div -> (prime-h? X Max (+ 1 Div))
            where (and (not (integer? (/ X Div)))(>= Max Div)))
```

Figure 3.14 An unoptimised encoding of the prime detector

---

[19] This is not an efficient way of testing for primes, and is simply used as a teaching example. .

Using our knowledge of the evaluation strategy of this program, some of the code in figure 3.12 can be eliminated. The (< 1 Div) test is redundant, because prime-h? is started with a divisor of 2. The (<= Div Max) is redundant too, because if (> Div Max), the program would have terminated. Similarly the (not (integer? (/ X Div))) (>= Max Div) tests can be dropped (they must be satisfied if the first two rules fail). After eliminating redundant code, the resulting program appears in 3.15.

```
(define prime?
  X -> (prime-h? X (isqrt X) 2))

(define isqrt
  X -> (isqrt-help X 1))

(define isqrt-help
  X Y -> Y                      where (= (* Y Y) X)
  X Y -> (- Y 1)                where (> (* Y Y) X)
  X Y -> (isqrt-help X (+ Y 1)))

(define prime-h?
  X Max Div -> true             where (> Div Max)
  X Max Div -> false            where (integer?[20] (/ X Div))
  X Max Div -> (prime-h? X Max (+ 1 Div)))
```

Figure 3.15 An optimised encoding of the prime detector

Guards do not give Shen any extra computational power; they are merely a convenient device for clarifying the control within a program. In fact all Shen function definitions can be coded with only one rewrite rule in each function! To do this, we transfer all the control information that appears to the left of the ->, to the right in the form of a nested case statement. What is left on the left of the -> is simply a series of variables called **formal parameters**. Here is a recoding of prime-h? along these lines.

```
(define prime-h?
  X Max Div -> (if (integer? (/ X Div))
                   false
                   (if (> Div Max)  true (prime-h? X Max (+ 1  Div)))))
```

Some functional languages such as Lisp, Scheme and Python require programs to be written in this style.   The introduction of significant structure to the left of -> is what pattern-directed or **pattern-matching** functional programming is about. The translation of Shen programs into this form is both purely mechanical and also an important stage in the compilation of Shen.[21]

---

[20] See appendix A; integer? is a system function.

[21] See chapter 15 for more on this.

3.6 Counting Change

How many ways can a one pound coin be changed? We can generalise the question and ask *"Given a sum of n pence, in how many ways can it be converted into change?"* To begin, we identify the units of currency existing in Britain of 2012; they are the 2 pound coin, the pound coin and the 50p, 20p, 10p, 5p, 2p and 1p coins. The problem has a simple recursive solution.   Let d be the value of the highest denomination, and n be the value of the money, which we are trying to break down.   Then the number of ways c of breaking n into change is c where

c = the number of ways of breaking n-d pence into change +
   the number of ways of breaking n pence into change using all
   remaining denominations *except* the highest denomination d.

What stops the recursion? We say that

1.   There is one way of changing 0 pence (give nothing back!).
2.   There are no (zero) ways of changing less than 0 pence.
3.   If there is no available denomination to use, there are 0 ways of changing any sum of money.

Putting this reasoning together gives the function count-change.

```
(define count-change
   Amount -> (count-change-h Amount 200))

(define count-change-h
   0 _ -> 1
   _ 0 -> 0
   Amount _ -> 0  where (> 0 Amount)
   Amount Fst_Denom
   -> (+ (count-change-h (- Amount Fst_Denom) Fst_Denom)
         (count-change-h Amount (next-denom Fst_Denom))))

(define next-denom
   200 -> 100
   100 -> 50
   50 -> 20
   20 -> 10
   10 -> 5
   5 -> 2
   2 -> 1
   1 -> 0)
```

Figure 3.16 Counting change in Shen

(count-change 100) provides the answer, 4563, to the original question.

3.7 Non-Terminating Functions

Recursion gives the ability to define **non-terminating** functions such as

```
(define silly
  X -> (silly X))
```

which calls itself forever. Here (silly X) is undefined for all values of X, since whatever input is submitted to silly, no normal form is computed.

There are other examples of functions, which are non-terminating only for certain inputs; for example the expression (factorial -1) has no normal form. The last example shows that functions that fail to terminate for all inputs are not always silly. To avoid non-termination we must ensure the input is a natural number.

However, there remain functions whose computation is not guaranteed to terminate and which are resistant to all safeguards.[22] A good example comes from number theory. Goldbach's conjecture suggests that every even number > 2 is the sum of two primes. The following program tests the conjecture.

```
(define slow-goldbachs-conjecture
  -> (slow-goldbachs-conjecture-h 4))

(define slow-goldbachs-conjecture-h
  N -> (slow-goldbachs-conjecture-h (+ N 2)) where (sum-of-two-primes? N)
  N -> N)

(define sum-of-two-primes?
  N -> (sum-of-two-primes-h? 2 N))

(define sum-of-two-primes-h?
  P N -> false                                   where (> P N)
  P N -> true                                    where (sum-of? P 2 N)
  P N -> (sum-of-two-primes-h? (next-prime (+ 1 P)) N))

(define sum-of?
  P1 P2 N -> true                                where (= N (+ P1 P2))
  P1 P2 N -> false                               where (> (+ P1 P2) N)
  P1 P2 N -> (sum-of? P1 (next-prime (+ 1 P2)) N))

(define next-prime
  X -> X                                         where (prime? X)
  X -> (next-prime (+ 1 X)))
```

Figure 3.17 Goldbach's Conjecture in Shen

---

[22] It was proved in 1936 by Alan Turing there is no algorithm for detecting all programs which may fail to terminate; a result known as the *Unsolvability of the Halting Problem.*

Currently the truth of Goldbach's conjecture is open to proof or disproof.[23] If conjecture is true, then the program in 3.17 will not terminate. If it is false, then it will halt and print out an integer that will refute the conjecture. Currently, mathematicians do not know what would happen. But from a programmer's viewpoint, the program is very inefficient because it uses next-prime to recalculate the same primes repeatedly. In the next chapter, we look at how lists can be used to store results for programs like this.

Exercise 3

1. Define the following functions.
   a. expt, that raises a number M to a natural number power N.
   b. round_n, that rounds a floating point number M to N places, rounding downwards.
   c. square?, that returns true if N is a perfect square. A perfect square is the result of multiplying a natural number by itself.
   d. gcd, which computes the greatest common divisor of two natural numbers a and b. This function returns the largest divisor common to a and b. The gcd of 12 and 16 is 4.
   e. lcm, which computes the least common multiple of two natural numbers a and b. This function returns the smallest number into which a and b both divide to give whole numbers. The lcm of 12 and 15 is 60.

2. *Define the 3-place function nth_root that receives the natural number N, the positive number M and the natural number P, where $P > 0$. nth_root finds the Nth root of M to an accuracy proportional to P as follows. Fix the conjectured value C for $\sqrt[N]{M}$ at M/2. Raise C to the power N and determine if C^N rounded to P places equals M. If so, return C. If C^N rounded to P places $> M$, reduce the value of C and repeat. If C^N rounded to P places $< M$, increase the value of C and repeat. The trick is seeing how to increase or decrease the value of C to converge on a solution.

3. Melvin Micro has defined his own version of if as follows:-

```
(define melvins_if
  true X _ -> X
  false _ Y -> Y
  Test _ _ -> (error "test ~A must be true or false. ~%" Test))
```

He defines factorial as

```
(define factorial
  X -> (melvins_if (= X 0) 1 (* X (factorial (- X 1)))))
```

What happens when Melvin tries to use this function to compute factorials? Give reasons.

---

[23] The Prussian mathematician Christian Goldbach suggested Goldbach's conjecture in 1742. It has been tested up to 4×10^{18} (April 2012). In 2001 a $1 million prize was announced in the Chicago Sun-Times for the first proof of Goldbach's conjecture. Two major publishers funded the money and the competition remained open until March 15th 2002. The prize was not won.

4. Melvin Micro has deposited $10,000 in a long term account in the year 2000. At 5% interest per year, he hopes to collect on this account for his retirement. Assuming he takes no money from his account, what will it be worth in 2040?

5. In 2005, the USA produced 10,900 billion dollars of goods and services with a growth rate of around 2.5% per annum. The same year China produced 6,400 billion dollars of goods and services with a growth rate of 9% per annum. Assuming these rates are maintained, at what year does the GNP of China exceed that of America?

6. In probability theory, the probability $P(A \lor B)$ of either or both of two independent events A or B occurring is given by the equation.

$$P(A \lor B) = 1 - ((1 - P(A)) \times (1 - P(B)))$$

$P(A)$ is the probability of A occurring and $P(B)$ is the probability of B occurring. 1 indicates certainty, 0 impossibility. Assume that the probability of a major global catastrophe in any one year is 1/200. What is the probability of a major global catastrophe in the next fifty years?

7. The factorisation of very large numbers is a key element in computer security. The prime factors of a number n are those primes which when multiplied together give n. Devise a program to compute the prime factors of the number 123456789.

8. *Two regiments of riflemen are facing each other. One side has 1000 men, the other 800. The smaller side fires first and then the larger and so on alternately. A riflemen hits and kills his enemy once in every 10 shots. Once a man is hit and killed he cannot fire back. The fight is to the finish. How many men are left in the stronger side at the end of the fight? What happens if the stronger side fires first?

9. *Implement a calendar program which determines what day of the week a particular date falls on. Use your program to calculate the day of the week on 13th July 2113.

10. A high-speed reconnaissance plane weighs 105,000 lb of which 70,000 lb is fuel. At a cruise speed of 1,800 mph, the plane uses 3lb of fuel per 10,000lb of weight per mile. The airforce need to know how long the plane will cruise and hence what is its effective radius of action. Write a program to compute a solution. Your program should allow the user to set the parameters of this problem for different aircraft.

Further Reading

The Fibonacci function in this chapter executes in exponential space relative to the input n. Henson (1987, chapter 4) shows how to derive a linear Fibonacci function definition from the tree recursive version using the rules for manipulating function definitions in Burstall and Darlington (1977). Bird (1984) and Wand (1980) extend this technique. Abelson and Sussman (1996) explain how to detect prime numbers using the square-root method used here and also present a much faster method based on the Fermat test. This book also has a good discussion of various types of recursion and the compilation strategies for dealing with them. The problem of showing that the evaluation of an arbitrary expression halts or showing it does not is, of course, unsolvable (being a corollary of the Halting Problem).

the problem of counting change is an old one. Kac and Ulam (1971) p.34-39 show how to calculate the number of ways of splitting a dollar without the use of a computer; their method uses simultaneous equations and polynomials. The computation used in this book is not particularly efficient since identical computations are repeated. Memoisation is a technique for recording the results of a computation so it need not be performed more than once. For more on memoisation see Field and Harrison (1988).

Web Sites

Chris Caldwell (http://www.utm.edu/research/primes/) maintains a site devoted to primes. http://www.fortunecity.com/meltingpot/manchaca/799/prime.html is a less detailed, but a more accessible account of primes.

4 Lists

4.1 Representing Lists in Shen

In Shen, a list begins with a [and ends with a]. So the list composed of 1, 2 and 3 would be written as [1 2 3]. Spaces are used to separate items; the list [123] is not the same as the list [1 2 3], since [123] is the list containing the single number 123. Shen evaluates lists according to the **list evaluation rule**.

The List Evaluation Rule

The normal form of a list $L = [x_1,...,x_n]$ is the list $[x'_1,...,x'_n]$ arrived at by evaluating the contents of L from left to right where for each x_j $(1 \leq j \leq n)$, x'_j is the normal form of x_j.

Suppose we wish to find the normal form of [(* 8 9) (+ 46 89) (- 67 43)] using the list evaluation rule. We evaluate (* 8 9) first.

(* 8 9) $\Rightarrow$ 72

Second we evaluate (+ 46 89)

(+ 46 89) $\cdot \Rightarrow$ 135

Last we evaluate (- 67 43).

(- 67 43) $\Rightarrow$ 24

So the result is [72 135 24].

Lists can be placed within lists (figure 4.1). The last example in that figure features one rather special sort of list - the empty list [ ]; a list which contains nothing and which evaluates to itself.[24] Shen requires all brackets to balance before undertaking an evaluation. If there are unequal numbers of (s and)s, or [s and]s, then Shen will wait for the user to balance them. ^ can be used to abort the line input in periods of confusion.

---

[24] The empty list can also be written as ( ) in Shen.

[[1]] $\Rightarrow$ [[1]]
[tom dick harry] $\Rightarrow$ [tom dick harry]
[[1 dick [3]]] $\Rightarrow$ [[1 dick [3]]]
[(+ 1 2) [(+ 2 3)]] $\Rightarrow$ [3 [5]]
[(+ 34 34) [(* 7 8) "foobar" [(- 9 8)]]] $\Rightarrow$ [72 [56 "foobar" [1]]]
[] $\Rightarrow$ []

Figure 4.1 Some examples of lists and their normal forms

4.2 Building Lists with cons

There is one primitive function for building up lists - cons. The function cons receives two inputs, an object *x* and a list *L* and builds a list *L′* through adding *x* to the front of *L*; this is **consing** *x* to *L* (figure 4.2).

```
(0-) (cons 1 [2 3])
[1 2 3]

(1-) (cons tom [dick harry])
[tom dick harry]

(2-) (cons tom (cons dick (cons harry [ ])))
[tom dick harry]
```

Figure 4.2 Using the cons function

Using cons, a supply of self-evaluating expressions, and the empty list [], any finite list can be built up. For instance, suppose we wish to construct the list [[a b] c [d e]]. The list [a b] is formed by consing a to the result of consing b to [].

$$[a\ b] = (cons\ a\ (cons\ b\ [\ ]))$$

[d e] is the result of consing d to the result of consing e to [ ]

$$[d\ e] = (cons\ d\ (cons\ e\ [\ ]))$$

The list [[d e]] is formed by consing [d e] to [ ].

$$[[d\ e]] = (cons\ [d\ e]\ [\ ])$$

The list [[a b] c [d e]] is the result of consing [a b] to consing c to [[d e]].

$$[[a\ b]\ c\ [d\ e]] = (cons\ [a\ b]\ (cons\ c\ [[d\ e]]))$$

Thus [[a b] c [d e]] is expressed in terms of consing operations.

[[a b] c [d e]] = (cons (cons a (cons b [ ])) (cons c (cons (cons d (cons e [ ])) [ ])))

When a list is described like this, using only cons, [ ] and self-evaluating expressions we say that it is in **cons form**. For practical purposes, writing lists in cons form is tedious and unnecessary. However, when we come to reason about programs, it is important to know that any list can be recast in cons form. The translation of a list to its cons form version is purely mechanical. Simply keep applying the following rules throughout any list representation until they can no longer be applied.

Cons Form Translation Rules

(i)   [ ] is translated as [ ].
(ii)   A non-list e remains the same.
(iii) $[e_1,...,e_n]$ where ($n \geq 1$) is translated as (cons e_1 [,...,e_n]).

A shorter way of expressing consing (as an alternative to writing "cons") is to use |; every expression to the left of | is consed in turn to the list on the right of | (figure 4.3).

(0-) [1 | [2 3]]
[1 2 3]

(1-) [tom dick harry | [ ]]
[tom dick harry]

Figure 4.3 Using | in Shen to cons expressions

We explain how to evaluate expressions containing | by showing how such expressions can be translated into expressions not containing |, but cons instead. The translation involves applying the following rules to every part of any given expression until the |s are gone.

| Elimination Rules

(i) $[e_1 | e_2]$ is translated to (cons e_1 e_2).
(ii) $[e_1 ,..., e_n | e_{n+1}]$ ($n \geq 2$) is translated to (cons e_1 [,..., e_n | e_{n+1}]).

We apply these rules to [tom dick harry | [ ]].

[tom dick harry | [ ]]
= (cons tom [dick harry | [ ]])   by rule (ii)
= (cons tom (cons dick [harry | [ ]]))   by rule (ii)
= (cons tom (cons dick (cons harry [ ]))) by rule (i)
⇒ [tom dick harry].

4.3 hd **and** tl **Access List Components**

cons builds lists out of component parts. hd and tl allow these component parts to be extracted from the assembled lists. hd receives a non-empty list and returns the first element in it; tl receives a non-empty list and returns all *but* the first element of that list (figure 4.4). hd and tl satisfy these equations.

$$hd(cons(x, y)) = x$$
$$tl(cons(x, y)) = y$$

Using hd and tl in composition, we can access any element in a list.

```
(0-) (hd [1 2 3])
1

(1-) (tl [1 2 3])
[2 3]

(2-) (hd (tl (tl [1 2 3])))
3
```

Figure 4.4 Using hd *and* tl *to extract elements from a list*

What happens if hd and tl are applied to the empty list? In this case the behaviour is platform dependent and unpredictable. There are two functions head and tail in Shen which are more predictable; they raise an error in that case. Both these function depend on testing the list to see if it is empty before applying hd or tl respectively.

The test for a non-empty list in Shen is cons? (another primitive function) which returns true to a non-empty list and false to anything else; so (cons? []) returns false, as does (cons? 67) etc. Obviously hd and tl are a little faster than head and tail.

An unusual feature of Shen (shared by another language Common Lisp) is that it is possible to cons together two objects neither of which are lists. The result is known as a **dotted pair**. This is printed in Shen using a bar |.

```
(0-) (cons 1 2)
[1 | 2]

(1-) [1 | 2]
[1 | 2]

(2-) (tl [1 | 2])
2
```

The utility of a dotted pair D versus a two element list L is that accessing the second element of a dotted pair requires only one operation (tl D) whereas for L it requires two (hd (tl L)).

A **lookup table** is an association of elements organised for the purpose of retrieving information. If a lookup table is coded as list in which various items are grouped together according to some criteria of interest then the list is called an **association list**. A telephone directory can be treated as a lookup table in which the leading item is a surname. A relational database for a hospital is functionally representable as a lookup table in which the leading item is (say) the patient's National Insurance number and the details associated with that are the medical details and identity of the patient.

Here is a simple association list for the capitals of the world and the respective countries, encoded as a list of dotted pairs in Shen.

[["London" | "Great Britain"] ["Paris" | "France"] ["Madrid" | "Spain"] ["Amsterdam" | "Holland"] ["Berlin" | "Germany"] ["Warsaw" | "Poland"] ["Vienna" | "Austria"]]

A function country maps a capital to a country using this list. In order to do that, the list has to be traversed. Our initial code begins easily.

```
(define country
  Capital -> (traverse Capital [["London" | "Great Britain"]
                                ["Paris" | "France"]
                                ["Madrid" | "Spain"]
                                ["Amsterdam" | "Holland"]
                                ["Berlin" | "Germany"]
                                ["Warsaw" | "Poland"]
                                ["Vienna" | "Austria"]]))
```

The definition of traverse comes next; plainly if the list is empty there is nothing constructive to return except "don't know". If the capital is found at the head of the table we return the country otherwise we recurse down the table.

```
(define traverse
  Capital Table -> (cases (= Table []) "don't know"
                          (= Capital (hd (hd Table))) (tl (hd Table))
                          true (traverse Capital (tl Table))))
```

In traditional functional languages like Lisp, Python and Scheme, programs are written in this way and what occurs to the left of the arrow is a series of variables or formal parameters. In fact in chapter 15 we shall see that all Shen programs are in fact compiled into this sort of idiom.

However in the previous chapter we got used to the idea that in Shen we could write other expressions to the left of the arrow and not just formal parameters. This is characteristic of **pattern-matching** found in modern functional programming languages like Shen, ML and Haskell. Let us see how to do this for lists in Shen. The first lines of our program were

```
(define traverse
   Capital Table -> (cases (= Table []) "don't know"
```

This can be replaced by a pattern directed invocation

```
(define traverse
   _ [] -> "don't know"
```

The second case was

```
(= Capital (hd (hd Table))) (tl (hd Table))
```

which can be replaced by several patterns; writing in cons form we can have

```
Capital (cons (cons Capital Country) _) -> Country
```

But practically the bar notation is far easier to use and we leave the task of compiling from bar notation to cons form to the Shen reader. Here is the sensible version. Note that Capital occurs twice indicating that the lead element has to be identical to the capital.

```
Capital [[Capital | Country] | _] -> Country
```

And the final case was

```
true (traverse Capital (tl Table))
```

which comes out as

```
Capital [_ | Table] -> (traverse Capital Table)
```

Putting it all together, here is the traverse function.

```
(define traverse
   _ [] -> "don't know"
  Capital [[Capital | Country] | _] -> Country
  Capital [_ | Table] -> (traverse Capital Table))
```

Now let's consider a slightly more complex problem; we have a set of 100 students all taking six compulsory exams; discrete maths, Java programming, algorithms and data structures, functional programming, databases and computer ethics. We have the task of printing out a sheet containing their names against each of these exams and later this sheet will be annotated with their marks. We have the 100 names to hand on the computer and the six compulsory exams are easy to write down in a list. We have to generate a 600 element list in which their names are set against the exam and this we do not want to do by hand.

What we actually need is to find the **Cartesian product** of the two lists. The Cartesian product of X and Y is formed by pairing every element of X with every element of Y. So (cartesian-product [1 2 3] [a b]) evaluates to [[1 | a] [1 | b] [2 | a] [2 | b] [3 | a] [3 | b]].

To compute the Cartesian product we take the first element of X and form all possible dotted pairs with the elements of Y; then the next element of X in the same way, and so on until X is emptied. The sets of pairs are then joined into one set. So to compute (cartesian-product [1 2 3] [a b]) we need to join [[1 | a] [1 | b]], [[2 | a] [2 | b]] and [[3 | a] [3 | b]] to make [[1 | a] [1 | b] [2 | a] [2 | b] [3 | a] [3 | b]].

'Joining' in this context means that the lists are *appended* together so that (e.g) joining [1 2 3] with [4 5 6] produces [1 2 3 4 5 6]. Note that appending is *not* the same as consing; consing [1 2 3] to [4 5 6] will produce [[1 2 3] 4 5 6]. append is a Shen system function. The code for Cartesian product is given in figure 4.5.

```
(0-) (define cartesian-product
       [] _ -> []
       [X | Y] Z -> (append (pairs X Z) (cartesian-product Y Z)))
cartesian-product

(1-) (define pairs
       _ [] -> []
       X [Y | Z] -> [[X Y] | (pairs X Z)])
pairs

(2-) (cartesian-product ["Harold Abelson" "John Backus"
                         "Rudolf Carnap" "Richard Dawkins"]
        ["discrete maths" "Java programming"
        "algorithms and data structures" "functional programming"
        "databases" "computer ethics"])
```

Figure 4.5 Cartesian products in Shen

The response is

[["Harold Abelson" "discrete maths"] ["Harold Abelson" "Java programming"] ["Harold Abelson" "algorithms and data structures"] ["Harold Abelson" "functional programming"] ["Harold Abelson" "databases"] ["Harold Abelson" "computer ethics"] ["John Backus" "discrete maths"] ["John Backus" "Java programming"] ["John Backus" "algorithms and data structures"] ["John Backus" "functional programming"] ["John Backus" "databases"] ["John Backus" "computer ethics"] ["Rudolf Carnap" "discrete maths"] ["Rudolf Carnap" "Java programming"] ["Rudolf Carnap" "algorithms and data structures"] ["Rudolf Carnap" "functional programming"] ["Rudolf Carnap" "databases"] ["Rudolf Carnap" "computer ethics"] ["Richard Dawkins" "discrete maths"] ["Richard Dawkins" "Java programming"] ["Richard Dawkins" "algorithms and data structures"]... etc]

Shen prints ... etc if list structures are so long that printing them in full seems unacceptably tedious.[25]

Combinatorial computations involving lists are not uncommon. Melvin Micro, an avid first year student of CS, decides to make a drink called a *porchcrawler* which consists of quantities of beer, gin, vodka, rum, and whisky sweetened perhaps with lemonade. Being devoid of plausible party conversation, but long on science and with an iron constitution, he decides to try all possible combinations of these ingredients in search of the perfect porchcrawler. The number of combinations being large, Melvin decides to compute them all and work through the list.

Melvin's problem is to compute the **powerset** of a set *S*; the set of all subsets of *S*. Thus *powerset*({*a, b, c*}) = {{*a, b, c*}, {*a, b*}, {*a, c*}, {*b, c*}, {*a*}, {*b*}, {*c*}, {}}. Melvin represents a set as a list that contains no duplicated elements. Since no spaces are involved in the names of the items he is manipulating, Melvin writes them as symbols and not strings. Here is his program (figure 4.6).

```
(define powerset
    [ ] -> [[ ]]
    [X | Y] -> (append (subsets X (powerset Y)) (powerset Y)))

(define subsets
  _ [ ] -> [ ]
  X [Y | Z] -> [[X | Y] | (subsets X Z)])
```

Figure 4.6 Melvin's coding of powerset

The response to (powerset [beer gin vodka rum whisky lemonade]) is

[[beer gin vodka rum whisky lemonade] [beer gin vodka rum whisky] [beer gin vodka rum lemonade] [beer gin vodka rum] [beer gin vodka whisky lemonade] [beer gin vodka whisky] [beer gin vodka lemonade] [beer gin vodka] [beer gin rum whisky lemonade] [beer gin rum whisky] [beer gin rum lemonade] [beer gin rum] [beer gin whisky lemonade] [beer gin whisky] [beer gin lemonade] [beer gin] [beer vodka rum whisky lemonade] [beer vodka rum whisky] [beer vodka rum lemonade] [beer vodka rum] [beer vodka whisky lemonade]... etc]

4.4 Local Assignments

Melvin's definition of *powerset* is inefficient because (powerset Y) is computed twice within the same expression. A better strategy is to compute the normal form of (powerset Y) once and store it for use the second time. This is done with **local assignments** using let.[26] (let *V E A*) receives three inputs *V*, *E* and *A* where;

---

[25] By default the maximum length for printing is set at 20 elements though this can be changed for any positive integer *n* by (set *maximum-print-sequence-size* *n*).

[26] Another primitive of the 46.

1. V is a variable, which is assigned a value which is …
2. the normal form N of E, and (let $V E A$) returns ……
3. the normal form of the expression that results from substituting N for all free instances of V within A.

Here is *powerset* redefined in figure 4.7 using let.

```
(define powerset
  [ ] -> [[ ]]
  [X | Y] -> (let Powerset (powerset Y)
                 (append (subsets X Powerset) Powerset)))
```

Figure 4.7 An efficient coding of powerset using local assignments

The assignment of (powerset Y) to Powerset is local because the assignment works within the scope of let. We cannot usefully employ Powerset outside the local assignment because Powerset would have no value attached to it and a free variable warning would be raised.

let allows multiple local assignments without nested parentheses. Thus

```
(let X 4
     Y 5
     Z 6
     (+ X (* Y Z)))
```

means exactly the same as (let X 4 (let Y 5 (let Z 6 (+ X (* Y Z))))).

4.5 Goldbach's Conjecture Revisited

The previous chapter closed with an example of a possibly non-terminating program to test Goldbach's conjecture. The wasteful recalculation of primes meant that the program ran unfeasibly slowly given even a three digit number on which to test the conjecture. Lists provide the solution; we carry around in the program a list of all the primes calculated up to the number being tested. We refactor this program using lists.

```
(define goldbachs-conjecture
  \\ begin with 4 and the list of primes < 4
  start -> (goldbachs-conjecture-help 4 [3 2]))

(define goldbachs-conjecture-help
  N Primes -> N    where (not (sum-of-two? Primes N))
  N Primes  -> (if (prime? (+ N 1))
       (goldbachs-conjecture-help (+ N 2) [(+ 1 N) | Primes])
       (goldbachs-conjecture-help (+ N 2) Primes)))
```

```
(define sum-of-two?
  \\ no primes left?  then return false
  [] _ -> false
  \\ If the X + any other prime = N return true
  [X | Primes] N  -> true      where (x+prime=n X [X | Primes] N)
  \* no?  then recurse.  *\
  [_ | Primes] N -> (sum-of-two? Primes N))

(define x+prime=n
  \\ no primes left, return false
  _ [] _ -> false
  \\ X + the first prime = N?, so return true
  X [Prime | _] N -> true      where (= (+ X Prime) N)
  \\ recurse and try the other primes
  X [_ | Primes] N -> (x+prime=n X Primes N))
```

Figure 4.8 A more efficient coding of Goldbach's Conjecture

Exercise 4

1. Give the cons-form representation of each of the following.
   [a b c], [[a] [b] [c]], [a [b [c]]], [[a | [b]] c], [a | [b | [c]]]

2. Using only hd and tl, isolate c in each of the expressions in question 1.

3. Define each of the following.
   a. A function total that returns the total of a list of numbers.
   b. A function remdup that removes all duplicated elements in a list.
   c. A function first_n that receives a list L and a natural number N and returns the list of the first N elements of L.
   d. A function flatten that receives a list L and flattens it by removing all internal brackets - so (flatten [a [b] [[c]]]) $\Rightarrow$ [a b c].
   e. *A function permute that returns all the permutations of a list; (permute [a b c]) = [[a b c] [a c b] [b a c] [b c a] [c a b] [c b a]]. The order of the permutation does not matter.
   f. *A function exchange that exchanges the mth and nth elements of a list L; so (exchange 3 5 [a b c d e f]) $\Rightarrow$ [a b e d c f].

4. Classify the recursive function definitions used to answer the previous question as tail-recursive, tree-recursive, mutually recursive or linear recursive.

5. Define a binary number as a non-empty list of 0s and 1s.

   a. *Define binary-add that adds two binary numbers.
   b. *Define binary-subtract that subtracts two binary numbers.
   c. Write a function decimal-to-binary that converts a decimal natural number into binary.
   d. Write a function binary-to-decimal that converts a binary number into decimal.

e. Define perfect?, that returns true if N is perfect. A perfect number is a natural number > 1 that is the sum of its divisors. 28 is perfect since 28 = 1 + 14 + 2 + 7. 6 is perfect since 6 = 1 + 2 + 3.

f. Define triangular?, that returns true if N is a triangular number. A triangular number is a natural number > 0 that is the sum of the first *n* natural numbers for some *n*. 1, 3, 6, 10, 15, 21 are all triangular since 1 = 0 + 1, 3 = 0 + 1 + 2, 6 = 0 + 1 + 2 + 3 and so on.

6. Rewrite the counting change program of the previous chapter so that it receives a list of the denominations in use and returns the answer. So our original result of 4563 would be returned by (count-change 100 [200 100 50 20 10 5 2 1]).

7. *Write a program that enumerates the powerset of a set [1,2,3,....20] by printing the elements of this powerset down the screen. Your program will also supply the millionth element of this enumeration in a second or less. The order of the elements in the enumeration does not matter.

8. *The ancient English game of *cribbage* is played in five and six card variations. We shall ignore some of the subtleties of scoring in this question. In cribbage a hand is scored as follows. Sets of cards whose total pip value is 15 score 2. Any number of cards can be in a set. For the purpose of totalling, face cards count as 10, ace as 1. Three or more cards in sequence (called a *run*) count 1 point for each card in the sequence. An ace is low in cribbage, so ace, two, three is a run, but not queen, king, ace. In five card cribbage, three or more cards of the same suit (called a *flush*) count one point for each card in the flush. In six card cribbage, *four* or more cards of the same suit count one point for each card in the flush. A *pair* (two cards of the same rank) counts 2 points. Here is a hand in six card cribbage.

J♥, Q♥, K♥, K♠, K♣, 5♥

The value of this hand is as follows. 10 points for cards totalling 15 (pair the 5 off with every other card); 6 points for runs (two runs of J, Q, K); 4 points for a flush (the four hearts) and 6 points for pairs (three distinct pairs made from the three kings) giving 26 points in all. Devise a program that scores hands in five and six card cribbage.

9. Cribbage requires the player to discard two cards from his hand. In six card cribbage this gives 30 possible discards and in five card cribbage, 20 possible discards. Devise a function that goes through all the possible discards and works out which is the best discard. The best discard will maximise the value of the remaining cards left in the player's hand (three cards in the case of five card cribbage and four in the case of six card cribbage).

10. *The Roman numeral system was used for many centuries in the ancient world. The table below shows Roman numerals and their decimal equivalents.

Roman	Decimal
I	1
V	5
X	10
L	50
C	100
D	500
M	1000

"The Roman counting system used tallies for numbers ending in 3 (III = 3, 33 = XXXIII). However, four strokes seemed like too many, so the Romans moved on to the symbol for 5 - V. Placing I in front of the V, or placing any smaller number in front of any larger number, indicates subtraction. So IV means 4. After V comes a series of additions - VI means 6, VII means 7, VIII means 8. IX means to subtract I from X, leaving 9. Numbers in the teens, twenties and thirties follow the same form as the first set, only with X's indicating the number of tens. So XXXI is 31, and XXIV is 24. 40 is XL, and 60, 70, and 80 are LX, LXX and LXXX. CCCLXIX is 369. As you can probably guess by this time, CD means 400. So CDXLVIII is 448." Implement a program that takes a Roman numeral from 1-3000 as a list and outputs the corresponding decimal number. (From www.novaroma.org/via_romana/numbers.html).

11. *(For readers with some logic). Implement a tautology tester which, by use of truth-tables, returns true if the input is a tautology and false if not. Thus (tautology? [[p & q] => q]) should return true.

Further Reading

The cons-cell representation of a list is the basis for the representation of a list within the architecture of the digital computer. Allen (1978) contains an account of cons-cell representations. There are other alternatives. Abelson & Sussman (1996) has a discussion of streams which can emulate lists of infinite length. Miranda[TM] uses schemas based on set comprehension as well as lists. The language SETL discussed in Schwartz J.T., Dewar R.B.K., Dubinsky, E., and Schonberg, E., (1986) uses the set instead of the list as its basic data structure. http://galt.cs.nyu.edu/~bacon/other-setl.html provides many links to ongoing work with SETL.

5 Strings

5.1 Strings and Symbols

A string is any series of characters flanked by double quotes ("). Strings behave ostensibly rather like symbols but with a greater degree of flexibility in allowing any standard keyboard character within the double quotes. Thus [a is not an acceptable symbol but "[a" is an acceptable string. In fact any symbol can be turned into a string by simply flanking it by double quotes.

In many languages, but not Shen, strings perform many of the duties of symbols as inputs to functions. Symbols which are simply used as inputs, without any intent to designate a variable or a function are called **idle symbols** in this text. Why allow symbols unless they are working as variables or calling functions? There are several reasons for freeing symbols from such roles.

First, an intellectually trivial but significant reason is that using symbols instead of strings saves time at the keyboard and the result is easier to type and prettier to read. If we are coding an algebra program then [x + [3 - y]] is easier to read and type than ["x" "+" [3 "-" "y"]].

The second reason for allowing idle symbols is that we can make effective use of a powerful idea called **programs as data**. As we shall see in chapter 11, we can represent Shen programs as complex lists containing symbols and write **metaprograms** (or programs that generate programs) which grab those lists and turn them directly into programs using either macros or a function called eval.

In contrast languages which do not allow idle symbols generally have to represent native programs as strings and this requires complex string parsing techniques which are generally more cumbersome to write and slower to execute than the list based ones. In effect, by having a pool of idle symbols to hand we can recruit them as needed for the various tasks which as programmers we might feel inclined to get them to perform.[27] Having established then, the right of idle

---

[27] In Shen, not only can symbols can be recruited for various purposes, but the same symbol can be recruited for different purposes making it a **multiple namespace** language. In a **single namespace** language like Scheme, ML or Python a symbol can only be recruited to mean one thing. The significance of this will become clearer in chapter 21.

symbols and strings to coexist in the same language, we now return to the subject of strings.

Any symbol can be turned into a string by means of the str function which is a primitive function. Thus (str cheese) returns "cheese". str, being one of the primitives, is fast in execution but limited in scope. In fact str is designed to work on Shen **atoms** – that is to say, either symbols, booleans, numbers or strings. (str "cheese") returns ""cheese"".

There is a converse function, intern, for turning a string into a symbol. (intern "cheese") produces cheese. intern is another primitive and will work on symbols and booleans that are effectively embedded within quotes. It can, depending on platform, sometimes extract from quotes objects that are not symbols, (e.g. numbers) but this is not guaranteed.

The basic recognisor for strings is string?, and cn will concatenate (join) two strings together. Both of these are primitive functions and are relatively fast. The correlate of the empty list [] is the **empty string ""**.

```
(0-) (string? "hello world")
true

(1-) (cn "H" (cn "i!" ""))
"Hi!"
```

Figure 5.1 Basic string operations

The set of acceptable strings is actually larger than the set of strings that we can construct from the keyboard characters. The **standard ASCII** character set (figure 5.2) evolved from a set of characters that are expressible within seven bits or 128 (2^7) combinations. Each character is associated with a number which is its **code point**. Later **extended ASCII** representing a set of characters expressible within eight bits or 256 (2^8) combinations was evolved. Still later **32-bit Unicode** was evolved providing enough space to encode the currently recognised 1,112,064 characters with room to spare.

All commonly used computer languages have provision to represent the standard ASCII character set and this includes Shen. Since some of these characters cannot be found on the keyboard, they are referred to through their code points.

ASCII	String	ASCII	String	ASCII	String	ASCII	String
0	blank	36	$	72	H	108	l
1	☺	37	%	73	I	109	m
2	☻	38	&	74	J	110	n
3	♥	39	'	75	K	111	o
4	♦	40	(	76	L	112	p
5	♣	41	)	77	M	113	q
6	♠	42	*	78	N	114	r
7	bell	43	+	79	O	115	s
8	"	44	,	80	P	116	t
9	tab	45	-	81	Q	117	u
10	newline	46	.	82	R	118	v
11	♂	47	/	83	S	119	w
12	♂	48	0	84	T	120	x
13	newline	49	1	85	U	121	y
14	♫	50	2	86	V	122	z
15	☼	51	3	87	W	123	{
16	►	52	4	88	X	124	|
17	◄	53	5	89	Y	125	}
18	↕	54	6	90	Z	126	~
19	‼	55	7	91	[	127	⌂
20	¶	56	8	92	\		
21	§	57	9	93	]		
22	▬	58	:	94	^		
23	↨	59	;	95	_		
24	↑	60	<	96	`		
25	↓	61	=	97	a		
26	→	62	>	98	b		
27	←	63	?	99	c		
28	∟	64	@	100	d		
29	↔	65	A	101	e		
30	▲	66	B	102	f		
31	▼	67	C	103	g		
32	blank	68	D	104	h		
33	!	69	E	105	i		
34	"	70	F	106	j		
35	#	71	G	107	k		

Figure 5.2 The ASCII Character Table for Windows

Shen allows non-keyboard characters to be embedded into strings by use of the c#*n*; notation; where *n* is a natural number. Thus in Windows the string "c#16;" is read and printed as "▶" because ▶ has the ASCII code point 16.[28] The table previous shows the list of ASCII code points and their associated characters.

The function n->string maps any ASCII code point to the corresponding **unit string**[29]. The domain of this function includes all of the ASCII codes from 0-127 and may, depending on the platform, incorporate a wider character set beyond 127, such as Unicode; however this is not guaranteed. For cases outside the ASCII code point space, this function may return an error. The inverse of n->string is string->n; both of these are primitive (figure 5.3).

```
(0-) "c#16;"
"▶"

(1-) (string->n "c#15;")
15

(2-) (n->string 67)
"C"

(3-) (string->n "G")
71
```

Figure 5.3 Using ASCII character codes

5.2 Building strings with make-string

The polyadic function make-string is rather more sophisticated than str; it accepts a string and a series of zero or more following arguments. One of these is ~%, which forces a new line (figure 5.4).

```
(4-) (make-string "goodbye cruel world,~%I bid you adieu.~%")
"goodbye cruel world,
I bid you adieu."
```

Figure 5.4 Using make-string

~A creates slots in the message, which can be filled in any way by placing expressions after the message string. The expressions are evaluated to their normal forms, and these normal forms are placed in the slots of the message and the result is printed. Figure 5.5 shows an example.

---

[28] For Linux and other operating systems, the appearance of non-keyboard characters may differ from those under Windows.

[29] A unit string is a single character flanked by quotes; such as "e" or "7".

(10-) (make-string "~A in ~A ~A made ~A ~A.~%" God his wisdom the fly)
"God in his wisdom made the fly."

Figure 5.5 Filling the slots in a string

The slots are determined by the following key sequences; ~A, ~S and ~R. ~A and ~S are identical except that when slot value is a string, ~A embeds it in the slot without quotes and ~S embeds it with quotes. ~R embeds a list into the slot using (...)s for [...]s which is useful for printing formulae.

(4-) (make-string "~S, said the fly.~%" "Why?")
""Why?" said the fly."

(5-) (make-string "~A, said the fly.~%" "Why?")
"Why? said the fly."

(6-) (make-string "~A = ~A~%" [1 + 1] 2)
"[1 + 1] = 2"

(7-) (make-string "~R = ~R~%" [1 + 1] 2)
"(1 + 1) = 2"

Figure 5.6 Building strings using different slots

5.3 Coercing Strings to Lists

A slower, but again more general function than intern, is read-from-string which will take any series of readable objects embedded in a string and return them as a list (figure 5.7).

(0-) (read-from-string "hello world")
[hello world]

(1-) (read-from-string "[hi there")
read error here:

[hi there

Figure 5.7 Reading from a string

explode is a useful function which explodes any object (including lists etc) into a list of unit strings. The expression (explode "hello") delivers ["h" "e" "l" "l" "o"]. Exploding [1 2 3] delivers ["[" "1" " " "2" " " "3" "]"] (the gaps between the numbers are marked by blank strings).

The expression ($ hello) is superficially similar in exploding its argument; however the exploding is done by the reader and ($ hello) is read in as if the user had typed in "h" "e" "l" "l" "o". This is useful to avoid typing multiple quotes. Thus the definition

```
(define remove-hello
  [($ hello) | X] -> X)
```

is equivalent to and is parsed as

```
(define remove-hello
  ["h" "e" "l" "l" "o" | X] -> X)
```

5.4 Programming with Strings

There are two basic primitives pos and tlstr for processing strings. pos takes two arguments, a string s and an integer n and returns the nth character of s counting from zero. tlstr returns all but the first character of s. Again both of these are primitive.

It is significant that hdstr, which returns the first element of a string, is not a primitive though it is provided as a courtesy (being equivalent to (pos *string* 0)). The reason for this is that many languages store strings in the form of vectors of characters, and in a vector v the nth element of v can be located in constant time. Hence it is just a quick to locate the 100th element of a string as the first and hence pos is a primitive and hdstr is not. A vector-based representation of strings has profound consequences for the speed of string handling operations and we will understand this better in chapter 8 on vectors.

Shen incorporates a function @s which acts as a polyadic version of cn. Thus (cn "H" (cn "i!" "")) can be written as (@s "H" "i!" "") or (@s "Hi" ""). The polyadicity is created by the Shen reader. Internally, the Shen reader inserts the missing brackets, and @s is read as a concatenation of *unit strings*. So the expression (@s "Hi!" "")) is read as (@s "H" (@s "i" (@s "!" ""))).

@s can be used in pattern-matching over strings and nearly all complex string manipulation programs are written in this style. Used in a function, (@s X Y) matches X to the head of the string and Y to the tail. @s therefore suffices to define all the primitive string operations. One such function tests a string to see if it is the prefix of another string.

```
(0-) (define string-prefix?
      "" _ -> true
      (@s S Str1) (@s S Str2) -> (string-prefix? Str1 Str2)
      _ _ -> false)
string-prefix?

(1-) (string-prefix? "123" "1234")
true

(2-) (string-prefix? "1234" "123")
false
```

Figure 5.8 Testing one string to see if it is a prefix of another

Now we have got the idea of string handling, let us consider again a problem we dealt with in the previous chapter; that of computing a list of students and the exams they had taken.

In order to do that we computed the Cartesian product of the students' names and the exams they took. In our scenario we had 100 names and 6 exams, but there was no supposition that the names were ordered alphabetically. If they are not ordered alphabetically then the Cartesian product will itself not be ordered alphabetically and we will end up with an unsorted 600 element list. Hence the student list should first be sorted alphabetically before the Cartesian product is computed.

Bubble sort is one of the simplest and least efficient sorting algorithms but it is sufficient for a 100 element list. Bubble sorting a list L into ascending or descending order works by traversing L comparing each item x with its successor y. If y is prior to x according to the sort relation, then the positions of x and y are exchanged. Bubble sorting is repeated until no change occurs, at which point L is sorted. Here it is in Shen.

```
(define bubble-sort
  X -> (bubble-again-perhaps (bubble X) X))

(define bubble
  [ ] -> [ ]
  [X] -> [X]
  [X Y | Z] -> [Y | (bubble [X | Z])]            where (prior? Y X)
  [X Y | Z] -> [X | (bubble [Y | Z])])

(define bubble-again-perhaps
  X X -> X
  X _ -> (bubble-sort X))
```

Figure 5.9 Bubble sort

One name is prior to another if the surname is prior.

```
(define prior?
  Name1 Name2 -> (string< (surname Name1) (surname Name2)))
```

The surname will be the series of characters that follow the last whitespace in a string. Whitespace is located by the code point, being either a new line, a tab or a blank.

```
(define surname
  Name -> (surname-help Name ""))
```

```
(define surname-help
  "" Surname -> Surname
  (@s S Name) _ -> (surname-help Name "") where (whitespace? S)
  (@s S Name) Surname ->  (surname-help Name (cn Surname S)))
```

```
(define whitespace?
  S -> (let N (string->n S) (element? N [9 10 13 32])))
```

```
 (define string<
   (@s S _) (@s S# _) -> true        where (< (string->n S) (string->n S#))
   (@s S Ss) (@s S Ss#) -> (string< Ss Ss#)
   "" (@s _ _) -> true
   _ _ -> false)
```

Finally the program can be run.

```
(9 -) (bubble-sort ["Rudolf Carnap"  "Richard Dawkins"
                "John Backus"  "Harold Abelson" ])
["Harold Abelson" "John Backus" "Rudolf Carnap" "Richard Dawkins"]
```

Exercise 5

1. Write a program that computes your initials from a string containing your full name and displays them as a list of unit strings.

2. An **anagram** is a word or a phrase made by transposing the letters of another word or phrase; for example, "parliament" is an anagram of "partial men," and "software" is an anagram of "swear oft." Write a program that figures out whether one string is an anagram of another string. The program should ignore white space and punctuation.

3. Design, then implement a program that sums the ASCII codes of all the letters of any string.

4. Divide a string into two halves. If the length is even, the front and back halves are the same length. If the length is odd, the extra character goes in the front half.

5. Write a program that given a natural number *n*, outputs a string in which *n* is embedded in an *n*X*n* square. For example, for the input 3 the square would be (numbers line up).

    a. "3 3 3
    b. 3 3 3
    c. 3 3 3"

6. Generalise intern to gen-intern so that you can read an expression of the form "[1 2 3]" and return [1 2 3]. Whether your platform already does this is not important.*

7. Write a function trimr to remove all trailing whitespace from the right of a string.

8. Write a function triml to remove all leading whitespace from the left of a string.

9. Write a function padr to add extra whitespace to the right end of a string to make it length *n*. If the string is already *n* characters or longer, do not change the string.

10. Write a function padl to add extra whitespace to the left end of a string to make it length *n*. If the string is already *n* characters or longer, do not change the string.

11. Write a function padc to centre a string by adding blanks to the front and back. If the string is already *n* characters or longer, do not change the string. If an odd number of blanks have to be added, put the extra blank on the right.

12. Write a function shorten which shortens a string to *n* characters. If the string is already shorter than *n*, the function should not change the string.

13. Write a function capitalise which capitalises the first letter in every word. Assume the first letter is any letter at the beginning or preceded by a blank. All other letters should be turned into lowercase.

14. Write a function count which counts the occurrences in a string, *a*, of the single character which is the second argument, *b*.

15. Write a function delete which deletes any occurrence in the first argument, *a*, of the single character which is the second argument, *c*.

Further Reading

String processing languages began with SNOBOL (string oriented and symbolic language) in 1962 (Emmer, 1985) developed by AT&T. More recent successors include TCL/tk (Ousterhout, 2006) and Perl (Wall et al., 2012). TCL/tk was popular in the '90s and Perl remains the language of choice for many people involved in text processing. The main feature of Perl in relation to strings is its regex pattern matching which allows the programmer write a single line to search for a string in a body of text.

6 Higher Order Functions

6.1 Higher Order Functions

Functions often seem insubstantial since they have no physical existence; the square root function, for instance, cannot be given a location; there is no moment when it was created, since it stands outside time and space. For people of a philosophical persuasion, this makes functions very strange objects. However a willingness to countenance functions as substantial objects is implicit in functional programming, where functions are treated as potential inputs or outputs to other functions, just as other objects like numbers or strings. In functional programming, functions enjoy the same rights of processing as other data objects; i.e. functions are **first-class objects**.

Higher-order functions receive functions as inputs or return them amongst the output. In Shen map is a higher-order system function. Its definition is:

```
(define map
   F [ ] -> [ ]
   F [X | Y] -> [(F X) | (map F Y)])
```

map receives a 1-place function F and a list L. If L is empty, then L is returned. But if L is of the form [X | Y] then the function F is applied to the first element X and the result is consed to the effect of recursing on the tail of the list using map. Figure 6.1 shows the use of map.

```
(0 -) (define double
        X -> (* X 2))
double

(1-) (map (function double) [1 2 3 4])
[2 4 6 8]
```

Figure 6.1 Using the map function

The significance of function is that we want to tell Shen that the symbol double is not just an idle symbol but is supposed to designate a function. In Shen a symbol may moonlight in a number of roles and it is necessary to be clear what we are asking of it. In this case we are asking for the function associated with that name.[30]

6.2 Abstractions, Currying and Partial Applications

The function that doubles a number is represented in Shen as (/. X (* X 2)). /. is the Shen ASCII substitute for the Greek lambda, and (/. X (* X 2)) is referred to as an **abstraction**. We can most easily read the notation of abstractions by taking /. to mean "the function that receives an input...". Thus (/. X (* X 2)) is read as "the function that receives an input X and returns the result of multiplying X by 2". Figure 6.2 shows the use of an abstraction.

```
(1-) (/. X (* X 2))
#<CLOSURE :LAMBDA [X] [* X 2]>

(2-) ((/. X (* X 2)) 5)
10
```

Figure 6.2 Using abstractions

The evaluation of an abstraction in Shen delivers an object called a **closure**, which is a compiled representation of the original abstraction with zero or more pieces of data attached to it.[31] In Shen, closures are represented as expressions beginning #<CLOSURE ...>.[32] These expressions are **internal expressions**; they cannot be read and evaluated in their computer-printed form (i.e. typing #<CLOSURE :LAMBDA [X] [* X 2]> will generate an error).

As shown, abstractions can be applied to expressions just like normal functions. They differ from conventional Shen functions in being applicable to only one input, for in these examples exactly one variable follows the /.. However it is possible to represent *n*-place functions with abstractions, where *n* is any value.

An example with the 2-place function + will illustrate the idea.

---

[30] This brings out the difference between Shen and single namespace languages mentioned earlier. In a single namespace language such as Python. ML or Haskell, a global symbol may only have a single role and hence the disambiguating function is not needed. Note that in the Lisp platform, the compiler is clever enough to figure out that the symbol is being used to denote a function. However this is not a portable feature and good practice requires us to use function.

[31] More precisely, a closure is a function represented as a pair composed of a lambda abstraction together with an assignment of values to the free variables of that abstraction. See chapter 14 of this book for a discussion of lambda expressions and chapter 21 for a discussion of closures.

[32] This representation may vary according to the platform being used. There is no obligation in Shen to print closures or streams or native objects of the platform in a specific form and if Shen cannot print such an object it is printed as a *funex* in the form funex*n* where *n* is a number. See chapter 9 on printing..

The 2-place function + can be represented as an interaction of two 1-place functions f and g. f receives a number x and produces a function g that waits to receive another number y. Whatever number y is supplied to g, y is added to x to produce the result $x + y$. Thus the function + is denoted by the expression

"the function that receives an input x and returns a function that receives an input y that then returns $x + y$".

Translating this into the notation of abstractions gives (/. X (/. Y (+ X Y))). Now suppose we tell Shen to apply this expression to the number 5.

```
(1-) ((/. X (/. Y (+ X Y))) 5)
#<CLOSURE :LAMBDA [Y] [+ X Y]>
```

Figure 6.3 Applying an abstraction to produce a function

Shen returns a closure which represents a function that adds 5 to its input.   If ((/. X (/. Y (+ X Y))) 5) is itself applied to 3, then the result is the same as applying this closure to 3, which produces 8. (/. X Y (+ X Y)) is an accepted abbreviation for (/. X (/. Y (+ X Y))).

```
(2-) (((/. X  Y (+ X Y)) 5) 3)
8
```

Figure 6.4 Using an abstraction to add two numbers

When an abstraction is applied to an input to produce a function (as in 6.3) then the application is called a **partial application**. Since the 2-place function symbol '+' and the abstraction '(/. X Y (+ X Y))' both denote the same operation of addition, it is reasonable to expect that we should be able to enter '(+ 5)' as a partial application in Shen and return a closure just as in figure 6.3.   This is correct; we can substitute '+' for '(/. X Y (+ X Y))' and gain the same function.

```
(3-) (+ 5)
#<CLOSURE :LAMBDA [Z1413] [+ 5 Z1413]>

(4+) ((+ 5) 3)
8
```

Figure 6.5 Currying + to add two numbers

Nearly every application[33] can be written to Shen in the form $(f\ i)$, consisting of a function f and a single input i. When an expression in this form is **curried** and the operation of placing it in this form is **currying**.[34]

---

[33] With few exceptions; the functions cons, let, output, make-string, error, @p, @v, @s, input are not curried or curryable in Shen and are referred to as **special forms**.

Partial applications can be incorporated into function definitions. This function receives a list of numbers and doubles each one.

```
(define double-everything
    X -> (map (* 2) X))
```

A function *f* may cite a function *g*, where the identity of *g* depends on the inputs supplied to *f*. This function, xn-map, when supplied with a number N and a list L, multiplies every element of L by N.

```
(define xn-map
    N L -> (map (* N) L))
```

The identity of the partial application (* N) depends on the value for N that is input to xn-everything. If N = 2, then the function behaves exactly as double-everything. Notice that though * is a *2-place* function, (* N) is a *1-place* function, since the first input N is fixed when xn-map is called.

Shen treats and compiles a 'function' call as shorthand for writing the corresponding abstraction. So (map (function double) [1 2 3]) is compiled into (map (/. X (double X)) [1 2 3]) and (map (function union) [[] [1] [2] [3]]) is compiled into (map (/. X (/. Y (union X Y))) [[] [1] [2] [3]]). Partial applications like (* N) are filled out by the Shen compiler to (/. X (* N X)).

Being able to fill out these shorthands correctly depends on knowing the arities of the functions involved. By default if a function *f* is applied whose arity is not known then Shen assumes the application is total. If a function *f* is partially applied in a definition *before f* is defined, then an error may result when the partial application is attempted e.g..

```
(18-) (define g
        X -> (f X))
g

(19-) (define f
        X Y -> Y)
f

(20-) (g 6)
APPLY: too few arguments given to #<COMPILED-CLOSURE f>
```

Figure 6.6 An attempted partial application

Using type checking, as discussed in the second part of this book, will activate a sentinel that guards against these mistakes.

---

[34] After Haskell B. Curry, the mathematical logician who is usually credited with inventing this technique, although Schonfinkel was the first to use it.

6.3 Programming with Higher Order Functions

Programming with higher-order functions enables us to

1. Get rid of unnecessary definitions using abstractions.
2. Use similarities in different processes to shorten our code.
3. Pass functions as data.

The Cartesian product program of 4.5 invoked a function pairs that paired an element X with each element of a list L. Rather than define a function like pairs, we use an abstraction; a similar optimisation works for the powerset function.

```
(define cartesian-product
  [] _ -> []
  [X | Y] Z -> (append (map (/. E [X E]) Z) (cartesian-product Y Z)))

(define powerset
  [] -> [[]]
  [X | Y] -> (let Powerset (powerset Y)
                  Sets (map (/. Z [X | Z]) Powerset)
                  (append Sets Powerset)))
```

Figure 6.7 Cartesian product and powerset recoded using abstractions

If two programs both share properties then rather than encode them separately, we can draw out the similarities using higher-order functions. Our case study compares the bubble sort algorithm of the last chapter with **Newton's method of approximations**. Here is the code for bubble sort again, but now as a higher-order program in which the priority relation is a parameter (figure 6.8).

```
(define bubble-sort
  R X -> (bubble-again-perhaps R (bubble R X) X))

(define bubble
  _ [] -> []
  _ [X] -> [X]
  R [X Y | Z] -> [Y | (bubble R [X | Z])]        where (R Y X)
  R [X Y | Z] -> [X | (bubble R [Y | Z])])

(define bubble-again-perhaps
  _ X X -> X
  R X _ -> (bubble-sort R X))
```

Figure 6.8 Bubble sort as a higher order program in Shen

The most common way is to compute square roots is to use Newton's method of approximations which says that if we want to find the square root of N, we take a guess Guess and average the result with N/Guess. This average will then be a better estimate of the value of √N than the original Guess. By repeating the process as many times as desired, we will derive the value of √N to a given degree of accuracy.

Suppose we decide to use Newton's method of approximations to derive the value of √N to three decimal places. We start our guess at √N by guessing that √N = N/2.0. Every time we derive a better value for √N using Newton's method, we compare the two values. Eventually the better value will be different from the old one by an absolute difference of less than (say) .001 which will be good enough. This value will be returned as our value for √N. The Shen program is given in figure 6.9.

```
(define newtons-method
  N -> (let Guess (/ N 2.0)
         (run-newtons-method N (average Guess (/ N Guess)) Guess)))

(define run-newtons-method
  _ Better_Guess Guess -> Better_Guess
               where (close-enough? Better_Guess Guess)
  N Better_Guess _
  -> (run-newtons-method N
       (average Better_Guess (/ N Better_Guess))
       Better_Guess))

(define average
  M N -> (/ (+ M N) 2.0))

(define close-enough?
  Better_Guess Guess -> (< (abs (- Better_Guess Guess)) .001))

(define abs
  N -> (if (> 0 N) (- 0 N) N))
```

Figure 6.9 Newton's method in Shen

The code for bubble sort and Newton's method share a common element in that they both apply a procedure to their input until no significant change is produced in the output. To make use of this observation to shorten the code we need to formalise the idea of *converging on a value*.

The basic idea of convergence is that we have a function F which is iteratively applied to a value X until the result differs from the result of the previous iteration within some agreed tolerance R. When that point is reached we have converged on a solution within the bounds of R. Figure 6.10 shows the higher-order function **converge,** that computes this.

```
(define converge
  F X R -> (converge-help F (F X) X R))

(define converge-help
  _ New Old R -> New  where (R New Old)
  F New _ R -> (converge-help F (F New) New R))
```

Figure 6.10 The converge function

Using converge, the top level of the bubble sort program can be rewritten; the bubble-again-perhaps function is now redundant (figure 6.11).

```
(define bubble-sort
   R X -> (converge (/. Y (bubble R Y)) X (function =)))
```

Figure 6.11 Rewriting the top level of the bubble sort program

Applying converge to Newton's method is a little more difficult since run-newtons-method is a 3-place function, not a 1-place function like bubble. However the number N whose square root we are to find is fixed when newtons-method is called and it always stays the same while the program is running. The newtons-method function can use a specialised version of run-newtons-method for that particular value of N. Since N is fixed, this specialised function could be a 2-place function.

Still one too many places! However, consider that run-newtons-method carries both the old value and the better value around in order to compare them for equality. If we use converge to derive the final value, such a comparison is not needed. Since the specialised version of run-newtons-method is defined only when newtons-method is called, it must be created "on the fly". Creating functions on the fly is a job for abstractions and so we use them to recode the original Shen program (figure 6.12). The recursion and comparison is driven by converge.

```
(define newtons-method
   N -> (converge (/. M (average M (/ N M)))
                  (/ N 2.0)
                  (function close-enough?)))
```

Figure 6.12 Newton's method recoded using a higher order function

The combined length of the two revised programs is less than half that of the originals. Higher-order functions can save us a lot of tedious code if we can learn to recognise the cases in which they are applicable. But if we want to seize these opportunities, we must be alert for high-level similarities between algorithms.

Higher order functions allow us to treat functions as data just like numbers or lists. This technique, called **procedural attachment,** is used in the next example - how to build a spreadsheet.

Imagine that we want to maintain a list of details about an employee Jim, including his salary and the amount he pays in tax. Suppose that he pays 25% of his wages in tax. If we enter his tax as a cash figure, then if he has a wage increase then the cash figure for tax will be wrong. Business managers cope with problems like this using *spreadsheets*; Jim's tax is stored, not as a number, but as a function that allows the calculation of his tax from other details on the spreadsheet. Our task is to model a spreadsheet in Shen.

Our spreadsheet will consist of a series of *rows*, each row consisting of an *index* and a series of *cells*. The index is a unique name that marks out that row and a cell is composed of an *attribute* (like tax or job) and a *value*. Values can be either *fixed values* which are **atoms** (booleans, numbers. strings or symbols) or they can be *dependent values* (functions) which when applied to the appropriate inputs, will return fixed values. To assess a spreadsheet, we replace all the dependent values by fixed values.

Figure 6.13 shows a sample spreadsheet in which Jim's wages are pegged to Frank's and his tax is pegged to .8 of whatever Frank pays. Frank is down as earning £20,000 a year and paying .25 of this in tax. We want to evaluate this expression so that the dependent values are replaced by fixed values, giving figures for wage and tax for both Jim and Frank.

```
[[jim [wages (/. Spreadsheet (get-val frank wages Spreadsheet))]
      [tax (/. Spreadsheet (* (get-val frank tax Spreadsheet) .8))]]
 [frank  [wages 20000]
      [tax (/. Spreadsheet (* .25 (get-val frank wages Spreadsheet)))]]]]
```

Figure 6.13 A sample spreadsheet in Shen

Figure 6.14 shows a spreadsheet program in Shen.

```
(define assess-spreadsheet
  Spreadsheet
  -> (map (/. Row (assign-fixed-values Row Spreadsheet))
          Spreadsheet))

(define assign-fixed-values
  [Index | Cells] Spreadsheet
  -> [Index |  (map (/. Cell (assign-cell-value Cell Spreadsheet))
              Cells)])

(define assign-cell-value
  [Attribute Value] _  -> [Attribute Value]
                              where (fixed-value? Value)
  [Attribute Value] Spreadsheet
              -> [Attribute (Value Spreadsheet)]])

(define fixed-value?
  Value -> (or (number? Value) (symbol? Value) (string? Value)))

(define get-val
  Index Attribute Spreadsheet
  -> (get-row Index Attribute Spreadsheet Spreadsheet))
```

```
(define get-row
  \\ looks for the right row using the index
  Index Attribute [[Index | Cells] | _] Spreadsheet
  -> (get-cell Attribute Cells Spreadsheet)
  Index Attribute [_ | Rows] Spreadsheet
  -> (get-row Index Attribute Rows Spreadsheet)
  Index _ _ _ -> (error "Index ~A not found" Index))

(define get-cell
  Attribute [[Attribute Value] | _] Spreadsheet
  -> (if (fixed-value? Value) Value (Value Spreadsheet))
  Attribute [_ | Cells] Spreadsheet
  -> (get-cell Attribute Cells Spreadsheet)
  Attribute _ _ -> (error "Attribute ~A not found" Attribute))
```

Figure 6.14 A spreadsheet program in Shen

The top level function **assess-spreadsheet** works along each row in turn, assigning fixed values to the cells; the entire spreadsheet is carried in this process, since a dependent value may access any part of the spreadsheet. **assign-fixed-values** takes a row and assigns a fixed value to every cell. **assign-fixed-values** will receive a cell and a spreadsheet; if the value in the cell is fixed, the cell remains the same. If it is dependent, then the value in the cell is applied to the spreadsheet to derive a fixed value.

The **get** function works along each row, carrying the full spreadsheet with it. We need to do this because a dependent value will access other values before returning a fixed value, and we will then need the spreadsheet again (e.g. Jim's tax accesses Frank's tax which accesses Frank's wages). We cope with this by creating two copies of the spreadsheet, one to work through row by row, and the other to hold in memory in case the whole spreadsheet is needed. This technique, of duplicating inputs to keep one for processing and one to remember, is called **spreading the input**. Finally **get-cell** looks for a cell corresponding to the attribute, and retrieves the value. If the value is fixed, then it is returned, if not then it is applied to the spreadsheet to retrieve the appropriate value.

Figure 6.15 shows our spreadsheet program in action.

```
(5-) (assess-spreadsheet
     [[jim  [wages (/. Spreadsheet (get-val frank wages Spreadsheet))]
        [tax (/. Spreadsheet (* (get-val frank tax Spreadsheet) .8))]]
      [frank  [wages 20000]
        [tax (/. Spreadsheet (* .25 (get-val frank wages Spreadsheet)))]]])

[[jim [wages 20000] [tax 4000.0]] [frank [wages 20000] [tax 5000.0]]]
```

Figure 6.15 Assessing a spreadsheet

Exercise 6

1. Define the following higher-order functions.

    a. A function count which takes a 1-place boolean function F and a list L and returns the number of elements in L that have the property F.
    b. A function some? which takes a 1-place boolean function F and a list L and returns true if some element of L has the property F and false otherwise.
    c. A function all? which takes a 1-place boolean function F and a list L and returns true if every element of L has the property F and false otherwise.
    d. A function compose that receives a non-empty list of 1-place functions and forms their composition. Thus (compose [(/. X (+ 1 X)) sqrt]) would generate a function that added one to the square root of a number.
    e. A function test-speed that receives a list input L and a natural number N. The list L is composed of a function symbol F followed by a series of elements $X_1,...,X_j$. test-speed should apply F to the inputs $X_1,...,X_j$, performing this operation N times, and timing the whole computation (hint: look at the function time in Appendix A).
    f. A function partition that receives a list L and an equivalence relation R on that list and generates the partition of L by R as a list of lists.

2. A progression is an object that mimics a possibly infinitely long list and can be represented as a three-element list [X F E]. X is the first element in the stream and F is the function that applied to any element of the stream gives the next element and E tests if the progression is exhausted. So the progression of natural numbers can be represented as [0 (/. X (+ 1 X)) (/. X false)].

    a. Write a function, lazy-nth, that given any progression P, gets the nth element of L.
    b. Devise a 2-place function some? that receives a 1-place boolean function f and a progression P, returning true if there is an object x in P such that $(f\,x)$ = true.
    c. If two progressions A and B have an infinite number of elements, then appending them together makes no computational sense because the stream that is tagged at the end will remain inaccessible to stream-nth. But we can interleave them by generating a progression composed of two-element lists where the nth element of this progression is composed of a list containing the nth element of A and the nth element of B . Write a function interleave which does just that.
    d. Write a function all? that receives a 1-place boolean function f and a progression, returning true if every object x in the stream is such that $(f\,x)$ = true.
    e. Write a function expand that takes a progression and generates the list that corresponds to it. So (expand [0 [(/. X (+ 1 X)) (/. X (= X 1000))]]) generates the list of numbers [0 1 2 3 .... 1000].

4. It is natural to think of lists as data objects and functions like head and tail as procedures which act on data-objects. But we can change this perception.

    a. Implement the list [1 2 3] as a higher-order function that receives the message head and returns 1 and the message tail and returns the corresponding higher-order function that represents the list [2 3]. Implement [ ] as a function that returns an error given the message head or the message tail.

b. Now implement the functions first and rest. first receives the higher-order function that represents the list and derives the first element from it. rest receives the higher-order function that represents the list and derives the corresponding higher-order function that represents the tail of the list.

c. Finally define constr as the analog of cons that builds a new list representing function from an old one. Show that (first (constr X Y)) = X.

5. *For this question and the following you need some background knowledge in the theory of search and some knowledge of resolution theorem-proving. Russell and Norvig (1995, 2002) provides a good introduction to these topics.

Implement *breadth-first search* as a higher-order function breadth-first that takes the following inputs.

a. A *start state* S.
b. A *state successor function* O that generates a list of states from a given state.
c. A 2-place function R that recognises when states are essentially the same and returns true when they are. (R is used to filter out redundant states.)
d. A function T that returns either true or false and that recognises only *goal states*.

Your function should return either true or false depending on whether a solution can be reached by breadth-first search.

6. Test your system by implementing a simple resolution theorem-prover where S is the initial clause set, O maps a set C of clauses to all the possible sets gained by resolving two clauses in C, R recognises when two clause sets are the same (they contain the same clauses) and T recognises a solution (the clause set contains the empty clause).

7. Implement *depth-first search* as a higher-order function depth-first that takes the same inputs as breadth-first but omits R.

8. Implement *hill climbing* and *best-first* search with all the parameters as depth-first plus an evaluation function E that maps a state to a number. Test your program with resolution by setting E to favour a *unit preference strategy*.

Further Reading

Hughes (1990) defends functional programming because of its ability to support higher-order programming. Abelson and Sussman (1996) has a very good discussion of higher-order programming. The classic reference for sorting algorithms is Knuth (1998).

Web Sites

Alejo Hausner (http://www.cs.princeton.edu/~ah/alg_anim/version2/sorts.html) at Princeton includes a description of several classical sorting algorithms (including bubble sort) which are implemented in Java.

7 Assignments

7.1 Simple Assignments

An assignment is an expression whose evaluation causes an object to be associated with a symbol in the environment so that we can call upon this object through invoking the symbol in an appropriate way. These objects are called **global values**.

If s is a symbol and e an expression, the simple assignment (set s e) does two things.

1. The normal form e^* of e is returned.
2. As a side-effect, e^* becomes the value of the global variable s; so that the expression (value s) will return e^*.

Figure 7.1 shows a short script that uses set and value. We follow the Lisp tradition of asterixing global variables.

```
(0-) (set *number* 6)
6

(1-) (+ (value *number*) 6)
12

(2-) (set *number* 5)
5

(3-) (+ (value *number*) 6)
11
```

Figure 7.1 Using simple assignments

Although conventionally, when computer scientists talk about assignment statements, they generally do not include function definitions under that category, the use of define is, strictly speaking, another example of an assignment. The effect of define is to change the environment in which the computation is carried out and in that sense it is an assignment.

The important difference between function definitions and other assignments is that, generally, function definitions do not and cannot change during the execution of a program, whereas simple assignments can change the value assigned. The basic similarity between assignments and function definitions can be brought out by assigning an abstraction to a global variable. The variable can then be used to invoke the function in almost the same way as a regular function definition. Figure 7.2 shows how a simple assignment can do this.

```
(0-) (set *factorial* (/. X (if (= X 0) 1 (* X ((value *factorial*) (- X 1))))))
#<CLOSURE :LAMBDA [X] [if [= X 0] 1 [* X [apply [value '*factorial*] [- X 1]]]]>

(1-) ((value *factorial*) 9)
362880
```

Figure 7.2 Using a simple assignment to hold an abstraction

Simple assignments can make programs shorter. For example, the get-val function of the previous chapter required the spreading of the input, 'Spreadsheet', in order to retain some memory of what the entire spreadsheet was like. However, if we assign the spreadsheet to a global variable (called *spreadsheet*), then this spreading is unnecessary and the program sheds an auxiliary function and becomes simpler (figure 7.3).

```
(define get-val
    Index Attribute [[Index | Cells] | _] -> (get-cell Attribute Cells)
    Index Attribute [_ | Rows] -> (get-val Index Attribute Rows)
    Index _ _ -> (error "Index ~A not found" Index))

(define get-cell
    Attribute [[Attribute Value] | _]
    -> (if (fixed-value? Value) Value (Value (value *spreadsheet*)))
    Attribute [_ | Cells] -> (get-cell Attribute Cells)
    Attribute _ -> (error "Attribute ~A not found" Attribute))
```

Figure 7.3 Using simple assignments in place of spreading

7.2 Destructive Operations

The function set used to perform simple assignment is an example of a *destructive function* because the effect of applying the operation is to change the global environment in which the computation is carried out by destroying or overwriting any previous value attached to the assigned symbol.

Destructive operations are a topic of contention in computer science. Pragmatically, as we shall see, being able to perform destructive operations on data allows us to simplify certain programs and can radically improve the performance of programs that are forced to modify large data structures.

On the minus side, there are several disadvantages to destructive operations. The first is that that there is no possibility of returning to the premodified version of the data structure unless we take care to keep it in memory.

The second is that the mathematical purity of functional programming is no longer maintained. We cannot reason about such programs using conventional logic because basic mathematical principles *apparently* break down. One such is self identity; i.e.

$$for\ all\ x,\ x = x$$

Interpreted *de re*[35], as a statement about objects, this principle is universally true; everything is itself. But interpreted *de dicto*, as a statement about languages, it is false. *De dicto* the principle reads that all substitution instances of '$x = x$' must receive the valuation *true*. In **extensional** languages this is true, but it is easy to show that this principle fails when we use destructive operations (figure 7.3).[36]

```
(0-) (define increment
      -> (set *counter* (+ 1 (value *counter*))))
increment

(1-) (set *counter* 0)
0

(2-) (= (increment) (increment))
false
```

Figure 7.4 Self identity failing de dicto in Shen

Figure 7.4 shows that if destructive operations are used then self-identity *apparently* breaks down. *De re*, this Law cannot fail, but the *de dicto* interpretation of it applied to Shen, based on the simple mathematical reading of a functional program, does break down here.

---

[35] The distinction between *de re* and *de dicto* comes from mediaeval logic; it literally means 'of things' and 'of speech'.

[36] In fact the principle fails even within the non-destructive subset of Shen. The expression (= (/. X (+ X X)) (/. X (* X 2))) returns false even though the functions are extensionally identical. Shen returns false because it compares the representation of the functions within the machine and not the functions themselves. The example illustrates the limitation of trying to capture the concept of identity within a functional language. To be of service in reasoning in Shen, the Law of Self Identity, *for all x, x = x* has to be qualified so that the variable x ranges only over objects of a particular kind; specifically symbols, strings and vectors and lists of such etc and destructive operations excluded. The ramifications of this approach leads into the area of typed or many-sorted logic, which lies beyond the province of this text, but is covered in the author's companion volume to this book, *The Specification of Programming Language*.

This failure means that standard logical tools are not fit for the job of reasoning about destructive programs and the programmer who wants to do this has to use something more complicated that appeals to the concept of *state* and *environment*. For functional programmers who prefer to be able to reason cleanly, destructive operations are avoided; and in *purely functional languages* they do not exist.

The last reason for avoiding destructive operations is concerned with *concurrency*; defined as the ability of a computer to sustain multiple simultaneous computational processes. Following the destructive model can create programs whose output is highly unpredictable.

For example, suppose we split a computation into two parallel processes; a process A that takes a global *counter* and destructively subtracts 2 and a process B that takes the same global and destructively doubles it. The final value of *counter* is inherently unpredictable. If *counter* = 4 and process A is applied and then process B; then *counter* is set to 2 by A and to 4 by B. But if B reaches *counter* before A, then *counter* is set to 8 by B and to 6 by A. The final value is therefore 4 or 6 depending on the order in which the processes are applied.

The debate can be argued at length. The advantage of operating in an impure language, of which Shen is one, is that the programmer can decide for himself which side to come down on and whether to use destructive operations or not. In the next chapter we will look at the time properties of destructive operations on *vectors*.

Further Reading

The question of concurrency and its representation is taken up in appendix C.

The original assault on the use of assignments, and the procedural programming style, that embodies them was made by Backus (1977) in his ACM Turing award address. "Can Programming be liberated from the von Neumann style? A functional style and its algebra of programs" belaboured procedural assignment based programming as "fat and weak".

Floyd-Hoare logic was an early attempt to come to grips with the challenge of reasoning about programs that required the use of state. A nice account is found in Gordon (1988). Boyer-Moore (1979, 1997) contrasts an approach to reasoning that involves purely functional programming.

A good discussion of the challenges of concurrent programming is found in the early chapters of Reppy (2007).

8 Vectors

8.1 Vectors

A vector is a sequence of items that can be constructed by the operation @v which adds an item to the front of a vector. The simplest vector is the **empty vector** written <>. The @v operation is polyadic, (@v 1 2 3 <>) is treated as (@v 1 (@v 2 (@v 3 <>))).

```
(1-) (@v 0 <>)
<0>

(2-) (@v 1 2 3 <>)
<1 2 3>
```

Figure 8.1 Some small vectors

Vectors are printed within angles < ... > for ease of reading but this is not a readable format (i.e. it cannot be typed in this form). Like @s, @v can be used within pattern-matching functions. For example, the following function receives a vector of numbers and outputs a vector in which each number is incremented by 1.

```
(define add1
  <> -> <>
  (@v N V) -> (@v (+ N 1) (add1 V)))
```

At this point, the similarity between vectors and lists will be so apparent that a reasonable question must arise; why should any language incorporate vectors *and* lists? The answer is that vectors and lists have different computational properties arising from their internal representation within the computer and we need to take time out to understand this.

8.2 Lists and Vectors

A list is held within memory as a chain of **cons cell** pairs which reflect the cons-form representation of a list. [1] in cons form is (cons 1 []) and represented as a cons cell pair in computer memory. One cell points to the location at which the first element may be found, the second to the location where the rest of the list may be found.

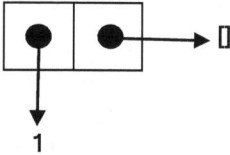

A longer list like [1 2 3] is simply a linked chain of such cons cells.

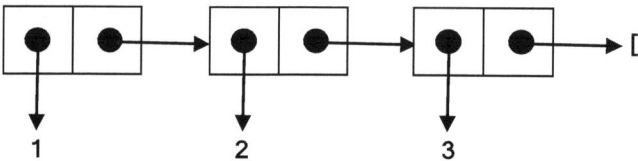

Consing an element to the front of the list (e.g. zero) requires only adding another cons cell pair which is a constant time operation.

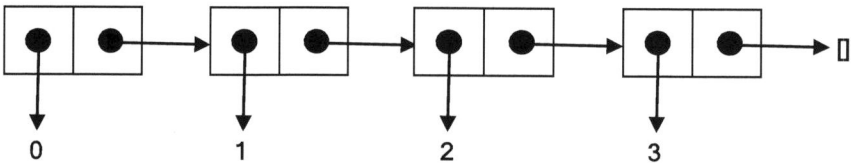

Locating the nth element of a list is *not* a constant time operation but a linear time operation; the third element of the list [1 2 3] can only be located by traversing three pointers.

In contrast to a list a vector is a series of pointers arranged by contiguous address in memory. In figure 8.2 our vector begins at a machine address that we have nominated as #523 which is the start address S of the vector.

#523 #524 #525

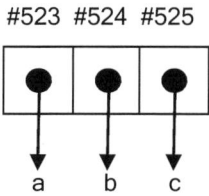

a   b   c

Figure 8.2 A representation of a vector

Every successive location of memory up to #525 contains a pointer (integer) that points to the address at which the vector element is found. If we want to find what the *n*th element of the vector contains we need only search in the address to find the right pointer. Hence locating the *n*th element of a vector is a constant time operation.

However if we want to add an element to a vector; say to splice an element into the first position of the vector without losing anything that is already in the vector, then we face the problem that the first element is already occupied. Replacing the first element is an option but then information contained in the original is lost. The only real option is to create a new vector and copy the contents of the old one and this is a linear time operation.

In the case of a list this problem is not so acute; given a list

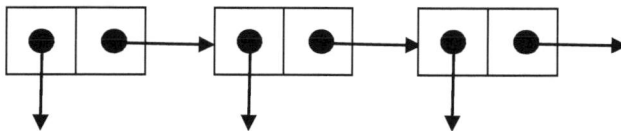

we can splice

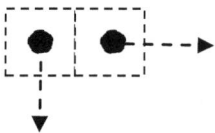

into the pole position by merely adding a pointer.

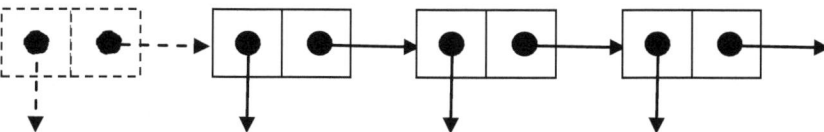

Hence consing to a list is a constant time operation.

It is important to know that vectors and lists have different time complexities in designing our programs. If our programs are intensively constructing and disassembling sequences of objects, then it makes sense to use lists for that purpose. If our sequences are relatively static and we are using them to store information then vectors are a logical choice. For this reason many languages, including Shen, contain both lists and vectors.

Because of the time penalties incurred in adding elements to a vector, @v is an expensive operation because every time it is invoked the vector has to be copied. For instance, the time taken to increment the contents of a vector V using **add1** is proportional to the summation $\Sigma(n)$ of the size n of V because each invocation of @v involves copying the vector. In the case of a list it would be linear.

This performance overhead is often reflected in the handling of strings in Shen. In many platforms, strings are held as vectors of characters or unit strings and hence @s is effectively a vector building operation. Hence for the same reasons @s is relatively slow and sometimes unacceptably slow if the string is very large. Downloading a large text file and processing it using @s is not practical, though for strings of a few hundred characters it works fine. In these cases, it makes sense to work with the file as a list of unit strings and in chapter 9 we will explore this more fully.

8.3 Handling Vectors

The @v operator theoretically allows us full control over vectors if we ignore the heavy time costs in using it. Locating the nth element of a vector is easily defined.

```
(define nth-vector
  1 (@v X _) -> X
  N (@v _ Vector) -> (nth-vector (- N 1) Vector))
```

However having followed the discussion so far, you will realise this is a colossally inefficient method of locating the nth element of a vector since we should be able to access the nth element directly. <-vector takes a vector and a number and does exactly that; (<- vector *vector* 56) will return the 56th element of *vector*.

Vectors in Shen are **1-indexed**; that is, the first index in them begins with 1 which is in contrast to vectors in other languages which are **zero indexed**. Because Shen vectors are often built on top of native vectors there is a zeroth element to a Shen vector whose contents Shen reserves for its own management and this cannot be accessed through <-vector. In **standard vectors**, which are the ones we mostly deal with, the zeroth index holds the size of the vector and is retrieved by the function (limit *vector*). Passing a number to <-vector which is larger than the limit of the vector is called an **out of bounds** vector call and will raise an error.

When a vector is created, there is a contiguous portion of memory laid aside for the contents of that vector. Using @v we are very much unaware of this fact since the portion of memory laid aside is exactly determined by the elements supplied to @v. However we can choose to create an **vacant vector** of say 1000 indices *none* of which are occupied by any chosen element. The function call (vector 1000) will create such a vector. The **empty vector**, which we abbreviated as <>, is in fact (vector 0).

The interaction between <-vector and a vacant vector is interesting; when we ask for the 56th element of a vacant vector using <-vector, an error message is returned telling us that there is nothing there. Similarly if we try to pattern-match over a vector with vacancies in it we can get an error telling us there is nothing there.

```
(5-) (define f
      (@v X _) -> X)
f

(6-) (f (vector 3))
hdv needs a non-empty vector as an argument; not <... ... ....>
```

Figure 8.3 Attempted pattern matching over a vacant vector

In fact there is something there, **the failure object** designated by the 0-place function (fail) and printed as ... . <-vector refuses to return this object for reasons of security that we shall understand in chapter 17. A vacant vector of limit 5 is printed in the form <... ... ...>.

A Shen vector is thus rather like a bank account in that we cannot take anything out unless it has first been put in. Vectors of other languages actually often allow a default element to be retrieved from a vacant vector. In 8.6 we shall see how to do that.

8.4 Timing Operations

In the previous section we remarked that an object could be spliced into a vector in constant time if we were willing to destructively overwrite part of the existing vector. Such a vector operation does exist in Shen.

(vector-> *vector* 56 a) will insert a into the 56th index of *vector* by destructively overwriting the data stored at that index. In computing terms, Shen vectors are **mutable** objects that can changed by the operations applied to them. For reasons explained in our section on assignments, destructive operations are a source of contention in computing because the behaviour of programs that use them is harder to fathom. However being able to destructively change a vector in constant time is extremely useful if we are using the vector to hold global information or we want to ensure our program runs quickly.

In this section we will learn the Shen technology for measuring the performance of programs by an examination of the contrasting performance between destructive and non-destructive vector programs. To get the timings we use the time function. We create a vector of 1000 numbers (rather slowly) using @v.

```
(define build-me-a-vector
  _ 0 -> <>
  X N -> (@v X (build-me-a-vector X (- N 1))))
```

Again we encode a version of add1; but this time the program cycles through the vector destructively changing the elements without using @v and hence without copying.

```
(define destructive-add1
  V -> (destructive-add1-loop V 1 (limit V)))

(define destructive-add1-loop
  V Limit Limit -> (vector-> V Limit (+ 1 (<-vector V Limit)))
  V Count Limit -> (destructive-add1-loop
                      (vector-> V Count (+ 1 (<-vector V Count)))
                      (+ Count 1)  Limit))
```

The program is longer and more abstruse than the pattern-directed version but runs in linear and not polynomial time.

```
 (11-) (set *v* (build-me-a-vector 0 1000))
<0 0 0 0 0 0 0 0 0 0 0 0 0 0 0 0 0 0 0 0... etc>

(12-) (time (add1 (value *v*)))
run time: 0.3739999532699585 secs
<1 1 1 1 1 1 1 1 1 1 1 1 1 1 1 1 1 1 1 1... etc>

(13-) (value *v*)
<0 0 0 0 0 0 0 0 0 0 0 0 0 0 0 0 0 0 0 0... etc>

(13-) (time (destructive-add1 (value *v*)))
run time: 0.0 secs

(14-) (value *v*)
<1 1 1 1 1 1 1 1 1 1 1 1 1 1 1 1 1 1 1 1... etc>
```

Figure 8.4 Destructively and non-destructively processing a vector

The profiler is a more detailed tool for measuring performance; the command (profile f) profiles the function f and the command (unprofile f) unprofiles the function f by removing the profiling code. The command (profile-results f) produces the timing for f, initialising the f counter to zero (figure 8.5). The results are displayed as an **ordered pair** – a structure we will meet again in chapter 17.

```
(2-) (profile add1)
add1

(3-) (profile build-me-a-vector)
build-me-a-vector

(4-) (time (do (add1 (build-me-a-vector 0 1000)) ok))

run time: 0.5460000187158585 secs
ok

(5-) (profile-results add1)
(@p add1 0.37400001287460327)
```

Figure 8.5 Running the profiler on vector operations

As can be seen, the tail recursive destructive version is much faster than the linear recursive non-destructive version. The lesson to be drawn from this is that if we merely want to interrogate the vector or process it without losing the original, then if time is not an issue or the vector is small, the non-destructive @v is useful. If we want to maintain a large global vector which is permanently updated by an operation f which is required to be fast, then it makes sense to use the destructive vector-> in defining f. In the next section we will apply this approach in earnest.

8.5 Hash Tables

Computers are extremely good at storing large amounts of information and retrieving it very quickly. In order to do this the computer needs to be able to associate a request for information with the location at which the information can be found and retrieve the information quickly.

A *hash function* is one way of doing this; it maps an object called a *key* to a natural number. If the request for information takes the form of a key, then a hash function can be applied to the request to get a natural number. The natural number can then be used to access the location at which the key can be found.
We have already seen that vectors give constant-time access to any item. A *hash table* can be viewed as a combination of a hash function h and a vector V, where the number produced by h is used to index into V.

There are cases where the hash function is not bijective; that is, when two different keys are mapped to the same number n; this is called a *collision*. In case of a collision, further search within the $h(n)$th entry of V may be needed to retrieve the answer.

The function hash in Shen allows us to create hash tables very easily. Given an expression *E* and a number *N* (hash *E N*) returns a number between 1 and including *N*. Hence by fixing *N* to be the limit of the vector *V*, we can effectively create a hash table for storing information.

We can use this technology to create a toy database system. We begin by creating a largish vector to serve as a database whose elements are all initially [] (indicating no information is stored there). The following two functions db-> and <-db create the means to insert and retrieve information into that vector. Figure 8.6 gives the code.

```
(set *db* (build-me-a-vector [] 1000))

(define db->
   Key Details -> (let DB (value *db*)
                       Hash (hash Key (limit  DB))
                       Entry (<-vector DB Hash)
                       (vector-> DB Hash [[Key | Details] | Entry])))

(define <-db
   Key -> (let DB (value *db*)
               Hash (hash Key (limit  DB))
               Entry (<-vector DB Hash)
               (find-details Key Entry)))

(define find-details
   Key [[Key | Details] | _] -> [Key | Details]
   Key [_ | Entries] -> (find-details Key Entries)
   _ _ -> void)
```

Figure 8.6 A toy database

Figure 8.6 shows our database in action.

```
(4-) (db-> "Mark Tarver" [[age 54] [nationality "British"]])
<[] [] [] [] [] [] [] [] [] [] [] [] [] [] [] [] ... etc>

(5-) (<-db "Mark Tarver")
["Mark Tarver" [age 54] [nationality "British"]]

(6-) (<-db "David Tarver")
void
```

Figure 8.7 Using a toy database

8.6 Property Vectors and Semantic Nets

The definitions of db-> and <-db are given to show the principle of working with hash tables in Shen. The Shen system functions put and get supply high-level access to hash tables in Shen. The function put receives

1. An expression e_1.
2. A pointer p which is used to point to ...
3. ... a value e_2 within ...
4. an (optionally user-specified) vector v.

put effectively does much of what db-> does in our previous program; it hashes e_1 into the property vector v index i and inserts e_2 into the information stored at this index. If no vector v is supplied Shen uses the system property vector built into the Shen installation.

get operates in a manner analogous to <-db; it receives three inputs e_1, p and an optional property vector v and searches i for the information placed by put and returns it. If v is not supplied the system property vector is used. If no information can be found, an error is returned.

```
(1-) (put "Mark Tarver" details [[age 54] [nationality "British"]])
[man]

(2-) (get "Mark Tarver" details)
[[age 54] [nationality "British"]]

(3-) (get "Mark Tarver" sex)
value not found
```

Figure 8.7 Using put and get with the system property vector

Semantic nets are a fun way of illustrating the usefulness of put and get. Semantic nets were introduced into Artificial Intelligence by **Quillian** (1968) as a model for the way humans hold information about objects and the relations between objects. Semantic nets are usually represented by **labelled directed graphs**, that is, as diagrams consisting of arrows (called **arcs**) with names or **labels** attached to the arrows. These arrows connect points or **vertices** that also have names. A semantic net which records the fact that I (Mark Tarver) am a man might consist of an arc labelled is_a leading from the vertex "Mark Tarver" to a vertex man.

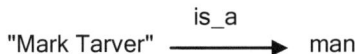

$$\text{"Mark Tarver"} \xrightarrow{\text{is\_a}} \text{man}$$

A statement of the form "All Xs are Ys" can be viewed as stating a relation between concepts; so "All men are human" becomes:-

$$\text{man} \xrightarrow{\text{type\_of}} \text{human}$$

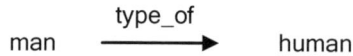

which states that the concept man is a **subtype** of the type of human, or (same thing) that human is a **supertype** of the type of man.

From "Mark Tarver is a man" and "All men are human" we can derive "Mark Tarver is human". Semantic nets allow for simple inferences like this by means of a search. Such a search starts from the "Mark Tarver" vertex and attempts to reach the vertex human, travelling in the direction of the arrows. If it succeeds it returns yes otherwise it returns no.

Property vectors are very good at representing the links in a semantic net. From "Mark Tarver" we construct a pointer that points to all the concepts $C_1,...,C_n$ which Mark Tarver is an instance. We call this pointer is_a. From each $C_1,..,C_n$ we can (if we want) create pointers in the same way, called type_of to show the supertypes of $C_1,..,C_n$.

Figuratively speaking, to find if Mark Tarver falls under a concept C, we place "Mark Tarver" in a 'box', and then we add to the box all the concepts $C_1, ...,C_n$ under which Mark Tarver falls in virtue of the is_a relation (i.e. all the concepts pointed to from "Mark Tarver" by the pointer is_a). For each of $C_1,...,C_m$, we add to the box every concept C_n which is a supertype of some C_i already in the box. We repeat this process until the box cannot be filled any more; at which point we look in the box to see if C is in the box. If it is, then Mark Tarver falls under the concept C and the answer is yes. If not, the answer is no.

The program that computes this algorithm is given in figure 8.8[37]; our box is a list that initially contains one object ([Object]), which is where our query begins.

```
(set *semantic-net* (vector 1000))

(define query
  [is Object Concept] -> (if (belongs? Object Concept) yes no))

(define belongs?
  Object Concept
  -> (element? Concept (fix[38] (function spread-activation) [Object])))

(define spread-activation
  [ ] -> [ ]
  [Vertex | Vertices]
  -> (union (accessible-from Vertex) (spread-activation Vertices)))
```

---

[37] Our program contains one feature explored in the next chapter; (trap-error (get ....) (/. E [])) has the effect that if get raises an error because no information is found then the empty list is returned instead of an error message. See 9.6 for an explanation.

[38] fix (short for fixpoint) iteratively applies a function to an input until no change can be produced. See appendix A.

```
(define accessible-from
  Vertex -> [Vertex | (union (is_links Vertex) (type_links Vertex))])

(define is_links
  Vertex -> (trap-error (get Vertex is_a (value *semantic-net*)) (/. E [])))

(define type_links
  Vertex -> (trap-error (get Vertex type_of (value *semantic-net*)) (/. E [])))

(define assert
  [Object is_a Type]
  -> (put Object is_a [Type | (is_links Object)] (value *semantic-net*))
  [Type1 type_of Type2]
  -> (put Type1 type_of [Type2 | (type_links Type1)] (value *semantic-net*)))
```

Figure 8.8 A simple semantic net in Shen

We can test this program.

```
(1-) (assert ["Mark Tarver" is_a man])
[man]

(2-) (assert [man type_of human])
[human]

(3-) (query [is "Mark Tarver" human])
yes
```

Figure 8.9 Using a semantic net to record information and ask questions

8.7 Native Vectors and Print Vectors

The standard vectors which discussed so far are built on top of the native vectors of the platform under which Shen runs. Shen imposes its own discipline on the native vectors in order to ensure that vectors behave uniformly across platforms.

Shen includes native vector functions which are primitive; these functions are address->, <-address, absvector and absvector?. They are the analogues of the functions vector->, <-vector, vector and vector? and behave similarly. Rather than reprise this material, we will just note the differences.

(absvector *n*) creates a native vector of *n* indices. The address-> function will access all the indices of a native vector, including the zeroth index which vector-> does not access. <-address will access even an index which is vacant (i.e. where no object has been inserted) but the nature of the object returned is platform dependent. The function absvector? will return true for all standard vectors but also vectors which are not standard. The Shen definitions of the standard vector functions are couched in terms of the native functions.

```
(define vector?
  V -> (and (absvector? V) (integer? (<-address V 0)))))

(define vector->
  V N X -> (if (= N 0) (error "index 0 used") (address-> V N X)))

(define <-vector
  _ 0 -> (error "index 0 used")
  V N -> (let X (<-address V N)
              (if (= X (fail)) (error "index is vacant") X)))

(define vector
  N -> (address-> (vector-fill (absvector N) 1 N) 0 N))

(define vector-fill
  V N N -> (address-> V N (fail))
  V M N -> (vector-fill (address-> V M (fail)) (+ M 1) N))
```

In terms of security and uniformity of behaviour, standard vectors are superior to native ones, but there is an advantage of performance in working with native vectors. Native vectors also allow us to define **non-standard vectors** and one important kind is a **print vector.**

A print vector is a non-standard vector where the zeroth element is not taken up by an integer (as with a standard vector) but by a symbol signifying a **print function**. A print function determines how that vector is printed off by mapping the vector to a string which is printed off as the print representation of that vector. This is highly useful if we want to define our own datatypes with special print conventions.

For example, suppose we want to add rational numbers as part of a number tower to Shen. We could choose a representation based on two element lists, but we may want a representation that allows rational numbers to be printed back in mathematical dress. So (rat 1 3) is printed as 1/3 and not [1 3] or <1 3>.

Internally our rational numbers will be held as a non-standard vector, a **print vector**, of two numbers with a tag in the zeroth index indicating that this vector is supposed to represent a rational number.

Since the vector is not a standard vector, we cannot use vector to create it and vector-> to set it up. Instead the print vector is created as a native vector and the address-> used to insert the appropriate elements. Here is the function rat (figure 8.10).

```
(4-) (define rat
 M N -> (let Vector (absvector 3)
             TagVector (address-> Vector 0 rational-number)
             Vector+M (address-> TagVector 1 M)
             Vector+N (address-> Vector+M 2 N)
             Vector+N))


 (5-) (rat 4 5)
 <<rational-number 4 5>>
```

Figure 8.10 Creating a rational number as a non-standard vector

The double angles indicate that the vector is a native vector. To turn this vector into a print vector we need to define rational-number as a print function. This function must build a string, given the vector in which it is embedded as an input. The string is built by taking the numerator and denominator and converting them into strings and placing them each side of the division sign (/). Entering (rat 4 5) returns a value printed in the accepted mathematical idiom.

```
(6-) (define rational-number
     Vector -> (@s (str (<-address Vector 1))
                 "/"
                 (str (<-address Vector 2)))))
rational-number

(7-) (rat 4 5)
4/5
```

Figure 8.11 Creating a rational number as a print vector

Exercise 8

1. Define each of the following functions; where appropriate, write a destructive version (using vector->) and non-destructive version (using v@) and compare timings.

   a. vector-append that appends two vectors together.
   b. vector-reverse that reverses a vector.
   c. vector-subst that substitutes one element for another throughout a vector.
   d. vector->list that maps a vector of elements to a list of the same elements
   e. list->vector that is the inverse of d.
   f. vector-extend that extends the size of a vector allowing more element to be written to it.

2. Define a function retract that allows you to remove assertions from the semantic net, so that stating (retract ["Mark Tarver" is_a man]) removes the corresponding assertion.

3. *Rewrite the function assert to include the backpointers instance_of and super_type so that if "Mark Tarver is a man" is stated then a backpointer instance_of then points from

man to a list containing Mark Tarver. Similarly if [man type_of human] is asserted then a backpointer super_type points from man to a list containing human. Amend the query program to allow the semantic net to cope with questions like (query [what is human]), so that it returns the list of all the humans of which it knows.

4. Extend the semantic net program to cope with disjunctive and conjunctive queries. For instance, (query [[Joe is_a man] or [Mark_Tarver is_a man]]) should return yes. (query [[Joe is_a man] and [Mark_Tarver is_a man]]) should return no.

5. *Extend the program to cope with conditional queries. For instance, (query [if [Joe is_a man] then [Joe is_a human]]) should return yes. To do this, you might want to assert the antecedent of the query during query time and test for the conclusion, and then retract the antecedent at the end of the computation.

Further Reading

Vectors are a fundamental data structure in computer science and are found in the early computer languages from Fortran onwards. Other data structures are often implemented in terms of vectors. In Common Lisp a string is implemented as a vector of characters; see Steele (1990) on strings and vectors. Matrix arithmetic, which is easily represented by 2 dimensional arrays, has been intensively studied in computing. See Sadler and Thorning (1993) for matrix arithmetic.

There are a number of data structures which attempt to combine the best features of vectors and lists – including binary trees and growable arrays

9 I/O

9.1 Streams

I/O, or input/output, covers all those aspects of a programming language that depend upon reading user input or printing the results of computation. In Shen both inputs and outputs are done through **streams**. A stream that is designed to receive input is called a **source** and one designed to display output is called a **sink**.

The basic stream that receives output for printing is the **standard output stream** which prints the results to the command window. pr receives a string and a sink and prints the string to the sink returning the string as a value. If only the string is supplied, then the sink defaults to the standard output stream.

```
(5-) (pr "hello world")
hello world"hello World"
```

Figure 9.1 Printing a string

When we use pr in this way, simply supplying a string input, Shen understands that the string is to be printed to the standard output i.e the command window. We can state this explicitly using the zero place function stoutput that returns the standard output stream.

```
(6-) (stoutput)
#<OUTPUT UNBUFFERED FILE-STREAM (UNSIGNED-BYTE 8)>

(7-) (pr "hello world" (stoutput))
hello world"hello World"
```

Figure 9.2 Invoking the standard output

Instead of using the standard output, we can choose to nominate some other form of sink which prints to a file. In order to do that we need to create a stream that acts as this sink. The function that does this is open which receives two arguments.

1. A string that indicates the path to the program or file required.
2. The keyword in or out which indicates whether the stream is a source or a sink.

When a stream is created in this way it is open until it is closed by the function close, which closes the stream and returns the empty list. Generally when we open a stream as a sink or a source we want to carry the stream around as an argument to a function like pr. Here we open a stream as a sink to a file and print hello world to it.[39]

```
(8-) (let Stream  (open "hello world.txt" out)
        Print (pr "hello world" Stream)
        (close Stream))
[]
```

Figure 9.3 Printing a string to a file

The file hello world.txt now contains the message hello world. Any previous content is overwritten. Notice the difference between writing to standard output and writing to some other stream. When we write to standard output the string we output is echoed back to us by being printed in the command window. When we write to a file, the string is not echoed back to us.

9.2 Print Functions

pr is a very basic print operation; the functions print and output are a little more flexible for printing to the standard output stream. print accepts any argument and prints it to standard output, returning that argument.

```
(2-) (print [1 2 3])
[1 2 3][1 2 3]

(3-) (print "hi there")
"hi there""hi there"
```

Figure 9.4 Printing arbitrary objects

print will attempt to print anything, including objects from within the native platform which are entirely foreign to Shen.[40] The polyadic function output is

---

[39] Writing to a sink is not a required feature of Shen. In the Javascript implementation of Shen, Javascript restricts access to the user's personal disk space for reasons of security.

[40] For example, in the Common Lisp platform of Shen, the expression (CODE-CHAR 54) returns an object called a **character** which is not part of the range of datatypes that Shen understands. Shen prints this as funex125 (the number component is computer generated), meaning that a functional object has been returned that Shen does not know how to print.

rather more sophisticated than print; it accepts a string and a series of zero or more following arguments. With zero following arguments it behaves much like pr with a single argument. But the output function shares the same features as make-string, except that it prints the resulting string. (figure 9.5).

```
(4-) (output "~A = ~A~%" [1 + 1] 2)
[1 + 1] = 2
 "[1 + 1] = 2"
```

Figure 9.5 Using output

The function nl, which returns zero, can be used to print *n* new lines. Without an argument it prints 1 new line.

```
(4-) (do (nl 2) (pr "Two blank lines! What a waste  of space") (nl))


Two blank lines! What a waste of space
0
```

When writing to a file, make-string and pr are used together to print formatted output to a file. In figure 9.6 (1 + 1) = 2 is printed to a file.

```
(12-) (let Stream  (open "simple sum.txt" out)
           String (make-string "~R = ~R~%"  [1 + 1] 2)
           Print (pr String Stream)
           (close Stream))
[]
```

Figure 9.6 Using make-string *and* pr *to print formatted output to a file*

write-to-file is a compact way of writing an object *x* to a file *f* in which a sink stream is opened to *f* and *x* is printed to *f*; the stream is then closed and *x* returned without the user having to go to the bother of creating a stream and then closing it. As with using open, any previous content in *f* is overwritten and if a string is written, the contents of the string appear in *f* without the enclosing quotes. The code in 9.7 creates a file containing (1 + 1) = 2.

```
(11-) (let String  (make-string "~R = ~R~%" [1 + 1] 2)
            (write-to-file "simple sum.txt" String))

"(1 + 1) = 2"
```

Figure 9.7 Using write-to-file *to output to a file*

All output that is produced by Shen, including error messages is filtered through the print and output functions. It is sometimes useful to be able to silence this output to enable silent loading of files. The assignment (set *hush* true) will silence printing from Shen.

9.3 Reading Input

Shen contains several functions designed to work on the standard input stream. The function read takes an input and parses it through the Shen reader *without* evaluating it. lineread works in the same way except several inputs terminated by a new line are read into a single list. input *both* reads in the user input *and* evaluates it.

```
(7-) (input)
(* 7 8)
56

(8-) (read)
(+ 7 8)
[+ 7 8]

(9-) (lineread)
1 2 3 4
[1 2 3 4]
```

Figure 9.8 Using input, read *and* lineread

If no arguments are given to these functions then they are defined relative to the standard input stream – that is the command window into which code is typed. But each of these functions is actually a 1-place function that receives as its second argument a source. If we supply a source using open then source is drawn from a file. Thus if we place the following in a file mytest.shen.

```
(* 3 7)
(+ 7 8)
"John" "loves"
"Mary"
```

Then the expression

```
(let Stream (open "mytest.shen" in)
     Print1 (input Stream)
     Print2 (read Stream)
     Print3 (lineread Stream)
     Close (close Stream)
     (output "~A ~A ~A" Print1 Print2 Print3))
```

will output the message

21 [+ 7 8] [John loves]

returning the string

"21 [+ 7 8] [John loves]"

Notice that all the read functions are destructive. If we read a source then we are consuming the contents of the source and hence

```
(let Stream (open "mytest.shen" in)
    (= (read Stream) (read Stream)))
```

will generally return false unless the second readable expression in the file is the same as the first.

If we want to simply read in the contents of a file into one large list without evaluating the contents then read-file just takes a file name and reads a file using Shen parsing. read-file may raise an error if it is used to parse files that fail Shen syntax requirements and is only to be used to read files, without evaluating the contents, that contain Shen programs or data. If we want to read *and* evaluate the contents of the file then the command is, of course, load.

The zero place function it is sometimes useful; it records verbatim the last input to the standard input and returns a string containing this input. This function is often useful in retaining a record of what the user actually typed in.

9.4 Bytes and Streams

All information within a computer is stored in **bits**, units of binary storage that exist in one of two states, represented figuratively in terms of 1 or 0. A **byte** (called an **octet** in recent literature) is a sequence of 8 bits. There is a conceptual connection between bytes and ASCII code. There are 128 ASCII characters numbered from 0 to 127 and these represent the characters that can be encoded in 7 bits. Extended ASCII covers 256 characters and this can be represented in 8 bits or one byte.

For many years in computing, the convention ruled that a byte represented one character of information. However in the late '80s, Joe Becker from Xerox and Lee Collins and Mark Davis from Apple realised there was a demand for a larger character set than could be represented in one byte. Initially they proposed two bytes, sufficient to represent 65,536 characters. This 16 bit representation was increased in 1996 to handle over a million characters and the Unicode consortium was formed. Eventually the Unicode consortium had classified over one million characters, giving each character a number or code point. This encoding requires a theoretical 20 bits per number or 3 bytes rounding up to the nearest whole byte.

The exact relation of the arrangement of bytes to the code point is called an **encoding**.

There are various encodings but one of the most popular is UTF-8 which is a variable length encoding which tries to save space and preserve backwards consistency with older standards by using the old convention of one byte to represent one character of the extended ASCII set – still by far the commonest character set in use since it encompasses the Roman alphabet.

How does this relate to Shen? Well, fundamentally the streams that Shen reads are **byte streams**. That is to say, the most basic operations on a Shen stream are reading a byte from a source or writing a byte to a sink. These two operations, read-byte and write-byte are the operations out from which all the other I/O primitives introduced so far are built. read-byte and write-byte are primitives of Kλ – the language from which Shen is built, discussed in chapter 15.

write-byte receives a byte – represented as a number between 0 and 255 – and a sink and writes the byte to the sink, returning that number as a result. read-byte receives a source and returns a byte, again as a number between 0 and 255.

```
(27-) (write-byte 145 (stoutput))
æ145

(28-) (read-byte (stinput))
10

(30-) (do (read-byte (stinput)) (read-byte (stinput)))
t
116
```

Figure 9.9 Using read-byte *and* write-byte *on standard input/output*

When write-byte sends a byte to the standard output stream, this byte is echoed to the command window where it appears as a **glyph** or shape printed on the screen and the number is returned (figure 9.9). Since write-byte can only return a number between 0 and 255, the glyph must be from the extended ASCII set.[41]

read-byte returns the first byte from the source, and if we invoke it in the command window it returns 10, which is the byte that represents the RETURN that we used to trigger Shen to evaluate the expression. In fact, to invoke it in standard input and get a result other than 10, we need to invoke read-byte twice. In figure 9.9 we do this and then type the letter t. read-byte reads the standard input and returns the byte 116 (the ASCII number of this character).

---

[41] In fact, Shen is only required to support the ASCII set so you should check to see if the extended ASCII glyphs can be printed. If you are interested in printing Unicode, in the standard library there are planned extensions to the specific ports that Shen uses which print glyphs outside extended ASCII.

Reading and writing bytes to a stream is easy. In figure 9.10 we write byte 145 to a file myfile. If we view this file under an appropriate editor, then the character æ appears in the file. If we read this file using read-byte then the byte 145 is read back. However if we attempt to read a byte from a stream where the stream is empty, -1 is returned.

```
(27-) (let Stream (open "myfile" out)
          Write  (write-byte 145 Stream)
          (close Stream))
[]

(28-) (let Stream (open "myfile" in)
          Read1 (read-byte Stream)
          Read2 (read-byte Stream)
          Close (close Stream)
          [Read1 Read2])
[145 -1]
```

Figure 9.10 Reading and writing bytes to a file

Now despite the limitations of only printing (at best) extended ASCII in the command window, there are several consequences of this arrangement, largely good. The first good consequence is that we can read any file into Shen using read-byte. Not just Shen text files, but graphic and audio files and we can manipulate these files inside Shen and reconstruct them and write these reconstructions to disk by using write-byte. The second good consequence is that Shen can handle files whose text is encoded using encodings other than UTF-8.

Such a stream is called here an **encoded stream** and an encoded stream is a higher-order object. It is effectively a pair <*S*, *f*> where *S* is a stream and *f* is an encoding function that reads the bytes off *S* and converts them to data. Instead of a stream being a passive source that waits to have data read off it, an encoded stream is an object that contains within it the information as to how it is to be read. This is an example of **object-oriented (O-O) programming**.

Using encoded streams allows us to write a higher-order read function for reading encoded streams.

```
(define read-encoded-stream
  [S F] -> (F S))
```

But again we need to preserve the idea of returning some designated object to indicate the end of the encoded stream. We'll assume that the reader in the encoding returns -1 if it attempts to read an empty encoded stream. Thus reading an encoded stream to a list also becomes a higher-order function.

```
(define read-encoded-stream-to-list
  [S F] -> (read-encoded-stream-to-listh [S F] (F S) []))
```

```
(define read-encoded-stream-to-listh
   _ -1 List -> (reverse List)
   [S F] Token List -> (read-encoded-stream-to-listh [S F] (F S) [Token | List]))
```

To see a practical application, in the chapter on vectors we observed that vectors are not suited to operations that involve adding elements to them. Since strings are often encoded as vectors, unsurprisingly string handling 'in the large' turns out to be a very inefficient process. If we are hoping to process a book, it pays to process it as a list of unit strings and not as a single string.

For example, we may wish to know how many times 'Alice' occurs in the text *Alice in Wonderland*. We can do this by treating the stream as an encoded stream of unit strings. The initial step is to download the text into a list of unit strings.

```
(define read-file-as-unit-string-list
   File -> (read-encoded-stream-to-list [(open File in) (function string-reader)]))

(define string-reader
  S -> (let Byte (read-byte  S)
            (if (= Byte -1)  -1 (n->string Byte))))
```

Processing the text in this form is not time consuming.

```
(5-) (define count-Alice
        [] -> 0
        [($ Alice) | Y] -> (+ 1 (count-Alice Y))
        [_ | Y] -> (count-Alice Y))
count-Alice

(6-) (time (count-Alice (read-file-as-unit-string-list "alice.txt")))
run time: 1.825211763381958 secs
395
```

Figure 9.11 Processing a large text file as a list of unit strings

Exercise 9

1. Define a function file-append that receives a string *s* as a name of a file *f* and an input *x* and appends *x* to *f*.

2. *Devise a reader fl for a functional language FL that works somewhat in the manner of ML. In FL, the factorial function is written

    factorial(0) = 1;
    factorial(x) = x * factorial(x − 1);

    and the append function

append(x,[]);
append(x::y,z) = x::append(y,z);

Your reader should read a file of FL definitions and compile them into Shen functions.

3. Devise a spellchecker; obtain from the internet a file containing list of recognised English words and write a function spellcheck that takes a file F as input and raises a spelling error warning whenever it encounters a word not in the word list. Create the system so that the line number of the spelling error is cited as well as the word. Arrange to give the user the option of dumping all these warnings to a file.

4. Devise a program text-file? that tests a file to see if it is a text file. A text file is defined as one which contains only characters which lie within the keyboard range.

5. Devise a function file-exists? that receives a string and tests if the corresponding file exists.

6. *Devise a program that communicates with a program P written in another language by scanning a file F for the output from P. Create a two ways exchange by arranging for Shen to write to a file which P can read. If you do not know any other language, use Shen and work with two processes.

7. Devise a program bytes that estimates the size of a file by returning the number of bytes in it.

8. *Devise a program html->text that reads an HTML file and strips the HTML leaving the bare text.

9. Create a front-end to the DB program so that details can be entered to the DB. Details should take the form Name, Age, Job, Salary. Place checks so that Name and Job are strings and Salary and Age are numbers with Age being no greater than 100. Allow the user to enter ^ to break off input without having to exit to the Shen top level from your front end.

10. Extend the DB program so that information is written to a file after leaving the DB and the information can be read from a file into the DB. In this way a permanent record can be kept of the data.

Further Reading

Byte streams in Shen are a lowest common denominator in terms of language design, because any language needs to have the capacity to handle them. Other languages contain a richer variety of streams, including program streams that connect directly to foreign processes and bidirectional streams that can act as both source and sink. For more on the latter and for a peek at how streams can be in other languages see the chapter on streams in Steele (1990). Haskell uses monads as a way of dealing with I/O that circumvents the non-functional aspect of I/O. See http://www.haskell.org/tutorial/monads.html for an introduction.

10 Macros and Packages

10.1 Macros

A Shen macro is a piece of code that modulates the way in which code is read into the working Shen image. Syntactically, a Shen macro looks like a standard function with three distinct differences.

1. The keyword defmacro is used instead of define.
2. Every macro takes one and only one input; i.e. its **arity** is 1.
3. Every macro has a default case X -> X inserted by Shen as a final rule. Thus the macro always behaves as the identity function if the rules supplied by the programmer fail to apply to an input.

Every Shen program, when loaded, is read in as a list of expressions. For example, the expression (+ 1 2) in a file is read in as a list [+ 1 2]. It is the task of the Shen reader to read in that expression and it is the task of the Shen evaluator to evaluate it. The program is read in as a series of **tokens**. Roughly, the set of tokens within an expression is the set of evaluable subexpressions found within it. For example, in [+ 1 2] the tokens are +, 1, 2 and [+ 1 2]. The application of the list of Shen macros to a token t is called **macroexpansion**. This process works as follows.

Let $f_1,...,f_n$ be macros in reverse order of their introduction; let t be a token. Let the application $(f_1... (f_n t)...) = t'$ represent the composition of all $f_1..,f_n$ on t. Then either

1. $t = t'$ in which case the macroexpansion acts as the identity function and t is unchanged.
2. $t \neq t'$ in which case the macroexpansion of t is identical to the macroexpansion of t'.

To begin with a simple case, suppose we wanted to create an infix +. The following macro does just that.

```
(defmacro +-macro
  [X + Y] -> [+ Y X])
```

+macro edits our infix notation into the acceptable prefix notation. Note if the token is not an infix addition then +-macro behaves as the identity function – hence X -> X is not needed as a default case in a macro.

Used accurately, macros allow us to create our own programming notation for many different types of problem.

Here is a slightly more advanced example; let us suppose we have defined a max function which given two numbers returns the larger (or if the numbers are the same, returns that number). Our max function works for two inputs, but we want max to be polyadic so that we can enter (max 1 2 3 4) and return 4. Figure 10.1 shows how we can create a macro to make our max function polyadic.

```
(0-) (defmacro max-macro
        [max W X Y | Z] -> [max W [max X Y | Z]])
macro
max-macro

(1-) (define max
  X Y -> X where (> X Y)
  _ Y -> Y)
max

(2-) (max 1 2 3 4)
4
```

Figure 10.1 Setting up a polyadic max function using a macro

The definition in 10.1 is deceptively simple and works because macros are repeatedly applied to all tokens of an input until no change can be produced by their application. (max 1 2 3 4) is read in as the list [max 1 2 3 4] and the first pass of the max-macro produces [max 1 [max 2 3 4]]. The macro is then applied to [max 2 3 4] to produce [max 2 [max 3 4]] and the whole expression that exits the reader is read as [max 1 [max 2 [max 3 4]]].

What exits from the reader is a list; it is the task of the evaluator to take that list and evaluate it to produce the appropriate result. Thus if we enter (+ 5 6), the Shen reader produces [+ 5 6] and the evaluator returns 7. What if we enter a list like [1 2 3] to the reader? This is read as a list expression too; the list [cons 1 [cons 2 [cons 3 []]]]. The evaluator then treats the square brackets as if they were round ones, evaluating [+ 5 6] as (+ 5 6) (i.e. 11) and [cons 1 [cons 2 [cons 3 []]]] as (cons 1 (cons 2 (cons 3 ()))) (i.e. [1 2 3]).

Though this sounds a little involved, the process actually allows the programmer a great deal of power and control as we shall see. The power arises from the fact that all Shen programs are read in as lists and Shen is *par excellence*, a list programming language. Therefore by reading in programs as lists and creating the facility to change the way that the reader treats those lists, we can effectively create our own programming environment and our own special notations. We shall see a few examples in this chapter.[42]

The evaluator that does the job of evaluating the lists produced by the reader is actually available as a function to the Shen programmer; it is called eval-kl.

```
(3-) (eval-kl [+ 7 8])
11

(4-) (eval-kl 16)
16
```

Figure 10.2 eval-kl *in action*

The kl suffix is a nod towards the underlying Kλ (K lambda) out of which Shen is built; eval-kl is one of the fundamental primitive functions out of which all of Shen is constructed.

eval-kl is actually a leaner cousin of a similar more programmer-friendly function eval which does the same job but applies all the macros to its input before applying eval-kl to the result. Since Shen uses a macros a lot in its construction, eval can work where eval-kl fails. The example in 10.3 works for eval but not eval-kl because define needs a macro within Shen to be evaluated.

```
(3-) (eval [define f
            1 -> 2])
f

(4-) (f 1)
2
```

Figure 10.3 eval *in action*

Is eval useful? Macros are more generally applicable, but sometimes eval and eval-kl can be used to effect as we shall see an example in chapter 15;. For example, we can run a Shen program P that *dynamically*[43] generates a list that represents a function definition and by evaluating it, generate a new program P*. Such a program is called a **metaprogram** (a program that generates programs). Even more intriguingly, the program P* that is generated can be a modification of P, so that the eval function opens the possibility of self-modifying programs. The

---

[42] One of the first languages to introduce macros and indeed the inspiration for Shen macros was Common Lisp. See Steele (1990) for an exposition.

[43] The emphasis is on *dynamic* here, because the program P' is created during the execution (evaluation) of P. Actually it is more common for programs to be generated during the *read* part of the read-evaluate-print loop, and in that case macros are the better approach.

eval function thus allows certain intriguing and alarming possibilities reminiscent of Skynet in *Terminator*. Self-modifying programs are outside the ambit of this book, but have been investigated within artificial intelligence.

10.2 Changing the Order of Evaluation

Macros enable the user to define polyadic functions in Shen which are not definable without their aid. But macros also allow us to create functions in which the usual applicative order of evaluation is suspended in favour of our own chosen version.

Suppose we are working with the task of modelling an electronic circuit which uses NOR gates, where (nor X Y) returns 1 just when both X and Y are 0. The straightforward Shen definition is.

```
(define nor
  0 0 -> 1
  _ _ -> 0)
```

But this function is driven by *strict evaluation*; if we are using it to model a circuit then nor will evaluate both inputs before returning 1 or 0. However if the first input is 1 then the evaluation of the second input need not be made. What is required is something more like the lazy evaluation of the conditional if. At the expense of readability (nor X Y) can be more efficiently rendered as (if (= X 0) (if (= Y 0) 1 0) 0).

Macros enable us to reconcile efficiency with readability. We define a macro in which every expression of the form (nor X Y) is replaced or **inlined** by the expression (if (= X 0) (if (= Y 0) 1 0) 0).

```
(3-) (defmacro nor-macro
      [nor X Y] -> [if [= X 0] [if [= Y 0] 1 0] 0])
macro
nor

(4-) (nor 0 1)
0
```

10.3 Defining our own Notation

In a calendar program, a 0-place function date generates the current date in the format day, month and year. Part of the calendar program's task is to generate the current date and print it in an acceptable format and for this purpose we have a function now which does exactly that.

```
(define now
  -> (let Date (date)
          Day (nth 1 Date)
          Month (nth 2 Date)
          Year (nth 3 Date)
          (output "~A, ~A, ~A~%" Day Month Year)))
```

In order to pass the output of date to the print function, we have to construct four local assignments that create local variables for the date, day, month and year. In other languages[44], local assignments can also be used to pattern-match on the input in the same way that patterns are used in Shen functions. i.e.

```
(define now
  -> (let [Day Month Year] (date)
          (output "~A, ~A, ~A~%" Day Month Year)))
```

Such a construction will not compile in Shen, but with macros it can be made to work. Here is the code.

```
(defmacro let-macro
  [let [X | Y] FCall Result] -> (let F (gensym (protect F))
                                     [let F FCall
                                         (recursive-let 1 [X | Y] F Result)]))

(define recursive-let
  _ [] _ Result -> Result
  N [cons V Vs] F Result
  -> [let V [nth N F] (recursive-let (+ N 1) Vs F Result)])
```

Figure 10.4 Setting up a pattern-matching local assignment

The macro accepts a pattern-matching let and expands it to a series of local assignments as in our original legal program. The pattern-matching let has the form [let [X | Y] FCall Result]. The FCall will be matched to some function call (like (date)) and we begin by storing the result of this call

```
(let F (gensym (protect F))
    [let F FCall ...
```

to a local variable in order not to repeat this computation. This local variable must be fresh to avoid clashes with any variables in the expression, so we use gensym to generate a new symbol for us. The recursive-let function then works through the list making the code for the appropriate local assignments.

---

[44] O'Caml being an example.

10.4 Packages

Our examples show how macros can be used to create polyadic functions, change the order of evaluation or create our own special notation. Metaprogramming really begins when we generate, not single functions, but whole programs from our chosen notation. In order to do this we need to look first at **packages**.

Packages are essentially a simple device to package up programs in order to minimise **name collisions**. A name collision occurs when we have two programs that accidentally choose the same identifier for a function or a global variable. In that case, loading both these programs will cause an error in one of the programs since one function or global will overwrite the other.

The accepted solution to this problem is to create a separate **name space** for each program so that these identifiers live in their separate name spaces. To do this in Shen, we place the two programs in different packages by creating an expression of the form

(package *place_package_name_here* [] ... *place_program_here* ...)

What goes in the place of *place_package_name_here* is the name of the package, which is a symbol beginning in lowercase. What goes in place of ... *place_program_here* ... is the program itself.

When a package P is loaded, Shen renames every function *f* defined in P by prefixing the name of P following by a dot (.) to *f*. In order to refer to a function defined in the package, we have to use the **fully qualified name** or **FQN.**

Hence as long as the package name is unique, we do not have to consider the possibility of name collisions when loading it.

More precisely, the Shen reader prepends the package symbol followed by dot before all the symbols when evaluating E_1 ... E_n apart from those symbols which are

1. Symbols listed as belonging to the system (such as ->, define, cons, append, =, == etc).
2. Symbols which are variables..
3. Symbols which are listed by the user to be exempted from renaming.
4. Symbols which are prefaced by shen..[45]

Symbols which are prepended we say are **internal** (to the package). Symbols which are not are **external**.

---

[45] All the code for Shen, which is written in Shen, is contained in the package 'shen'..

Thus to illustrate, we can package the square root program of chapter 6 within our own maths package called my-maths-stuff. When we do that Shen compiles all the functions within that package printing off the FQNs of each function. To access any of these functions in the top level, we need to use the FQN.

```
(0-) (package my-maths-stuff []

(define sqrt
  N -> (let Guess (/ N 2.0)
        (run-newtons-method N
         (average Guess (/ N Guess)) Guess)))

(define run-newtons-method
  _ Better_Guess Guess -> Better_Guess
                    where (close-enough? Better_Guess Guess)
  N Better_Guess _
  -> (run-newtons-method N
      (average Better_Guess (/ N Better_Guess))
       Better_Guess))

(define average
  M N -> (/ (+ M N) 2.0))

(define close-enough?
  Better_Guess Guess -> (< (abs (- Better_Guess Guess)) .001))

(define abs
  N -> (if (> 0 N) (- 0 N) N)) )
my-maths-stuff.sqrt
my-maths-stuff.run-newtons-method
my-maths-stuff.average
my-maths-stuff.close-enough?
my-maths-stuff.abs

(1-) (my-maths-stuff.sqrt 2)
1.414
```

Figure 10.5 Using a package

A package contains a list after the package name which in 10.5 is empty. This list contains the list of symbols that are external to the package and that are not subject to the renaming conventions of the package and are exempted from renaming by the choice of the user. The function external takes a package name and returns the list of all those symbols which have been declared external to that package at the point the function is called.

We may decide that some of the functions in the maths package should be accessible without having to type my-maths-stuff. The functions that stand out as generally useful to a user are sqrt average and abs. Hence we can change our declaration by replacing [] by [sqrt average abs].

```
(2-) (package my-maths-stuff [sqrt average abs]

(define sqrt
  N -> (let Guess (/ N 2.0)
         (run-newtons-method N
           (average Guess (/ N Guess)) Guess)))

(define run-newtons-method
  _ Better_Guess Guess -> Better_Guess
                    where (close-enough? Better_Guess Guess)
  N Better_Guess _
  -> (run-newtons-method N
       (average Better_Guess (/ N Better_Guess))
         Better_Guess))

(define average
  M N -> (/ (+ M N) 2.0))

(define close-enough?
  Better_Guess Guess -> (< (abs (- Better_Guess Guess)) .001))

(define abs
  N -> (if (> 0 N) (- 0 N) N)) )
sqrt
my-maths-stuff.run-newtons-method
average
my-maths-stuff.close-enough?
my-maths-stuff.abs

(3-) (sqrt 2)
1.414
```

Figure 10.6 Exporting from a package

Now the list of functions printed off shows that sqrt, average and abs are all functions directly accessible to the user; only the auxiliary functions are hidden in the package. The expression (external maths-stuff) will retrieve all the external functions of that package.

```
(4-) (external maths-stuff)
[sqrt average abs]

(5-) (external whatsthis)
package whatsthis has not been used

(6-) (external shen)
[! } { --> <-- && : ; :- := _ *language* *implementation* *stinput*
*home-directory* *version* *maximum-print-sequence-size* *macros* *os*
*release* *property-vector*... etc]
```

Since Shen is written in Shen it also inhabits a package called (unsurprisingly) shen. Typing (external shen) returns the list of keywords and symbols used in Shen that are accessible to the user. This list is quite long and is truncated by ... in printing.

The system functions of Shen are all external to the Shen package and are found in this long list. These external symbols have a special status in that function definitions attached to them cannot be overwritten and they are accessible to every package. It is open to the programmer to give his function symbols the same status by applying systemf to them.

```
(4-) (define append X Y -> X)
append is not a legitimate function name.

(5-) (sysemf sqrt)
sqrt

(6-) (define sqrt  X -> X)
sqrt is not a legitimate function name.
```

Now let us suppose that you wish to devise some engineering package that uses your my-maths-stuff package. You write

(package engineering [...] ...)

Within the engineering package the sqrt, abs and average functions are used. Since these are cited in the engineering package they will be prefixed by engineering which is not what we want. To escape that we can exempt them by typing (package engineering [sqrt abs average] ...)

However this is a bind, if we add more maths functions from our maths package, then we may want these to be accessible to the engineering package. We can avoid having to look up these functions by making *all* the external maths functions accessible within the engineering package.

(package engineering (append (external my-maths-stuff) [...] ...)

The external function allows us to spread a package over several files. For example if we have our engineering package spread out in files A and B, to be loaded in that order, we can write in A.

(package engineering []

   Code for file A)

In file B we write

(package engineering (append (external engineering) *symbols external in file B*)

    Code for file B)

The invocation of external means that the symbols external in file A will be inherited by the program in file B.

10.5 The Null Package and Macros

One very special package is the **null package**, signified by writing the word null in place of the package name. The effect of incorporating a program within this package is precisely zero. No symbols are changed within the package and the program is read in as it is written. It looks, at first sight, that the null package is entirely useless. In fact, the null package is extremely useful and is the key to metaprogramming in Shen and liberating the full power of macros.

In order to be able to do metaprogramming, we need freedom to develop our own notation, and if necessary, generate significant programs from this notation. Macros allow this to a limited degree. The limitation arises from the fact that macros are essentially 1-1 functions; as taught so far they can at best replace one token by another token. What is missing is a way of replacing a token by an entire series of expressions which constitutes a program. However if we have a means of parcelling up *n* arbitrary expressions into one package, then effectively we also have a means of using macros to generate programs. The null package provides exactly that means.

A simple example uses macros and packages to add **anonymous functions** to Shen. An anonymous function is a function defined in the usual manner, but which lacks an identifier. For example in the following program, there are two functions enter-choice and process-choice which receive an input and process it.

```
(define enter-choice
  -> (do (output "Choose: ") (process-choice (input))))

(define process-choice
  1 -> (print hi)
  2 -> (print why)
  3 -> (print die))
```

Figure 10.7 A basic program for processing user input

In a language with anonymous functions, we can choose not to name the second function but instead use it anonymously thus;

```
(define enter-choice
  -> (do (output "Choose: ")
        ((anon 1 -> (print hi)
               2 -> (print why)
               3 -> (print die)) (input))))
```

Figure 10.8 The same program recoded using an anonymous function

Here (anon .....) is an anonymous function which effectively works a little like an abstraction except its internal structure mirrors a Shen defined function. To achieve the effect of anonymous functions, we use packages and macros. Given the expression of 10.8, we generate a packaged expression (figure 10.9) in which the anonymous function is extracted and given a machine-generated name.

```
(package null []

  (define enter-choice
    -> (do (output "Choose: ") (f479  (input))))

  (define f479
    1 -> (print hi)
    2 -> (print why)
    3 -> (print die))  )
```

Figure 10.9 The generated code

The program for compiling an anonymous function is shown in figure 10.10.

```
(define find-anon-funcs
  [anon | X] -> [[anon | X]]
  [X | Y] -> (append (find-anon-funcs X) (find-anon-funcs Y))
  _ -> [])

(define process-anon-macros
  Def [] -> Def
  Def Anons -> [package null [] | (replace-anon-calls Def Anons)])

(define replace-anon-calls
  Def [] -> [Def]
  Def [[anon | Rules] | Anons] -> (let F (gensym f)
                                    FDef [define F | Rules]
                                    NewDef (subst F [anon | Rules] Def)
                                    [FDef | (replace-anon-calls NewDef Anons)]))

(defmacro anon-macro
  [define F | X] -> (process-anon-macros [define F | X]
                      (find-anon-funcs [define F | X])))
```

Figure 10.10 Using a macro and the null package for anonymous functions

The working program is shown below.

```
(5-) (define enter-choice
  -> (do (output "Choose: ")
          ((anon 1 -> (print hi)
                 2 -> (print why)
                 3 -> (print die))  (input))))
f479
enter-choice

(9-) (enter-choice)
Choose: 1
hihi
```

10.6 Macro and Package Management

Are macros a good thing? Having followed the chapter so far, you will probably consider the answer must be 'yes'. As a friend Dr Gyorgy Lajos once said 'You can have sharp tools with which you can also cut yourself, or you can have blunt tools which do not cut well but protect you from harm.' Macros are a razor sharp tool.

For this reason software managers do not always welcome macros precisely because they are so powerful. The ability to define your own personal notation is a delight for experimental programmers, but is not welcome in commercial settings where third-party readability is at a premium.

Shen macros are particularly open to abuse; for example here is a lethal specimen that rewrites 3 as 2.

```
(7-) (defmacro def3
        3 -> 2)
def3

(8-) (+ 3 3)
4
```

Apart from being an April Fool's joke on unsuspecting Shen programmers, a macro of this sort is of little use. It is in fact an example of a **red macro**, that is, a macro that changes the global run-time environment of the Shen system by changing the semantics of Shen itself. A red macro is not necessarily a toxic macro, because the let macro of section 11.3 changed the semantics of local assignments but in a more benign way than the def3 macro. Nevertheless red macros are far-reaching in their effects. (undefmacro def3) removes this macro.

A macro that is not red is a **green macro**. Can this categorisation be calculated by computer? Substantially - assuming the code is packaged - yes. If the external symbols on the left-hand side of the macro are a subset of the external symbols of the Shen then the macro is red. In the case of def3 the set of symbols involved is the empty set which is obviously a subset of the external symbols of the Shen. If a macro is internal to a package and contains symbols on the left-hand side which are internal to that package then the macro is green and the effects are local to the package. Thus it is possible to effectively compute the existence of red macros.

The package system of Shen is somewhat different from the package system of other languages and is designed for the construction of a **standard library**. A library is a repository of programs each aimed at a specific purpose and the standard library for a programming language is the standard repository of code for that language.

In the standard library all the external functions of a package are systemfed, so that standard functions when loaded cannot be overwritten and, assuming unique package names, the standard library naming conventions are thus guaranteed to be free of name clashes (merely loading all the standard library ensures this). The motivation for this is to establish a standard means of referring to basic functions (tan for tangent etc).

Outside of the standard library the safest and most acceptable way of building packages is to only make external those symbols which are used in the standard library, which assuming the uniqueness of the package name that is chosen for the package, ensures no name collisions.

Exercise 10

1. Devise a macro that makes > polyadic so that (> 3 2 1) returns true.

2. Write a macro that allows you to use standard 2 digit hex notation \xNN for characters in strings. Thus "\x12" should print out in the same way as "c#18;".

3. Devise a version of let that allows pattern matching; given (let [Y Z] (foo X)), the is version of let takes the two element list produced by foo and binds the first element to Y and the second to Z.

4. Devise a version of /. that uses pattern matching; (/. [Y Z] Z) receives a 2 element list and returns the second element and if the input is not a 2 element list returns an error.

5. Devise a notation that allows Miranda-style constructions like

   (define pred (+ 1 X) -> X)

   in a Shen definition. Your macro should rectify the result to be legal Shen but preserve the intent of defining the predecessor function.

Further Reading

Metaprogramming was very much a feature of the first functional programming language Lisp. Macros are very much part of the Lisp tradition and are well explained in Seibel (2005) which also includes a chapter on Lisp packages.

11 Exceptions and Continuations

The two topics covered in this chapter deal with the control flow of a program, that is, the order in which instructions are executed. Exceptions allow us to break the execution of a program and return the control to an earlier point or to surface to the top level with an error message. Continuations allow us to carry computations as actual objects which can be activated at our will. Both of these are powerful tools in the hands of experienced programmers. We begin with looking at exceptions.

11.1 Exceptions

A basic feature of any programming language is the ability to stop the flow of computation when an anomalous condition is realised and signal an error. The simple-error function is one of the primitive functions in which Shen is written and its role is to raise an error whenever such a condition is encountered. simple-error receives a string and maps it to an **exception**; a computational object that, unless trapped, surfaces to the top level in which the contents of the string are printed as an error message.

For example, suppose we maintain a vector of employee names in which every employee is uniquely identified by a number which indexes into the vector. If we supply a number which lies outside the range of the vector then the system signals an out of bounds error message vector call is out of range. This is not precisely informative to a naive user of our system who may know nothing of vectors. One solution is substitute our own error message by first testing to see if the index lies outside the limit of the vector

```
(define get-employee
   N Vector -> (if (> N (limit Vector))
                (simple-error "this number is larger than our database!")
                (<-vector Vector N)))
```

This works fine except that in cases where we try to access a number within the limit, but one which has not been assigned any employee, the system crashes with an error message because nothing has been stored at the vector index. One way round this is to plug all the vector spaces with void as we did in 8.3. But a more elegant solution is to trap the error and substitute one of our own error messages. This has the advantage that we can also trap out of bounds error messages too.

For this purpose we use a higher-order function trap-error that receives two inputs; an expression *x* and a function *f*. If the evaluation of *x* raises an exception *e*, then this exception is passed to *f* and (*f e*) is returned. If *x* does not raise an exception, then the normal form of *x* is returned. In figure 11.1, we use an abstraction that receives the system exception as an argument E and then discards it, replacing it by our own error message.

```
(define get-employee
  N Vector -> (trap-error (<-vector Vector N)
                 (/. E (simple-error "this number does not occur our database!"))))
```

Figure 11.1 Trapping an error

Since an error can be raised for one of two reasons; either an out of range call or a call to an unassigned index, it would be useful if we could determine which error is involved and tailor our response accordingly.

The function error-to-string allows us to map an exception to the string from which it was generated. Using this function we can arrange our response.

```
(define get-employee
  N Vector -> (trap-error (<-vector Vector N)
                 (/. E (simple-error (error-response (error-to-string E))))))

(define error-response
  "vector element not found" -> "this number is not in our database"
  _ -> "this number is larger than our database!")
```

A slightly more sophisticated function than simple-error is error which does what simple-error does but includes all the formating facilities of output. The program below now prints (e.g.) #123 is not in our database.

```
(define get-employee
  N Vector -> (trap-error (<-vector Vector N)
                 (/. E (let ErrorString (error-response (error-to-string E))
                          (error "#~A ~A ~%" N ErrorString)))))
```

Error trapping can be useful if we want to incorporate a global into our program but only initialise it if and when it is called. The function push allows us to push values onto a variable without having to initialise it. push uses trap-error to initialise the variable to [Value] when push is first invoked avoiding the need to initialise the variable in the program or the top level.

```
(define push
  Value  Variable -> (set Variable (trap-error [Value | (value Variable)]
                                                 (/. E [Value])))))
```

Hence we can write (push 0 *stack*) without having to consider whether *stack* has been initialised.

11.2 Continuations

Lazy evaluation is the technique of delaying a computation until such time as the result of the computation is known to be needed. Examples of lazy evaluation appeared in chapter 2 with the introduction of if, and and or. All these functions selectively evaluate their arguments only when these evaluations need to be made. An elegant way of performing lazy evaluation in Shen is to use the services of freeze and thaw.

freeze receives an expression x and instead of evaluating x, returns a promise called a **continuation** to evaluate x if asked. This promise will be honoured if it is **thawed**. thaw will receive the frozen expression and thaw it to produce the normal form of x. Figure 11.2 shows a simple example.

```
(3-) (freeze (+ 1 2))
#<CLOSURE :LAMBDA NIL [+ 1 2]>

(4-) (thaw (freeze (+ 1 2)))
3
```

Figure 11.2 Using freeze and thaw

freeze and thaw allows us to explore interesting computational paradigms. For instance, nearly forty years ago, in a paper *Cons Should not Evaluate its Arguments,* Friedman and Wise argued that cons should not be strict in its evaluation but should hold suspended evaluations. The result is a **lazy list** used in languages like Haskell. To do this in Shen we construct a lazy cons that allows us to build lazy lists.

```
(defmacro @c-macro
  [@c X Y] -> [cons [freeze X] [freeze Y]])
```

The lazy list composed of 1 and 2 is written (@c 1 (@c 2 [])). For convenience we also define the equivalent of a polyadic list operator which allows the lazy list composed of 1 and 2 to be written (@l 1 2).

```
(defmacro @l-macro
  [@l] -> (freeze [])
  [@l X | Y] -> [@c X [@l | Y]])
```

The lazy equivalent of hd and tl is @hd and @tl.

```
(define @hd
  X -> (thaw (hd X)))

(define @tl
  X -> (thaw (tl X)))
```

```
(6-) (@l 1 2 3)
[#<CLOSURE LAMBDA NIL 1> | #<CLOSURE LAMBDA NIL (CONS (freeze
2) (freeze (CONS (freeze 3) (freeze NIL))))>]

(7-) (@hd (@l 1 2 3))
1

(8-) (@tl (@l 1 2 3))
[#<CLOSURE LAMBDA NIL 2> | #<CLOSURE LAMBDA NIL (CONS (freeze
3) (freeze NIL))>]
```

Lazy lists allow the possibility of constructing data structures that mimic the effect of computing with infinitely large lists such as the list of all prime numbers. Let's define the set of all primes as a lazy list.

```
(define primes
  -> (primes-from 2))
```

(primes-from 2) will construct a lazy list of all the primes from 2 onwards.

```
(define primes-from
  N -> (@c N (primes-from (next-prime (+ N 1)))))

(define next-prime
  X -> X                          where (prime? X)
  X -> (next-prime (+ 1 X)))
```

The task of finding the first prime divisor of a number can be defined as an operation on the lazy list of all primes.

```
(define first-prime-divisor
  N -> (first-prime-divisor-help N (primes)))

(define first-prime-divisor-help
  N Primes -> (let D (@hd Primes)
                (if (divisor? D N)
                    D
                    (first-prime-divisor-help N (@tl Primes)))))

(define divisor?
  D N -> (integer? (/ N D)))
```

Figure 11.3 shows a test.

```
(38-) (first-prime-divisor 1257)
3

(39-) (first-prime-divisor 1261)
13

(40-) (first-prime-divisor 1246681)
29
```

11.3 A prime divisor using lazy lists

For efficiency and convenience, freeze is one of the primitive functions, but actually we can define freeze and thaw in terms of abstractions using macros.

```
(defmacro freeze-macro
  [freeze X] -> [/. (gensym⁴⁶ (protect Y)) X])
```

```
(defmacro thaw-macro
  [thaw X] -> [X 0])
```

Exercise 11

1. Represent the Cartesian product program of chapter 4 as a lazy list.

2. Represent the powerset program of chapter 4 as a lazy list.

3. Represent the Goldbach's conjecture program as a lazy list; if the user enters RETURN, the program returns a new instance of the Conjecture.

4. Devise a simulation of a UNIX operating system that allows the user to place a job in background by typing bg *command*. Your job will be held as a continuation and bg will return a job number *n*. Typing fg *n* will execute the job.

5. In object-oriented (OO) programming, objects are not just data but data with 'intelligence'; that is, an object can respond to commands sent to it. Implement an OO version of a database program where the database is held as an abstraction that receives user input and can modify itself accordingly.

---

[46] (gensym (protect Y)) generates a new symbol such as Y4567. The purpose is to protect from accidental variable capture if the symbol Y occurs in the expression denoted by X.

Further Reading

Scheme (Abelson and Sussman, 1984) was famous for introducing many ideas which became standard including continuations. The idea of a continuation was present in operating systems in the form of a **thread**; a computational process that could be passed around or activated. Such technology has become more common with the development of concurrent programming.

Websites

See http://www.sbcl.org/manual/Threading.html for an exposition of threads for SBCL which are held a continuations.

12 Non-Determinism

It's choice - not chance - that determines your destiny.

Jean Nidetch

12.1 Non-deterministic Algorithms

An important class of algorithms is grouped under the heading of **non-deterministic algorithms**. In a deterministic algorithm, every step is determined and there is no possibility of choice. Non-deterministic algorithms present a series of steps in which, at some point, there is an undetermined choice as to what step to take out of a set of possibilities, and the algorithm leaves it to us to determine how the right choice is made. The stage of a non-deterministic algorithm where such a choice arises is called a **choice point**.

The problem in programming a non-deterministic algorithm into a computer is that computers do not *choose* anything; they only do what they are told to do. One way of representing non-determinism to a computer is to get it to order the choices available and to try each one in turn. If a choice turns out to be unsuccessful, then the computer **backtracks** to the choice point and tries the next choice in the ordering.

12.2 Depth First Search

Non-deterministic algorithms are common in **search** where the solution may not be obvious and computations may have to be undone when initial choices turn out to be wrong.

A search problem is a triple $<s, f, g>$ composed of a start state s, a state function f that maps a state to a set of states and a goal function g that maps a state to a boolean and recognises when the search problem has been solved. If $(g\ s) =$ true then s is a **goal state**.

An example of a search problem is the problem of finding, from a given set s of natural numbers, a series of numbers whose summation is equal to some given natural number n. For instance, if $s = \{2, 7, 9\}$ and $n = 27$, then a solution is [2 7 9 9]. Our start state s is composed of the empty list and the state function f

generates from any state s_i, a list of states $[[2 \mid s_i] \, [7 \mid s_i] \, [9 \mid s_i]]$. The goal function g returns true just when S' totals 27 and false otherwise.

The challenge of search is to conduct the generation of new states efficiently so that a goal state is reached with the minimum computation. This may not be easy because the further into the seach we go, the greater the number of possible paths of computation. In our example, every application of f to a state generates three new states and iterating f over those states generates three more from every state. Hence every level l of search raises the number of possible paths to 3^l. For this reason search programs can get bogged down in possibilities; a phenomenon known as the **combinatorial explosion**.

There are ways of coping with this explosion; a popular method, **depth–first search**, is good at constraining the memory requirements of search because, instead of generating every layer of search, depth-first search chooses only one possible solution and runs with it. This is a choice point of course. The immediate problem that the choice might be wrong and the possible solution may turn out to be a dead end. At this point the computer will have to return to the last choice point and choose again.

One nasty possibility is that the wrong choice is taken and the computer never gets to recognise it. Depth–first search may fail to find a solution, preferring to beaver away endlessly on the wrong path. A useful adjunct is a **failure function** which recognises if a state can never lead to a solution. In our problem, if the summation (sum) of the numbers in a state exceeds 27, we know that the state is a failure state and we need not persevere with it. Such a function can be built into f to filter out useless states. The various pieces of our search problem can be easily coded.

```
(define goal?
  S -> (= (sum S) 27))

(define f
  S -> (remove-if-no-good  [[2 | S] [7 | S] [9 | S]]))

(define remove-if-no-good
  Ss -> (remove-if (/. X (> (sum X) 27)) Ss))

(define remove-if
  _ [] -> []
  F [X | Y] -> (remove-if F Y)        where (F X)
  F [X | Y] -> [X | (remove-if F Y)])
```

The challenge is to join these bricks of code together to form a coherent program. The mortar in this case is a **search strategy** and the one we have chosen to implement is depth-first search. Since two of the elements of search are functions, it follows that depth-first search will be implemented as a higher-order function. Implementing depth-first search is a 7 line program in Shen, but to achieve this economy we need to look at the resources Shen supplies for computing with choice points.

In Shen, rules that mark choice points are signalled by the use of <- instead of -> within a function definition. The effect of this change is that the expression R to the right of <- is returned only provided R does *not* evaluate to the **failure object**. The failure object is returned by the 0-place function (fail) and is printed out as three dots ... . If R *does* evaluate to the failure object, then the rule is skipped and Shen **backtracks** to this point the next rule is tried. For instance the function

```
(define return-n
  10 <- (fail)
  10 -> 9
  N -> N)
```

returns 9 for 10 and n for any other number n. The input 10 on the first line causes (fail) to be evaluated. However the result of (fail) is not returned because the back arrow <- is used. The rule is thus skipped and the second line returns 9.. The following equivalence is convenient way of grasping the use of <- in Shen.

The rule $P_1,...,P_n$ <- R is equivalent to $P_1,...,P_n$ -> R where (not (= R (fail)))[47]

Another means of forcing backtracking is through the higher-order fail-if function which takes two arguments; a function f and an object x and triggers failure if $(f\ x)$ is true. fail-if is a powerful means of controlling backtracking which allows the elements of an infinitely large class to count as failure objects. In figure 12.1 return-n acts as the identity function for numbers less than or equal to 45 but triggers failure if the number is greater. Shen skips to the next rule in this case, but since there is no next rule an error is triggered.

```
(5-) (define return-n
       N <- (fail-if (/. X (> X 45)) N))
return-n

(6-) (return-n 45)
45

(7-) (return-n 46)
error: partial function return n
```

Figure 12.1 Invoking backtracking

A convenient way of grasping the use of fail-if in Shen is to remember the following equivalence

---

[47] The rule is declaratively accurate but inefficient, because the result R returned from the rewrite rule is evaluated twice in the right-hand side of the equivalence, but only once on the left hand side. In chapter 15 we shall see how continuations are used to compile these constructions efficiently.

P₁,...,Pₙ <- (fail-if F R)   is equivalent to   P₁,...,Pₙ -> R where (not (F R))

Preliminaries over, the depth-first program can be encoded (figure 12.2).

```
(5-) (define depth
       State F G?  -> (depth-help [State] F G?))
depth

(6-) (define depth-help
       [State | _] _ G? -> State                    where (G? State)
       [State | _] F G? <- (depth-help (F State) F G?)
       [_ | States] F G? -> (depth-help States F G? )
       _ _ _ -> (fail))
depth-first

(7-) (depth [] (function f) (function goal?))
[7 2 2 2 2 2 2 2 2 2 2 2]
```

Figure 12.2 Depth first search in Shen

Certain beautiful programs, and this is one of them, are best left to contemplation.

12.3 Recursive Descent Parsing

Languages, whether natural like English or French, or artificial, like Pascal or Shen, possess a syntax whereby certain series of symbols are grammatically acceptable and others are not.   To take English as an example, "John kicks the ball" is an acceptable English sentence but "the kicks ball John" is not. One basic facility that every competent programmer needs is that of being able to design, upon request, programs that recognise whether a certain series of symbols is grammatically acceptable according to the syntax rules of a given language. Such programs are called **recognisers** for the sentences of the language in question.

A recogniser for a language may only return two values; indicating either that its input is grammatical or that it is not. Rather more useful is a *parser* which returns either the verdict that the input is not grammatical or else, if the input is grammatical, returns a description of the **grammatical structure** of the input. [48]

For example, a linguist would say that "John kicks the ball" is a grammatical sentence composed of two parts - a *noun phrase* comprising the *name* "John" and a *verb phrase* "kicks the ball". The verb phrase is composed of two parts, a *transitive verb* "kicks" and another *noun phrase* "the ball". Finally the concluding noun phrase is built out of a *determiner* "the" and a *noun* "ball". This

---

[48] Such programs can be a big challenge to write because of the size of the grammars for English. For instance, realistic grammars will contain several thousand rules, which pose a severe computational challenge for any parser. Happily most programmers do not set themselves such an ambitious task and the techniques taught in this chapter will suffice to solve simple parsing problems.

analysis is sometimes represented as a tree structure in which *sent* stands for *sentence*, *np* stands for *noun phrase*, *vp* stands for *verb phrase*, *vtrans* stands for *transitive verb*, *det* stands for *determiner* and *n* stands for *noun*. Such a tree is called a **parse tree** (figure 12.3).

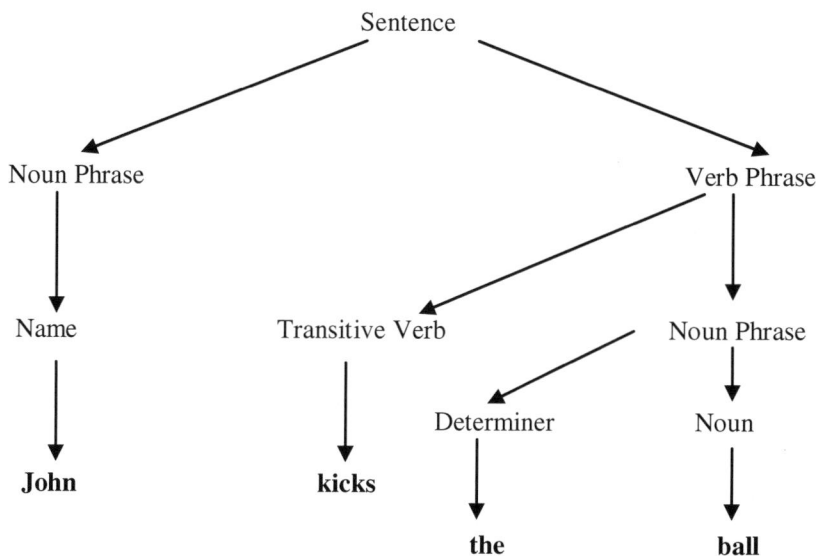

Figure 12.3 A parse tree representing the syntax of "John kicks the ball"

The choice of representation is conventional; the same information can be given as a list.

```
[[sent  -->  np  vp]  [np  -->  name]  [name  -->  "John"]  [vp  -->  vtrans  np]
[vtrans -->"kicks"]  [np --> det n]  [det -->"the"]  [n-->"ball"]]
```

Grammar rules are rules that attempt to define what counts as grammatical in the language studied. The shape and form of these grammar rules vary according to the system used, but by far the commonest form is the **context-free grammar** (also called a **type 2 grammar**). A context-free grammar consists of a series of context-free grammar rules. Each such rule consists of a left-hand side and a right-hand side separated by some agreed symbol (generally →, but also sometimes ::=). The left-hand side has but one symbol and the right-hand side one or more symbols. For example, here is a simple grammar which parses our specimen sentence.

1.	*sent → np vp*	9.	*det →* "this"
2.	*np → name*	10.	*n →* "ball"
3.	*np → det n*	11.	*n →* "girl"
4.	*name →* "John"	12.	*vp → vtrans np*
5.	*name →* "Bill"	13.	*vp → vintrans*
6.	*det →* "the"	14.	*vtrans →* "kicks"
7.	*det →* "a"	15.	*vtrans →* "likes"
8.	*det →* "that"	16.	*vintrans →* "jumps"

Figure 12.4 A grammar for a simple fragment of English

One symbol, called **the distinguished symbol,** occurs to the left of the arrow but never to the right; in our example this is *sent*. A series of expressions $e_1,...e_n$ are **expansions** of an expression e if there is a rule $e \rightarrow e_1,...e_n$ in the grammar. The expressions that occur in the grammar but never on the left of $\rightarrow$ are called **terminals**. A **lexical category** is a non-terminal whose expansions are always terminals. In order to prove a sentence S is grammatical according to the grammar rules we can follow a non-deterministic procedure the **naive top down parsing procedure**.

Naive Top Down Parsing Procedure.

Let i = the list containing only the distinguished symbol, let S be the sentence to be parsed.

Repeat.

If i consists of only terminals and i = S, then halt. S is grammatical. Print the proof.[49]

If i consists of only terminals and $i \neq$ S, then halt. The proof has failed.

Otherwise choose a non-terminal i_n in i. Choose an expansion of i_n and set the new value of i to the result of replacing i_n in the old value of i by the chosen expansion.

To illustrate, we wish to prove ["John" "kicks" "the" "ball"] is grammatical according to *G*. The symbol $\rightarrow n$ indicates that a symbol may be expanded according to the *n*th rule in *G*. The following chain of expansions constitutes a proof that ["John" "kicks" "the" "ball"] is grammatical.

---

[49] Most usually, this proof is presented as a parse tree, but there is no necessity to do so. The parse tree is only significant in rendering graphically the history of the expansions that were used to prove the sentence grammatical. The difference between a parser and a recogniser is not that the parser produces a parse tree and the recogniser does not, but that the parser produces a proof of its verdict whereas the recogniser does not.

[*sent*] $\rightarrow_1$ [*np vp*] $\rightarrow_2$ [*name vp*] $\rightarrow_4$ ["John" *vp*] $\rightarrow_{12}$ ["John" *vtrans np*] $\rightarrow_{14}$ ["John" "kicks" *np*] $\rightarrow_3$ ["John" "kicks" *det n*] $\rightarrow_6$ ["John" "kicks" "the" *n*] $\rightarrow_{10}$ ["John" "kicks" "the" "ball"]

Though the basic top down parsing procedure is perfectly sound it requires modification for three reasons.

1. It cannot show a sentence is ungrammatical. A negative result from this procedure could be due to a faulty choice of expansions earlier in the proof. For instance if [*np vp*] $\rightarrow_3$ [*det n vp*] had been chosen instead of [*np vp*] $\rightarrow_2$ [name vp], then the parse would have failed.

2. The basic top down parsing procedure provides no clue as to which expansions to use.

3. The basic top down parsing procedure provides no clue as to which non-terminals to expand.

The solution to the second problem is also a solution to the first. We mimic the non-determinism in the basic top down parsing procedure by arranging to backtrack if the procedure has led to a dead end. Since by this method all available expansions will be tried, if a negative result is still returned then this must be because the input sentence is ungrammatical and so our improved procedure can return a message to this effect. The solution to the final problem is to adopt a convention as to which non-terminal will be expanded first and the most convenient choice is to work on the leftmost or leading non-terminal in *i*.

In this revised form, the top down parsing procedure is still inefficient because it has to convert all non-terminals to terminals before comparing the result with the input sentence to see if they are identical. But it is often possible to spot dead-ends before this stage. For instance, if the chain [*np vp*] $\rightarrow_3$ [*det n vp*] $\rightarrow_6$ ["the" *n vp*] had been followed, then the failure of "the" to match the input "John" would signify straight away that further expansion of ["the" *n vp*] was a waste of time.

A much improved performance arises when we arrange that whenever the leading expression i_l of *i* is a terminal, that further expansion proceeds only if $i_l = S_1$ (where S_1 is the first element of S). Computationally it is then convenient to remove i_l from *i* and S_1 from S so that the parse finally succeeds when every word in S has been accounted for; i.e. S has been reduced to an empty list. This adaptation of the basic top down parsing procedure is called **recursive descent parsing**.

12.4 A Recursive Descent Parser in Shen

Building a recursive descent parser for *G* in Shen is not too difficult. Each non-terminal *N* in *G* is represented by a function in Shen. The nature of this representation varies according to whether *N* is a lexical category or not. Let us deal with the case where *N* is a lexical category using an example. These are the rules dealing with the lexical category *n* (Noun).

$$n \rightarrow \text{"ball"}$$
$$n \rightarrow \text{"girl"}$$

An initial attempt to construct a function for *n* would simply receive the input list and check to see if the head of the list was "girl" or "ball". If so, following recursive descent parsing, the head of the list is removed. If not, then (fail) is returned showing the function has failed to find a noun.

```
(define n
  ["ball" | Words]  -> Words
  ["girl" | Words] -> Words
  _ -> (fail))
```

This is almost adequate except that if the head of the list is a noun, then the fact that the relevant expansion has been used must be recorded so that it can be returned at the end of the parse. A solution is to make the input a pair composed of (a) the sentence being parsed (a list of strings) and (b) a list of the rules used to parse it so far. This second list will be returned at the end of the parse as a proof that the sentence is grammatical. The revised version now reads.

```
(define n
  [["girl" | Words] Proof]  -> [Words [[n --> "girl"] | Proof]]
  [["ball" | Words] Proof]  -> [Words [[n --> "ball"] | Proof]]
  _ -> (fail))
```

Now consider the construction of a function for a non-lexical category; for example *vp*. *vp* has two expansions *vp → vtrans np* and *vp → vintrans*. If the first expansion is used then (a) the front of the sentence will be scanned for a transitive verb and (b) if there is one, the remainder of the sentence will be scanned for a noun phrase. However either of these procedures might fail in which case the failure object will be found. In such an event we will want to try the second expansion. So the outline form of the function vp will be

```
(define vp
  Sentence
    <- ( <parse-noun-phrase> (parse-transitive-verb> Sentence)))
  Sentence -> ( <parse-intransitive-verb> Sentence))
```

The gaps *<parse-transitive-verb>*, *<parse-noun-phrase>* and *<parse-intransitive-verb>* will be taken up by the functions that encode *vtrans*, *np* and *vintrans* respectively so the function will look like this.

```
(define vp
  Sentence <- (np (vtrans Sentence))
  Sentence <- (vintrans Sentence)
  _ -> (fail))
```

But since the input is a pair, we need again to record the expansion used. So the final form is:-

```
(define vp
  [Sentence Proof]
    <- (np (vtrans [Sentence [[vp --> vtrans np] | Proof]]))
  [Sentence Proof] -> (vintrans [Sentence [[vp --> vintrans] | Proof]])
  _ -> (fail))
```

Dealing with all the other expansions in the same way generates the program in figure 12.5.

```
(define sent
  [Input Proof] <- (vp (np [Input [[sent --> np vp] | Proof]]))
  _ -> (fail))

(define np
  [Input Proof] <- (n (det [Input [[np --> det n] | Proof]]))
  [Input Proof] <- (name [Input [[np --> name] | Proof]])
  _ -> (fail))

(define name
  [["John" | Input] Proof] -> [Input [[name --> "John"] | Proof]]
  [["Bill" | Input] Proof] -> [Input [[name --> "Bill"] | Proof]]
  _ -> (fail))

(define det
  [["the" | Input] Proof] -> [Input [[det --> "the"] | Proof]]
  [["a" | Input] Proof] -> [Input [[det --> "a"] | Proof]]
  [["that" | Input] Proof] -> [Input [[det --> "that"] | Proof]]
  [["this" | Input] Proof] -> [Input [[det --> "this"] | Proof]]
  _ -> (fail))

(define n
  [["ball" | Input] Proof] -> [Input [[n --> "ball"] | Proof]]
  [["girl" | Input] Proof] -> [Input [[n --> "girl"] | Proof]]
  _ -> (fail))

(define vp
  [Input Proof] <- (np (vtrans [Input [[vp --> vtrans np] | Proof]]))
  [Input Proof] <- (vp [Input [[vp --> vintrans] | Proof]])
  _ -> (fail))
```

```
(define vtrans
  [["kicks" | Input] Proof] -> [Input [[vtrans --> "kicks"] | Proof]]
  [["likes" | Input] Proof] -> [Input [[vtrans --> "likes"] | Proof]]
  _ -> (fail))

(define vintrans
  [["jumps" | Input] Proof]
  -> [Input [[vintrans --> "jumps"] | Proof]]
  _ -> (fail))
```

Figure 12.5 A parser for our simple fragment of English

All that is needed to complete the program is the driver function that builds the input and applies the function representing the distinguished function and tests to see if the parse is successful (figure 12.6).

```
(define parse
  Sentence -> (let Parse (sent [Sentence []])
                 (if (parsed? Parse)
                     (output_parse Parse)
                     ungrammatical)))

(define parsed?
  [[] _] -> true
  _ -> false)

(define output_parse
  [_ Parse_Rules] -> (reverse Parse_Rules))
```

Figure 12.6 The top level of the parser

The program can now be used to parse sentences according to the grammar rules (figure 12.7).

```
(22-) (parse ["the" "girl" "likes" "the" "ball"])
[[sent --> np vp] [np --> det n] [det --> "the"] [n --> "girl"] [vp --> vtrans np]
[vtrans --> "likes"] [np --> det n] [det --> "the"] [n --> "ball"]]

(23-) (parse ["the" "cat" "likes" "the" "girl"])
ungrammatical
```

Figure 12.7 The parser in action

The extraction of a program like the above from a grammar is actually a mechanical process, so it is more sensible to program the computer to generate the parser than to code it by hand. Such a program is a **parser-generator** – a metaprogram that receives a grammar as input and generates a parsing program as an output. We will examine the use of such a program in the next chapter.

Exercise 12

1. Bratko (1990) "A **non-deterministic finite state machine** (NDFSM) is a machine that reads a series of symbols and decides whether to accept or reject that series. A NDFSM has a number of states and upon receipt of a symbol will change from being in one state to being in another. There is a privileged set of states called **final states** and if the automaton is in one of these states when it finishes reading a series then it accepts that series, otherwise it rejects it. If there is one state that has to be chosen in order for the whole list to be accepted, then the NDFSM will choose that state and not one that will cause the list to be rejected." The operation of a NDFSM can be represented by a labelled directed graph in which the nodes of the graph represent the states of the NDFSM, and the labels on the arcs are the inputs required to get the NDFSM to jump from one state to the next. The figure below shows a NDFSM as a labelled directed graph.

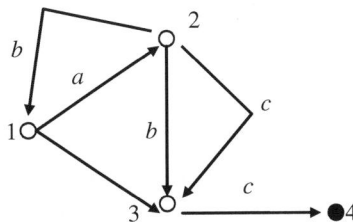

There is one final state in this NDFSM, state 4. Initially the NDFSM is in state 1. This automaton accepts the input $a\ b\ a\ b\ a\ c$ in the following way. The input a causes the automaton to go to state 2, the b to state 1, the a to state 2, the b to state 1, the a to state 3 and the c to state 4. Write a program to simulate this NDFSM.

The next problems are all taken from Werner Hett's web site of *Ninety-Nine Prolog Problems*.

3. **The eight queens problem.** This is a classical problem in computer science. The objective is to place eight queens on a chessboard so that no two queens are attacking each other; i.e., no two queens are in the same row, the same column, or on the same diagonal. Write a program that computes all the solutions for this problem. Your program will systematically place queens and force a backtrack when a queen cannot be added to the board without attacking another queen already on it.

4. **The knight's tour.** Another famous problem is this one: how can a knight jump on a chessboard in such a way that it visits every square exactly once?

5. ***Graceful labelling problem**. This problem is taken from Werner Hett who records.

> "Several years ago I met a mathematician who was intrigued by a problem for which he didn't know a solution. His name was Von Koch, and I don't know whether the problem has been solved since.

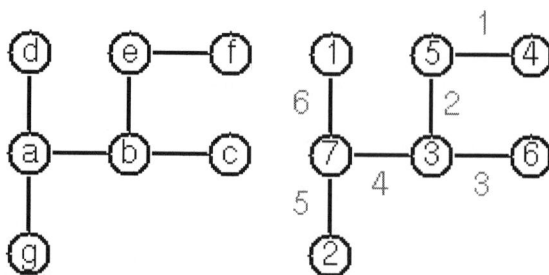

Anyway the puzzle goes like this: Given a tree with N nodes (and hence N-1 edges). Find a way to enumerate the nodes from 1 to N and, accordingly, the edges from 1 to N-1 in such a way, that for each edge K the difference of its node numbers (labels) equals to K. The conjecture is that this is always possible. [The diagram above shows a solution for one tree].

For small trees the problem is easy to solve by hand. However, for larger trees, (and 14 is already very large), it is difficult to find a solution. And remember, we don't know for sure whether there is always a solution!"

Write a program that calculates a labeling scheme for a given tree.

6. *Again from Werner Hett.

"Given a list of integer numbers, find a correct way of inserting arithmetic signs (operators) such that the result is a correct equation. Example: With the list of numbers [2,3,5,7,11] we can form the equations 2-3+5+7 = 11 or 2 = (3*5+7)/11 (and ten others!)."

Write a program that finds the list of all possible solutions to this problem.

7. Write a function path to find an acyclic path P from node A to node B in the graph G. The function should return all paths via backtracking.

8. Write a function cycles to find a closed path (cycle) P starting at a given node A in the graph G. The function should return all cycles from A via backtracking.

9. Two graphs G_1 and G_2 are *isomorphic* if there is a 1-1 function from the set of nodes of G_1 onto the set of nodes of G_2 such that for any nodes X,Y of G_1, X and Y are adjacent in G_1 if and only if f(X) and f(Y) are adjacent in G_2. Write a function that determines whether two graphs are isomorphic.

Further Reading

The use of backtracking in programming dates at least as far back as Hewitt's (1969) PLANNER and became widely used when Prolog (Kowalski (1979)) made its appearance. A more restrictive version of the backtracking used in Shen appeared in the MetaLisp programming language (Lajos (1990)) and in Wright (1991). Liu and Staples (1993) introduce a backtracking extension into C. Haynes (1987) and more recently Sitaram (1993) experimented with backtracking in Scheme, a functional language that is a dialect of Lisp. Charniak and McDermott (1985), discuss improvements to our implementation of basic backward chaining which involve applying rules that generate the fewest subgoals. Chapter 6 of that book contains a very readable exposition of the issues involved in using backward chaining in implementing reasoning systems. Chronological backtracking is not the only form of backtracking; **dependency-directed backtracking** aims to intelligently analyse the reasons for why a search ends in a failure node and tries to undo those decisions that are directly responsible for the failure. This area is also studied within **constraint programming**, which studies the **constraint satisfaction problem** of assigning values to each element of a set of variables in such a way that a set of constraints is satisfied. Problems which fall under this category range from DNA sequencing to scheduling.

13 Shen-YACC

13.1 A Short History of Shen-YACC

Programs which generate parsers in the manner of the last chapter are very much a commodity now in computing and most major languages field such programs, although the parsing strategies vary. A more useful tool than a parser-generator is a **compiler-compiler**, which generates a compiler - that is to say, a program that not only parses the input but transforms it into some representation in another formal language. The study of compilers spans not only computer languages, but also natural language processing (NLP). NLP involves encoding assertions in languages like English and German into artificial or formal languages used for information storage.

The compiler-compiler studied in this chapter is Shen-YACC[50] which was built to service the requirements of parsing Shen into Kλ. The genealogy of the system goes back to the Ph.D. work described in Lajos (1990) which in turn was derived from the **TDPL** (top down parsing language) formalism of Alexander Birman, documented in Aho and Ullman (1973). Shen-YACC uses the recursive descent parsing strategy described in the last chapter, but augments this strategy by adding **semantic actions** that translate the input to an output, instead of simply producing a parse tree. Shen-YACC incorporates certain familiar constructions such as guards, and the less familiar constructions, <e>, <!> which we will come to grips with in this chapter.

---

[50] The terminology YACC means 'yet another compiler-compiler'; a now generic title for compiler-compilers derived from Steve Johnson's YACC (Johnson, 1970); a compiler-compiler developed at AT&T for the language B – a predecessor of C.

13.2 Programming in Shen-YACC

A computable relation exists between the grammar rules of the last chapter and the parse that represented them. Rather than hand code a parser, it is easier to use Shen-YACC to generate the parser (figure 13.1).

```
(defcc <sent>
  <np> <vp>;)

(defcc <np>
  <name>;  <det> <n>;)

(defcc <name>
  "John";  "Bill";)

(defcc <det>
 "a"; "that"; "the";)

(defcc <n>
  "ball"; "girl";)

(defcc <vp>
 <vtrans> <np>; <vintrans>;)

(defcc <vtrans>
 "kicks"; "likes";)

(defcc <vintrans>
 "jumps";)
```

Figure 13.1 A Shen-YACC program acting as a recognisor

In Shen-YACC, non-terminals are identified by angles <...>. Every rule within a Shen-YACC definition is terminated by a semi-colon and there can be several rules relating to one non-terminal, as in this example. Warnings are generated whenthis program isloaded e.g.

```
(defcc <np>
    <name>;  <det> <n>;)
warning: <name> has no semantics.
warning: <det> <n> has no semantics.
```

because no **semantic actions** have been issued as to what to do with the input when it is parsed. By default, if no semantic action is given for a rule *r*, then Shen-YACC practises a technique called **semantic completion**. Semantic completion allots to *r* an action that collects the list of those terminals that fall under *r*. The semantic action is separated from the syntactic component by :=. Thus the rule <np> <vp>; is completed by the Shen compiler to <np> <vp> := (append <np> <vp>) and "ball" is completed to "ball" := ["ball"].

The higher-order function compile invokes a Shen-YACC non-terminal on an input (figure 13.2). Since semantic completion has been used in every rule, if the input is grammatical, it is returned as an output. If it is not grammatical, a parse error is raised.

```
(10-) (compile (function <sent>) ["the" "girl" "likes" "the" "ball"])
["the" "girl" "likes" "the" "ball"]

(11-) (compile (function <sent>) ["the" "girl" "likes" "the" "cat"])
parse error
```

Figure 13.2 Invoking compile

The program that Shen-YACC has generated is a recogniser for the sentences of the grammar which produces only two outputs; one output for grammatical sentences and another for non-grammatical ones.

By overriding the semantic completion and inserting our own actions, we can arrange for Shen-YACC, not only to parse an input, but also to generate some significant output. To start gently, here is a Shen-YACC program that returns true if the numbers of as and bs are the same. Figure 13.4 shows it in action.

```
(defcc <asbs>
     <as> <bs> := (= (length <as>) (length <bs>));)

(defcc <as>
     a <as>;
     a;)

(defcc <bs>
     b <bs>;  b;)
```

```
(3-) (compile (function <asbs>) [a a a b b b])
true

(4-) (compile (function <asbs>) [a a a b b b b])
false

(5-) (compile (function <asbs>) [a a a c b b b b])
parse error
```

Figure 13.3 A simple Shen-YACC program that counts tokens of two kinds

The program incorporates a semantic action in the definition of the top level non-terminal; the as and the bs are collected into two lists and the lists are compared.

Since no semantic actions are given for <as> and <bs>; these non-terminals simply collect all the tokens that fall under them, returning a list in each case. The compiler can give three verdicts, true, false or an error if the list contains other than as followed by bs. An alternative encoding (13.4) avoids lists and counts the tokens on the fly.

```
(6-) (defcc <asbs>
       <as> <bs> := (= <as> <bs>);)
<asbs>

(7-) (defcc <as>
       a <as> := (+ 1 <as>);
       a := 1;)
<as>

(8-) (defcc <bs>
       b <bs> := (+ 1 <bs>);
       b := 1;)
<bs>

(9-) (compile (function <asbs>) [a a a a a b b b b b])
true

(10-) (compile (function <asbs>) [a a a a a b b b b b])
false

(11-) (compile (function <asbs>) [a a a a a b b b b b c])
parse error
```

Figure 13.4 Optimising our counting program

13.3 The Empty Expansion and Guards

A more advanced case allows 'dead characters' between the as and the bs, so that in [a a a c c % b b b] the c c % is ignored (figure 13.5).

```
(10-) (defcc <asXbs>
        <as> <dead> <bs> := (= <as> <bs>);)
<asXbs>

(11-) (defcc <dead>
        X <dead> := skip   where (not (= X b));
        <e>;)
<dead>

(12-) (compile (function <asXbs>) [a a a a a c c % b b b b b])
true
```

Figure 13.5 Using the empty expansion and a guard

The first line of <dead> says that dead characters can consist of an element X followed by dead characters on the condition that X is not b. Here, like Shen, a guard places an extra condition on the rule. The second line introduces a special non-terminal <e>, the **empty expansion** which consumes no input and always succeeds and under semantic completion returns the empty list. This line allows <dead> to be called without consuming any characters and hence allows there to be no dead characters.

13.4 Non-Terminals and Semantic Actions

Consider the following grammar for a language L

```
(defcc <asbas>
   <as> b <as>;)

(defcc <as>
     a <as>;   a;)
```

Figure 13.6 A language L characterised by repeating a non-terminal

The set of L sentences defined by this grammar is the set a_m b a_n where m and n are greater than zero. If we submit an input to the parser generated from this grammar we get an interesting result.

```
(12-) (compile (function <asbas>) [a b a a a a a])
[a a a a a b a a a a a]
```

The output is not the same as the input. The semantic completion that Shen-YACC uses is

```
(defcc <asbas>
   <as> b <as> := (append <as> [b | <as>]);)
```

The problem here is that the grammar uses <as> for both the as preceding the b and the as following it. Since there is no way of disambiguating from the description, which <as> is invoked in the semantics, Shen follows the course of associating the output with the last occurrence of the repeated non-terminal. In this case, this is the <as> that is bound to the list of as following b. Hence the output consists of five as followed by a b followed by five more as.

To make our intentions unambiguously clear, we need to rename one of the repeated <as>.

```
(defcc <asbas>
   <as> b <as+>;)

(defcc <as>
     a <as>;     a;)

(defcc <as+>
   <as>;)
```

Figure 13.7 Disambiguating the characterisation of L

The renamed <as+> has the same properties as <as>. But renaming means that the semantic completion uses two styles of non-terminal; one for the as preceding the b and one for the as after it. Using this grammar, the compiler acts as the identity function on all L sentences.

The example illustrates the importance of understanding semantic completions in Shen-YACC. The method of semantic completion follows three rules.

1. The output from a non-terminal is *appended* to the output.
2. A terminal is *consed* to the output.
3. In cases of ambiguity where a non-terminal is repeated, the output of the non-terminal is the output associated with its final occurrence.

Though these rules are not hard to follow, it is useful, when mastering Shen-YACC, not to rely on semantic completion but to program in the actions oneself – especially if there is doubt on the result of the compilation. For example the language L can be characterised by this grammar.

```
(defcc <asbas>
   <as> <b> <as+>;)

(defcc <as>
      a <as>;
      a;)

(defcc <b>
  b;)

(defcc <as+>
   <as>;)
```

Figure 13.8 Another characterisation of L

The program works as before; however if we change the definition of <b> to include a semantic action of returning b, the program crashes.

```
(defcc <b>
  b := b;)
<b>

(compile (function <asbas>) [a a a b a a a a a])
The value b is not of type LIST.
```

The reason this happens is that Shen-YACC constructs the semantic completion

```
(defcc <asbas>
   <as> <b> <as+> := (append <as> <b> <as+>);)
```

Since <b> is returning a symbol and not a list, the attempt at appending fails. Since we want to override the default completion we would add

```
(defcc <asbas>
  <as> <b> <as+> := (append <as> [<b> | <as+>]);)
```

13.5 Handling Lists in Shen-YACC

Shen-YACC accepts lists and wildcards except | is not recognised to the left of :=. The following compiler recognises all inputs, and outputs the input stripped of all lists of as including the empty list.

```
(defcc <remove>
  [<as>] <remove> := <remove>;
  _ <remove>;
  <e>;)

(defcc <as>
  a <as>
  <e>;)
```

A common confusion is to forget that the input to compile is *always* a list itself in which the sentence is read. Thus

```
(defcc <xs>
  [x x];)
```

fails in (compile (function <xs>) [x x]) which fits the definition

```
(defcc <xs>
  x x;)
```

and the correct input is (compile (function <xs>) [[x x]])

13.6 Stripping Comments

A common parsing problem is removing structured 'noise' from a file where 'noise' is defined as unwanted data and 'structured' denotes that the beginning and end of the noise is well defined. Examples of structured noise are program comments in relation to a compiler. Let's suppose we are writing a compiler for a language in which <& is used to open a multiline comment and &> is used to close it. The task is to strip the comments from the code. We open with

```
(defcc <strip>
  <comment> <strip> := <strip>;
  X <strip>;
  <e>;)
```

The tricky part is <comment>. A comment consists of stuff between <& and &>.

```
(defcc <comment>
  <& <stuff> &>;)
```

<stuff> reads the input subject to the condition that it is not &>.

```
(defcc <stuff>
  X <stuff> := skip  where (not (= X &>));
  <e>;)
```

Unfortunately this does not work.

```
(46-) (compile (function <strip>) [hi <& ignore this &> there])
The value skip is not of type LIST.
```

This occurs because <comment> uses semantic completion in which <stuff> is supposed to return a list, and not skip. We change this to:

```
(defcc <comment>
  <& <stuff> &> := skip;)
```

and it works fine

```
(48-) (compile (function <strip>) [hi <& ignore this &> there])
[hi there]
```

However the guard in

```
(defcc <stuff>
  X <stuff> := skip  where (not (= X &>));
  <e>;)
```

is invoked only *after* the <stuff> expansion is used and not *before* and this is expensive in time. It is better is to apply the guard immediately (figure 13.9).

```
(defcc <strip>
  <comment> <strip> := <strip>;
  X <strip>;
  <e>;)

(defcc <comment>
  <& <stuff>  &>;)

(defcc <stuff>
  <token> <stuff> := skip ;
  <e>;)

(defcc <token>
  X := skip  where (not (= X &>));)
```

Figure 13.9 A comment stripper

13.7 Consuming the Input

Shen-YACC requires that any parse consume all the input and failure to 'clean one's plate' will cause parse failures. A simple example containing this mistake is a program <look> that tests to see if a sentence occurs embedded in the input. A naive encoding is

```
(defcc <look>
  <sent> := true;
  _ <look>;)
```

But this only works if the sentence is at the end of the input. If it is not then the unconsumed input will cause a parse failure. We can easily write an auxiliary which simply recursively consumes the remaining input.

```
(defcc <look>
  <sent> <skip> := true;
  X <look>;)

(defcc <skip>
  _ <skip> := skip;
  <e>;)
```

But this is unnecessary and computationally inefficient because <!> will immediately consume the remaining input and return it as the result. Thus

```
(defcc <look>
  <sent> <!> := <!>;
  _ <look>;)
```

returns all of the input after the first sentence encountered. <!> can be used within a list to consume the contents of a list.

```
(45 -) (defcc <asbs>
        [a <!>] b := <!>;)
<asbs>

(46-) (compile (function <asbs>) [[a 1 2 3] b])
[1 2 3]
```

Figure 13.10 Using <!>to consume input

The issue of consuming the input arises in several contexts. For example the recursive definition of <as> as

```
(defcc <as>
  a;
  a <as>;)
```

will fail on the following input.

```
(compile (function <as>) [a a])
parse error here: ...a
```

The message indicates that part of the input has not been consumed in the parse and that unconsumed input is returned in the error message. The reason for this is that <as> is called with the base case first, which succeeds, returning control to the top level with the second a unconsumed. The common solution, given overlapping rules of this kind, is to place the longest expansion first.

The non-terminal <end> is will fail if the entire input has not been consumed; if it succeeds the input and output are unchanged. It is sometimes useful to use this non-terminal in a toplevel concept to ensure that all input has been consumed.

13.8 Limited Backtracking

Shen-YACC practices backtracking between expansions of a non-terminal. If one expansion fails, then the next is tried. However backtracking takes place *between* expansions and not *within* expansions and this limited backtracking affects the declarative reading of Shen-YACC. Here is an example that defines a language L.

```
(defcc <?bscs>
  <?s> <bs> <cs>;)

(defcc <?s>
  a <?s>;
  a;
  b <?s>;
  b;)

(defcc <bs>
  b <bs>;
  b;)

(defcc <cs>
  c <cs>;
  c;)
```

Figure 13.11 An example of limited backtracking

Declaratively the above rules admit the sentence [a a a b b b c c c] as a sentence of L. But (compile (function <?bscs>) [a a a b b b c c c]) generates a parse error, because Shen-YACC does not backtrack *within* the expansion <?bscs> ::= <?s> <bs> <cs> to consider the possibility that <?s> may be expanded ambiguously with respect to the input. Instead the rule <?bscs> ::= <?s> <bs> <cs> is interpreted to make <?s> a greedy consumer of the input. In this case it consumes [a a a b b] leaving no bs left for <bs>.

The limited backtracking model can pose problems if the behaviour interacts with the 'longest expansion first' requirement. We'll see an example of this in the next section.

13.9 Left Recursion

Direct left-recursion is fairly common in grammars. A definition is directly left recursive if it has the form

```
(defcc v
  .......
  v ...
  ......)
```

A simple example is an NLP program that expresses the idea that a sentence can be a conjunction of sentences, a natural expression is:

```
(defcc <sent>
  <sent> "and" <sent>;
  <np> <vp>; )
```

However this function will causes a memory stack overflow if asked to parse a conjunction, since in the first rule, the non-terminal <sent> directly calls itself without consuming any of the input.[51] The solution is to rephrase the definition to eliminate the left-recursion.

```
(defcc <sent>
  <np> <vp> "and" <sent> := [<np> <vp> & <sent>];
  <np> <vp>;)
```

Figure 13.12 Eliminating left recursion

Another common example involving left-recursion is the specification of the language of arithmetic expressions of which 1 + x - 3, 6 * (y / z) are examples. Suppose we want to convert such expressions to fully parenthesised prefix. This is most naturally encoded as a left-recursive grammar.

---

[51] **Indirect left recursion** is more insidious and occurs when there is a mutual recursion between non-terminals. Here <sent> calls <sent*> which calls <sent>.

```
(defcc <sent>
  <sent*> "and" <sent> := [<sent*> & <sent>];
  <np> <vp>; )

(defcc <sent*>
  <sent>;)
```

```
(defcc <expr>
   <expr> <op> <expr+> := [<op> <expr> <expr+>];
   [<expr> <op> <expr+>] := [<op> <expr> <expr+>];
   <number> := <number>;)

(defcc <expr+>
   <expr>;)

(defcc <number>
   N := N            where (number? N);)

(defcc <op>
   X := X            where (element? X [+ - * /]);)
```

This fails because the first expansion of <expr> is left-recursive. Arriving at a non-left recursive definition is an interesting exercise in understanding Shen-YACC. To begin we try

```
(defcc <expr>
   <number> <op> <expr> := [<op> <number> <expr>];
   [<expr> <op> <expr+>] := [<op> <expr> <expr+>];
   <number> := <number>;)
```

This works on inputs that are entirely unparenthesised, but fails to work on inputs that are parenthesised– even inputs that we think should parse!

```
(125-) (compile (function <expr>) [1])
1

(126-) (compile (function <expr>) [1 + 2 + 3])
[+ 1 [+ 2 3]]

(127-) (compile (function <expr>) [[1 + 2]])
parse error
```

The failure of the last case is interesting because it looks at first as if it should succeed. The parse is the victim of the dual strategy of placing the longest expansion first together with the limited backtracking model used in Shen-YACC.

Given the input [1 + 2], the second expansion   [<expr> <op> <expr+>] is used. So far, so good. But the <expr> function then uses the expansion <number> <op> <expr> to consume *all* the input, leaving nothing for <op> and <expr+> to process. We could fix this by abandoning the 'longest expansion first' rule and writing

```
(defcc <expr>
   <number> := <number>;
   <number> <op> <expr> := [<op> <number> <expr>];
   [<expr> <op> <expr+>] := [<op> <expr> <expr+>]; )
```

This does solve the errant case, but now (compile (function <expr>) [1 + 2 + 3]) does not work since the short expansion is used which does not consume all the input. Hence however we order these definitions, the result is not a working model.

In this case, the simplest method is to define a class of *terms*. An arithmetic expression is just a series of terms linked by operations or a term on its own.

```
(defcc <expr>
  <term> <op> <expr> := [<op> <term> <expr>];
  <term> := <term>;)
```

A term is then defined as either a number or something which can be parsed as an expression. The second alternative is covered by an invocation to the compiler.

```
(defcc <term>
  N := N  where (number? N);
  E := (parse-term E);)

(define parse-term
  E -> (compile (function <expr>) E))
```

And this works.

```
(140-) (compile (function <expr>) [[1 - 0 * 8] + [5 + 8] * 7])
[+ [- 1 [* 0 8]] [* [+ 5 8] 7]]

(141-) (compile (function <expr>) [[1 - 0 * 8] + [5 + 8] * a7])
parse error
```

Figure 13.13 Parsing arithmetic

13.10 The Compilation of Shen-YACC

A few words in closing need to be said about the relation of Shen-YACC to Shen. Shen-YACC compiles into Shen using an approach not far removed from the approach of the parser-generator in the previous chapter. Every non-terminal v applied to an input will return an output which is either (fail) or some other object. If the object returned is the failure object then v is deemed to have failed and another expansion (if possible) is found. Hence a program such as

```
(defcc <abcd>
   <as> <bs>;
   <cs> <ds>;)
```

is compiled into a function *somewhat* resembling

```
(define <abcd>
  Input <- (let Parse<as> (<as> Input)
              (if (= Parse<as> (fail))
                  (fail)
                  (<bs> Parse<as>)))
  Input <- (let Parse<cs> (<cs> Input)
              (if (= Parse<cs> (fail))
                  (fail)
                  (<ds> Parse<cs>)))
  Input -> (fail))
```

This is in essence very similar to the parser generator of chapter 12. Semantic completion means that what is *actually* compiled is the following.

```
(defcc <abcd>
  <as> <bs> := (append <as> <bs>);
  <cs> <ds> := (append <cs> <ds>);)
```

The resulting code is therefore much more like

```
(define <abcd>
  Input <- (let Parse<as> (<as> Input)
              (if (= Parse<as> (fail))
                  (fail)
                  (let Parse<bs> (<bs> Parse<as>))
                      (if (= Parse<bs> (fail))
                          (fail)
                          (append Parse<as> Parse<bs>)))))
  Input <- (let Parse<as> (<cs> Input)
              (if (= Parse<cs> (fail))
                  (fail)
                  (let Parse<ds> (<ds> Parse<cs>))
                      (if (= Parse<ds> (fail))
                          (fail)
                          (append Parse<cs> Parse<ds>)))))
  Input -> (fail))
```

Being able to perform semantic actions requires that the input and the output and carried around together. Hence Input is matched to a two element list [ι o] composed of an input ι and an output o and it is the second element o ((hd (tl Input))) that is returned in the semantic action. Hence a closer approximation to the actual code is

```
(define <abcd>
  Input <- (let Parse<as> (<as> Input)
              (if (= Parse<as> (fail))
                  (fail)
                  (let Parse<bs> (<bs> Parse<as>))
                      (if (= Parse<bs> (fail))
                          (fail)
                          (append (hd (tl Parse<as>)) (hd (tl Parse<bs>)))))))
```

```
Input <- (let Parse<as> (<cs> Input)
             (if (= Parse<cs> (fail))
                 (fail)
                 (let Parse<ds> (<ds> Parse<cs>))
                     (if (= Parse<ds> (fail))
                         (fail)
                         (append (hd (tl Parse<cs>)) (hd (tl Parse<ds>)))))))))
         Input -> (fail))
```

Exercise 13

1. Devise a Shen-YACC program that

    a. Reverses a list.
    b. Divides an even numbered list into two lists. If the list is not even numbered then a parse error is returned.
    c. Removes all numbers from a list and returns them as a output.
    d. Gives the length of a list.
    e. Sums a list of numbers to a total.
    f. Recognises if a list is sorted high to low.

2. Devise a YACC program for a fragment of English and show that it can recognise sentences. Include adjectives, prepositions and sentence connectives in your grammar.

3. *Build a natural language front-end to a database system that enables database queries to be conducted in your native language and answered by the computer.

4. Write an HTML stripper in YACC that extracts raw text from HTML pages.

5. Our arithmetic expression parser will also allow (compile <expr> [[[1 - 0]]]). Amend the program so this example raises an error.

6. *Find a procedural language that you know, such as C or Java and write a YACC program that parses programs in it.

7. *Write a compiler for the language ML that compiles ML into Shen.

Further Reading

Meta II was a very early compiler-compiler introduced by D. V Schorre (1964). The original YACC was developed at AT&T by Steve Johnson and the technology was ported to various languages including ML. Aho and Ullman (1973) gives an overview of YACC. Lajos (1990) introduced MetaLisp which was the foundation of Shen-YACC.

Websites

http://www.techworld.com.au/article/252319/a-z_programming_languages_yacc gives an interview with Johnson on YACC.

14 Lambda Calculus

In this chapter, we are going to delve more deeply into some of the theory behind Shen. The lambda calculus, invented by **Alonzo Church** (1940), provides a notation for talking and reasoning about functions. Understanding lambda calculus is important to understanding of Shen for two reasons. First because the lambda calculus is the basis of the notation Kλ into which Shen is compiled. Second, because the type theory of the lambda calculus forms part of the underlying type theory of Shen (studied in part II of this book) and of every typed functional language since ML.

14.1 The Notation of the Lambda Calculus

The syntax of the pure lambda calculus is very simple.

Syntax Rules for the Pure Lambda Calculus

1. $x, y, z, x', y', z',....$ are all variables.
2. Any variable on its own is an expression of the lambda calculus.
3. If e_1 and e_2 are lambda expressions then the **application** $(e_1\ e_2)$ of e_1 to e_2 is an expression of the lambda calculus.
4. If e is an expression of the lambda calculus and v is a variable then $(\lambda\ v\ e)$ (called an **abstraction**) is an expression of the lambda calculus.
5. Nothing else is an expression of the lambda calculus.

Just as in Shen, when we wish to apply a function f to an input i, the lambda calculus requires us to write $(f\ i)$. The function *square* is said to be **applied** to 3, and the whole expression (square 3) is called an **application**.

Strictly speaking, the syntax of the pure lambda calculus makes no explicit allowance for referring to numbers, so (square 3) is not an expression of the pure lambda calculus. Many authors allow the pure lambda calculus to be enriched by a set of constants (Hindley and Seldin (1986) call this an **applied lambda calculus**), and they allow these constants to count as lambda calculus expressions. We will follow this example, and for the moment admit numbers and names of functions into the lambda calculus. Later in this chapter, we shall see how they can be reduced to expressions of the pure lambda calculus. The syntax rules for the pure lambda calculus are given next.

Abstractions are used within the lambda calculus to reveal the internal structure of a function. An abstraction has the form (λ v e), where v is a variable and e is an expression of lambda calculus. "(λ v e)" signifies a function that given some input v, returns the output e. The simplest example is the abstraction (λ x x), which denotes the **identity function** that receives any input x and returns x. Here are some more examples.

Abstraction	Interpretation
(λ x 3)	receives any input x and returns 3.
(λ x y)	receives any input x and returns y.
(λ x (x 5))	receives any input x and returns the result of applying x to 5.
(λ x (x x))	receives any input x and returns the result of applying x to x.
(λ x (λ y (x y)))	receives any input x and returns a function (λ y (x y)) which receives any input y and applies x to y.

Figure 14.1 Some abstractions and their interpretations

An occurrence of a variable v is **bound** in an abstraction if v occurs within an expression of the form (λ v e), and if it is not bound it is **free**. It is important to distinguish between *occurrences* of variables and variables themselves. The same type of variable may occur several times in one lambda expression and, in relation to that expression, some of the occurrences can be free and some can be bound. For example, in the application ((λ x (y x)) x) there are three occurrences of the variable x. Reading from left to right, the first two are bound and the last is free. A lambda expression where all variables are bound is said to be a **closed lambda expression** or **combinator**.

We perform a **substitution for the free variable occurrences** within a lambda expression when we uniformly replace all free occurrences of that variable throughout the lambda expression. For example, substituting z for free occurrences of x in ((λ x (y x)) x) gives ((λ x (y x)) z)); the first two occurrences of x are not replaced because they are bound. A substitution of an expression y for the free occurrences of a variable x in a lambda expression e is written $[e]_{y/x}$. Here are some more examples.

Expression	Result
$[(\lambda\ x\ x)]_{y/x}$	(λ x x)
$[(\lambda\ y\ x)]_{z/x}$	(λ y z)
$[(\lambda\ x\ (x\ y))]_{y/z}$	(λ x (x y))
$[(\lambda\ x\ (y\ (\lambda\ y\ (x\ y))))]_{z/y}$	(λ x (z (λ y (x y))))

Figure 14.2 Performing substitutions

14.2 Reasoning with the Lambda Calculus

The lambda calculus was originally designed as a formal system for proving the equality of functions expressed in lambda calculus notation. We write $e_1 = e_2$, where e_1 and e_2 are lambda calculus expressions, to state that e_1 and e_2 denote the same function. Obviously if e_1 and e_2 are syntactically identical then $e_1 = e_2$ holds. This is the first rule of the lambda calculus.

$e = e$

The next rules deal with the obvious properties of =; symmetry and transitivity.

From $e_1 = e_2$ derive $e_2 = e_1$.
From $e_1 = e_2$ and $e_2 = e_3$ derive $e_1 = e_3$.

The next three rules state the principle that equals may be substituted for each other.

From $e_1 = e_2$ derive $(e_3\ e_1) = (e_3\ e_2)$
From $e_1 = e_2$ derive $(e_1\ e_3) = (e_2\ e_3)$
From $e_1 = e_2$ derive $(\lambda\ v\ e_1) = (\lambda\ v\ e_2)$

In addition, there are three more rules for proving lambda expressions equal; the rules of **α conversion, β reduction** and **η conversion**.

$(\lambda\ x\ x)$, $(\lambda\ y\ y)$ and $(\lambda\ z\ z)$ are all ways of referring to the identity function. Consequently the equations $(\lambda\ x\ x) = (\lambda\ y\ y)$ and $(\lambda\ y\ y) = (\lambda\ z\ z)$ are both true, and should be provable in the lambda calculus. α conversion allows this proof by legitimising the uniform replacement of a bound variable within an abstraction by some other variable. We write $(\lambda\ x\ x) \rightarrow_\alpha (\lambda\ y\ y)$ to show that $(\lambda\ x\ x)$ is convertible to $(\lambda\ y\ y)$ by α conversion. It does not matter what replacement variable is used, provided that the replacement is performed uniformly and there is no **variable capture**.

A variable capture occurs when the effect of inserting the replacement variable is to bind a free variable. For instance the function $(\lambda\ x\ (x\ y))$ can be α converted to $(\lambda\ z\ (z\ y))$, but it cannot be α converted to $(\lambda\ y\ (y\ y))$ without capturing or binding the previously free y. We formulate the rule for α conversion so that variable captures are not allowed.

The Rule of α Conversion

Any expression $(\lambda\ v\ e)$ may be α converted to $(\lambda\ v'.[e]v_{/v})$ provided v' does not occur free in e.

If e_1 and e_2 can be made identical by α conversions alone then they are **congruent** to each other and this is written $e_1 \approx e_2$.

The application of the function ($\lambda\, x$ (square x)) to 3 produces (square 3). We can write this as (square 3) or (($\lambda\, x$ (square x)) 3). In any event, the following equation must be true.

$$((\lambda\, x \text{ (square } x)) \text{) } 3) = (\text{square } 3)$$

Deriving (square 3) from (($\lambda\, x$ (square x)) 3) requires replacing each free occurrence of x within (square x) by 3 and eliminating the $\lambda\, x$; an operation called **β reduction**. This operation is written (($\lambda\, x$ (square x)) 3) $\rightarrow_\beta$ (square 3). Here is an example where β reduction is applied twice.

$$((\lambda\, x ((\lambda\, y\ (x\ y))\ z))\ z) \rightarrow_\beta ((\lambda\, x\ (x\ z))\ z) \rightarrow_\beta (z\ z)$$

As with α conversion, there is a proviso to β reduction. We must take care with expressions where a variable has both free and bound occurrences. Thus suppose we attempt to β reduce (($\lambda\, x$ ($\lambda\, y$ ($x\ y$))) y) without regard to the fact that y occurs both free and bound in different occurrences; we derive

$$((\lambda\, x\ (\lambda\, y\ (x\ y)))\ y) \rightarrow_\beta (\lambda\, y\ (y\ y))\ ???$$

However if we should first do α conversion on (($\lambda\, x$ ($\lambda\, y$ ($x\ y$))) y) to get (($\lambda\, x$ ($\lambda\, z$ ($x\ z$))) y), and then perform β reduction we derive ($\lambda\, z$ ($y\ z$)); but plainly ($\lambda\, z$ ($y\ z$)) $\neq$ ($\lambda\, y$ ($y\ y$)).[52]

The reduction of (($\lambda\, x$ ($\lambda\, y$ ($x\ y$))) y) to ($\lambda\, y$ ($y\ y$)) is wrong because the second occurrence of y in (($\lambda\, x$ ($\lambda\, y$ ($x\ y$))) y) (which is free) becomes bound if placed in the scope of $\lambda\, y$. In this case, to perform β reduction, it is first necessary to rename the bound occurrences of y using α conversion, and only then can β reduction be performed. The rule of β reduction, like the rule for α conversion, has a clause within it stipulating that variables may not be captured.

The Rule of β Reduction

(($\lambda\, v\ e_1$) e_2) may be transformed by β reduction to $[e_1]e_2/v$ provided no free occurrence of a variable in e_2 becomes bound.

In some cases, the result of performing all possible β reductions is an expression free of λs. This need not always be so. The expression (($\lambda\, x$ (($\lambda\, y$ (($z\ x$) y))) 3) β

---

[52] In case there is doubt on this issue, reflect that ($\lambda\, z$ ($y\ z$)) designates a function that receives an input and applies y to it, and ($\lambda\, y$ ($y\ y$)) designates a function that receives an input and applies it to itself.

reduces to $(\lambda\ y\ ((z\ 3)\ y))$ and the λ is retained after the β reduction. If the result of a β reduction is an abstraction, then the operation of β reduction is said to be a **partial application**.

The η conversion rule is the least intuitive of the lambda calculus rules.

The Rule of η Conversion

Any abstraction $(\lambda\ v\ (e\ v))$ may be transformed by η conversion to e if v does not occur free in e.

An example of η conversion is $(\lambda\ x\ ((y\ z)\ x)) \rightarrow_\eta (y\ z)$. The principle of **Functional Extensionality** justifies η conversion. This principle says that two functions are identical if they produce the same outputs given the same inputs. That is:-

$$\text{If for all } x, (f\ x) = (g\ x) \text{ then } f = g.$$

The argument in defence of η conversion is as follows. η conversion is justified if we can show that, if e is any lambda calculus expression and v is a variable is not free in e, $(\lambda\ v\ (e\ v)) = e$. By the Principle of Functional Extensionality, the proof is secured if it can be proved that, for any a, $((\lambda\ v\ (e\ v))\ a) = (e\ a)$. β reduction on $((\lambda\ v\ (e\ v))\ a)$ gives $(e\ a)$ (since e contains no free occurrences of v, β reduction leaves e unchanged), so the equation is proved.

A **redex** is an expression that can be reduced by any of the rules of the lambda calculus; a β-redex is a redex that can be reduced by the β rule.

14.3 The Church-Rosser Theorems

When working with the lambda calculus, the goal is often to reduce a lambda expression to its simplest form. For example, the simplest form of $(((\lambda\ x\ (\lambda\ y\ ((+\ x)\ y)))\ 3)\ 5)$ is $((+\ 5)\ 3)$ (or 8 if the rules of arithmetic are added to the lambda calculus). The expression $((+\ 5)\ 3)$ is a **normal form** of $(((\lambda\ x\ (\lambda\ y\ ((+\ x)\ y)))\ 3)\ 5)$. We say that e is **lambda convertible** to e' when e can be converted to e' by α, β or η conversion rules. In the context of the lambda calculus, a normal form of an expression e is any expression e' where

(a) e is lambda convertible to e' and
(b) at most only α conversion can be applied to change e'.

An important theorem called the **first Church-Rosser theorem** has a bearing on the search for normal forms. Let $e_1 \geq e_2$ obtain when e_1 is reducible to e_2 by zero or more α conversions and/or β reductions. The first Church-Rosser theorem states that if $e_1 \geq e_2$ and $e_1 \geq e_3$ and e_2 and e_3 are not syntactically identical, then there is an e_4 such that $e_2 \geq e_4$ and $e_3 \geq e_4$.

An immediate corollary of the first Church-Rosser theorem is that all normal forms are congruent to each other.

Proof: suppose e_1 reduces to two non-identical normal forms e_2 and e_3, then by the first Church-Rosser theorem there exists an expression e_4 to which e_2 and e_3 are reducible. However, since e_2 and e_3 are normal forms, e_2 and e_3 are convertible to e_4 by α conversion alone. Since $e_2 \approx e_4$ and $e_3 \approx e_4$, then $e_2 \approx e_3$.

This theorem is a basis for the lambda calculus as a foundation for functional programming. If the theorem did not obtain, then two equally acceptable computations of the same lambda expression could terminate with significantly different results. This would make computation with lambda calculus quite hopeless.

A **reduction strategy** for the lambda calculus is a strategy that determines how reductions are performed. Two reduction strategies are **normal order** and **applicative order evaluation**.

The rule of normal order evaluation is that β-redexes must always be reduced from the outside inwards, and where there is a choice, working from the leftmost such redex. The rule of applicative order evaluation is that the leftmost most deeply embedded β-redex must always be reduced first. Another way of expressing this is to say that, given an expression $(e_1\ e_2)$ to evaluate, applicative order evaluation first performs β reduction on e_1 and then $e2$ before attempting β reduction on the whole expression.

For example, reducing $((\lambda x\ (x\ x))\ ((\lambda y\ y)\ z))$ to a normal form by normal order evaluation involves three steps; the β-redexes are bolded.

$$((\lambda x\ (x\ x))\ ((\lambda y\ y)\ z)) \rightarrow_\beta (((\lambda y\ y)\ z)\ ((\lambda y\ y)\ z)) \rightarrow_\beta (z\ ((\lambda y\ y)\ z)) \rightarrow_\beta (z\ z)$$

Applicative order evaluation derives the same result in two steps.

$$((\lambda x\ (x\ x))\ ((\lambda y\ y)\ z)) \rightarrow_\beta ((\lambda x\ (x\ x))\ z) \rightarrow_\beta (z\ z)$$

When bound variables are repeated, applicative order evaluation is often more efficient than normal order evaluation. However, sometimes, normal order evaluation will find a normal form where applicative order evaluation fails.

For instance $((\lambda x\ z)\ ((\lambda x\ (x\ x))\ (\lambda x\ (x\ x))))$ has the normal form z, but using applicative order evaluation, this normal form is not computed since $((\lambda x\ (x\ x))\ (\lambda x\ (x\ x))) \rightarrow_\beta ((\lambda x\ (x\ x))\ (\lambda x\ (x\ x)))$! Applicative order evaluation repeats this step endlessly. The **second Church-Rosser theorem** states if a lambda expression has a normal form, then normal order evaluation will find it.

The expression $((\lambda x \ (x \ x)) \ (\lambda x \ (x \ x)))$ itself has no normal form. An important theorem of the lambda calculus is that there is no mechanical procedure for accurately determining, in all cases, whether a lambda expression has a normal form. This theorem is a corollary of another important theorem about the lambda calculus that was proved by Church, namely, that it is **Turing-equivalent**. This means that the lambda calculus is powerful enough to serve as a programming language. If there was an algorithm $\mathcal{H}$ that could determine if the normal order evaluation of any lambda expression terminated, we would also have a decision procedure for finding if *any* program terminated (i.e. translate it into lambda calculus and then apply $\mathcal{H}$). However, Turing's proof of the **Unsolvability of the Halting Problem**, states that there is no such procedure to be found.[53]

14.4 Conditionals

It is surprising that a formal system as basic as the pure lambda calculus should have the expressive power of a programming language. The usual control features of conventional programming languages are not in evidence; there are no commands like **if.... then ....else** or **and**. There are no commands like **do ... while** or **for ... next**. There are not even integers or booleans in the lambda calculus.

The basic technique for dealing with this problem is to identify a set of equations that describe the behaviour of the wanted features and then to choose representations in the lambda calculus which reflect those equations. Thus in the case of if ...then ...else, true and false, we have two essential equations.

$$\text{(if true then X else Y)} = X$$
$$\text{(if false then X else Y)} = Y$$

The boolean true can be identified with the lambda expression $(\lambda x \ (\lambda y \ x))$ and the boolean false with $(\lambda x \ (\lambda y \ y))$. The conditional **if...then...else** is identified with $(\lambda z \ (\lambda x \ (\lambda y \ ((z \ x) \ y))))$. If these identifications are correct, then the lambda equivalent of (if true then a else b) should evaluate to a.

Calculating this identity by hand is tedious and error prone – and unnecessary, because the task is computational and an interpreter for an applicative order evaluator for lambda calculus is a short program in Shen (figure 14.3).

---

[53] Turing's result shows that there is no algorithm which can determine for any arbitrary computer program (Turing machine) whether it will halt for any arbitrary input. This is one of the most famous proofs in computer science and is intimately related to the proof of the undecidability of first-order logic. See Boolos and Jefferies (1977) for more on this.

```
(define aor
  [lambda V [E V]] -> E        where (not (free? V E))
  [lambda X Y] -> [lambda X (aor Y)]
  [[lambda X Y] Z] -> (let Alpha (alpha [lambda X Y])
                          (aor (beta Alpha (aor Z))))
  [X Y] -> (let AOR [(aor X) (aor Y)]
              (if (= AOR [X Y])
                  AOR
                  (aor AOR)))
  X -> X)

(define free?
  V V -> true
  V [lambda V _] -> false
  V [lambda _ Y] -> (free? V Y)
  V [X Y] -> (or (free? V X) (free? V Y))
  _ _ -> false)

(define alpha
  [lambda X Y] -> (let V (gensym x)
                      [lambda V (replace X (alpha Y) V)])
  [X Y] -> [(alpha X) (alpha Y)]
  X -> X)

(define beta
  [lambda X Y] Z -> (replace X Y Z))

(define replace
  X [lambda X Y] _ -> [lambda X Y]
  X X Z -> Z
  X [Y Y'] Z -> [(replace X Y Z) (replace X Y' Z)]
  X [lambda Y Y'] Z -> [lambda Y (replace X Y' Z)]
  _ Y _ -> Y)
```

Figure 14.3 An applicative order evaluator for pure lambda calculus

The most awkward rule to program is the alpha rule and here we use it to prevent capture by renaming *all* the bound variables in an abstraction before performing beta reduction.[54]

Armed with this program we can test our conjecture; we define (t) to mean the lambda abstraction standing for true and (f) for false and if' for the lambda expression for if.

```
(2-) (define t
       -> [lambda x [lambda y x]])
t

(3-) (define f
       -> [lambda x [lambda y y]])
f

(4-) (define if'
       -> [lambda z [lambda x [lambda y [[z x] y]]]])
if'

(5-) (aor [[[(if') (t)] a] b])
a

(6-) (aor [[[(if') (f)] a] b])
b
```

Figure 14.4 Proving that (((if true) a) b) = a in lambda calculus

The equations work, but working with our evaluator is still laborious; both at the human end, because the expressions are deeply bracketed, and at the computing end, because the enforced α conversion makes computation very expensive. We can begin to approach some of the functionality of a programming language by arranging for the reader to curry expressions for us.

```
(define curry
  [lambda X Y] -> [lambda X (curry Y)]
  [W X Y | Z] -> (curry [[W X] Y | Z])
  [X Y] -> [(curry X) (curry Y)]
  X -> X)
```

We define aor+ as;

```
(define aor+
  X -> (aor (curry X)))
```

Now (aor+ [(if') (f) a b]) evaluates as (aor [[[(if') (f)] a] b]).

14.5 Weak Head Normal Form

Our evaluator delves into abstractions to evaluate them. The abstraction [lambda x [[lambda y y] a]] is evaluated to [lambda x a]. But functional languages do not carry evaluation to that length; the internals of an abstraction are not evaluated. If we type (/. X (+ 1 "a")) to Shen the evaluator compiles it without raising an error message, showing the body of the abstraction remains unevaluated.

Blocking the evaluation of a body of an abstraction means that the evaluator does not return, in all cases, a normal form, but returns an expression in **weak head**

normal form (WHNF). Generally returning an expression in WHNF is sufficient for computational purposes.

Formally an expression is in WHNF if one of the following hold.

1. It is an abstraction (λ x y) for *any y*.
2. It is a constant. In an applied lambda calculus, this might include strings, numbers and booleans and function symbols.
3. It is a partial application of some *n*-place function *f* in an applied lambda calculus to a series of arguments $x_1...x_m$ where $n > m$.

If we insist that the objects of computation must be closed lambda expressions then η reduction (which depends on free variables) becomes unnecessary *and* in addition, if we agree to reduce only to WHNF, then α conversion becomes unnecessary because the variable capture problem disappears too.

The expression (λ x ((λ **y** (λ **x** (+ **x** y))) x)) is in WHNF because it is an abstraction; it contains a constant, the addition symbol '+'. It contains a redex which is bolded which if applied naively (without α conversion) results in a variable capture of x. However since the expression is in WHNF, no reduction is applied and no α conversion is needed.

If this expression is applied to, say, the number 8, then the whole expression is a redex which reduces to ((λ y (λ x (+ x y))) 8) and then to (λ x (+ x 8)). However note that if we allow the free variable x to replace 8 in ((λ y (λ x (+ x y))) 8) we get ((λ y (λ x (+ x y))) x) in which variable capture is again possible unless the bound x is renamed. However by blocking the use of free variables, this case is prevented. Bringing these changes into a model means that the code for the evaluator becomes much simpler (figure 14.5) and the model is easier to operate and faster to execute.

```
(define aor
  [[lambda X Y] Z] -> (aor (replace X Y Z))
  [X Y] -> (let AOR [(aor X) (aor Y)]
             (if (= AOR [X Y]) AOR  (aor AOR)))
  X -> X)

(define replace
  X [lambda X Y] _ -> [lambda X Y]
  X X Z -> Z
  X [Y Y'] Z -> [(replace X Y Z) (replace X Y' Z)]
  X [lambda Y Y'] Z -> [lambda Y (replace X Y' Z)]
  _ Y _ -> Y)
```

Figure 14.5 An evaluator for WHNF

14.6 Tuples

Continuing with the reconstruction of programming concepts in lambda calculus, the operation of forming the pair $<x, y>$ of two elements x and y gives us a **tuple**. Tuples can be treated as the analogue of lists because the three element list $[x\ y\ z]$ can be represented as the tuple $<x, <y, z>>$.

We represent the tupling operation by the curried expression $((\text{tuple } x)\ y)$. Together with this pairing operation are two operations first and second that take first and second elements of a pair. These operations must satisfy the equations.

$$(\text{first } ((\text{tuple } X)\ Y)) = X$$
$$(\text{second } ((\text{tuple } X)\ Y)) = Y$$

We define these concepts as follows. Our $=_{df}$ notation means "is defined as".

$$\text{tuple} =_{df} (\lambda\ x\ (\lambda\ y\ (\lambda\ z\ ((z\ x)\ y))))$$
$$\text{first} =_{df} (\lambda\ x\ (x\ \text{true}))$$
$$\text{second} =_{df} (\lambda\ x\ (x\ \text{false}))$$

Figure 14.6 gives the Shen equivalents.

```
(7-) (define tuple
        -> [lambda x [lambda y [lambda z [[z x] y]]]])
tuple

(8-) (define first
        -> [lambda x [x (t)]])
first

(9-) (define second
        -> [lambda x [x (f)]])
second

(10-) (aor+ [(first) [(tuple) a b]])
a

(11-) (aor+ [(second) [(tuple) a b]])
b
```

Figure 14.6 Lambda calculus tuples in Shen

14.7 Numbers

Lambda calculus lacks any natural numbers, but there are many ways of representing them. Each representation treats natural numbers as built up by compositions of the successor function to 0.

i.e. 1 = (succ 0), 2 = (succ (succ 0)),..... etc.

The differences lie in how succ and 0 are defined. We use a definition from **Barendregt** (1984) that defines the natural numbers in terms of the progression.

0 = (λ x x)
1 = ((tuple false) 0)
2 = ((tuple false) 1) .....

We introduce succ as a function that adds 1 to a natural number, a zero test function zero? which, when applied to 0, evaluates to the lambda calculus representation of true. We also introduce the predecessor function pred that subtracts 1 and $\perp$ as a constant indicating the error condition of attempting to find the predecessor of 0. The following definitions meet those constraints.

succ =$_{df}$ (λ x ((tuple false) x))
zero? =$_{df}$ (λ x (x true))
pred =$_{df}$ (λ x (((if (zero? x)) $\perp$) (second x))) (λ x (x false))

```
(8-) (define zero
       -> [lambda x x])
zero

(9-) (define succ
       -> [lambda x [(tuple) (f) x]])
succ

(10-) (define zero?
         -> [lambda x [x (t)]])
zero?

(11-) (define pred
       -> [lambda x [(if') [(zero?) x] error! [(second) x]]])
pred

(12-) (aor+ [(zero?) (zero)])
[lambda x [lambda y x]]

(13-) (aor+ [(pred) [(succ) (zero)]])
[lambda x x]
```

Figure 14.7 Arithmetic in lambda calculus

14.8 Recursion and the Y combinator

The lambda calculus is rich enough to provide surrogates for conditionals, booleans, tuples, natural numbers and the basic arithmetical operations of adding and subtracting 1 from a number. What is still missing is some construction that will do the job of a **do ... while** or **repeat .. until** of a conventional procedural programming language. To illustrate how lambda calculus copes with this challenge, we will consider the definition of addition in lambda calculus. Two equations give the properties of addition.

$$0 + Y = Y$$
$$X + Y = (\text{succ } ((\text{pred } X) + Y))$$

To represent these equations in lambda calculus, we use an expression called the **fixpoint combinator Y** or **Y combinator** whose behaviour is described by the following equation.

$$(\mathbf{Y} f) = (f (\mathbf{Y} f))$$

It is possible to define **Y** in pure lambda calculus, and there are several ways of doing so; we leave it as an exercise to show that the following definition satisfies $(\mathbf{Y} f) = (f (\mathbf{Y} f))$.

$$\mathbf{Y} = (\lambda f (V\ V)) \text{ where } V = (\lambda x (f (x\ x)))$$

We can use the **Y** combinator to represent addition (here written *add*) over the natural numbers. We first transcribe the equations for addition into lambda calculus. For clarity we omit currying and use the usual if ... then .. else notation.

$$add =_{\text{df}} (\lambda x (\lambda y (\text{if } (\text{zero? } x) \text{ then } y \text{ else } (\text{succ } (add (\text{pred } x)\ y)))))$$

add mentions itself within its own definition; from our studies we know that this is a recursive definition of *add*. We could compute additions with this definition if we added a rule that said that we were allowed to replace any occurrence of '*add*' in a lambda expression by the right-hand side of this definition. In doing so, we would be enriching the rules of the lambda calculus by allowing replacement according to a definition as an extra rule in the lambda calculus. This is precisely the step taken in the next chapter, but in this section we want to show that, in principle, the pure lambda calculus can represent addition without needing this extra rule.

In our next step, we replace the occurrence of "*add*" by a new bound variable. We abbreviate this expression as ADD.

$$\text{ADD} =_{\text{df}} (\lambda f (\lambda x (\lambda y (\text{if } (\text{zero? } x) \text{ then } y \text{ else } (\text{succ } (f (\text{pred } x)\ y))))))$$

Now we define + as (**Y** ADD). This new definition of + will add numbers. Figure 14.8 shows the evaluation of ((+ 1) 2).

Expression	Justification
((+ 1) 2)	
(((**Y** ADD) 1) 2)	definition of +
(((ADD (**Y** ADD)) 1) 2)	definition of **Y**

(((λ *f* (λ *x* (λ *y* (if (zero? *x*)
    then *y*
    else (succ (f (pred *x*) *y*))) (**Y** ADD))))) 1) 2)
	definition of ADD

((λ *x* (λ *y* (if (zero? *x*) then *y* else (succ ((**Y** ADD) (pred *x*) *y*)))))) 1) 2)	β reduction
((λ *y* (if (zero? 1) then *y* else (succ ((**Y** ADD) (pred 1) *y*)))) 2)	β reduction
(if (zero? 1) then 2 else (succ ((**Y** ADD) (pred 1) 2)))	β reduction
(succ (((**Y** ADD) 0) 2))	(zero? 1) is false
(succ (((ADD (**Y** ADD)) 0) 2))	definition of **Y**

(succ (((λ *f* (λ *x* (λ *y* (if (zero? *x*)
    then *y*
    else (succ (*f* (pred *x*) *y*))) (**Y** ADD))))) 0) 2))
	definition of ADD

(succ ((λ *x* (λ *y* (if (zero? *x*) then *y* else (succ ((**Y** ADD) (pred *x*) *y*)))))) 0) 2))	β reduction
(succ ((λ *y* (if (zero? 0) then *y* else (succ ((**Y** ADD) (pred 0) *y*)))) 2))	β reduction
(succ (if (zero? 0) then 2 else (succ ((**Y** ADD) (pred 0) 2))))	β reduction
(succ 2)	(zero? 0) is true

Figure 14.8 Evaluation using Y-combinators

If we try to reproduce this behaviour using our evaluator, the program crashes with a memory error. This arises from the feature of applicative order evaluation; that *all* the arguments to a function are always evaluated before the function is applied; and this applies to *if* as well. This leads to the rather disastrous result in the penultimate line of figure 14.8 that the recursive call is evaluated even though (zero? 0) is true. For normal order evaluation, the correct result is returned.

One solution is to replace applicative order evaluation by normal order evaluation. Alternatively we retain applicative order, but introduce the evaluation of the conditional as a special case to be treated in a non-strict manner. The addition of special rules for *if*, + etc. to a lamba calculus L are δ **rules** of L. In our study of the SECD machine we will pick up this story again.

Exercise 14

1. Which variable occurrences are free and which are bound in the following expressions?

    a. $((y\ x)\ y)$,
    b. $((\lambda\ y\ (y\ x))\ y)$,
    c. $(x\ x)$,
    d. $(y\ (\lambda\ y\ (x\ (y\ z))))$

2. Perform the necessary substitutions on the following.

    a. $[(y\ x)\ y]_{z/y}$,
    b. $[(y\ x)\ y]_{z/x}$,
    c. $[(\lambda\ y\ ((y\ x)\ y))]_{z/y}$,
    d. $[(y\ (\lambda\ y\ (x\ (y\ z))))]_{z/y}$
    e. $[(x\ x)]_{z/x}$,

3. Reduce the following to a normal form using α, β and η conversion.

    a. $((y\ x)\ y)$,
    b. $((\lambda\ x\ (\lambda\ y\ (x\ x)))\ y)$,
    c. $((\lambda\ x\ (\lambda\ y\ (x\ y)))\ (\lambda\ x\ (x\ y)))$

4. *Implement an interpreter for the pure lambda calculus that reduces lambda expressions to a normal form using normal order evaluation.

Further Reading

Gordon (1988) (chapters 4-7) gives a nice introduction to the lambda calculus. For the encyclopaedic accounts, Barendregt (1984) and Hindley and Seldin (1986), but Barendregt (1992) (pp 118-147) for a quick look.

Web Sites

(http://www.santafe.edu/~walter/AlChemy/software.html) provides a standalone lambda calculus interpreter written in C. Colin Taylor provides a version (http://drcjt.freeyellow.com), including source code) which will run on a Palm Pilot. http://worrydream.com/AlligatorEggs/ is a delightful explanation of lambda calculus based on alligators.

15   Kλ

15.1 From Lambda Calculus to Kλ

Chapter 14 showed that it is possible to program in the pure lambda calculus but programming at this level of detail is not attractive. For example the number 2 in our pure lambda calculus is:-

$$(((\lambda\,x\,(\lambda\,y\,(\lambda\,z\,((z\,x)\,y))))\,(\lambda\,x\,(\lambda\,y\,y)))$$
$$(((\lambda\,x\,(\lambda\,y\,(\lambda\,z\,((z\,x)\,y))))\,(\lambda\,x\,(\lambda\,y\,y)))\,(\lambda\,x\,x)))$$

Practical programming requires a barrier of abstraction between the programmer and the complexity of these expressions. We answered this problem in our evaluator by *naming* lambda calculus expressions, so that instead of writing [lambda x [lambda y x]] we wrote (t).

But the result is still not a practical functional programming language. Functional programming languages do not rely on Y-combinators for recursion or represent numbers as lambda expressions, but make use of δ rules that come with the instruction set in the resident hardware, treating numbers as primitive objects. Like Shen, functional programming languages also facilitate the definition of functions by not requiring function applications to be curried. If we introduce these changes, and add facilities for I/O and recursion, we end up with an enriched lambda calculus that is suitable for the purposes of programming.

Hidden inside of Shen is a miniature functional language of just this capability called **Kλ**. Though it is not much used in applications, it has a vital role within the internals of Shen because all Shen function definitions are ultimately compiled and defined within this tiny language. If we contrast Kλ with pure lambda calculus; then we find these differences.

1. Kλ allows expressions to be named within definitions; so a function can call itself in its definition without having to use a Y-combinator.
2. Applications do not have to be curried.
3. Numbers can be written as decimal numbers, and not as lambda expressions. The same applies to booleans.
4. There are 46 primitive functions built in for the manipulation of lists, vectors, numbers, strings and symbols.

The syntax of Kλ is very simple. The basic concept is a **symbolic expression** or s-expr which is defined as follows

An **atom** is either a boolean, a Shen number (but excluding e-numbers which are not assumed by Kλ), a symbol, a string or the empty list (). All atoms are symbolic expressions.

An **abstraction** is of the form (lambda *symbol s-expr*) and corresponds to an abstraction of the lambda calculus. This too is a symbolic expression.

An **application** is a series of *n* (*n* ≥ 0) symbolic expressions encased in parentheses (....). An application can be curried but Kλ does not require it. An application is a symbolic expression.

A Kλ **definition** is of the form (defun *symbol* (*parameters*) *s-expr*) where *symbol* is a symbol, *parameters* is a series of *n* (*n* ≥ 0) non-identical symbols and *s-expr* is a symbolic expression.

Since the Shen compiler compiles Shen into Kλ, Kλ is in a sense the *lingua franca* of the implementation and we can converse with Shen in the notation of Kλ. Generally this is not useful for programming purposes, because Kλ is much more prolix than Shen, but it is educational in understanding how Kλ works. Another good reason for understanding Kλ is that Kλ is a **Lisp**; one of a family of languages of which the oldest was Lisp 1.5 and the progenitor of all other functional languages.

Applications in Kλ and Shen have much the same form; a function is applied to arguments in prefix form. Abstractions are written with lambda rather than /. and Kλ follows strictly the notation of the lambda calculus (/. X Y Y) must be written (lambda X (lambda Y Y)). Currying and partial applications are allowed; (+ 5 8) and ((+ 5) 8) are equivalent.

A function definition in Kλ can be treated as effectively giving a name to an abstraction. The definition of the successor function in Kλ can be written (defun succ () (lambda x (+ x 1))). Typing this into Shen shows this to work.

```
(0-) (defun succ () (lambda x (+ x 1)))
succ

(1-) ((succ) 5)
6
```

Kλ contains 46 primitive functions, most of which we have met in the preceding pages (figure 15.1).

Boolean operations:	if, and, or, cond.
Symbol operations:	intern
String operations:	pos, tlstr, cn, str, string?, n->string, string->n
Global operations:	set, value
Exception handling:	simple-error, trap-error, error-to-string
List operations:	cons, hd, tl, cons?
Vector operations	absvector, address->, <-address, absvector?
Stream operations	write-byte, read-byte, open, close
Numeric operations:	+, -, *, /, >, <, >=, <=, number?
Function definitions	defun
Abstraction builders	lambda
Local Assignments	let
Equality	=
Evaluation	eval-kl
Continuations	freeze
Type declarations	type
Time	get-time

Figure 15.1 The primitive instructions of Kλ

Any Shen function can be constructed out of these primitives. Here is a function that totals the numbers in a list. () is the empty list in Kλ.

```
(0-) (defun total ()
   (lambda x (if (= () x)  0
                 (+ (hd x) (total (tl x))))))
total

(1-) ((total) (cons 3 (cons 7 ())))
10
```

This function tests two lists to see if the first is a prefix of the second

```
(2-) (defun prefix ()
  (lambda x (lambda y (if (= () x) true
                          (if (= y ())  false
                            (if (= (hd x) (hd y))
                              (prefix (tl x) (tl y))
                              false))))))
prefix

(3-) ((prefix) [1] [1 2])
true
```

We have chosen our coding to emphasise the continuity of Kλ with the lambda calculus of the last chapter. However it is not usual to write Kλ functions in the form above; it is more natural to place the lambda bound variables in the list of formal parameters after the name of the function. This style allows functions to be applied without extensive parenthesising.

Lastly Kλ, like nearly all members of the Lisp family, contains a construction cond for avoiding heavily nested conditionals which does very much the same job that cases does in Shen.

```
(4-)  (defun prefix (x y)
          (cond ((= () x)  true)
                ((= y ())     false)
                ((= (hd x) (hd y)) (prefix (tl x) (tl y)))
                (true  false)))
prefix

(5-) (prefix [1 2] [1 2 3])
true
```

Figure 15.2 Using cond *in Kλ*

Kλ is a very simple functional language; pattern-matching and the use of @s, @p, |, [...] are all missing from Kλ. A list of three numbers 12 45 67 has to be written in cons form in Kλ as (cons 12 (cons 45 (cons 67 ()))). This makes Kλ a very cumbersome language to program in, but it was not designed to be such but to serve as a sort of functional assembly language for porting Shen. For this reason there are no comment conventions for Kλ programs.

However one side-effect of embedding Kλ into the Shen environment is that many of the Shen idioms can be embedded into Kλ. This arises because the Shen reader actually translates these conventions into the language of Kλ. The result is a sort of pidgin language which allows Kλ to compete in brevity and clarity with established Lisps used for programming. For example the following computes in Shen because the reader translates the list notation into cons form.

```
(defun cons-10 (x)
  [0 1 2 3 4 5 6 7 8 9 | x])
```

The technique is interesting but not so important because the purpose of Kλ is to serve as a target language into which Shen is compiled.

15.2 Manipulating Kλ

Every Shen function f is compiled into Kλ and the Kλ source can be read by the command (ps f) (print source) which prints the Kλ source as a list. This source can be itself manipulated and the result can be evaluated to result in a new definition. This feature is useful in the manipulation of Kλ because the source can be evaluated to produce a new program.

Our case example is production of a trace stack, whereby the list of functions called in a program is stored. The usefulness of the trace stack is that, if our program crashes, the stack will show the last function f to be called, which is generally the source of the error.

To construct such a facility in Shen, we need to construct a **wrapper function** f_w for any function f which acts exactly as f does but places a record of every call on the trace stack. In order to do this f_w will assume the same name as f in order that programs that calls f will be intercepted by f_w from wherever they originate. The call will be recorded on the stack and the arguments will be sent to a function f' whose coding will be exactly that of f. In other words, our trace program will do two things.

1. The Kλ source for f will be called up and a copy f' will be created and evaluated.
2. The body of f will be changed to point to f', but in addition a piece of code recording the call to f will be inserted.

These operations will not affect the results returned by (ps f) which records the Kλ source generated from the Shen definition. Hence we use this original code to restore the system once we decide not to trace the stack of calls any more. The program is very short (figure 15.3).

```
(define trace
  F -> (trace-h (gensym f') (ps F)))

(define trace-h
  F' [defun F Params Body]
  -> (do (eval-kl [defun F' Params Body])
         (eval-kl [defun F Params [do [record F] [F' | Params]]])))

(define record
  F -> (set *callstack* [F | (trap-error (value *callstack*) (/. E []))]))

(define untrace
  F -> (eval-kl (ps F)))
```

Figure 15.3 A trace program for Kλ

15.3 From Shen to Kλ

In this section we will look at how Shen is compiled to Kλ. Shen is compiled to Kλ in two steps; first Shen is compiled to an intermediate language $\mathcal{I}$ and then $\mathcal{I}$ is compiled to Kλ. The language $\mathcal{I}$ is an extension of the lambda calculus designed to support the compilation and type checking of pattern-directed function definitions. $\mathcal{I}$ will play a significant part in proving the credentials of Shen and we shall encounter it again in chapter 25.

$\mathcal{I}$ contains one significant addition to lambda calculus, which is the appearance of pattern-matching abstractions. A conventional abstraction is part of lambda calculus, but pattern-matching abstractions are not part of lambda calculus; they are, however, part of $\mathcal{I}$. The syntactic difference between a conventional abstraction and a pattern-matching abstraction is that a conventional abstraction may contain only a variable after the λ, whereas a pattern-matching abstraction may have a pattern.

For our purposes, a pattern is either a base expression (i.e. a symbol, string, number or boolean) or the empty list, or an expression built out of patterns by the use of cons, @s, @p and @v. Thus the expression, (λ X X) is a conventional lambda abstraction, but the expression (λ (cons 1 [ ]) 2) is a pattern-matching abstraction. Here are some more examples with their attendant interpretations.

Expression	Interpretation
(λ (cons 1 [ ]) 2)	A function that if it receives an input (cons 1 [ ]) returns 2.
(λ 1 2)	A function that if it receives an input 1 returns 2.
(λ [ ] [ ])	A function that if it receives the input [ ] returns [ ].
(λ (cons X [ ]) X)	A function that if it receives a one-element list returns its first element.

What happens if (λ (cons 1 [ ]) 2) is applied to, say, the number 3? Intuitively the input 3 does not match the pattern (cons 1 [ ]) and so the application fails. In such a case we designate the object ⊗ as being the result of this application - indicating a match failure.

We shall explain how Shen is compiled to $\mathcal{I}$ by reference to the compilation of the member function. Here is the initial function.

```
(define member
   _ [] -> false
   X [X | _] -> true
   X [_ | Y] -> (member X Y))
```

1. All lists are translated to cons form, and all wildcards are replaced by unique variables. We emphasise the process by bolding the parts that change.

    (define member
      V [] -> false
      X **(cons X W)** -> true
      X **(cons Z Y)** -> (member X Y))

2. Ensure that each rule is **left linear**, where a left linear rule is one that does not contain the same variable twice to the left of the arrow. This entails renaming repeated variables and adding a guard.

    (define member
      V [] -> false
      X **(cons U W)** -> true   **where (= U X)**
      X (cons Z Y) -> (member X Y))

3. Determine the arity n of the function f by counting the number n of patterns to the left of each arrow in each rule $r_1,...,r_m$. If there is a different number in any two rules, then an error is raised. Let $v_1,...,v_n$ be a list of fresh variables. From a function (define f $r_1,..,r_m$) generate $f =_{df} (\lambda v_1 \ .. \ (\lambda v_n \ r_1,..,r_m))$.

    member $=_{df}$ (λ A (λ B (V [ ] -> false
                  X (cons U W) -> true where (= U X)
                  X (cons Z Y) -> (member X Y))))

4. Replace each rule

    $p_a \ ...p_n$ -> q where g

    by

    $p_a \ ...p_n$ -> (where g q)

    member $=_{df}$ (λ A (λ B (V [ ] -> false
                  X (cons U W) -> (where (= U X) true)
                  X (cons Z Y) -> (member X Y))))

5. Change the definition from $f =_{df} (\lambda v_1 \ .. \ (\lambda v_n \ r_1,..,r_m))$ to $f =_{df} (\lambda v_1 \ .. \ (\lambda v_n$ (cases $r_1,..,r_m$)).

    member $=_{df}$ (λ A (λ B **(cases** V [ ] -> false
                  X (cons U W) -> (where (= U X) true)
                  X (cons Z Y) -> (member X Y))))

6. Given $f =df (\lambda v_1 \ .. \ (\lambda v_n$ (cases $r_1,..,r_m$))) replace each $r_i = p_a \ ...p_n$ -> q by a **rule application** of the abstraction $(\lambda p_a \ ... \ (\lambda p_n q))$ to the arguments $v_1,...,v_n$

member =_{df} (λ A (λ B

    (cases (((λ V (λ [ ] false)) A) B)

        (((λ X (λ (cons U W) (where (= U X) true))) A) B)

        (((λ X (λ (cons Z Y) (member X Y)) A) B))))

This completes the transformation of Shen to $\mathcal{L}$. The generation of $\mathcal{L}$ expressions is an intermediate step in the compilation of Shen. The target is to generate expressions in Kλ. This involves eliminating the rule applications.

7.   For each rule application $r = ((\lambda\,p\;q)\;v)$ apply the following recursively throughout r.

   a.   If p is a variable apply β reduction to r.

   b.   If p is a constant, (i.e. a non-variable symbol, string, boolean, number etc) then substitute $((\lambda\,v_f\;(if\;(=\,v_f\;p)\;q\;\otimes))\;v)$ for r, where v_f is a fresh variable and $\otimes$ is a symbol indicating match failure

   c.   If $p = (cons\;p_1\;p_2)$ substitute $((\lambda\,p_1\;(\lambda\,p_2\;(if\;(cons?\;v)\;\otimes)\;(tl\;v)\;(hd\;v))$ for r.

Step 7 is the most complex transformation, let's see how this works out in the case of the member expression from step 6. The first line is

   (((λ V (λ [ ] false)) A) B)

which by 7a. using β reduction gives ((λ [ ] false) B). Applying 7b to this expression gives

   (if (= B []) false ⊗)

The second rule was

(((λ X (λ (cons U W) (where (= U X) true))) A) B)

The outermost application is covered by 7a., β reduction gives

((λ (cons U W) (where (= U A) true)) B)

This expression is covered by 7c. and the result is

((λ U (λ W (if (cons? B) (where (= U A) true) ⊗)) (tl B)) (hd B))

Two steps of β reduction gives

((λ W (if (cons? B) (where (= (hd B) A) true) ⊗)) (tl B))

   (if (cons? B) (where (= (hd B) A) true) ⊗)

The final rule was

$(((\lambda \ X \ (\lambda \ (cons \ Z \ Y) \ (member \ X \ Y)) \ A) \ B))$

By 7a. and β reduction

$((\lambda \ (cons \ Z \ Y) \ (member \ A \ Y)) \ B)$

By 7c.

$((\lambda \ Z \ ((\lambda \ Y \ (if \ (cons? \ B) \ (member \ A \ Y) \ \otimes)) \ (tl \ B)) \ (hd \ B))$

Two steps of β reduction gives

$((\lambda \ Y \ (if \ (cons? \ B) \ (member \ A \ Y) \ \otimes)) \ (tl \ B))$
$(if \ (cons? \ B) \ (member \ A \ (tl \ B)) \ \otimes)$

So in total the function appears after step 7 as follows.

> member $=_{df} (\lambda \ A \ (\lambda \ B$
> (cases (if (= B []) false $\otimes$)
> (if (cons? B) (where (= (hd B) A) true) $\otimes$)
> (if (cons? B) (member A (tl B)) $\otimes$))))

8. Replace (where $p \ q$) by (if $p \ q \ \otimes$).

> member $=_{df} (\lambda \ A \ (\lambda \ B$
> (cases (if (= B []) false $\otimes$)
> (if (cons? B) **(if (= (hd B) A) true $\otimes$) $\otimes$)**
> (if (cons? B) (member A (tl B)) $\otimes$))))

9. Replace (if p (if $q \ r \ \otimes$) $\otimes$) by (if (and $p \ q$) $r \ \otimes$).

> member $=_{df} (\lambda \ A \ (\lambda \ B$
> (cases (if (= B []) false $\otimes$)
> **(if (and (cons? B) (= (hd B) A)) true $\otimes$)**
> (if (cons? B) (member A (tl B)) $\otimes$))))

10. Replace cases by cond. To adapt the syntax to the use of cond, apply the following transformation τ recursively to $f =_{df} (\lambda v \ ... \ \lambda v_n \ (cond \ c_1 \ ... \ c_n))$ to generate $f =_{df} (\lambda v \ ... \ \lambda v_n \ (cond \ \tau(c_1 \ ... \ c_n)))$ where τ is defined as

$\tau((if \ p \ q \ \otimes) \ c_i \ ...) = (p \ q) \ \tau(c_i \ ...)$
$\tau((if \ p \ q \ \otimes)) = (true \ (error \ "partial \ function \ f"))$

```
member =df (λ A (λ B
                (cond ((= B []) false)
                      ((and (cons? B) (= (hd B) A)) true)
                      ((cons? B) (member A (tl B)))
                      (true (error "partial function member)))))
```

11. Replace $f =_{df} (\lambda v \ ... \ \lambda v_n \ p)$ by $(\text{defun} f \ (v \ ... \ v_n) p)$.

(defun member (A B)
```
        (cond ((= B []) false)
              ((and (cons? B) (= (hd B) A)) true)
              ((cons? B) (member A (tl B)))
              (true (error "partial function member)))))
```

Step 11 completes the transformation into Kλ. There remains two points of interest.

The first is that we have not explained how to compile backtracking constructions that use <-. There is a missing step 1.5.

1.5 Replace every rule $p_a \ ... p_n \ \text{<-} \ q$ by $p_a \ ... p_n \ \text{->} \ (\copyright \ q)$

$\copyright$ is the choice point operator and remains in the code to indicate a choice point. These choice points will remain in the Kλ to be compiled out. A function which contains such a choice point will generally be of the form $(\text{defun} \ f \ (v_1 \ ... \ v_n)$ $(\text{cond} \ c_1 \ ... \ c_k \ (p \ (\copyright \ q)) \ c_{k+2} \ .... \ c_{k+m}))$ where $(p \ (\copyright \ q))$ contains the first occurrence of the choice point operator in the function definition. The trick is to isolate the code after the choice point and turn it into a continuation, thus delaying the computation; this continuation is then thawed when needed (figure 15.4). The process is repeated throughout $c_{n+2} \ .... \ c_{n+m}$ to eliminate the choice point operators.

```
(defun f (v₁ ... vₙ)
  (cond c₁ ... cₖ
        (true  (let Freeze (freeze (cond cₖ₊₂ .... cₖ₊ₘ))
                    (if p  (let Result q
                                (if (= Result (fail))
                                (thaw Freeze)
                                Result))
                           (thaw Freeze))))))
```

Figure 15.4 Compiling out a choice point in Kλ

The second point of interest concerns efficiency. The code generated from our compilation process is not optimally efficient.

The (cons? B) test occurs twice, and this means that in the recursive case the extra (cons? B) test is unnecessary since the result of this test has already been determined if control reaches this clause. There is a general principle at work here.

Let (defun f $(v_1 \ldots v_n)$ (cond $c_1 \ldots c_x \ldots c_{x+y}$ $c_{x+y+1} \ldots c_{x+y+1+z}$)) be any K$\lambda$ definition where for each c_i of $c_x \ldots c_{x+y}$ is of the form ((and p p_i) q_i) or (p q_i). In this case each clause c_i is repeating a common test p. **Factorisation** involves removing this repeated test.

Let χ be such that for all c_i of $c_x \ldots c_{x+y}$, if c_i = ((and p p_i) q_i) then $\chi(c_i)$ = (p_i q_i) and if c_i = (p q_i) then $\chi(c_i)$ = (true q_i). An encoding which does eliminate the repeated p tests is shown in figure 15.5.

```
(defun f (v₁ ... vₙ)
  (cond c₁ ...
        (true (if p (cond χ(cₓ)

                         ...

                     χ(c_{x+y})
              (true (cond c_{x+y+1} ... c_{x+y+1+z})))
        (cond c_{x+y+1} ... c_{x+y+1+z})))))
```

Figure 15.5 Factorising out p

There are two main problems with this code. The first is that it leads in the worst cases to exponential code growth since (cond $c_{x+y+1} \ldots c_{x+y+1+z}$) occurs twice. This can be offset by using the device for choice points - that is, by freezing (cond $c_{x+y+1} \ldots c_{x+y+1+z}$) once and locally assigning the result and then invoking the continuation as needed. The second problem, which is not avoided, is that tail-recursive code is buried in the detail of factorisation which means that the compiler has to be very clever to detect the tail recursion. For choice points this loss is acceptable because they are used sparingly, but for factorisation, which is very common, it is not.

For this reason Kλ code is not factorised and the optimisation of factorisation is deferred to a platform level. Efficient factorisation relies on having a platform which can jump out of the flow of control and direct it to the procedural code corresponding to (cond $c_{x+y+1} \ldots c_{x+y+1+z}$) under some label or heading. An earlier version of Shen, Qi, was optimised for Common Lisp and did exactly that, using the Common Lisp GO (a version of the notorious *goto*). The resulting code was highly unreadable, but so efficient than faster code could only be written by a Lisp programmer with considerable effort.

Exercise 15

1. *Build a compiler from $\mathcal{L}$ into Kλ.

2. *Implement a compiler from Shen into $\mathcal{L}$.

3. *Write a compiler for compile Kλ into Common Lisp that factorises Kλ.

4. *Find a language of your choice and implement a compiler or interpreter for Kλ.

Further Reading

The compilation of pattern-matching code into extended abstractions and then into lambda calculus is discussed in Peyton-Jones (1988). The generation of Kλ represents the end of this chapter, but in the complete compilation of Shen, the production of Kλ is only an interim in the compilation of a functional program into executable object code. The optimisation of pattern-matching is described in Peyton-Jones (1987).

16 Writing Good Programs

The previous chapter covered the last elements of what may be called the *core* Shen language. Core Shen is a very powerful programming language and it is possible to write a great number of good and useful programs in it. Many textbooks say little about how to write good programs, preferring to teach by example, rather than through precept. But because we have now covered enough to know how powerful and elegant functional programming can be, it is worth pausing to try and distil what we have learnt about how to write functional programs.

First it must be said that functional programming is a *craft*. Like any craft, it takes practice and practice is the best teacher. The more exercises you do, the better you become, and hopefully you should outgrow the exercises in this book, and go on to pursue ideas of your own. In course of working on programs, you will develop an intuitive appreciation of how to tackle problems and, with luck, you will become a craftsman. Here are 11 precepts, designed to help you improve your technique, which tell you what to aim at and what to avoid.

1. *Employ top down programming methodology to tackle difficult problems.*

Most significant programming tasks are too difficult for you to know exactly how they are to be solved. Functional programmers respond by a top down methodology, whereby the top level functions of the program are coded first, then the functions immediately below the top level, and so on down to the system functions. At each step they postpone the consideration of exactly how the given functions they cite in a definition are themselves implemented until they come to define them. Use the same technique and don't be afraid of being banal. For example, suppose you are given the task of getting a computer to make a move in chess and you have decided to employ some method whereby the computer generates a list of likely moves and analyses them. However you are still a little hazy about how the best moves are selected. No matter; you can make an appropriate beginning by writing.

```
(define play-move
  Position -> (select-best-move (generate-likely-moves Position)))
```

2. Make a program clear before you try to make it efficient.

Inexperienced programmers are sometimes tempted into trying to optimise before they have fully understood what they are doing. Even if the program then works, the programmer is not quite sure what is going on, and debugging the program becomes very difficult. Aim to be clear initially and forget about being clever until later. Often clear programs tend to be efficient anyway.

3. Get used to throwing away code.

Declarative programmers talk about **throwaway designs** - programs that are written in order to help the understanding, but which are thrown away and replaced by something better once that understanding has been achieved. Don't be afraid to throw things away instead of patching them up.

4. Use significant variable and function names.

If a variable is supposed to stand for a list of towns, then use Towns rather than X. Similarly if a function is supposed to sort towns by population call it sort-by-population rather than sbp. You may think you know what sbp means now, but returning after 3 weeks holiday it may mean nothing to you (or your co-workers). Suitable variable and function names remove the need to attach copious comments.

5. Look for a common pattern in different processes, and try to capture it with higher-order functions.

We covered this in the chapter on higher-order programming. Acquire the habit of looking for common patterns in diverse processes and of using higher-order functions to capture these patterns. Apart from being an excellent mental training, forming this habit will lead you to simpler and often faster programs.

6. If a procedure is used more than once, then it should be defined within its own function.

If there is a procedure, which is called again and again within your program, hive it off into a separate function and give it a name. Not only does this lead to a shorter program, since you can just invoke the procedure through the name of the function instead of typing in the whole procedure, but also the program becomes easier to maintain. If the procedure has to be changed, then only its definition need be altered, rather than everywhere it is called.

7. Avoid writing large function definitions.

Students who have attained some experience in functional programming, but are not yet expert, often write large unwieldy functions into which a large amount of activity is squeezed. Keep functions small. In terms of clarity, it is better to have a lot of short simple functions than a few large complex ones.

8. Avoid heavily parenthesised expressions.

This maxim is best bracketed with 7. Creating expressions with deep parentheses is visually confusing. Compare this function from the text.

```
(define <-db
   Key -> (let DB (value *db*)
              Hash (hash Key (limit  DB))
              Entry (trap-error (<-vector DB Hash) (/. E []))
              Details (assoc Key Entry)
              (if (empty? Details)
                  (error "information not found~%")
                  Details)))
```

with the equivalent function stripped of the elucidating local assignments.

```
(define <-db
   Key -> (let Details (assoc Key (trap-error (<-vector (value *db*)
                             (hash Key (limit (value *db*)))) (/. E [])))
              (if (empty? Details)
                  (error "information not found~%")
                  Details)))
```

The first version breaks up the logical stages of querying a DB and uses local assignments to annotate these stages. The second saves two lines, but requires a bracket balancing editor to write it, and cannot be comprehended without spending as much time as was needed to code it.

9. Try to avoid using assignments to hold information unless the information is of a permanent non-changing kind.

A source of "spaghetti code", where the thread of control is lost, is due to assignments over-playing their role. Ideally global values should be used to represent information which remains almost unchanged throughout the execution of program. In this role, they reduce the need to create extra inputs to functions, since a function can consult the global value if it needs to access this information. However, if a global value changes throughout a program, then the program is in danger of being a "spaghetti program". It is very difficult to correct mistakes in the program since the source of the error involving the global value cannot be easily localised.

10 . Tackle complex problems by successive approximation.

Some problems are too complex to be solved in the first pass. A good technique is to use *successive approximation*. Begin by simplifying the problem to something manageable and add the complexities in each approximation until you achieve the desired solution.

11 . If you find yourself feeling discouraged, tired or annoyed then don't continue to hack away at your program. Give it up and do something else and return to it later.

Writers of computer science texts often neglect the truism that programming is a human activity and that human beings get upset. Being upset and writing good code just do not go together. Anything you do while you tired or unsettled is liable at best to be worthless and at worst to be counterproductive. Most experienced programmers can recall making mistakes when feeling like this (a favourite is deleting some vital file). Save your work, log off, and walk away.

Part II

Working with Types

17 Types

Socrates: *Well then, since we have agreed that kinds of things can similarly mix with each other, is there not some sort of knowledge that one needs to take one's progress through the realm of statements, if one is going to point correctly which kinds will harmonise with which, and which are mutually discordant?*

Theaetetus: *Of course one needs knowledge, and possibly the greatest there is.*

Plato *Theaetetus*

17.1 Types and Type Security

The observations that Plato made over 2,300 years ago also hold true in computing. Programmers manipulate objects of many types, and for each type there is a set of specific legitimate operations that can be performed on the objects which belong to or **inhabit** that type. It is sensible to multiply two numbers or to take the head of a list. It is not sensible to try to take the head of a number or multiply two lists. The ability to recognise and avoid discordant **type errors** of this kind is one important form of knowledge that the programmer needs to possess if his programs are to work.

Since type errors must be avoided in order to have a properly working program, computer languages provide varying degrees of support to ensure that programs written in them are free from type errors, or **type secure**. In languages like Lisp and Python, type errors are often found when programs crash. Both these languages support **dynamic type checking;** only when programs are run, are the type errors in them detected.

In statically typed languages, type errors are detected in programs without having to run them. Statically typed languages are almost invariably **strongly typed languages** - i.e. every object of computation and every function must belong to a type, and the set of recognised types is rigorously laid down. This is a condition of being able to analyse programs to determine their type-security. The **type discipline** of the language is given by the rules, which determine how objects and types are associated. When functional programmers talk of typed programming languages, they mean languages that are statically and strongly typed.

17.2 Modifying the Read-Evaluate-Print Loop

In statically typed functional programming languages, the read-evaluate-print loop is modified to become a read-check-evaluate-print loop. The extra steps in the loop are italicised.

The Read-Check-Evaluate-Print Loop

Do until the user exits.

1. Read in the user's input.
2. *Type check it.*
3. *If there is a type error, output an error message and go to 1.*
4. If there is no type error, evaluate it to give the normal form.
5. Print the normal form together with its type.

If (tc +) is typed to the Shen top level, the Shen switches over to this loop.[55] After evaluation, the normal form and its type are printed separated by a colon, so 6 : number means 6 belongs to the type number. '6 : number' is an example of a typing (i.e. a functional expression together with a type). Typings can be entered to the evaluator. If a typing $e : t$ is typed to the top level, the Shen interpreter performs two operations.

1. If $e : t$ is not provable, then a type error is signalled.
2. Else e is evaluated to a normal form $e\Downarrow$, and $e\Downarrow : t$ is printed.

Figure 17.1 shows a session with the typechecker.

```
(0-) (tc +)
true

(1+) (* 7 8)
56 : number

(2+) (* 7 a)
type error

(3+) howdy
howdy : symbol

(4+) true
true : boolean
```

Figure 17.1 Base types in Shen

---

[55] (tc -) switches back to dynamic type checking.

Every typed functional language has a set of predefined types called **base types**, and operators called **type operators** for creating new types out of old ones. Shen has five base types.

1. symbol; e.g. a21, computer_studies, myname.
2. string; e.g. "my name is".
3. boolean; true, false.
4. number; e.g. ..., -3, -2, -1, 0, 1, 2, 3,... , 3.1462.
5. unit

A **type operator** is a means of building new types out of old. Shen has six inbuilt type operators:

1. list
2. vector,
3. *
4. lazy
5. stream
6. -->.

We will explain the semantics of many of these operators by giving the conditions under which objects inhabit the types constructed by them.

17.3 Lists, Vectors and Tuples

Lists, vectors and tuples are ways of grouping objects together; they each have their own type rule.

Rule for the Type Operator list

Where A is any type, list L : (list A) just when for each x in L, x : A.

Figure 17.2 shows a session with lists in typed Shen.

```
(6+) [3 4]
[3 4] : (list number)

(7+) ["a" "b" "c"]
["a" "b" "c"] : (list string)

(8+) [["a"]]
[["a"]] : (list (list string))
```

Figure 17.2 Typed lists in Shen

[3 4] inhabits the type (list number) which is the type of all lists whose elements are all number; a list of strings inhabits the type (list string); a list of lists of strings inhabits the type (list (list string)). What if we submit a list of symbols and integers to Shen?

```
(9+) [76 trombones]
type error
```

There is no type to which each element of the list belongs, the list does not inhabit a list type and consequently is treated as badly typed by Shen. Strongly typed functional languages do not naturally tolerate lists containing objects of different types.

Tuples restore some of the flexibility that is lost by imposing type homogeneity on lists. A tuple in Shen is strictly a **pair**, written in set theory as $<x, y>$ and in Shen as (@p x y). A tuple is a nested series of pairs in formal set theory where $<x, y, z>$ is shorthand for $<x, <y, z>>$. Similarly in Shen, @p is a polyadic function so that (@p 1 2 3) is parsed and printed as (@p 1 (@p 2 3)).

@p builds a tuple from x and y of types A and B respectively; the resulting tuple inhabits the **product type** (A * B) .

Rule for the Product Type *

(@p x y) : (A * B) just when x : A and y : B.

The function fst isolates the first element of a tuple and the function snd isolates the second element (figure 17.3). Pattern matching with tuples is part of Shen.

```
(1+) (@p 76 trombones)
(@p 76 trombones) : (number * symbol)

(2+) (fst (@p 1 a))
1 : number

(3+) (snd (@p 1 a))
a : symbol

(4+) (define foo
      {(number * symbol) --> number}
      (@p 76 trombones) -> 76)
foo : ((number * symbol) --> number)
```

Figure 17.3 Tuples in typed Shen

The rule of the vector type is similar to the rule for lists; vector contents must belong to the same type.

Rule for the Type Operator vector

Where A is any type, vector v : (vector A) just for any $i > 0$ within the limit of v, $i(v)$: A.

The type rule for vectors only applies to standard vectors. A native vector that contains unassigned indices will have those indices filled with some platform-dependent object. Hence in general it is not possible to guarantee that a native vector will contain objects of a uniform type because a retrieval from it can yield an arbitrary object. For standard vectors, since nothing can be retrieved unless it is first entered, this problem does not arise.

```
(8+) (@v 76 0 <>)
<76 0> : (vector number)

(9+) (@v 76 trombones <>)
type error
```

Figure 17.4 Vectors in typed Shen

17.4 Lazy Types

Objects which inhabit lazy types are generated by the freeze function; the rule is straightforward.

Rule for the Type Operator lazy

Where A is any type, (freeze x) : (lazy A) just for x : A.

---

freeze generates objects which belong to lazy types and thaw removes the laziness.

```
(8+) (freeze (* 7 8))
#<CLOSURE LAMBDA NIL (shen.multiply 7 8)> : (lazy number)

(9+) (thaw (freeze (* 7 8)))
56 : number
```

Figure 17.5 Lazy types

17.5 Arrow Types

The next rule relates to the types of functions and gives the conditions under which a function inhabits a type constructed by the infix **arrow operator** →.

Rule for the Type Operator →

For any types A and B, $f : (A \rightarrow B)$ just when for all x, if $x : A$ then $(f\,x) : B$.

Here is an example entered to Shen. The symbol --> is used for the type operator →.

```
(10+) (define double
         {number --> number}
         X -> (* X 2))
double : (number  --> number)
```

Figure 17.6 Type checking a function in Shen

double has the type number → number, because if x is a number then (double x) is a number.

Unlike the previous cases, in typed mode Shen will not verify the type of any function unless this type is specified in the function definition. This marks Shen out as an **explicitly typed** language in the manner of Hope (Burstall et al. 1980) rather than one of the group of **implicitly typed** languages like ML or Haskell which do not require this information.[56] The type or **signature** of the function is entered in curly brackets immediately after the name of the function.

The rule for → applies only to 1-place functions; but from chapter 6 we recall that this is no limitation on the expressive power of a functional notation because currying allows us express n-place functions in terms of 1-place ones. We consider the function + as being a 1-place function that when applied to an number m returns a function that adds m to whatever number n is supplied to it.

If we apply + to 1, we return an expression that adds 1 to an object. If we apply that expression to another number, we derive the successor of that number (figure 17.7)

---

[56] There is a very good reason why this information is required in Shen which has to do with the issue of the combinatorial explosion; a phenomenon we touched on in chapter 12 but did not actually witness. We will return to this theme in chapter 26.

```
(1+) (+ 1)
#<CLOSURE :LAMBDA [Z1414] [+ 1 Z1414]> : (number --> number)

(2+) ((+ 1) 2)
3 : number
```

Figure 17.7 Type checking and using a partial application

By the rule for the type operator $\to$, the function + has the type number $\to$ (number $\to$ number). If + is defined in the manner of chapter 2, this is the type that Shen allocates to the function.

```
(3+) (define plus
       {number --> (number --> number)}
       0 X -> X
       X Y -> (+ 1 (plus (- X 1) Y)))
plus : (number --> (number --> number))
```

In many textbooks the internal parentheses for the type operator $\to$ are omitted, so that number $\to$ (number $\to$ number) is written as number $\to$ number $\to$ number. Shen permits this shorthand and automatically inserts the missing parentheses, as in this example.

```
(8+) (define average
       {number --> number --> number}
       M N -> (/ (+ M N) 2.0))
average : (number --> (number --> number))
```

This notational shorthand is used throughout this book. Figure 17.8 shows two functions from previous chapters together with their types.

```
(define add1
  ((vector number) --> (vector number)}
  <> -> <>
  (@v N V) -> (@v (+ N 1) (add1 V)))

(define whitespace?
  {string --> boolean}
  S -> (let N (string->n S) (element? N [9 10 13 32])))
```

Figure 17.8 Some functions from the previous chapters with types

The arrow operator is polyadic in Shen; it may be used as a monadic operator for zero place functions. Thus

```
(define pi
  {--> number}
  -> 3.142)
```

is legitimate.

17.6 Polymorphic Types

A **polymorphic function** is a function that can be applied to arguments of different types. For example the append function can be used to append lists of numbers or list of symbols or lists of strings. We could say that append has the type (list string) $\rightarrow$ (list string) $\rightarrow$ (list string), but with equal reason we could also say that it has the type (list symbol) $\rightarrow$ (list symbol) $\rightarrow$ (list symbol).

In fact there is an infinite set Σ of variable-free types to which append belongs and there is no reason to single out one element of Σ as *the* type of append. Instead we say append inhabits the type (list A) $\rightarrow$ (list A) $\rightarrow$ (list A) for any type A that one cares to mention.[57]

The type (list A) $\rightarrow$ (list A) $\rightarrow$ (list A) is the **most general type** with respect to the types in Σ; because every member of Σ is a substitution instance of it. The presence of a variable in the type of append shows that the type of this function is a **parametric polytype**.[58] The inhabitation rule for a polytypes is as follows:-

---

Rule for Polytypes

If A is a polytype, x : A just when, for any type B which results from the uniform substitution of types for variables in A, x : B .

Figure 17.9 reproduces the Cartesian product program of chapter 4 with the appropriate polytypes.

---

[57] Most of the standard list handling functions in Shen are polymorphic, reverse : (list A) $\rightarrow$ (list A) and element? : A $\rightarrow$ (list A) $\rightarrow$ boolean; these functions and their types can be seen in appendix A. In contrast the functions of the previous section were **monomorphic** and their variable-free types are **monotypes**.

[58] The qualifier 'parametric' implies that there are non-parametric polytypes; indeed there are. An object x displays non-parametric polytyping or **ad hoc polymorphism** when it belongs to two types a and b such that $a \neq b$ and there is no type c of which a and b are instances where x : c. We will see an example in the next chapter. The terms 'parametric polymorphism' and 'ad hoc polymorphism' were coined by Strachey. ML was the first language to introduce parametric polytyping.

```
(define cartesian-product
  {(list A) --> (list A) --> (list (list A))}
  [ ] _ -> [ ]
  [X | Y] Z -> (append (pair X Z) (cartesian-product Y Z)))

(define pair
  {A --> (list A) --> (list (list A))}
  _ [ ] -> [ ]
  X [Y | Z] -> [[X Y] | (pair X Z)])
```

Figure 17.9 A type secure version of the Cartesian product program

The old program computed the Cartesian product of a list of symbols and a list of numbers forming a list of lists containing symbols and numbers. The type checked version is more restrictive; both input lists must contain elements of the same type.

A way of recapturing some of the functionality of the old program is to generate tuples rather than two element lists. Figure 17.10 shows the revised program that uses @p in place of the previous list constructor. The types are revised in line with the new approach.

```
(define cartesian-product
  {(list A) --> (list B) --> (list (A * B))}
  [ ] _ -> [ ]
  [X | Y] Z -> (append (pair X Z) (cartesian-product Y Z)))

(define pair
  {A --> (list B) --> (list (A * B))}
  _ [ ] -> [ ]
  X [Y | Z] -> [(@p X Y) | (pair X Z)])
```

Figure 17.10 A revised version using tuples instead of lists

Since lists are built by consing to the empty list, the empty list must be capable of accepting an arbitrary object of any type. The empty list is a polymorphic object; typing '[ ]' reveals the type of [ ] to be (list A).[59] For similar reasons, the empty vector is also polymorphic.

```
(11+) [ ]
[ ] : (list A)

(12+) <>
<> : (vector A)
```

---

[59] For those who know first-order logic and prefer a formal explanation, this follows from our rule R for list types. Let L be a list and let $x \varepsilon L$ be the relation between x and L when x is an element of L. R states that $\forall A \, L : (list \, A)$ iff $\forall x \, x \varepsilon L \rightarrow x : A$. Since $\sim \exists x \, x \varepsilon []$, then it follows that $\forall A \, [] : (list \, A)$.

Higher order functions are generally polymorphic and their nature means that arrow types are found embedded in their signatures. The converge program of chapter 6 is typed as follows.

```
(define converge
  {(A --> A) --> A --> (A --> A --> boolean) --> A}
  F X R -> (converge-help F (F X) X R))

(define converge-help
  {(A --> A) --> A --> A --> (A --> A --> boolean) --> A}
  _ New Old R -> New                          where (R Old New)
  F New _ R -> (converge-help F (F New) New R))
```

Here F has the type $A \rightarrow A$ since it is recursively applied to X to generate new values; since F may be applied to its own output, it must have the same type as its input. X has to have the type A if F has the type $A \rightarrow A$ and since R compares X and (F X), R : $A \rightarrow A \rightarrow$ boolean.

A very important polymorphic function is the equality function =. Objects can be compared using = only when they are of the same type. [60]

```
(13+) (= 6 6)
true : boolean

(14+) (= a 6)
type error
```

17.7 Stream Types

A stream in Shen is either of the type (stream in) or (stream out) depending on whether it is a source or a sink. (open <filename> in) creates a stream of the type (stream in) and (open <filename> out) of type (stream out).

The function read-byte has the type (stream in) $\rightarrow$ number and pr has the type string $\rightarrow$ (stream in) $\rightarrow$ string. stinput and stoutput will return objects of the form (stream in) and (stream out) respectively. The function open does not have a type that can be directly expressed as an arrow type.

---

[60] Shen also provides a more inclusive equality function == which operates exactly as does =, but allows comparison of objects of different types. The type of == is $A \rightarrow B \rightarrow$ boolean. In most statically typed languages, == is not supported. The reasoning is that since objects of different types can never be equal, there is no point comparing objects of different types to see if they are the same. We can think of an analogy in a world where every person is the citizen of only one country. In such a world the question "Is Mr Jules, French citizen of Paris, one and the same as Mr Jules, resident of London and British citizen" must always be answered in the negative. In the real world, where dual citizenship abounds, such questions are sensible and are sometimes answered positively. The world of programming is closer to the real world in allowing objects to have "dual citizenship" and so Shen caters for this. We shall see a real application in chapter 19.

input+ is the typed correlate of input.   Unlike input, input+ receives two arguments; a type A and a stream. If the stream is omitted, then the standard input is used. The expression entered is then type checked and if it inhabits the type A, then it is evaluated. If not an error is returned. Here is an example.

```
(7+) (input+ number)
(* 5 6)
30 : number

(8+) (input+ symbol)
(* 5 6)
type error: (* 5 6) is not of type symbol
```

Since input+ can be used to read any stream, we can use it to read a file item by item and return just those items which belong to a desired type. In figure 17.11 we use it to filter a file of junk for expressions which evaluate to numbers. The higher-order function chomp takes a reader and applies it to the input stream, terminating when the stream is empty.

```
(define filter-numbers
  {string --> (list number)}
  File -> (chomp (/. S (input+ number S)) (open File in)))

(define chomp
  {((stream in) --> A) --> (stream in) --> (list A)}
  Reader Stream -> (trap-error [(Reader Stream) | (chomp Reader Stream)]
                        (/. E (if (eos? (error-to-string E))
                              (close Stream)
                              (chomp Reader Stream)))))

(define eos?
  {string --> boolean}
  "error: empty stream" -> true
  _ -> false)
```

Figure 17.11 Filtering a file using input+

Here is a test case - a readable file junk.txt
```
---------------------------------------------
        1 2 a gg
        "3455"
        456          7890
        (* 7 8 9)

        true
        isk;k;vk;vk
---------------------------------------------
```
Filtering the numbers using our program yields a list of numbers.

```
(14+) (filter-numbers "junk.txt")
[1 2 456 7890 504] : (list number)
```

17.7 The unit Type

The unit type is a special type that is used by a few system functions; one of them being read-file which has the type string → (list unit). When an object is assigned the type unit, it means that it is simply an object of some kind to which no type information is attached. Hence there is no inhabitation rule for the unit type. 'read-file : string → (list unit)' asserts that read-file accepts a string and returns a list of objects about which no type information can be assumed.

The main utility of the unit type is that units are still susceptible to polymorphic functions; that is to say, we can use functions like print and output on the output of read-file and maintain type security. Macros in Shen are given the type unit by the typechecker to allow them to be read into Shen.

17.8 Types and Optimisation

When a function is type checked, the type information gleaned from this process can be attached to the Kλ in the form of type declarations. Entering (optimise +) allows this to happen. (figure 17.13).

```
(11+) (optimise +)
true

(12+) (define identical?
       {string --> string --> boolean}
       X X -> true
       _ _ -> false)
identical? : (string --> (string --> boolean))

(13+) (ps identical?)
[defun identical? [V547 V548]
   [cond [[= [type V548 string] [type V547 string]] [type true boolean]]
         [[type true boolean] [type false boolean]]]] : (list unit)
```

Figure 19.13 Automatically generating type annotations

The degree to which Shen makes use of these type annotations when compiling Kλ depends on the platform. It is legal and feasible to ignore them completely, but some compilers may choose to act on them in order to optimise the resultant code. Hence the function identical? above may actually be optimised to work only with strings. Whether this occurs or not, a basic principle to which Shen adheres is that all purely declarative type secure programs must behave in the same way when given type secure inputs. This condition is called the **weak portability requirement** which all platforms for Shen must respect. **Strong portability** requires that all programs must behave in the same way irrespective of whether the program or the input is type secure. Strong portability is not a condition in Shen and indeed several ports do not obey it.[61]

17.9 The Limits of Inbuilt Types

The set of types whose members can be constructed by means of the type operations and base types built into Shen constitutes the set Σ^S of inbuilt types that Shen can compute. Σ^S is infinitely large and incorporates the types of many of the functions of the previous chapters, but not all. The lambda calculus evaluator aor in chapter 14 cannot be given a type within Σ^S because it manipulates λ expressions. λ expressions are not uniform lists in the ordinary sense, nor are λ expressions necessarily lists at all since they can be symbols.

Practically speaking, for static typing to be useful in a language there has to be a way for the user to extend the set of recognisable types beyond the limits of the inbuilt types of the system. Such a facility exist within Shen in the form of the **sequent calculus** studied in the next chapter.

Exercise 17

1. Define the following functions with types (problems inspired by Werner Hett).

    a. a function last that returns the last element of a list;
    b. a function mirror which tests to see if a list is of even length and if its first half is a mirror image of its second; thus [a b c c b a] would pass this test;
    c. a function remdup that removes duplicates of a list;
    d. a function partition that takes an equivalence relation and a list and partitions the list by the relation. Thus (partition (function ==) [1 1 3 4 2 7 8 5 8 9]) = [[1 1] [3] [4] [2] [7] [8 8] [5] [9]]. The order of the elements does not matter.
    e. run-length; which takes a list as an input and returns a list of pairs giving the frequency of each element. Thus (run-length [1 1 3 4 2 7 8 5 8]) = [(@p 1 2) (@p 3 1) (@p 4 1) (@p 2 1) (@p 7 1) (@p 8 2) (@p 5 1) (@p 9 1)].
    f. duplicate; which duplicates the elements of a list; (duplicate [a b c] 3) = [a a a b b b c c c].
    g. drop; which drops every nth element from a list. (drop [a b c d e f g h i k] 3) = [a b d e g h k]
    h. split; which splits a list into two parts. So (split [a b c d e f g h i k] 3) = [[a b c] [d e f g h i k]].

2. Provide correct types to all the functions contained in the following programs.
    a. the prime program of chapter 3;
    b. the change counting program of chapter 3;
    c. the powerset program in figure 4;
    d. the Goldbach conjecture program of chapter 4;

3. Attach to each of the following functions, its most general type.

---

[61] E.g the Javascript port of Shen in which + will append two strings as well as adding two numbers.

```
(define prim
  0 X F -> X
  N X F -> (F (- N 1) (prim (- N 1) X F)))

(define mapf
  _ _ [] -> []
  C F [X | Y] -> (C (F X) (mapf C F Y)))

(define prependX
  X -> (append X))

(define has?
  Test [ ] -> false
  Test [X | Y] -> (or (Test X) (has? Test Y)))

(define b
  F Test States -> true          where (has? Test States)
  F Test States  -> (let NewStates (mapf append F States)
                      (if (empty? NewStates)
                          false
                          (b F Test NewStates)))))

(define s*
  _ [ ] -> [ ]
  _ [X] -> [X]
  R [X Y | Z] -> [Y | (s* R [X | Z])]        where (R Y X)
  R [X Y | Z] -> [X | (s* R [Y | Z])])

(define s
  R X -> (fix (/. Y (s* R Y)) X))

(define a
  F -> (/. X (/. Y (F X Y))))
```

4. Reimplement the semantic net program in figure 8.8 so that a semantic net appears as a list of pairs; each pair being composed of a symbol, and another pair composed of a pointer (is_a or type_of) and a list of properties. Thus asserting that Mark Tarver is both male and a teacher would be represented by the nested pair (@p Mark_Tarver (@p is_a [male teacher])). Since you will not be using a property list, your program will contain a top level function that maintains the semantic net as bound to a formal parameter. This same top level function will query the user as to whether she wishes to assert or query the system. Your program must pass the type checker.

Further Reading

Types that are not polytypes are **monotypes**, and languages that allow polytypes are **polymorphic languages**. Languages, which are strongly typed but do not admit polytypes are called **monomorphic languages**. An example of a monomorphic procedural language is Niklaus Wirth's **Pascal** to which Holmes (1993) provides a good introduction. Edinburgh ML (Gordon, Milner and Wadsworth (1979)) was the first statically typed polymorphic functional programming language. Discussions of the relative advantages of typed languages (like SML) and untyped languages (like Lisp) have appeared in user groups. The introduction to Abelson and Sussman (1996) contains some interesting observations on this topic as does Backhouse (1990).

18 Sequent Calculus

18.1 Sequent Calculus and Computer Science

Sequent calculus was developed by a German mathematician and logician Gerhard Gentzen during the unpromising conditions of World War II as an alternative to the **axiomatic** or **Hilbert systems** of logic that had existed up to his time. Gentzen's groundbreaking development was to offer two alternative presentations of logic – **natural deduction** and **sequent calculus**.

Gentzen's work originally arose within the framework of first-order logic, but was quickly taken up to present deductive systems of many different kinds including type theory. In 1984 Cardelli represented the type theory of a simple functional language using sequent notation and so it has been known for more than 30 years both that type checking within computer languages is a deductive process and that deductive processes can be represented in sequent calculus notation.

It would seem that building in sequent calculus into a programming language would offer the quickest route to providing type security. In fact this did not happen and instead developers produced special purpose algorithms like Milner's $\mathcal{W}$ algorithm to drive type checking, even though they often wrote their theory papers with the help of sequent calculus. Most modern functional languages are derived from the Hindley-Milner approach including ML and Haskell.

There are at least two reasons why computer science took this direction. First during the 70s and early 80s there was little understanding of how to compile sequent calculus rules into efficient code. As we shall see in chapter 23, an essential intermediate step in effecting this compilation is to compile sequent calculus into Horn clause logic.

Horn clause logic is the basis of **logic programming**, studied in chapter 22. But logic programming entered computing relatively late in 1973 and only received a generally portable high-performance encoding 10 years later with the development of the Warren Abstract Machine and 5 years after Milner had introduced and worked out the theory for ML.

Torkel Franzen (1988) wrote a report explicitly noting the close connection between intuitionistic (single-conclusion) sequent calculus and logic programming. But the practical fusion of sequent calculus with functional programming had to wait until machine performance and the diffusion of logic programming technology allowed the author to make the first experiments in 1992 in using sequent calculus to drive type checking.

The second reason for not specifying types in sequent calculus is that the sequent calculus in its undiluted form is enormously powerful; in fact it is a programming language in its own right. In 2007, J. T. Gleason proved the Turing equivalence of the Shen type notation by writing an SKI combinator machine in it (a kind of λ calculus evaluator). Designers of SML and Haskell to a degree consciously or unconsciously shunned giving the user this power. We will look at the issues here in the second part of chapter 21.

The sequent calculus introduced here is a notational restriction of the original sequent calculus introduced by Gentzen. In particular, the multiple conclusion format of Gentzen is not used and what we study is single conclusion sequent calculus, generally a more natural idiom for reasoning and one with close connections to Prolog. Readers interested in comparing the classical approach of Gentzen, and in particular natural deduction, are referred to the further reading.

18.2 Introducing Sequent Calculus

The primordial material for any argument is a set of assumptions and a proposition which is to be proved. A sequent is an ordered pair $<\Delta, \chi>$ of just such a set of assumptions Δ and a proposition χ. From the point of view of mathematical and logical reasoning, the important question is whether the proposition χ follows from the assumptions Δ. If it does then the sequent $<\Delta, \chi>$ is said to be **valid**. If the assumptions are true and the sequent is valid then the sequent is said to be **sound**. Plainly the conclusion of any sound sequent is true.

In logic and mathematics, the focus is on the question of validity which is supposed to be a matter of pure thought. That is to say, no empirical investigation is required to establish validity of a sequent, although empirical investigation may be required to demonstrate the truth of the assumptions. The sequent

$$<\{\text{mercury boils at } 356.73 \text{ °C}\}, \text{mercury's boiling point} > 100 \text{ °C}>$$

is undoubtedly valid and can be established by reflection, but the soundness of the argument requires an empirical investigation in chemistry.

In logic and mathematics, the announcement of a sequent as valid is presented in the form of a proof. Nothing that is non-obvious should be stated unless it is accompanied by some form of proof. The revolution in logic that took place in the late 19th and early 20th centuries was concerned with the formalisation of this concept of proof. The notation that became preeminent was **first-order logic**.

Though this revolution predated the computer revolution by more than half a century, what the logicians achieved was the reduction of the process of proof recognition to something that required no understanding of meaning, and only a recognition of the proper relations between the symbols involved. That is to say, the correctness of a fully formalised proof became a computable matter.[62]

The formalisation of proof requires that the steps of any proof be broken down to a level where each step is the product of a mechanical procedure. In functional terms, each step represents the application of a computable function to the previous steps of the proof. Such a computable function is an **inference rule**.

The structure of such a formal proof suggests that the form of an inference rule ρ must be

ρ: 'Any sequent of the form $S = \langle \Delta, \chi \rangle$ is provable if ... are provable.'

In cases where ... is empty, the inference rule is stating that S is unconditionally provable. Such an inference rule is called an **axiom**. Some more terminology. The elements of ... are the **premises** of ρ, S is the **conclusion** of ρ, Δ is the **context** of the S, the elements of Δ are **hypotheses** and χ is the **succeedent** of S.[63]

Generally sequent calculus inference rules are presented with the premises placed above a line with the conclusion placed below it. 'S is valid if $S_1,...,S_n$ are all valid' is written as

$$\frac{S_1,...,S_n}{S}$$

In certain textbooks, whitespace is used to separate premises which is slightly inconvenient in computing. Shen notation, which we will come to in the next chapter, uses semi-colons to separate premises and commas to separate items within a context. Also it is common to write the sequent not as $\langle \Delta, \chi \rangle$ but as $\Delta \gg \chi$ or sometimes $\Delta \vdash \chi$ - the $\gg$ or $\vdash$ symbol being read as 'therefore'. From now on we will follow these conventions.

---

[62] For some years it was an open question as to whether it was also possible to not only computably check proofs in first-order logic, but also to computably check validity. It fell to Turing and Church independently in the '30s and '40s to demonstrate that, as far as first-order logic was concerned, there was no algorithm for demonstrating the validity in first-order logic. This did not hamper the subsequent attempts by scientists to develop reasoning engines which would compete with human beings. This endeavour marks the beginning of **automated deduction**, a fascinating field which abuts on some of the topics in this book, including logic programming.

[63] The terminology is confusing. Logic is the unfortunate victim of naming conventions whereby 'sound' has at least three meanings and 'premise' has two. In logic, 'premise' is sometimes applied to the assumptions of an argument, what here we call hypotheses.

18.3 Propositional Calculus

Courses of elementary logic generally begin with **propositional calculus** (PC) and here we use it here to illustrate the application of sequent notation because we suppose some familiarity with this system. PC is a proof system which captures some basic patterns of inference involving & (and), v (or), ~ (not), → (if ... then ...) and ↔ (if and only if).

As well as these symbols there is an unlimited supply of propositional variables p, q, r,... ,p', q', r', ... These propositional variables can be made to stand for sentences.

The syntax of our propositional calculus can be stated quite simply.

    1.   A propositional variable on its own is a formula of PC. Such a formula is a **PC atom**.
    2.   The special atom *falsum* (explained later) is a formula of PC.
    3.   If P and Q are formulae of PC so is each of the following:
       $(\sim P)$, $(P \,\&\, Q)$, $(P \rightarrow Q)$, $(P \vee Q)$, $(P \leftrightarrow Q)$.

Identifying p with the sentence 'Logic is easy' and q with the sentence 'Students like logic' determines the meaning of all propositional wffs containing only p and q as variables (figure 18.1).

Wff	*Interpretation*
$(p \rightarrow q)$	If logic is easy then students like logic.
$(p \vee q)$	Either logic is easy or students like logic.
$((\sim p) \vee q)$	Either logic is not easy or students like logic.
$((\sim p) \,\&\, (\sim q))$	Logic is not easy and students do not like logic.
$(p \leftrightarrow q)$	Logic is easy if and only if students like logic.

Figure 18.1 A reading of some propositional calculus wffs

In logical parlance, $(\sim p)$ is the **negation** of p. $(p \,\&\, q)$ is the **conjunction** of p and q, $(p \vee q)$ is the **disjunction** of p and q.

In terms of sequent calculus, the proof theory of PC can be explained by giving the inference rules associated with &, v, ~, → and ↔. These symbols are the **logical constants** of PC in contrast to p, q, r,... ,p', q', r', which are the **logical variables**.

The logical constant & has two derivation rules. Here is the first. The first rule defines how to deal with a conjunction that forms the succeedent which is to the right of the >>. For this reason it is called the **right rule** for &.

Δ >> P;
Δ >> Q;
Δ >> (P & Q);

The rule states effectively that (P & Q) is provable from a context Δ if P is provable from Δ and so is Q. Generally when the nature of the context is irrelevant, then it is omitted and the rule is written as

&-*right*
P;
Q;_____
(P & Q);

The variables Δ, P and Q are **metavariables**; that is variables used in the rule to mark places where the nature of the input is not important. The term 'metavariable' arises from the fact that sequent calculus is essentially a metalanguage evolved for the purpose of describing other languages like PC. In Shen uppercase is used to mark variables and again we follow suit.

The left rule for & says a conjunction that forms a hypothesis is split into its components

&-*left*

Δ, P, Q >> R;
Δ, (P & Q) >> R;

Again Δ is read as given and the whole is written as

P, Q >> R;
(P & Q) >> R;

The &-*left* rule can be applied to any hypothesis and the nature of the rule does not determine, if there is a choice to be made, which hypothesis is to be unpacked. Hence this rule is non-deterministic in application.

The left (L) and right (R) rules for & are symmetrical; they both involve splitting a conjunction into its parts. In Reeves and Clarke (1990) a useful shorthand is introduced whereby these two rules are expressed in a shorthand as an **LR rule** using the double underline

P;
Q;
======
(P & Q);

This shorthand is optional but is used later in Shen. When using this notation it is important to always remember that it is only a shorthand for writing two rules in longhand.

The rules for v are *asymmetrical* – there two right rules and one left rule.

v-*right1*
$$\frac{P;}{(P \vee Q);}$$

v-*right2*
$$\frac{Q;}{(P \vee Q);}$$

A disjunction is provable if *either* of its components is provable. The left rule for v is sometimes called a **proof by cases** in mathematics.

v-*left*

$$\frac{P \gg R;\quad Q \gg R;}{(P \vee Q) \gg R;}$$

R is provable from (P v Q) if R is provable from P and R is provable from Q. The rules for → are also asymmetrical.

→-*right*

$$\frac{P \gg Q;}{(P \rightarrow Q);}$$

→-*left*

$$\frac{(P \rightarrow Q) \gg P;}{(P \rightarrow Q) \gg Q;}$$

The →-*left* is a restriction of a more general rule called *modus ponens*.

$$\frac{(P \rightarrow Q); P;}{Q}$$

The difference in formulation may appear to be slight but they are significantly different. The →-*left* rule requires that the implication occur in the context whereas *modus ponens* makes no such restriction. The modus ponens rule is an example of a **synthetic** inference rule, because the set of metavariables in the premises is not a subset of those in the conclusion. Inference rules that are not synthetic are said to be **analytic**. Synthetic rules are less common in type checking than analytic ones and in the next chapter we will look at some of the dangers of using them carelessly.

The rules for ~ and ↔ are simple and symmetrical. (~ P) is shorthand for (P → falsum) where falsum is placeholder for any absurd proposition. (P ↔ Q) is defined as ((P → Q) & (Q → P)).

def~
(P → falsum);
=========
(~ P);

def↔
((P → Q) & (Q → P));
===============
(P ↔ Q);

The definition of negation has its origins in the idea that one way of denying a proposition P is to assert that if P is true then some absurdity follows. (e.g. 'If Nixon was innocent then my aunt is my uncle').

The next rule *lemma* allows us to introduce a new succeedent and, having proved it, to incorporate this into the new context.

lemma
P;
P >> Q;
Q;

In mathematics this is called **introducing a lemma**. If we are proving Q, then we can break or cut into the proof to prove P and then add P to the context and return to proving Q. In logic this is a form of the **cut rule**. The cut rule is an example of a **structural rule** since no logical constant is involved here. Two other structural rules are *swap* – that allows us to change the order of hypotheses and *thin*, that allows us to remove hypotheses.

swap
Q, P >> R;
P, Q >> R;

thin
Q;
P >> Q;

Finally there needs to be an axiom to ensure that proofs terminate; *hyp* states that a sequent is valid if the succeedent is also an hypothesis.

hyp

P >> P;

These rules collectively define a system called **minimal logic** that is somewhat weaker than PC. To construct full PC, two more rules are needed. First, a rule for deriving a proposition from a proof of an absurdity. If falsum is provable then anything follows. This is sometimes called the *principle of explosion*.

explosion
falsum;
P;

This rule set now defines a weaker version of PC called **intuitionistic propositional calculus**. Adding the *law of the excluded middle* gives full classical PC.

lem

(P ∨ (~ P));

18.4 First Order Logic (FOL)

In propositional calculus, atomic sentences are simple symbols. If we take the two sentences "Tarver likes the *Guardian*" and "Tarver likes the *Independent*", and represent them in PC we derive two sentences p (representing "Tarver likes the *Guardian*") and q (representing "Tarver likes the *Independent*"). Neither of these representations gives any clue that these two sentences share anything - that they both concern me and what I like.

First-order logic (FOL) captures these similarities by allowing atomic sentences, unlike those of PC, to have an internal structure. In FOL, an atomic sentence is composed of a **predicate** followed by zero or more **terms**. The predicate ascribes properties to the objects denoted by the terms. So in FOL, "Tarver likes the *Guardian*" is represented as "likes(Tarver, *Guardian*)" and "Tarver likes the *Independent*" as "likes(Tarver, *Independent*)".

A term in FOL can be structured, "likes((father-of Tarver), *Guardian*) represents the proposition that the father of Tarver likes the *Guardian*.

If we replace "Tarver" in "likes(Tarver, *Guardian*)" by a variable "*x*", we derive the **open sentence** "likes(*x*, *Guardian*)" in which the *x* is **free**.

Though both "Tarver likes the *Guardian*" and "Tarver likes the *Independent*" are true, an open sentence such as "likes(*x*, *Guardian*)" is neither true nor false because variables do not denote objects. One way to turn open sentences into sentences that are true or false is to replace the variables by denoting terms (like "Tarver", or "the man next door to me in #28"). Another way is to **bind** the variables by the **quantifiers** ∀ or ∃. Here is an example.

for every substitution for x, "likes(x, *Guardian*)" is true.

which in FOL is written "∀x likes(x, *Guardian*)", which is plainly false. Another way is to assert

for some substitution for x, "likes(x, *Guardian*)" is true.

which is itself true, and which in FOL is written "∃x likes(x, *Guardian*)". Since FOL includes all of the logical constants of PC, as well as quantifiers and structured atomic sentences, its expressive capacity is much greater than PC. Correspondingly, the syntax of FOL is more complex than PC.

Syntax Rules for First Order Logic

1. A variable is any of x, y, z, x', y', z'...
2. A predicate is any non-variable symbol other than ~, &, →, ∨, ↔, ∃, ∀.
3. A name is any non-variable symbol/string/number/boolean other than ~, &, →, ∨, ↔, ∃, ∀.
4. A functor is non-variable symbol other than ~, &, →, ∨, ↔, ∃, ∀.
5. A term is either
   a. a name or ...
   b. a variable or ...
   c. an expression $(f\, t_1,...,t_n)$ made of a functor f followed by n ($n \geq 0$) terms.
6. $\sigma(t_1,..t_n)$ is a formula of FOL if σ is a predicate and $t_1,...,t_n$ ($n \geq 0$) are terms. $\sigma(t_1,..t_n)$ is a **first-order atom**.
7. If A and B are formulae of FOL so are (~ A), (A & B), (A → B), (A ∨ B), (A ↔ B).
8. If A is a formula of FOL and v is a variable then (∃v A) and (∀v A) are formulae of FOL .

Our syntax for FOL allows for 0-place predicates, but these are, in effect identical to the propositional variables of PC. Hence we will borrow on the syntax of PC and write $(p \lor q)$ rather than $(p(\,) \lor q(\,))$. All the inference rules of PC are also inference rules of FOL. In addition, there are left and right rules for the quantifiers.

∀−*right*
$A_{t/v}$ is the result of replacing all free instances of v by a fresh name t.
$\underline{A_{t/v};}$
(∀v A);

The ∀–*right* rule contains a novelty; a **side condition**, '$A_{t/v}$ *is the result of replacing all ....*' when placed on the inference rule, both explicates and restricts its application.

This side condition calls for a **fresh** or arbitrary name. The meaning of 'arbitrary' is a little subtle. In conventional usage to select something arbitrarily is to select it at random. This is not the sense of 'arbitrary' needed here. For instance, one could 'prove' that all numbers are odd by arbitrarily selecting 3 and stating that since 3 is odd and selected arbitrarily, all numbers are odd. This is obviously wrong.

The problem thus arises of how we show that our choice of name is genuinely arbitrary, or arbitrary in sense that allows us to claim that the name chosen stands proxy for all cases. The philosopher's answer is that the object chosen must have no special conditions attached to it. This is correct, but changes the problem into - how are we supposed to recognise that no special assumptions are attached?

The logician supplies a syntactic criterion; the object supplied should be given a unique name, which does not occur anywhere else in the proof; such a name is **fresh**. This shows up immediately what is wrong with the 'proof' that all numbers are odd. We begin with the sequent

$$odd(3) >> \forall x \, odd(x)$$

We select our so-called arbitrary case, 3.

$$odd(3) >> odd(3)$$

However, here the proof fails, since "3" is not a fresh name and so is not arbitrary in the required sense.

The ∀–*left* rule allows the instantiation of a universally quantified formula. Given the assumption '$\forall x \, physical(x)$' (everything is physical), then the assumption 'physical(5)' (the number 5 is physical) can be added.

∀–*left*
$A_{t/v}$ is the result of replacing all free instances of v by any term t.
$\underline{A_{t/v}, (\forall v \, A) >> P;}$
$(\forall v \, A) >> P;$

The ∃-*right* rule states that an existentially quantified succeedent can be proved if some instance of can be proved. '$\exists x \, prime(x)$' can be proved if some instance e.g. '$prime(5)$' can be proved.

∃–*right*
$A_{t/v}$ is the result of replacing all free instances of v by any term t.
$\underline{A_{t/v};}$
$(\exists v \, A);$

The ∃-*left* rule states that an existentially quantified hypothesis can be replaced by some arbitrary instance.

∃–*left*
$A_{t/v}$ is the result of replacing all free instances of v by a fresh name t.
$A_{t/v}, \gg P;$
$(\exists v\, A) \gg P;$

In justification, consider the proposition; '$\exists x\; man(x)$'. As one of a list of assumptions, this statement may be replaced by '$man(c)$' as long as 'c' is fresh. The validity of this move can be justified by pointing out that if we know that something is a man, then there is no harm in stating 'and let c be the man in question', provided that no assumptions are smuggled in about c.

18.5 Proof Trees and Goal Stacks

Framed in terms of sequents, each inference rule maps a sequent S to a series of sequents $S_1,...,S_n$ where S is valid if $S_1,...,S_n$ are all valid. Such a process can be represented in the form of a **tree**, a familiar computing data structure, whereby S is a node and $S_1,...,S_n$ are daughter nodes. In automated deduction, S is sometimes called the **goal** and $S_1,...,S_n$ are **subgoals**. In order to avoid an infinite regress, it must be supposed that some sequents can be treated as valid without generating daughter nodes.

A **proof tree** is a labelled tree which at the root contains the sequent that is to be solved, sometimes called the **proof obligation**. The labels on the tree are the inference rules to be invoked in the proof. When a sequent is solved then that path on the tree is sealed with ☐. Figure 18.2 shows a sequent proof from our version of PC.

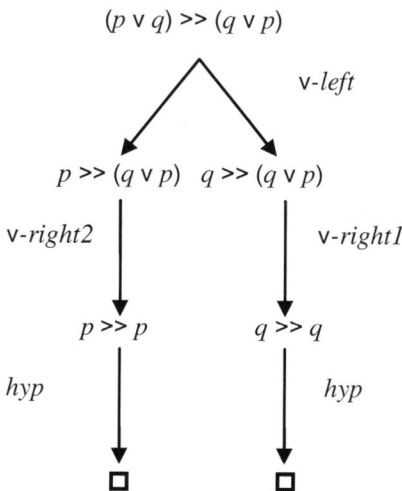

$$(p \vee q) \gg (q \vee p)$$

∨-*left*

$$p \gg (q \vee p) \quad q \gg (q \vee p)$$

∨-*right2*   ∨-*right1*

$$p \gg p \quad\quad q \gg q$$

hyp   *hyp*

☐   ☐

Figure 18.2 A tree proof of $(p \vee q) \gg (q \vee p)$

In producing a proof with the aid of a computer, at any stage in a the proof, the computer will be trying to prove one of the nodes on the proof tree. A simple way of keeping track of them is to place them all in a list and work from the front. Such a list is a **stack**; i.e. a series of elements in which elements are always added (pushed) or removed (popped) from the front. A stack to keep track of goals in a proof is a **goal stack**. Every proof begins with the proof obligation as the only goal on the goal stack. At any stage in the proof, the only available goal is the goal at the front of the stack.

It is important to see the difference between a proof tree and a goal stack. A proof tree keeps the entire history of the proof process, including the proof obligation that started the proof off. The goal stack only keeps those goals that remain to be solved. At the end of the proof, the proof tree is a record of the way the proof was done. At the end of proof, the goal stack is merely an empty stack. A proof tree does not correspond to a single stack, but rather a series of stacks, where each stack results from its predecessor by some act of inference. A goal stack is thus a snapshot of the leaves of a growing proof tree. This is illustrated in figure 18.3, which shows how a proof tree changes and grows in relation to the goal stack.

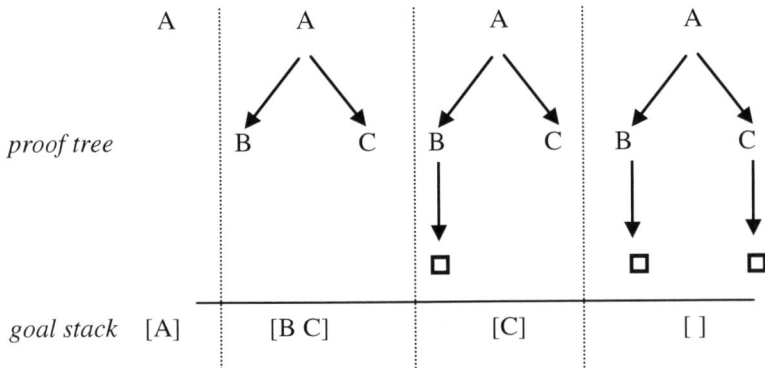

	A	A	A	A
proof tree				

goal stack   [A]   [B C]   [C]   [ ]

Figure 18.3 Representing the state of a proof tree using a stack

The computational advantages of a goal stack are that it is simple to represent as a list, and efficient in terms of memory usage, since it does not retain those parts of the proof tree which are irrelevant to the completion of the proof. Shen maintains such a stack in the implementation of type checking.

18.6 Implementing a Stack Based System: Proplog

We'll now look at the implementation of a very simple stack based reasoning program based on a very simple logic called **Proplog** (Maier and Warren (1988)). Proplog is a subset of PC suitable for automated reasoning on the computer. In fact Proplog is precisely the propositional subset of **Horn clause logic,** (studied in chapter 22), an important subset of first-order logic and significant for forming the basis of logic programming and type checking in Shen.

We introduce Proplog here as a way of both preparing the ground for the examination of Horn clause logic in chapter 22 and to illustrate the implementation of a stack-based sequent theorem prover. The syntax of Proplog is simple.

1. A propositional variable on its own is a formula of Proplog. This is generally referred to as an **atom** or a **fact** in logic programming
2. A conjunction of Proplog atoms is a Proplog formula
3. If A is either a conjunction of Proplog atoms or an atom and B is an atom then $(A \rightarrow B)$ is a Proplog formula. This is referred to as a **rule** in logic programming.

If we allow first-order atoms to supplant Proplog atoms then what we derive is precisely Horn clause logic.

There are three sequent rules for Proplog

hyp

P >> P;

→-left
$(P \rightarrow Q) >> P$;
$(P \rightarrow Q) >> Q$;

&-*right*
P;
Q;

(P & Q);

A Proplog context consists of a set of rules and facts and a Proplog succeedent is an atom or a conjunction of atoms. In order to automate Proplog inferencing on the computer, a **control strategy** had to be developed for applying these inference rules. The simplest strategy is to place the proof obligation $\Delta >> Q$ on a stack S and perform **backward chaining** (figure 18.4).

A Backward Chaining Proof Procedure for Proplog

Do until success or failure

1. If S = [] signal success and halt.
2. If S = [S_1 | S_n] and S_1 = Δ >> Q then
    a. If Q ∈ Δ set S to S_n. (*hyp*)
    b. If Q = (Q_1 & Q_2), set S to [Δ >> Q_1; Δ >> Q_2; | S_n] (&-*right*).
    c. If (P → Q) ∈ Δ, set S to [Δ >> P; | S_n] (→-*left*).
    d. Else signal failure and halt.

Figure 18.4 The Proplog proof procedure

Here is a simple schematic problem to illustrate the approach. The assumptions are

$(p \rightarrow q), (r \rightarrow q), ((s \& t) \rightarrow r), (u \rightarrow r), ((s \& v) \rightarrow r), v, s.$

We can prove q by backward chaining as follows:-

Begin with *q*.
  Prove *q* by proving *r*.
   Prove *r* by proving (*s* & *v*).
    Prove *s*.
    Prove *v*.
    Signal success and halt.

As a proof tree this is shown in figure 18.5.

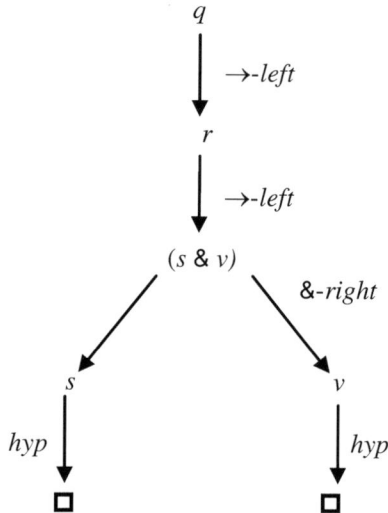

Figure 18.5 A completed proof tree

The snag comes in programming the computer to do proofs like this, because in the above proof we unconsciously avoided the obvious dead ends (like trying to prove q by using $(p \rightarrow q)$). These dead-ends are called **failure nodes** and are sometimes marked by a single daughter node ∎. A failure node is a node of the proof tree which cannot be closed with a ☐, nor can it be extended to produce subgoals. A proof tree cannot count as a completed proof if it contains a failure node.

Since the computer has no intelligence of its own, we need to program some technique into it to avoid being stuck in failure nodes. The problem is that our proof procedure is non-deterministic; it assumes that the right choice of rule is always made without providing any means of finding it.

The solution we will follow is to order all the choices open to the computer and try each one in the ordering, backtracking if needed to try a new choice. The backtracking we will use is chronological backtracking to the last point at which a goal was solved.

Implementing a backward chaining inference engine of the kind needed is an eleven line program in Shen (figure 18.6). To make things even easier for us, we arrange to maintain the context as a separate argument because the nature of the proof process in Proplog means that the context never changes.

```
(define backchain
   Context Succeedent  -> (backchain* Succeedent Context Context))

(define backchain*
   P [P | _] _ -> true \\ hyp
   [P & Q] _ Context
   -> (and (backchain* P Context Context)
           (backchain* Q Context Context)) \\ &-right
   Q [[P => Q] | Hypotheses] Context
   -> (or (backchain* P Context Context) \\ →-left
          (backchain* Q Hypotheses Context)) \\ choice point!
   _ _ _ -> false)
```

Figure 18.6 Backward chaining for Proplog implemented in Shen

18.7 Soundness and Completeness

Our little program is an example of an **inference engine** or **theorem-prover** for Proplog. A theorem-prover is a program that is designed to automate the process of formal proof. Let us write $\Delta \gg_{Proplog} P$ to mean that from a context Δ, the conclusion P can be derived by the rules of inference for Proplog. Let us write $\Delta \gg_{program} P$ when P can be derived from Δ using our program. What is the relation between $\gg_{Proplog}$ and $\gg_{program}$? One desirable relation is

If $\Delta \gg_{program} P$ then $\Delta \gg_{Proplog} P$

This should certainly be true for any Δ and P; if our program says that P follows from Δ, then, according to the rules of inference for Proplog, we should be able to derive P from Δ. A theorem-prover which has this property is said to be **sound**. The converse relation is

If $\Delta \gg_{Proplog} P$ then $\Delta \gg_{program} P$

A theorem-prover with this property is said to be **complete**. If a theorem-prover is both sound and complete and guaranteed to terminate then it constitutes a decision procedure for the formal system in question. If no such theorem-prover exists then the system is said to **undecidable**.

Backward chaining with chronological backtracking is complete as a proof procedure provided that:-

1.   there is no proof tree which has a branch which can be grown to infinity and
      …
2.   … at any stage in a proof there are only a finite number of ways that the proof tree can be grown.

Our theorem-prover for Proplog is sound but incomplete because condition 1. is not met. For example, the problem

$$\text{(backchain [[p => q] [r => q] [q => r] [[s \& v] => r] v s] r)}$$

causes an infinite loop, even though the conclusion is derivable from the assumptions according to the rules of inference of Proplog. The reason why is that assumptions [r => q] [q => r] are used by our theorem-prover to backward chain from r to form a branch which can be infinitely extended.

$$r \longrightarrow q \longrightarrow r \longrightarrow q \longrightarrow r \longrightarrow \quad \ldots\ldots$$

The construction of a complete and terminating theorem-prover for Proplog requires detecting and trapping these loops; a not too difficult problem that is left as an exercise to this chapter.

Exercise 18

1. Give proof trees for the following

   a. $\forall x\ (F(x) \rightarrow \sim G(x)),\ \forall x(H(x) \rightarrow G(x)) >> \forall x\ F(x) \rightarrow \sim(H(x))$
   b. $\forall x\ (F(x) \lor G(x)) \rightarrow H(x),\ \forall x\ \sim(H(x)) >> \forall x\ \sim F(x)$
   c. $\forall x(G(x) \rightarrow \sim H(x)),\ \exists x(F(x)\ \&\ G(x)) >> \exists x\ F(x)\ \&\ \sim(H\ (x))$
   d. $\forall x(F(x) \lor G(x)) \rightarrow H(x),\ \exists x \sim(H(x)) >> \exists x \sim(F\ (x))$
   e. $\forall x \forall y \forall z\ F(x,y,z) >> \forall z \forall y \forall x\ F(x,y,z)$
   f. $\forall x \exists y \forall z F(x,y,z) >> \forall x \forall z \exists y F(x,y,z)$
   g. $\exists x \exists y \forall z\ F(x,y,z) >> \forall z \exists y \exists x\ F(x,y,z)$
   h. $>> \exists y \exists x(F(x)) \rightarrow (F(y)))$
   i. $>> \forall x \exists y(R(x,y) \rightarrow \exists x \exists y R(x,y))$
   j. $R(x,x),\ \forall x \forall y \forall z((R(x,y)\ \&\ R(y,z)) \rightarrow R(x,z))$
      $>> \forall x \forall y(R(x,y) \rightarrow \sim(R(y,x)))$
   k. $>> \exists y(\exists x(F(x)) \rightarrow (F(y)))$

2. Write a proof assistant for FOL based on the rules given here.

3. *Can you to some degree automate your proof assistant so that it gives advice on what to do or even does it for you?

Further Reading

The best introduction to the material in this chapter is Tarver (2014).

The sequent based notation used to define types in Shen was introduced by Gentzen (1934), and Diller (1990) and Duffy (1991) provide good introductions to the use of this notation in modern logic.

There are many introductions on FOL including Hodges (1977) which is based on (non-automated) tableau. For a natural deduction treatment see Lemmon (1978); and Mendelson (1987) for a Hilbert (or axiomatic) approach. Smullyan (1968) and Fitting (1990) deals with tableau; Fitting provides Prolog code for implementing it. Beckert and Posegga (1997) implement a high-performance Prolog version.

Tarver (1992) described a machine learning algorithm to get the computer to learn to use sequent calculus. The experiment was conducted on a theorem-prover for PC and uses genetic programming techniques. Lopes (1998) developed this algorithm for a range of systems including modal, intuitionistic and second-order logics and showed that in certain cases, the computer-generated programs were superior to the humanly created ATPs for the same logic.

Proof assistants based on sequent calculus include, Gordon, Milner and Wadsworth (1979)., Constable et al (2012) and Paulson (1990). Milner was responsible for introducing the idea of tactics for proof assistants that automated proof steps in a type secure way.

19 Concrete Types

19.1 Enumeration Types

In the previous chapter , we covered the elements of sequent calculus. In this chapter, we begin to use sequent calculus to define types within programs beginning with the simplest type - an **enumeration type.** There are a finite number of inhabitants of an enumeration type which are given by stating each one. For example the days of the week can be stated as an enumeration type.

if $x \in \{$ "Monday", "Tuesday", "Wednesday", "Thursday", "Friday", "Saturday", "Sunday"$\}$
    then x : day

Written in sequent calculus, this statement emerges as seven axioms

---

"Monday" : day;

"Tuesday" : day;

"Wednesday" : day;

"Thursday" : day;

"Friday" : day;

"Saturday" : day;

"Sunday" : day;

In Shen derivation rules are entered in the form (datatype *<name>* *<derivation rules>*), where the *<name>* is a symbol and the *<derivation rules>* are written in sequent notation. Conventionally the name of the datatype is generally used as *<name>*. A notational convenience is that Shen does not require typings (i.e. expressions of the form X : A) to be entered with the outer brackets in datatype definitions. The underlines in are represented in Shen by 1 or more underscores

---
.

```
(1+) (datatype day

_____
"Monday" : day;
_____
"Tuesday" : day;
_____
"Wednesday" : day;
_____
"Thursday" : day;
_____
"Friday" : day;
_____
"Saturday" : day;
_____
"Sunday" : day;)
type#day

(2+) "Sunday"
"Sunday" : string

(3+) "Sunday" : day
"Sunday" : day

(4+) "Mardi": day
type error
```

Figure 19.1 Recognising days of the week

The effect of this datatype definition is to allow these strings to be of more than one type: "Sunday" is both of type string and of type day. This string now exhibits overloading or what Strachey called *ad hoc polymorphism* mentioned in chapter 17. It belongs to two types which are not instances of any type less general than the universal type A which is the type of all objects that have some type or other.

Entering "Sunday" to the Shen top level returns the verdict that "Sunday" : string. Given that "Sunday" is overloaded, Shen always defaults to the base type if possible. To get Shen to agree that "Sunday" is now also of type day, a typing must be entered (figure 19.1).

The definition works, but 7 axioms occupy a deal of space which was not reflected in our set theory notation. Side conditions enable derivation rules to be condensed. There are two forms of side condition in Shen – **tests** and **local assignments**; we deal with the use of local assignments in 19.5 but by far the most common side conditions are tests.

A test side condition uses the if keyword which, placed before the derivation rule and followed by some boolean expression *E* creates a side-condition. If *E* evaluates to false when the derivation rule is applied, then the derivation rule fails in its application. Figure 19.2 shows the use of a test to shorten the definition of the datatype day.

```
(datatype day

if (element? Day ["Monday" "Tuesday" "Wednesday"
                  "Thursday" "Friday" "Saturday" "Sunday"])
_____
Day : day;)
```

Figure 19.2 Using a side condition to simplify a definition

Once we have defined day, we can define month.

```
(datatype month

if (element? Month ["January" "February" "March"  "April"
                    "May" "June" "July" "August" "September"
                    "October" "November" "December"])
_____
Month : month;)
```

And we can easily write a function that maps a number from 1-12 to a month.

```
(define decode-month
   {number --> month}
    1 -> "January"
    2 -> "February"
    3 -> "March"
    4 ->  "April"
    5 -> "May"
    6 ->  "June"
    7 -> "July"
    8 -> "August"
    9 ->  "September"
   10 -> "October"
   11 -> "November"
   12 ->  "December")
```

Side-conditions permit us to define types where itemising each inhabitant by name is unacceptable for practical purposes. For example, we might have a list of 50,000 employees in a file and wish to define an employee as a member of this list.

```
(datatype employee

        if (element? E (read-file "employees.txt"))
        _____
        E : employee;)
```

It is also common to find that **intervals** are commonly used in programming because it often transpires that an entry must fall within a certain interval to be admitted for computation. For example, we may insist that employees must be aged between 18 and 64.

```
(datatype age

if (number? Age)
if (>= Age 18)
if (<= Age 64)
_____
Age : age;)
```

Figure 19.3 Age as an interval type

These formulations have in common with enumeration types the feature that their specification can be done using only axioms; we can call them **axiomatic types** of which enumeration types are a special case.

19.2 Left and Right Rules

Enumeration types are the simplest examples of defined types and employ only axioms in their formulation. More complex types require derivation rules that are not axioms. We consider as a case in point a database system for a company which holds employee details, including the department in which they work.

The list of acceptable departments is [wages recruitment sales advertising]. We add this as an enumeration type to the previous types

```
(datatype department

if (element? D [wages recruitment sales advertising])
_____
D : department;)
```

An employee record is a list composed of a name (a string), an age (a number) and a department (a symbol) in which the person works. Our database is a list of such records. We want a database retrieval function get-age which given a person's name and our database extracts the person's age from it.

A record is a list, but it is not a homogeneous list, being composed of three different types. We need to define it and we wish to assert proposition Φ

Φ: [N A D] : record if and only if N : string and A : age and D : department

Such an assertion cannot be made within an axiom but requires premises. In sequent notation we write

```
(datatype record

  N : string; A : Age; D : department;
  [N A D] : record;)
```

Now equipped we write our **get-age** function

```
(define get-age
  {string --> (list record) --> number}
  _ [] -> (error "no details for this name~%")
  N [[N A D] | _] -> A
  N [_ | Records] -> (get-age N Records))
```

When we enter this function to Shen we get the result

type error in rule 2 of get-age

Why has this happened? The answer is that our derivation rule is too weak to capture the 'if and only if' in Φ. What we have asserted is Φ_R.

Φ_R: if N : string and A : age and D : department then [N A D] : record

To validate our function we need more information. Line 2 states

N [[N A D] | _] -> A

But by knowing [N A D] : record we cannot deduce A : age according to what we have entered. To complete the formalisation we have to add that from [N A D] : record as an hypothesis we can derive N : name and A : age and D : department. We want to capture

Φ_L: if [N A D] : record then N : string and A : age and D : department

The second rule captures the other side of the equivalence

```
(datatype record

  N : string; A : Age; D : department;
  [N A D] : record;

  N : string, A : Age, D : department >> P;
  [N A D] : record >> P;)
```

Now the function checks and compiles. Note that commas separate the hypotheses in the premise.

Looking at what we have done, we have in fact treated records in the same manner in which logical constants were treated in the previous chapter. To complete the definition of a record we have had to construct a right rule and a left rule. The original rule was a R rule, dealing with decomposing record types in the consequent. The rule above is a L rule, dealing with the decomposition of the record type as a hypothesis. Both are needed to make the program work.

Symmetrical right-left pairs like this are very common and Shen uses the Clarke-Reeves shorthand introduced in chapter 18 to combine such rules into an LR rule. Because of keyboard restrictions the double underlines are replaced by one or more equals signs.

```
(datatype record

N : string; A : Age; D : department;
===========================
[N A D] : record;)
```

There is an alternative way of doing all this; represent records as tuples. A record is then an object of type (string * age * department) and get-age becomes.

```
(define get-age
  {string --> (list (string * age * department)) --> age}
  _ [] -> (error "no details for this name~%")
  N [(@p N A D) | _] -> A
  N [_ | Records] -> (get-age N Records))
```

This works fine, although typing '(string * age * department)' is rather a bore compared to typing 'record'. Shen permits us to define our own shorthand for types. (synonyms $t_1,...,t_n$) where n is even defines a shorthand for types so that every t_i, where i is odd, is a symbol and every t_{i+1} is the type which defines it. Hence we can avoid always typing '(string * age * department)' by entering at the top of any file containing our program.

```
(synonyms record (string * age * department))
```

After this Shen will **demodulate** (replace) record within every type entered or loaded by (string * age * department). The two techniques seem almost equivalent in effect and for most cases they are, however there are subtle differences between using an LR rule to define a type and using synonyms. The latter is rather stronger as we shall see in the next section.

19.3 Handling Global Variables

Global variables need to be declared with respect to their type. To declare a global variable *test* to be of type (list number), the type of the value of *test* has to be declared of type (list number).

```
(datatype some-globals
  _____
  (value *test*) : (list number);)
```

An interesting example provided by Aditya Siram shows how using synonyms differs from using the corresponding LR rule. Siram defined *test* as

(datatype some-globals

    ——————————
    (value *test*) : numbers;)

Where numbers was taken as a synonym for (list number). However the expression (head (value *test*)) did not return a number as expected but a type error.

The source of the error was the definition of numbers which was defined as

```
X : (list number);
=============
X : numbers;
```

This definition is equivalent to

```
X : (list number) >> P;
X : numbers >> P;
```

```
X : (list number);
X : numbers;
```

Here the first (L) rule is no use to the proof of (head (value *test*)) : number. Let us try to prove (head (value *test*)) : number from (value *test*) : numbers, the R rule above and the type for head. Applying the rule for head first derives (value *test*) : (list number) which cannot be proved by the R rule. However if the ordering of the LR rule was reversed to

```
X : numbers;
============
X : (list number);
```

then (head (value *test*)) would typecheck. But far better is to declare numbers and (list number) to be synonyms.

(synonyms numbers (list number))

The example shows two important things. First that LR rules are not indifferent with respect to ordering; these two forms are not equivalent

$$\frac{\alpha}{\beta} \quad \text{and} \quad \frac{\beta}{\alpha}$$

Second an LR rule is not logically equivalent to the corresponding synonyms declaration; these two forms are not equivalent.

(synonyms α β)   and   α
                                     ===
                                     β

19.4 Recursive Types (I): the Lambda Calculus

The user-defined types studied so far are non-recursive; they consist either of atoms or finite or homogeneous sequences of non-recursive objects. But some of the data objects manipulated in the previous chapters are not like that. We shall look at two cases from the previous chapters.

1. The lambda calculus interpreter of chapter 14.
2. The Proplog theorem prover of chapter 18.

The lambda calculus interpreter was designed to evaluate lambda expressions represented as nested lists. To type check such a program we need to manipulate recursive types.

The simplest lambda expression is a symbol which is not lambda. An application is a two element list [x y] where x and y are lambda expressions and an abstraction is a three element list [lambda x y] where x is a symbol which is not lambda and y is a lambda expression. Figure 19.4 lays this out in Shen. The fact that lambda-expr occurs both in the premises and the conclusion of the last two rules defining it marks out lambda-expr as recursive.

```
(datatype lamba-expr

          if (not (= X lambda))
          X : symbol;
          _____
          X : lambda-expr;

          X : lambda-expr; Y : lambda-expr;
          =================================
          [X Y] : lambda-expr;

          if (not (= X lambda))
          X : symbol; Y : lambda-expr;
          ============================
          [lambda X Y] : lambda-expr;)
```

Given this type we can annotate the lambda calculus evaluator of chapter 14 with the right types (19.4).

```
(define aor
  {lambda-expr --> lambda-expr}
  [lambda V [E V]] -> E        where (not (free? V E))
  [lambda X Y] -> [lambda X (aor Y)]
  [[lambda X Y] Z] -> (let Alpha (alpha [lambda X Y])
                           (aor (beta Alpha (aor Z))))
  [X Y] -> (let AOR (type [(aor X) (aor Y)] lambda-expr)
             (if (= AOR [X Y])
                 AOR
                 (aor AOR)))
  X -> X)

(define free?
  {lambda-expr --> lambda-expr --> boolean}
  V V -> true
  V [lambda V _] -> false
  V [lambda _ Y] -> (free? V Y)
  V [X Y] -> (or (free? V X) (free? V Y))
  _ _ -> false)

(define alpha
  {lambda-expr --> lambda-expr}
  [lambda X Y] -> (let V (gensym x)
                     [lambda V (replace X (alpha Y) V)])
  [X Y] -> [(alpha X) (alpha Y)]
  X -> X)

(define beta
  {lambda-expr --> lambda-expr --> lambda-expr}
  [lambda X Y] Z -> (replace X Y Z))

(define replace
  {lambda-expr --> lambda-expr --> lambda-expr --> lambda-expr}
  X [lambda X Y] _ -> [lambda X Y]
  X X Z -> Z
  X [Y Y*] Z -> [(replace X Y Z) (replace X Y* Z)]
  X [lambda Y Y*] Z -> [lambda Y (replace X Y* Z)]
  _ Y _ -> Y)
```

Figure 19.4 A type secure lambda calculus evaluator

A demonstration.

```
(5+) (aor [[lambda x x] a])
a : lambda-expr

(6+) (aor [[lambda x [x x]] a])
[a a] : lambda-expr

(7+) (aor [[lambda x [lambda y x]] y])
[lambda x1220 y] : lambda-expr
```

19.5 Recursive Types (II): Proplog

This example is a little more complex than the lambda calculus case; mainly because there is an asymmetry between Proplog succeedents and the hypotheses used to process them. Succeedents are essentially conjunctions or atoms, but hypotheses are either atoms or implications.

Let's begin by tackling atoms and conjunctions. A Proplog atom is a symbol other than & or =>.

```
if (not (element? P [& =>]))
P : symbol;
P : atom;
```

We make atoms a limiting case of conjunctions – a conjunction with only one proposition in it.

```
P : atom;
P : conjunction;
```

In all other cases a conjunction is defined recursively

```
P : conjunction; Q : conjunction;
=========================
[P & Q] : conjunction;
```

An implication is one form of hypothesis; being composed of an conjunction, an implication sign and an atom.

```
P : conjunction; Q : atom;
===================
[P => Q] : hypothesis;
```

An hypothesis can be an atom.

```
P : atom;
P : hypothesis;
```

Putting all this into a datatype definition and entering it allows the program of chapter 18 to be type checked. Notice that == is used in this program to test the equality of objects under different types.

```
(define backchain
  {(list hypothesis) --> conjunction --> boolean}
  Context Succeedent -> (backchain* Succeedent Context Context))

(define backchain*
  {conjunction --> (list hypothesis) --> (list hypothesis) --> boolean}
  P [Q | _] _ -> true         where (== P Q) \\ hyp
  [P & Q] _ Context
  -> (and (backchain* P Context Context)
          (backchain* Q Context Context)) \\ &-right
  Q [[P => Q] | Hypotheses] Context
  -> (or (backchain* P Context Context) \\ &-left
         (backchain* Q Hypotheses Context)) \\ choice point!
  Q [_ | Hypotheses] Context -> (backchain* Q Hypotheses Context)
  _ _ _ -> false)
```

Figure 19.5 Proplog as a type secure program

A short demonstration.

```
(5+) (backchain [p q [[p & q] => r]] r)
true : boolean

(6+) (backchain [[s => r] p [p => q] [q => r]] r)
true : boolean

(7+) (backchain [[s => r] [p => q] [q => r]] r)
false : boolean
```

19.6 Dynamic Type Checking

We now consider the simulation of a simple calculator. Our calculator program takes numbers or lists and evaluates them to a number result (figure 19.6). Having loaded the program and set it running, we can calculate the answers to problems like [88.9 + 8.7] and [56.8 * [45.3 - 21.7]].

```
(define do-calculation
  [X + Y] -> (+ (do-calculation X) (do-calculation Y))
  [X - Y] -> (- (do-calculation X) (do-calculation Y))
  [X * Y] -> (* (do-calculation X) (do-calculation Y))
  [X / Y] -> (/ (do-calculation X) (do-calculation Y))
  X -> X)
```

Figure 19.6 A calculator function

However, as soon as type checking is switched on, entering the program produces a type error, because do-calculation is designed to deal with mixed lists and strong typing does not allow such lists. Recursive types provide a way of tackling this problem (figure 19.7).

```
(datatype arith-expr

X : number;
X : arith-expr;

if (element? Op [+ - * /])
X : arith-expr; Y : arith-expr;
========================
[X Op Y] : arith-expr;)
```

Figure 19.7 An attempt at defining a datatype of arithmetic expressions

Armed with these datatype rules, we define our calculator (figure 19.8).

```
(2+) (define do-calculation
      {arith-expr --> arith-expr}
      [X + Y] -> (+ (do-calculation X) (do-calculation Y))
      [X - Y] -> (- (do-calculation X) (do-calculation Y))
      [X * Y] -> (* (do-calculation X) (do-calculation Y))
      [X / Y] -> (/ (do-calculation X) (do-calculation Y))
      X -> X)
type error: rule 1 of do-calculation
```

Figure 19.8 An erroneous attempt to produce a type secure calculator

do-calculation fails to type check because + produces numbers and not arith-exprs as required by our type assignment. Suppose we change the type of do-calculation to arith-expr → number.

```
(3+) (define do-calculation
      {arith-expr --> number}
      [X + Y] -> (+ (do-calculation X) (do-calculation Y))
      [X - Y] -> (- (do-calculation X) (do-calculation Y))
      [X * Y] -> (* (do-calculation X) (do-calculation Y))
      [X / Y] -> (/ (do-calculation X) (do-calculation Y))
      X -> X)
type error: rule 5 of do-calculation
```

Figure 19.9 Another erroneous attempt to produce a type secure calculator

Now the final rewrite rule fails to typecheck because Shen finds that it cannot prove that the input X is a number from the assumption that X is an arith-expr (remember that our rules say that all numbers are arith-exprs; not that all arith-exprs are numbers).

Our solution is to use a **tag** to mark out the numbers within an arith-expr. Figure 19.10 introduces the tag num as a way of marking out numbers.

```
(datatype arith-expr

     X : number >> Y : A;
     [num X] : arith-expr >> Y : A;

     X : number;
     [num X] : arith-expr;

     if (element? Op [+ - * /])
     X : arith-expr; Y : arith-expr;
     ======================
     [X Op Y] : arith-expr;)
```

Figure 19.10 Using tags

This solution works with the following definition of do-calculation.

```
(define do-calculation
  {arith-expr --> number}
  [X + Y] -> (+ (do-calculation X) (do-calculation Y))
  [X - Y] -> (- (do-calculation X) (do-calculation Y))
  [X * Y] -> (* (do-calculation X) (do-calculation Y))
  [X / Y] -> (/ (do-calculation X) (do-calculation Y))
  [num X] -> X)
```

The use of tags makes for confusing reading - typing in [[num 2] + [num 3]] is a counterintuitive way of adding 2 and 3. **Verified objects** make life easier. A verified object is an object that inhabits the type verified. The inhabitation rule for this type is: X : verified just when the normal form of X is true. No self-evaluating object of Shen is recognised as belonging to this type - not even true! At this point you will wonder what the point of such a type is.

Actually, this type is very useful. When Shen dynamically type checks definitions that include guards, it assumes that if the rule fires, then the guard must evaluate to true and hence Shen assumes that, in that circumstance, the guard is of the type verified. For instance, we can assume that if an input X passes the guard (number? X) (which tests for numberhood) that X is a number so, we can write:

     _____
     (number? X) : verified >> X : number;

If we insert this rule in the datatype rules for arith-expr, and place a guard in the do-calculation function, then the whole thing typechecks.

```
(datatype  arith-expr

    _____
    (number? X) : verified >> X : number;

    X : number;
    X : arith-expr;

    if (element? Op [+ - * /])
    X : arith-expr; Y : arith-expr;
    ====================
    [X Op Y] : arith-expr;)

(define do-calculation
    {arith-expr --> number}
    [X + Y] -> (+ (do-calculation X) (do-calculation Y))
    [X - Y] -> (- (do-calculation X) (do-calculation Y))
    [X * Y] -> (* (do-calculation X) (do-calculation Y))
    [X / Y] -> (/ (do-calculation X) (do-calculation Y))
    X -> X                      where (number? X))
```

Figure 19.11 A type secure version of do-calculation using verified objects

19.7 Analytic and Synthetic Rules

A sequent rule is **analytic** just when every variable that occurs above the line in the rule either occurs below the line or is bound in a local assignment using let. When a variable occurs above the line which neither occurs below the line nor is bound in a local assignment within a side condition then that variable is said to be **free**. An analytic rule is thus a rule that contains no free variables. Most datatype rules used in sequent rules are analytic, and in fact all the examples used so far are analytic rules.

A **synthetic** rule is a rule that is not analytic and thus does contain free variables. A simple example of such a rule is the rule defining couples which are two element lists of possibly diverse types.

```
    X : A; Y : B;
    [X Y] : couple;
```

In this definition A and B are free variables standing for any given type. Shen programmers working with advanced types will eventually encounter synthetic rules and should be aware of the pitfalls of dealing with them. There is nothing specifically toxic about such rules if they are properly understood, but one mistake is common with such rules.

In defining a synthetic rule, it is important to grasp the interplay between the free variables and their position in the sequent. For example it seems intuitive that the proper definition of the type couple of two element list of different objects should be

```
X : A; Y : B;
=========
[X Y] : couple;
```

Recall that the double underline is really only a conventional shorthand and that the above rule is really asserting two inference rules.

```
X : A; Y : B;
[X Y] : couple;

X : A , Y : B >> P;
[X Y] : couple >> P;
```

However the second rule is wrong; it asserts that from the assumption that [X Y] : couple that X : A and Y : B for *any* A and for *any* B can be inferred. Essentially the free variables A and B now stand proxy for any type. The correct rule asserts that from the assumption that [X Y] : couple that X : A and Y : B for *some* A and for *some* B can be inferred.

Shen allows the use of local assignments within side conditions. Since the nature of A and B is not fixed; the correct rendition uses gensym to generate arbitrary symbols for these types.

```
let A (gensym a)
let B (gensym b)
X : A , Y : B >> P;
[X Y] : couple >> P;
```

The new version uses local assignments to bind the free variables to arbitrary values indicating that the identity of A and B are not known. The new rule is now analytic.

Exercise 19

1. Define the enumeration type coin for British coinage and type check the next-denomination function in chapter 3 using this type (count 0 as of type coin for this question).

2. [a [b c d] [e] [f]] describes a tree

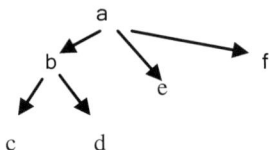

Define tree as a polymorphic type operator which can take a type argument; the type of the above is (tree symbol). Define

a. A function leaves that takes an object of type (tree A) and returns a list of leaves of type (list A).
b. A function size of type (tree A) --> number that returns the number of nodes in the tree.
c. A function paths of type (tree A) --> (list (list A)) that returns all the paths from the root node.
d. A function nodes of type (tree A) --> (list A) that returns the list of nodes in the tree.
e. A function subtree? of type (tree A) --> (tree A) --> boolean that tests to see if the first argument is a subtree of the second. Here [b c d] is a subtree.
f. A function prune of type (tree A) --> (tree A) --> (tree A) that removes the first argument as a subtree from the second.
g. A function graft of type (A --> A --> boolean) --> (tree A) --> (tree A) that orders the daughters of every node by an ordering relation R so that if x precedes y as a daughter then Rxy.

3. Devise a database which takes employee records of the form Id (number), Name (string) Age (a number from 18 to 100), Position (worker, manager, tycoon), Wages (fixed as 10,000 for workers, 30,000 for managers and 1000,000 for tycoons). Create the following functions.

h. A function find of type number --> database --> record that takes an id and the database and returns the record that holds the person's details.
i. A function payroll of type database --> number that totals the wages for the company.
j. A function level of type position --> (list string) that returns the list of all those people in that position in alphabetical order.
k. A function year of type age --> (list string) that returns the list of all those people of that age in alphabetical order.

Further Reading

Enumeration types are found in all the main statically typed functional languages including ML (Wikstrom, 1988) and Haskell (Thompson, 1999). The use of sequent calculus to define types is not a feature of those languages and the algebraic approach (discussed in chapter 21) is used instead.

Web Sites

http://homepages.inf.ed.ac.uk/stg/NOTES/node79.html gives a good account of abstract datatypes in ML. http://www.haskell.org/haskellwiki/Abstract_data_type provides the equivalent for Haskell.

20 Proof and Control

Type checking is computationally expensive, sometimes involving hundreds of thousands of inferences for a single program. The Shen type checker executes at the rate of many thousands of such inferences per second, but even so there can be instances where the type checker spends a longer time than necessary validating the program. In some cases, type checking may be subject to timeout. This almost always occurs at the site of a type error; hence localising and fixing these errors is often the key to avoiding timeouts.

This chapter deals with techniques for controlling the search space in Shen type theories and improving the performance of type checking. Specifically we will

1. See how to adjust the timeout feature.
2. See how to use cuts to control the search space.
3. See how to use type annotations to guide the type checker and to improve the performance of our code.
4. How to use mode declarations to control potential infinite loops.
5. How to use the Shen spy tool for tracing the type checker at work.
6. How to order type rules to get the maximum performance.
7. The use of preclude and include to marshal type theories.

20.1 Controlling Timeout

By default Shen includes a timeout feature that cuts off the type checker when it has expended more than a million inferences in solving a problem. When this occurs, the process is aborted and the error

maximum inferences exceeded

is raised. In 9 out of 10 of cases, when this message arises then the type checker has encountered a type error and is backtracking furiously in an attempt to find some non-existent solution.

It is possible to reset the timout limit by the maxinferences function that receives a number n and sets the limit at n. However, generally, increasing n will have little effect other than to delay the return of a negative response. It is better at this point, to roll up one's sleeves and seek the source of the error.

20.2 Using spy to Trace Type Checking

When Shen raises a type error or experiences timeout then the messages it raises give a strong indication as to the location of the error.   If a type error is raised then the message

type error in rule n of f

is often raised. If you have experienced timeout, then the timeout message will be preceded by a series of messages about the functions that have been successfully type checked.   Hence your error will be certainly located immediately after the last expression that has been successfully type checked.

If you have examined the offending expression and cannot determine the source of the problem, then it is best to turn on the spy feature.

The spy feature is enabled by (spy +) and disabled by (spy -). When enabled, the spy feature will print off interactively the steps of reasoning that the type checker is making. At each step, spy will display the problem it is working on and pause the process. Each step is printed as a sequent; that is, as a consequent to be proved and a list of hypotheses from which it is to be proven.

Starting with a simple example; we want to type check a list of two numbers [1 2]; the list is converted to cons form and printed out as a consequent (cons 1 (cons 2 ())) : Var2. There are no hypotheses. The variable Var2 is a place holder for a type; the proof obligation is

Prove there exists a value for Var2 *such that* (cons 1 (cons 2 ())) : Var2

With spying enabled Shen prints out this problem.

```
(8+) (spy +)
true : boolean

(9+) [1 2]
                                                                 3 inferences
?- (cons 1 (cons 2 ())) : Var2

>
```

Figure 20.1 Tracing the type checker

The proof will be a **constructive existence proof**; that is, we not only want to demonstrate that there is such a value, we want to do so by finding a specific value that does the job.[64] Hitting RETURN to the > prompt moves the proof on.

```
_____ 12 inferences
?- 1 : Var5
```

The proof now focuses on the first item; effectively Shen has applied the rule

$$X : A; Y : (list\ A);$$
$$\overline{(cons\ X\ Y) : (list\ A);}$$

Hitting RETURN moves the proof on again.

```
_____ 16 inferences
?- (cons 2 ()) : (list number)
```

The transition from the previous step to this one is important. The variable has disappeared and the type checker is hunting for a list of numbers. How did this happen? Effectively the type checker is armed with the following rule.

$$\frac{if\ (number?\ N)}{N : number;}$$

The conclusion N : number is compared to the consequent of the previous problem which is 1 : Var5. The variable Var5 is bound to number and the binding is transmitted to the rest of the proof.

Once the type checker has grasped the right direction, the proof runs smoothly. The inference counter does not go up in increments of one, because Shen makes several low level inference steps which are not displayed here.

```
_____ 21 inferences
?- 2 : number

>
_____ 25 inferences
?- () : (list number)

>
[1 2] : (list number)
```

---

[64] The difference can be thought of in these terms; if we are investigating a suspicious death we may prove that it was a murder and hence somebody was the murderer without knowing who. A constructive existence proof of the murder would produce the actual murderer.

Here is another example involving a simple numerical function

```
(4+) (define double
      {number --> number}
      N -> (* 2 N))
_____ 3 inferences
?- (define double { number --> number } N -> (* 2 N)) : Var2

>
_____ 23 inferences
?- &&N : number

1. &&N : Var9

>
```

We assume &NN is of type number and prove ((* 2) &&N) (the curried form) is of type number. &&N is a placeholder for an arbitrary object.

```
_____ 33 inferences
?- ((* 2) &&N) : number

1. &&N : number
2. double : (number --> number)

>
_____ 43 inferences
?- (* 2) : (Var15 --> number)

1. &&N : number
2. double : (number --> number)

>
_____ 52 inferences
?- * : (Var17 --> (Var15 --> number))

1. &&N : number
2. double : (number --> number)

>
_____ 55 inferences
?- 2 : number

1. &&N : number
2. double : (number --> number)
>
_____ 59 inferences
?- &&N : number

1. &&N : number
2. double : (number --> number)

double : (number --> number)
```

Generally it is useful to place (spy +) into your file immediately before the expression that triggers the type failure. In that way spy is invoked only at the point of failure and not throughout the entire program.

20.3 Using Cuts

Suppose we have defined a type constant to mean any boolean, string, symbol or number. We can write this as follows.

(datatype constant

V : boolean;
V : constant;

V : string;
V : constant;

V : number;
V : constant;

V : symbol;
V : constant;)

constant is effectively a sum of a series of **subtypes** boolean, string etc. Moreover all these subtypes are disjoint because nothing can be an inhabitant of two different subtypes of constant. However if we track a proof involving constant, we find that in cases of type failure, the type checker will backtrack through all these cases even though success in one of these cases means that the remainder are not worth considering.

The **cut,** written !, controls the unrestricted backtracking so that these unnecessary cases are not considered. Syntactically, the cut will fit anywhere a premise will fit. Proof theoretically any goal which is a cut succeeds. However if the control backtracks to the point at which the cut was called, then all rules which are subsequent to the cut in the datatype in which the cut was invoked will not be considered as alternatives for that choice point.[65] Effectively the cut commits the type checker to the choice in which it occurs (figure 20.2).

---

[65] Students of Prolog will recognise the similalrity to the Prolog cut. In fact, the cut here is compiled into a Prolog cut. See chapters 23 and 24 for details.

(datatype constant

V : boolean; !;
V : constant;

V : string; !;
V : constant;

V : number; !;
V : constant;

V : symbol; !;
V : constant;)

Figure 20.2 Using cuts in a type

The above cuts are **green** because they makes the process of proof more efficient but do not change what is derivable. A **red cut** changes what is derivable and is often the result of a mistake in the placing of !. Here is an example

(datatype constant

!; V : boolean;
———————
V : constant;

!; V : string;
———————
V : constant;

!; V : number;
———————
V : constant;

!; V : symbol;
———————
V : constant;)

Here as soon as the type checker encounters the first rule, the cut causes the proof to be committed to that choice *before* it is established that V is a boolean. Hence effectively the cut has eliminated all the other rules apart from the first one from the definition of constant.

20.4 Type Annotations

The 'function' type is one of the 46 primitives in Kλ. type receives two arguments; first an expression e of some kind and secondly a type t. The result returned is the normal form of e, but if type checking is enabled, then the typechecker will typecheck $e : t$. Used within a function definition type places the constraint that e has to be proved to be of type t (figure 20.3).

```
(11 +) (type (+ 8 9) number)
17 : number

(12+) (type (+ 6 7) symbol)
type error

(13+) (define paren
        {A --> (list A)}
         X -> [(type X number)])
type error in rule 2 of paren
```

Figure 20.3 Using type

In cases where the user wants to disambiguate his intention, it can be occasionally useful to annotate the program with this function. The scare quotes in the opening sentence to this section are an indication that type is not a function in the sense that append or cons are, but is a construction that is handled in a special way by the compiler – rather as define is.

20.5 preclude and include

The next method is a means for controlling large search spaces when there are a great many types in use. Generally in large Shen programs, the program is generally the product of more than one hand. In such a case, the programmer working on one part of the system might actually use only a fragment of the type discipline of the whole system. Nevertheless, the type checker, unless instructed, will slog through the program armed with the entire type system.

The commands preclude, include, preclude-all-but and include-all-but allow the programmer to optimise the type checker to the program at hand. Thus it is possible to have a massive type system in Shen and programs of many thousands of lines, and yet type check them in reasonable speed by configuring the type checker to ignore those types whose rules are not needed.

The command preclude accepts a list of symbols which are names of datatypes or synonyms and sets them aside from use in type checking. Placing the command (preclude [lazylist]) at the head of a file will cause the type checker to ignore the rules for the lazylist datatype. The command (include [lazylist]) works the opposite way, placing the rules back into the type environment. The command (preclude-all-but [lazylist]) will preclude all user defined datatypes apart from lazy lists, whereas (include-all-but [lazylist]) will include all user defined datatypes apart from lazy lists. Reasonably enough, (preclude-all-but [ ]) will set aside all user defined datatypes and (include-all-but [ ]) will include all of them.

20.6 Ordering Rules: Subtypes

A is a **subtype** of B when every *x* that inhabits A, inhabits B. We can say that integers are a subtype of numbers.

(datatype integer

  if (integer? N)
  _____
  N : integer;

N : integer;
_____
N : number;)

This does the trick; but a more general method is to define subtype as a type operator

(datatype subtype

(subtype A B); X : A;
_____
  X : B;)

We can then simply write as an axiom

_____
(subtype integer number);

And then treat integers just like other numbers.

(8+) (+ (input+ integer) (input+ integer))
5
6
11 : number

The power and simplicity of this approach is beguiling; it does conceal one pitfall. Lets define a type integer as a subtype of numbers. If we type

(define increment-integers
  {(list integer) --> (list number)}
   L -> (map (+ 1) L))

then we get a type error; which *prima facie* we should not, since integers are simply a type of number. If we track this proof then we get this:

```
(8+) (define increment-integers
      {(list integer) --> (list number)}
      L -> (map (+ 1) L))
```
_____ 3 inferences
```
?- (define increment-integers { (list integer) --> (list number) }
      L -> (map (+ 1) L)) : Var2

>
```
_____ 23 inferences
```
?- &&L : (list integer)

1. &&L : Var9

>
```
_____ _____ 32 inferences
```
?- ((map (+ 1)) &&L) : (list number)

1. &&L : (list integer)
2. increment-integers : ((list integer) --> (list number))
```
_____ 41 inferences
```
?- (map (+ 1)) : (Var15 --> (list number))

1. &&L : (list integer)
2. increment-integers : ((list integer) --> (list number))

>
```
_____ 50 inferences
```
?- map : (Var17 --> (Var15 --> (list number)))

1. &&L : (list integer)
2. increment-integers : ((list integer) --> (list number))

>
```
_____ 53 inferences
```
?- (+ 1) : (Var19 --> number)

1. &&L : (list integer)
2. increment-integers : ((list integer) --> (list number))

>
```
_____ 62 inferences
```
?- + : (Var22 --> (Var19 --> number))

1. &&L : (list integer)
2. increment-integers : ((list integer) --> (list number))

>
```
_____ 65 inferences
```
?- 1 : number

1. &&L : (list integer)
2. increment-integers : ((list integer) --> (list number))

>
```

```
_____ 69 inferences
?- &&L : (list number)

1. &&L : (list integer)
2. increment-integers : ((list integer) --> (list number))

>
_____ 84 inferences
?- (subtype Var30 (list number))

1. &&L : (list integer)
2. increment-integers : ((list integer) --> (list number))
```

Past this point the proof fails since (subtype Var30 (list number)) is not provable. A little later the computer tries &&L >> (list integer) >> &&L : (list number) which also fails, and for the same reasons. In fact given that A is a subtype of B and x : (ƒ A), the conclusion x : (ƒ B) is not formally derivable from our subtype definition. This also holds for any type operator ƒ, not merely list. There are several ways round this; we can redefine increment-integers so that the list is decomposed item by item into its elements

```
(define increment-integers
  {(list integer) --> (list number)}
  [] -> []
  [N | Ns] -> [(+ 1 N) | (increment-integers Ns)])
```

which works fine. Alternatively we can define a function that coerces a list of integers to a list of numbers.

```
(define intlist->numlist
  {(list integer) --> (list number)
  [] -> []
  [N | Ns] -> [N | (intlist->numlist Ns)])
```

and the original definition of increment-integers becomes

```
(define increment-integers
  {(list integer) --> (list number)}
  L -> (map (+ 1) (intlist->numlist L)))
```

So we can invoke this definition of subtype if we are willing, in perhaps a few cases, to work around the limits of our short definition in this manner.

Subtypes, whether explicitly defined using a subtype operator as in this example, or simply by listing the special cases are computationally expensive; for example here is a case where the inferences stack up.

```
(datatype expr

          E : symbol;
          E : expr;

          E : number;
          E : expr;

          E : boolean;
          E : expr;

          E : string;
          E : expr;

          E : expr; Es : (list expr);
          ==================
          [E | Es] : expr;)
```

Given any problem of the form (cons x ... y) : expr, Shen will first attempt to prove that (cons x ... y) is a symbol, a number ... etc. before using the final LR rule to decompose the expression. In such cases significant improvement can be found by simply placing the LR rule first in these list of rules.

20.7 Controlling Infinite Loops: Mode Declarations

In section 20.3 we defined a type constant as composed of several subtypes. Melvin has a better idea; define a type operator union so that X : (union string symbol boolean number) states in one rule what took four separate rules to do previously. But what are the rules for union? Having learnt macros, Melvin decides to make union a 2-place type operator and rely on macros to insert the missing elements.

```
(defmacro union-macro
 [union W X Y | Z] -> [union W [union X Y | Z]])
```

So far, so good. Now the rules for union; Melvin knows that there should be a left and a right rule for union. Melvin's right rule states that you can prove X : (union A B) if you can prove X : A.

Rule a

```
X : A;
X : (union A B);
```

Spurred on, Melvin adds the other right rule

Rule b

```
X : B;
X : (union A B);
```

The left rule follows the familiar pattern for disjunction

Rule c

X : A >> P;
X : B >> P;
———————————
X : (union A B) >> P;

Placing these all into a datatype definition; Melvin tries it out. At first it works beautifully.

```
(5+) [1 a]
[1 a] : (list (union number symbol))

(6+) (@v 1 a 2 b <>)
<1 a 2 b> : (vector (union number symbol))
```

But then when Melvin types an expression in that should produce an error, the type checker goes into an infinite loop and the top level topples over.

```
(7+) (* 1 a)

*** - Program stack overflow. RESET
*** - Program stack overflow. RESET
```

Now let's see, courtesy of **spy**, what happens when Shen is supplied with the rule for **union** and (* 1 a) is checked. The initial stages are routine, the expression is curried and checked as ((* 1) a).

```
(4+) (* 1 a)
                                                    3 inferences
?- ((* 1) a) : Var2

>
                                                    12 inferences
?- (* 1) : (Var5 --> Var2)

>
                                                    17 inferences
?- * : (Var7 --> (Var5 --> Var2))

>
                                                    20 inferences
?- 1 : number

>
                                                    24 inferences
?- a : number
```

This proof obligation cannot be discharged, and after this point, the computer becomes involved in futile attempts to discharge the proof. None of these work and lead to an infinite regress. The reasons are clear in the structure of Melvin's rules. Let x be any expression which is not type secure (like $((* 1) a)$). We begin by trying to constructively prove that $x : V$ for some V. Since V is a variable we can invoke the conclusion of *rule a* on it; i.e.

X : (union A B);

and the new target is X : A – which when instantiated is just $((* 1) a) : A$. But this conclusion is essentially just what we started with, except with a change of variable. Hence the computer repeats this move *ad infinitem*.

One way of stopping this is to constrain the inferences the computer is allowed to make using **mode declarations**.

(datatype union

> $\dfrac{X : A;}{X : (mode (union A B) -);}$
>
> $\dfrac{X : B;}{X : (mode (union A B) -);}$
>
> $\dfrac{X : A >> P;\quad X : B >> P;}{X : (mode (union A B) -) >> P;)}$

Figure 20.4 Using mode declarations

The mode declaration (mode ... -) enforces an exact match between the expression in its scope and what it is matched to. In effect, (union A B) cannot be matched to a variable. The consequence is that the bizarre loop goes away. The declaration (mode ... +) restores the default and the innermost mode has priority. Thus (mode (f (mode c +) b) -) would use the default over c but restricted matching over the rest of the formula.

This actually works quite nicely for functions that use Melvin's union types because the explicit typing attached to these functions means that union types appear explicitly in the type and unification is rarely needed. But [1 a] no longer typechecks as (union number symbol), since there is not an exact match. This problem can be circumvented by entering the expression as a typing [1 a] : (list (union A B)) which will trigger the appropriate search.

Further Reading

The use of cut derives from logic programming and is explained in Sterling and Shapiro and Bratko. Mode declarations derive from DEC-10 Prolog, see http://www.cs.cmu.edu/afs/cs/project/ai-repository/ai/lang/prolog/doc/intro/prolog.doc although the mode declarations in DEC-10 Prolog were slightly different. preclude and include relate to the assert and retract predicates of Prolog.

21 Abstract, Semi-Abstract & Algebraic Datatypes

21.1 Concrete and Abstract Datatypes

Our exposition of types has so far ranged only over what are generally referred to as **concrete datatypes**. A concrete datatype is fixed by identifying inhabitants of that type as constructable from a finite number of operations over generally recognised data structures. If we define a database as a concrete datatype, say as an association list, then we identify a database with a specific list structure.

However when we do this we are in fact making a contingent choice about how to represent databases because there are several alternative ways organising data e.g. hash tables and binary trees. It is often useful to be able to build our database program without having to pre-emptively decide on one representation. That is to say, we can construct our database program by building a **barrier of abstraction** between the basic operations needed to drive our database program and how we choose to implement them.

A good example is a **stack**. A stack is a structure into which objects are placed or **pushed** one by one. Objects can also be removed or **popped** one by one. The basic rule governing stacks is that the object popped is the last object that was pushed onto the stack. A concrete example is the magazine of a rifle, in which the last bullet pushed into the magazine is the first to be fired.

First lets see what we know about stacks. We assume that we have a function **empty-stack** for making the empty stack.

(datatype stack

_____
 empty-stack : (--> (stack A));

We also assume that there is an operation **push** that pushes objects on a stack.

_____
 push : (A --> (stack A) --> (stack A));

and finally operations **top** and **pop** that return the object on the top of the stack and pop the stack respectively.

$$\overline{\text{top} : ((\text{stack A}) \dashrightarrow \text{A})};$$

$$\overline{\text{pop} : ((\text{stack A}) \dashrightarrow (\text{stack A}))};$$

We assume the following equations

$(\text{pop } (\text{push } x \text{ s})) = s$
$(\text{top } (\text{push } x \text{ s})) = x$
$(\text{pop } e) = (\text{top } e) = \perp$ where e is the empty stack

$\perp$ signifies the undefined value, generally an error condition, created when we try to pop an empty stack.

We have defined a stack as an **abstract datatype**; that is, as a datatype defined by the types of the functions used to manipulate it and by the equations that describe the behaviour of those functions. The abstract specification is separated from the **concrete implementation** that represents our contingent choice of a particular datatype to play the role of a stack.

For instance one possible concrete representation is to use [] for the empty stack, **cons** for **push** and **head** and **tail** for **top** and **pop** respectively. This is not an inevitable choice; figure 21.1 shows another encoding in which a stack is a lambda expression.

```
(define empty-stack
  _ -> (/. X (if (or (= X pop) (= X top))
              (error "~this stack is empty~%")
              (error "~A is not an operation on stacks.~%"))))

(define push
  X S -> (/. Y (if (= Y pop) S
              (if (= Y top) X
                (error "~A is not an operation on stacks.~%")))))

(define top
  S -> (S top))
```

Figure 21.1 Encoding a stack as an abstract datatype

Lets try it.

```
(3+) (empty-stack)
#<COMPILED-CLOSURE empty-stack-1> : (stack A)

(4+) (push 0 (empty-stack))
#<COMPILED-CLOSURE push-1> : (stack number)

(5+) (push a (push 0 (empty-stack)))
type error

(6+) (top (push 0 (empty-stack)))
0 : number
```

By hiding inessential information on how the abstract datatype is implemented and allowing access to the data structure only through the accessor functions, abstract datatypes build a barrier of abstraction between the essential properties of the datatype and the accidental properties of how we choose to implement it. This in turn, reduces information load and allows flexibility in making changes to the representation without having to rewrite large stretches of code.

21.2 Abstract Datatypes in Sequent Calculus

If we contrast the type theory for stacks in the previous section with the type theory for concrete recursive types like lambda expressions in chapter 19, we see that there are significant differences. The type rules for a concrete datatype are of the form

$$\frac{\varphi_1;...;\varphi_m;}{(C\ x_1\ ...x_n):\ t_0;} \qquad \text{or} \qquad \frac{\varphi_1,...,\varphi_n >> P;}{(C\ x_1\ ...x_n):\ t_0 >> P;}$$

where C is a recognised constructor function for building structures e.g. cons, @p, @s, @v and $\varphi_1;...;\varphi_m$ is some series of typings. Alternatively they are of the form

$$\frac{x:t_1;}{x:t_0;} \qquad \text{or} \qquad \frac{\text{if } (h\ x)}{x:t_0;}$$

stating that an atomic expression has the given type t_0 if it can be proved to belong to some given subtype t_1 or it satisfies some computable test h. The process of typechecking proceeds by recursively decomposing $(C\ x_1\ ...x_n)$ into its components. In the abstract datatype definition nothing like that is presented; only the types of the functions needed to construct, deconstruct and recognise the objects of the type.

Midway between these two cases are cases which involve **semi-abstract** datatypes; where the formalisation of the type theory may make use of both forms of rule. As a case example we will look at the formalisation of Hilbert proof systems.

21.3 A Semi-Abstract Datatype: Proofs in a Hilbert System

A **Hilbert proof system** or Hilbert-Ackermann proof system is characterised by proofs which consist of a series of *steps*, each step being either the instantiation of an axiom scheme or derived from previous steps by some rule of inference. Formally a Hilbert proof system is a triple $<F, A, R>$; where F is a set of formation rules for the wffs of the system, A is a set $\{A_1,...,A_n\}$ of *axiom schemes* such that any uniform substitution for the metavariables in A_i results in a wff called an *axiom* and R is a set of inference rules or functions of the type *wff ... → wff* .

Typically R is a singleton set composed of a single rule *modus ponens* or *mp* which maps p and $p \rightarrow q$ to q. Before the work of Gentzen, Hilbert systems were the basis of much formal work in logic, including Russell and Whitehead's *Principia Mathematica*.

The particular Hilbert system that is studied in this section found in Mendelson's (1997, p.35) formalisation of propositional calculus where it is referred to as system L. System L takes as primitive the connectives ~ and →.. The rules of formation are simple.

1. An atom is any one of p, q, r, p', q', r' ....
2. If A is an atom then A is a wff.
3. If A and B are wffs, then $(\sim A)$, $(A \rightarrow B)$, are wffs.

In our formalisation we will use => for → and allow an atom to be any symbol other than ~ or =>.

```
(define atom?
  {A --> boolean}
  P -> (and (symbol? P) (not (== P =>)) (not (= P ~))))
```

The concrete datatype for wffs in this system is:

```
(datatype wff

 if (atom? P)
 _____
 P : atom;

 P : atom;
 _____
 P : wff;
```

```
P : wff;
========
[~ P] : wff;

P : wff; Q : wff;
============
[P => Q] : wff;)
```

There are three axiom schemes and a rule of detachment for system L (figure 21.2). Each axiom scheme α asserts an infinite set of axioms S_α where $x \in S_\alpha$ just when x is a wff that results from the uniform substitution of all the metavariables in α by wffs.

Axiom Schemes

A1. $(B \rightarrow (A \rightarrow B))$,
A2. $((A \rightarrow (B \rightarrow C)) \rightarrow ((A \rightarrow B) \rightarrow (A \rightarrow C)))$
A3. $(((\sim A) \rightarrow (\sim B)) \rightarrow (((\sim A) \rightarrow B) \rightarrow A))$

Rule of Detachment (*mp*): from A and $(A \rightarrow B)$, derive B.

Figure 21.2 The axiom schemes of system L

Here is a proof.

$\vdash (p \rightarrow p)$

1. $((p \rightarrow ((p \rightarrow p) \rightarrow p)) \rightarrow ((p \rightarrow (p \rightarrow p)) \rightarrow (p \rightarrow p)))$
   by A2 *p/A*, $(p \rightarrow p)$/*B*, *p/C*
2. $(p \rightarrow ((p \rightarrow p) \rightarrow p))$ by A1 $(p \rightarrow p)$/*A. p/B*
3. $((p \rightarrow (p \rightarrow p)) \rightarrow (p \rightarrow p))$ by *mp* 2 1
4. $(p \rightarrow (p \rightarrow p))$ by A1 *p/A, p/B*
5. $(p \rightarrow p)$ by *mp* 4 3

The natural formalisation of these schemes is to consider that they are functions which fill in the slots in a template when supplied by wffs. Accordingly each axiom scheme is represented by a function of type *wff* → ... *wff*.

```
(define scheme1
  {wff --> wff --> wff}
  P Q -> [Q => [P => Q]])

(define scheme2
  {wff --> wff --> wff --> wff}
  P Q R -> [[P => [Q => R]] => [[P => Q] => [P => R]]])

(define scheme3
  {wff --> wff --> wff}
  P Q -> [[[~ P] => [~ Q]] => [[[~ P] => Q] => P]])
```

Likewise, the rule of detachment is also a function of type $wff \rightarrow wff \rightarrow wff$.

```
(define mp*
  {wff --> wff --> wff}
  P [P => Q] -> Q)
```

The crucial aspect of these schemes is that they are involved in the recursive definition of a Hilbert proof. A proof is defined as a series of steps in which each step is either an axiom (i.e. an instance of axiom scheme) or derived from previous steps by *mp*. In order to capture this recursive structure we need to characterise a proof as a list structure built up by certain permitted operations. The operations are not those defined by the familiar constructor functions of cons, @p, @s and @v; they are instead defined using the scheme functions given above. A Hilbert proof therefore shares some of the characteristics of an abstract datatype though in part the specification is concrete i.e. we can see that a Hilbert proof must be a list. Such a type can be called **semi-abstract**.

First an axiom is defined as a substitution instance of an axiom scheme i.e. the result of supplying wffs to the scheme functions. In our terms axioms constitute an abstract datatype.

```
(datatype axiom

  P : wff; Q : wff;
  (scheme1 P Q) : axiom;

  P : wff; Q : wff; R : wff;
  (scheme2 P Q R) : axiom;

  P : wff; Q : wff;
  (scheme3 P Q) : axiom;)
```

A proof is a list structure; the base case is that the proof is empty.

```
(datatype proof

  _____
  [] : proof;  .....
```

Secondly we can add an axiom to the end of the proof and the result is a proof.

```
  Step : axiom; Proof : proof;
  (append Proof [Step]) : proof;
```

Third, applying *modus ponens* to two elements of a proof and adding the result to the end of the proof is also a proof.

```
  M : number; N : number; Proof : proof;
  (append Proof [(mp* (nth M Proof) (nth N Proof))]) : proof;
```

Last, if we are given to assume something is a proof, we can also assume it is a list of wffs.

```
Proof : (list wff) >> P;
Proof : proof >> P;)
```

We can now define and typecheck a function mp that performs *modus ponens* on a proof. If *modus ponens* is misapplied, this function returns the proof unchanged.

```
(define mp
  {number --> number --> proof --> proof}
  M N Proof -> (trap-error (append Proof [(mp* (nth M Proof) (nth N Proof))])
               (/. E (do (output "mp failure~%") Proof))))
```

Similarly these three functions, which involve the axiom scheme functions, generate proofs.

```
(define a1
  {wff --> wff --> proof --> proof}
  P Q Proof -> (append Proof [(scheme1 P Q)]))
```

```
(define a2
  {wff --> wff --> wff --> proof --> proof}
  P Q R Proof -> (append Proof [(scheme2 P Q R)]))
```

```
(define a3
  {wff --> wff --> proof --> proof}
  P Q Proof -> (append Proof [(scheme3 P Q)]))
```

Our top level functon is hilbert which receives a wff to be proved and outputs an annotated proof; that is, a proof together with a list of strings which shows the rules and axioms invoked to justify the step.

```
(synonyms ann string)
```

```
(define hilbert
  {wff --> (proof * (list ann))}
  P -> (hilbert-loop P [] []))
```

This passes control to a function hilbert-loop which first tests to see if the proof is complete and if so returns it together with the annotation. If not, then the proof is printed and the user is asked to supply a rule or axiom which is then used to drive the proof forward. Note the use of (it) to record the user input as a string to be used in the annotation. If the user types **stop** then the proof is aborted.

```
(define hilbert-loop
  {wff --> proof --> (list ann) --> (proof * (list ann))}
  P Proof Ann -> (@p Proof Ann)            where (end-proof? Proof P)
  P Proof Ann -> (let NL (nl)
                   Show (print-proof 1 Proof Ann)
                   Ask (ask)
                   It (it)
                     (if (= It "stop") (error "exit~%")
                         (hilbert-loop P (Ask Proof) (append Ann [It])))
```

```
(define stop
  {proof --> proof}
  X -> X)
```

A proof ends when the final wff is identical to what is to be proved.

```
(define end-proof?
  {(list wff) --> wff --> boolean}
  [P] P -> true
  [_ P | Ps] Q -> (end-proof? [P | Ps] Q)
  _ _ -> false)
```

print-proof prints the proof as a series of annotated steps.

```
(define print-proof
  {number --> (list wff) --> (list ann) --> symbol}
  _ [] [] -> skip
  N [Step | Proof] [Ann | Anns] -> (do (output "~A. ~R   ~A~%" N Step Ann)
                                       (print-proof (+ N 1) Proof Anns)))
```

ask asks for a function that will produce a step; no error is accepted.

```
(define ask
  {--> (proof --> proof)}
  -> (let Prompt (output "~%> ")
       (trap-error (input+ (proof --> proof))
                   (/. E (do (output (error-to-string E))
                             (nl)
                             (ask)))))))
```

Here is 'hilbert' in action.

```
(4+) (hilbert [p => p])
```

```
> (a2 p [p => p] p)
```

```
1. ((p => ((p => p) => p)) => ((p => (p => p)) => (p => p)))   (a2 p [p => p] p)
```

Since a2 has the type *wff* → *wff* → *wff* → *proof* → *proof*; (a2 p [p => p] p) constitutes a partial application of type *proof* → *proof*. The rest of the proof follows the expected pattern.

> (a1 [p => p] p)

1. ((p => ((p => p) => p)) => ((p => (p => p)) => (p => p)))   (a2 p [p => p] p)
2. (p => ((p => p) => p))   (a1 [p => p] p)

> (mp 2 1)

1. ((p => ((p => p) => p)) => ((p => (p => p)) => (p => p)))   (a2 p [p => p] p)
2. (p => ((p => p) => p))   (a1 [p => p] p)
3. ((p => (p => p)) => (p => p))   (mp 2 1)

> (a1 p p)

1. ((p => ((p => p) => p)) => ((p => (p => p)) => (p => p)))   (a2 p [p => p] p)
2. (p => ((p => p) => p))   (a1 [p => p] p)
3. ((p => (p => p)) => (p => p))   (mp 2 1)
4. (p => (p => p))   (a1 p p)

> (mp 4 3)
(@p [[[p => [[p => p] => p]] => [[p => [p => p]] => [p => p]]] [p => [[p => p] => p]] [[p
=> [p => p]] => [p => p]] [p => [p => p]] [p => p]] ["(a2 p [p => p] p)" "(a1 [p => p] p)"
"(mp 2 1)" "(a1 p p)" "(mp 4 3)"]) : (proof * (list string))

21.4 Shen and ML

A reader with experience of other statically typed functional programming like
ML may wonder how the type theory in Shen relates to that in ML. The
characterising notation for most other functional languages, including ML, is
based on the so-called **algebraic datatype** notation. This notation might be more
accurately described as a form of limited BNF.

In ML, a type is described by expressing the formation rules for that type in terms
of simple objects and constructors over types. Thus the suits of a playing deck
are described in ML as

datatype suit = hearts | clubs | diamonds| spades;

which corresponds to the enumeration type

(datatype suit

if (element? suit [hearts clubs diamonds spades])
_____
Suit : suit;)

A recursive type, such as the type of natural numbers, would be expressed in ML
as

datatype natnum = zero | succ of natnum;

and in Shen

(datatype natnum

---
zero : natnum;

Natmum : natnum;
====================
[succ Natnum] : natnum;)

The answer then, to the question of the relations of ML type notation to Shen sequent calculus notation *is that the ML type notation maps into a proper subset of sequent calculus.* Let t be the type that is defined algebraically; then this subset is characterised by the following restrictions. Then either t is an inbuilt type of Shen or it is defined in a sequent calculus such that:

1. Side conditions are not used.
2. t does not contain a pre-existing type.
3. Every R rule has the form

    $s : t;)$

    where s is a symbol which is not a variable.
4. Every LR rule for t has the form

    $x_1 : t_1;...,x_n : t_n;$
    ============
    $[c\ x_1\ ...\ x_n] : t;$

    where $t_1;...,x_n : t_n$ are algebraic types.

We can call this fragment the **algebraic sequent calculus.**

We can introduce ML notation into Shen and arrange for this mapping into algebraic sequent calculus to be done by a macro. For convenience, we change the notation slightly; datatype suit = hearts | clubs | diamonds| spades; becomes (ml-datatype suit = hearts, diamonds, clubs, spades) and datatype natnum = zero | succ of natnum; becomes (ml-datatype natnum = zero, succ of natnum). The code is given in 21.4.

```
(package ml [ml-datatype of ,]

(define parse-ml
  ML-Rules -> (compile (function <ml-rules>) ML-Rules))

(defcc <ml-rules>
  <ml-rule> , <ml-rules> := [<ml-rule> | <ml-rules>];
  <ml-rule> := [<ml-rule>];)

(defcc <ml-rule>
  Constructor of <datatypes> := [Constructor | <datatypes>];
  <datatype> := <datatype>;)

(defcc <datatypes>
  <datatype> <datatypes> := [<datatype> | <datatypes>];
  <e>;)

(defcc <datatype>
  Datatype := Datatype where (not (= Datatype ,));)

(define ml->shen
  Datatype [Constructor | Datatypes] -> (let Vars (map (function var) Datatypes)
                        Conclusion (conclusion Constructor Datatype Vars)
                        Premises (premises Vars Datatypes)
                        (append Premises
                             [=============]
                             Conclusion))
  Datatype Instance -> [_____
                        Instance : Datatype;])

(define conclusion
  Constructor Datatype Vars -> [(cons-form [Constructor | Vars]) : Datatype;] )

(define premises
  [] [] -> []
  [V | Vs] [D | Ds] -> [V : D ; | (premises Vs Ds)])

(define cons-form
  [X | Y] -> [cons (cons-form X) (cons-form Y)]
  X -> X)

(define var
  _ -> (gensym (protect X)))

(defmacro ml-macro
  [ml-datatype Datatype = | ML-Rules] -> [datatype Datatype
                        | (mapcan (/. ML-Rule (ml->shen Datatype ML-Rule))
                          (parse-ml ML-Rules))]) )
```

Figure 21.4 Embedding ML datatypes into Shen

We can demonstrate the effectiveness of our transcription by comparing the ML version with Shen.

Standard ML of New Jersey v110.74 [built: Tue Jan 31 16:19:10 2012]

```
- datatype natnum = zero | succ of natnum;
datatype natnum = succ of natnum | zero
- succ(succ zero);
val it = succ (succ zero) : natnum
- fun add zero n = n
= |    add (succ m) n = (succ(add m n));
val add = fn : natnum -> natnum -> natnum
- add (succ zero) zero;
val it = succ zero : natnum
```

In Shen this appears as

```
 (9+) (ml-datatype natnum = zero, succ of natnum)
type#natnum : symbol

(10+) [succ [succ zero]]
[succ [succ zero]] : natnum

(11+) (define add
      {natnum --> natnum --> natnum}
      zero N -> N
      [succ M] N  -> [succ (add M N)])
add : (natnum --> (natnum --> natnum))

(12+) (add [succ zero] zero)
[succ zero] : natnum
```

When we compare the expressive power of Shen and ML, it is obvious that the elimination of side-conditions and the restrictions placed on the structure of sequent calculus makes ML a less expressive language than Shen. The type of all natural numbers was expressed in 20.6 using side-conditions, but cannot be so expressed in ML. The direct and elegant treatment of Hilbert proofs uses a fragment of sequent calculus outside that allowed by ML.

However there is another aspect of working with algebraic sequent caluclus; which is that absurd and non-terminating rules cannot be added to the type system. We've already seen examples of non-terminating rules. We can also identify derivation rules which allow us to formulate types which collapse the Shen type system; one such is the universe type $ to which supposedly everything belongs.

```
(datatype universal

  _____
  X : $;)
```

This type rule causes (* 3 a) to be evaluated because the expression is taken to inhabit the universe type. This rule is not part of the algebraic sequent calculus because X is a variable.

Similarly

(datatype string

---

3 : string;)

is admissible in Shen, but not in ML or algebraic sequent calculus because string is a pre-existing type. We can also entirely eliminate the type system by declaring everything to be provable.

(datatype anything-goes

P;)

All these rules fall outside the algebraic sequent calculus.

To put the matter succinctly, there is a space of things that can be done in a programming language; some are which are useful, progressive and interesting and some of which are foolhardy and dangerous. What we now know, and see clearly in the gap between Shen and ML, is that these spaces are not *linearly separable*. There is no straight line that leaves the useful and interesting on one side and the foolhardy on the other.[66]

Exercise 21

1. ML is an implicitly typed language whose functions do not need a type within {...}. Design a macro that accepts ML-style functions and compiles them into an internal representation that does not need an attached signature.
2. A theorem in a Hilbert system is any step of a proof. Upgrade the program so that a theorem that has been demonstrated in a past proof can be introduced in a new proof.
3. Design a proof assistant for the sequent calculus system described in chapter 18.
4. Design a database system using the abstract datatype approach. Show how you can use two different approaches to storing and retrieving data using the same type theory.

---

[66] This fact is still not understood in programming circles, and much discussion of Shen and it's predecessor, Qi, was marred by the inability to recognise that a value judgement was being played out under a scientific guise. There is no *scientific* reason to prefer ML to Shen or Shen to ML in this matter.

Further Reading

Helma and Veroff (2005) explore abstract datatypes and the importance of barriers of abstraction is explained in Abelson and Sussman (1996). Mendelson explores system L. Wikstrom (1987) and Paulson (1996) both cover concrete and abstract datatypes in ML.

22 The SECD Machine

22.1 Formal Semantics

In the first part of this book we studied Shen as a programming language, taking for granted the basic operating principles of the language. Such features as pattern matching were introduced by example, rather than being formally defined. From a pedagogic view this makes sense. However in the specification of a language, it is often important to define these operating principles formally and not just by example. The study of how to do this belongs to **formal semantics**.

There are three approaches to formal semantics; operational, denotational and axiomatic. An **operational semantics** for a language L provides the rules by which programs in L are executed. **Denotational semantics** provides a meaning for L programs by mapping then to a denotation which is held to be the meaning of the program. An **axiomatic semantics** for L provides a meaning by mapping the programs in L to some description within a formal language, of which first-order logic is one example. An examination of Shen from all these perspectives would require a book of comparable size to this one, and so for reasons of space we will limit ourselves to examining Shen from the operational perspective.

We asserted that an operational semantics is important without explaining why. There are two reasons for constructing a formal semantics for a computer language L. The first is to provide a formal basis for making proofs or predictions about L programs. The second is to provide some accurate model for implementing L.

In this chapter we will be concerned with operational semantics from the point of view providing a model of how to implement Kλ. Our operational semantics for interpreting Kλ is based on the SECD machine of Peter Landin. In chapter 25 we cover operational semantics from the other perspective – as a ground for proving the correctness of the type checking algorithm in Shen.

22.2 The Basic SECD Machine

Landin's SECD machine arose out of a landmark paper (Landin (1964)) in which he explained a method for evaluating a restricted lambda calculus which later proved to be immensely influential in the design of functional language compilers. However the relations between the SECD and the lambda calculus are rather indirect. The SECD is not an evaluator for pure λ calculus expressions for several reasons.

1. The output of the SECD is not always a λ calculus expression.
2. The SECD extracts the normal form of λ expressions in WHNF.
3. Because λ calculus applications involving free variables like $(x\ y)$ can raise an error from the SECD.
4. Because the SECD is generally adapted for processing an enriched λ calculus with δ rules.

In practice these restrictions are not so important as they first seem. In order to adapt a pure formalism like lambda calculus to the practical requirements of efficient computation, some additions and also restrictions have to be made to the derivations within those formalisms. We will begin with a basic SECD machine and gradually enrich it to a machine capable of compiling Kλ.

The SECD is most conveniently viewed as a program and so to explain the SECD, we will code directly into Shen. We begin with a version of the SECD directed specifically to λ calculus expressions and λ calculus reasoning. Subsequently we will enrich the SECD to incorporate δ rules.

The objects produced and manipulated by the SECD machine we will call *obs*. An *ob* can be any of the following

1. A λ expression.
2. A closure.

A closure consists of a symbol, an *ob*, and an environment E which associates symbols with *obs*.

```
X : symbol; L : ob; E : environment;
============================
[closure X L E] : ob;
```

An *ob* can be a λ expression, that is a symbol, an application or an abstraction.

X : symbol;
―――――――――
X : ob;

X : symbol; Y : ob;
==============
[lambda X Y] : ob;

X : ob; Y : ob;
==========
[X Y] : ob;

The SECD machine is based on a quadruple <S, E, C, D> comprised of a **stack**, an **environment**, a **control**, and a **dump**. We'll first describe the basic machine and its expression in Shen, before considering how this machine can be augmented to fit the requirements of Kλ.

The stack is a list of *ob*s. The environment is a list of pairs comprised of an identifier (symbol) and an *ob*. The control is another list of *ob*s and the dump is a list of triples composed of a stack, an environment and a control.

```
(synonyms      stack (list ob)
               environment (list (ob * ob))
               control (list ob)
               dump (list (stack * environment * control)))
```

The function of these elements of the SECD is as follows. The stack S maintains the function and the argument to which it is applied (using λ calculus, all functions are 1-place). The environment E contains a list of identifiers which are bound to the *ob*s with which they are paired. The control C contains the expression currently under evaluation and the dump D contains the memory of the previous states of the SECD should these need to be restored.

The SECD program is given in figure 22.1.

```
(define secd
  {ob --> ob}
  X -> (evaluate [] [] [X] []))

(define evaluate
  {stack --> environment --> control --> dump --> ob}
  [Result] E [] [] -> Result
  [X] _ [] [(@p S E C) | D] -> (evaluate [X | S] E C D)
  [[closure X Y E] Z | S] E' [@ | C] D
  -> (evaluate [] [(@p X Z) | E] [Y] [(@p S E' C) | D])
  S E [X | C] D -> (evaluate [(lookup X E) | S] E C D)   where (symbol? X)
  S E [[lambda X Y] | C] D -> (evaluate [[closure X Y E] | S] E C D)
  S E [[F X] | C] D -> (evaluate S E [X F @ | C] D))
```

```
(define lookup
  {A --> (list (A * A)) --> A}
  X [(@p X Y) | _] -> Y
  X [_ | Y] -> (lookup X Y)
  X _ -> X)
```

Figure 22.1 The SECD without δ rules

The transitions of the SECD machine can be described by a function evaluate of type stack → environment → control → dump → ob. The first line states that if the stack contains one element and the control and dump are empty, then the head of the stack is returned.

[Result] E [] [] -> Result

The second line states that if the stack is non-empty and the control is empty but the dump is non-empty, that the dump is to be used to restore the previous values of S, E, and C.

[X] _ [] [(@p S E C) | D] -> (evaluate [X | S] E C D)

The third line states if the stack is topped by a closure an followed by an *ob*, and the leading symbol of the control is @ (indicating that an application on the stack is to be evaluated) then the leading variable of the closure is to be bound to the argument in the environment and the body of the closure becomes the new control, the stack is emptied and the previous states of S, E and C are placed on the dump.

```
[[closure X Y E] Z | S] E' [@ | C] D
         -> (evaluate [] [(@p X Z) | E] [Y] [(@p S E' C) | D])
```

Fourth, if a symbol is found at the head of the control, that the value of the symbol is to be found in the environment and placed on the stack. If there is no such value, the value of the symbol is the symbol itself.

S E [X | C] D -> (evaluate [(lookup X E) | S] E C D)   where (symbol? X)

```
(define lookup
  {A --> (list (A * A)) --> A}
  X [(@p X Y) | _] -> Y
  X [_ | Y] -> (lookup X Y)
  X _ -> X)
```

Fifth, if the control is fronted by an abstraction, then a closure is to be formed from the bound variable of the abstraction, its body and the current environment and placed on the stack.

S E [[lambda X Y] | C] D -> (evaluate [[closure X Y E] | S] E C D)

Sixth, if the control is headed by an application then the elements of the application are placed in reverse order on the control followed by the application symbol @. If the operator is placed after the operands in this manner then the notation is said to be in postfix or **reverse Polish**.

S E [[F X] | C] D -> (evaluate S E [X F @ | C] D)

The evaluation of an *ob* X begins by evaluating (evaluate [] [] [X] []).

We add to the definition of evaluate, a rule that shows a window on the evaluation process.

```
S E C D <- (do (output "S = ~R~%E= ~R~%C = ~R~%D = ~R~%"
                    S E C D)
           (read-byte (stinput))
           (fail))        where (value *track*)
```

22.3 Computing with the SECD Machine

The basic SECD can compute (secd [[[lambda x [lambda y x]] a] b]) returning the normal form which is a. The following is a trace of the basic SECD machine with a commentary.

> (secd [[[lambda x [lambda y x]] a] b])

The initial step begins with placing the expression to be evaluated on the control.

```
S = ()
E = ()
C = ((((lambda x (lambda y x)) a) b))
D = ()
```

The application is then placed in reverse Polish.

```
S = ()
E = ()
C = (b ((lambda x (lambda y x)) a) @)
D = ()
```

The argument b to the lambda expression is placed on the stack.

```
S = (b)
E = ()
C = (((lambda x (lambda y x)) a) @)
D = ()
```

The application is then placed in reverse Polish

S = (b)
E = ()
C = (a (lambda x (lambda y x)) @ @)
D = ()

The argument a to the lambda expression is placed on the stack.

S = (a b)
E = ()
C = ((lambda x (lambda y x)) @ @)
D = ()

The lambda expression is turned into a closure and placed on the stack. The environment is empty of bindings .

S = ((closure x (lambda y x) ()) a b)
E = ()
C = (@ @)
D = ()

Since the @ symbol is now at the top of the control, the closure is applied to the argument a. x is now bound to a and the computation involving b is deferred and placed on the dump.

S = ()
E = ((@p x a))
C = ((lambda y x))
D = ((@p (b) (@p () (@))))

Again the control contains a lambda expression so this is converted to a closure. The stack contains only one element but the dump is not empty.

S = ((closure y x ((@p x a))))
E = ((@p x a))
C = ()
D = ((@p (b) (@p () (@))))

Hence the contents of the dump are retrieved and the closure is applied to b.

S = ((closure y x ((@p x a))) b)
E = ()
C = (@)
D = ()

The result is x which is placed on the control.

S = ()
E = ((@p y b) (@p x a))
C = (x)
D = ((@p () (@p () ())))

x is bound to a, so a replaces x.

```
S = ()
E = ((@p y b) (@p x a))
C = (a)
D = (((@p () (@p () ()))))
```

a is now placed on the stack.

```
S = (a)
E = ((@p y b) (@p x a))
C = ()
D = (((@p () (@p () ()))))
```

The stack contains one element but the dump is not empty. Retrieving the remaining computation from the dump empties the dump and shows that nothing more remains to be done.

```
S = (a)
E = ()
C = ()
D = ()
```

a

Since the control and dump are empty, what remains is the answer and a is returned.

22.4 Adding δ Rules to the SECD Machine

The SECD machine as described is extremely basic, and it uses strict evaluation. As we saw in chapter 14, with strict evaluation it is impossible to compute recursive definitions because the conditional if computes the values for all its arguments. Moreover we have no facility to do arithmetic in any practical way. The simplest solution is to introduce many of these facilities as δ rules to the SECD machine.

The basic types for *stack*, *environment* and *dump* remain the same. But we widen the concept of an *ob* so that an *ob* becomes either an element of the base types (string, symbol, boolean, number) or an empty list or a non-empty list of *ob*s. Such an object is generally referred to in the literature as a **symbolic expression** or **s-expr**. Lastly we also require that closures be considered *ob*s.

```
if (not (= X closure))
[X | Y] : (list ob);
============
[X | Y] : ob;

X : ob; Y : ob; E : environment;
========================
[closure X Y E] : ob;

X : number;
X : ob;

X : boolean;
X : ob;

X : symbol;
X : ob;

X : string;
X : ob;


[] : ob;
```

We will need two special functions whose task it is to reduce *ob*s by δ rules; these will be given declared types.

```
reduce1 : (ob --> ob --> ob);
```

```
reduce2 : (ob --> ob --> ob --> ob);
```

Last, a global variable to hold function definitions within a **global environment**.

```
(value *global*) : environment;
```

The SECD machine in figure 22.2 changes to accommodate function definitions. If a function definition is entered, then the action is to associate a lambda function with the name of the function.

The coding here reflects the fact that defun is a **top level form**; that is, it is designed to be evaluated outside the scope of any other expression.   An alternative approach would be to evaluate definitions within the main body of evaluate, which would allow a definition to be embedded within an expression. Such an arrangement is found within other members of the Lisp family such as Scheme. But here we follow the approach of Kλ.

```
(define secd
 {ob --> ob}
 [defun F [Param | Params] Body]
 -> (newdef F (lambda-form [Param | Params] Body))
 X -> (evaluate [] [] [X] []))

(define lambda-form
 {(list ob) --> ob --> ob}
 [] Body -> Body
 [Param | Params] Body -> [lambda Param (lambda-form Params Body)])

(define newdef
 {ob --> ob --> ob}
  F X -> (do (set *global* [(@p F X) | (value *global*)]) F))

(set *global* [])
```

Figure 22.2 An SECD machine including a global environment

The evaluate function is expanded.

```
(define evaluate
 {stack --> environment --> control --> dump --> ob}
 [Result] E [] [] -> Result
 [X] _ [] [(@p S E C) | D] -> (evaluate [X | S] E C D)
 S E [[if P Q R] | C] D -> (evaluate S E [P if @ Q R | C] D)
 S E [@ | C] D -> (apply S E C D)
 S E [X | C] D -> (evaluate [X | S] E C D)    where (self-evaluating? X E)
 S E [X | C] D -> (evaluate S E [(lookup X E) | C] D) where (isbound? X E)
 S E [[lambda X Y] | C] D -> (evaluate [[closure X Y E] | S] E C D)
 S E [[closure X Y E'] | C] D -> (evaluate [[closure X Y E'] | S] E C D)
 S E [[F | X] | C] D -> (evaluate S E (append (reverse [F | X]) [@ | C]) D))
```

Figure 22.3 An SECD machine including δ rules

The changes are as follows.

1.   **S E [[if P Q R] | C] D -> (evaluate S E [P if @ Q R | C] D)**

     The test part of the conditional is separated from the branches by the apply symbol **@** which allows the test to be evaluated before the branches.

2.   **S E [@ | C] D -> (apply S E C D)**

     If the application symbol arises then control is sent to a special apply function which, amongst other duties, applies the δ rules.

3.   S E [X | C] D -> (evaluate [X | S] E C D)
                          where (self-evaluating? X E)

Here the rule allows any self-evaluating expression to be placed on the stack.

4.   S E [[closure X Y E'] | C] D
     -> (evaluate [[closure X Y E'] | S] E C D)

This rule allows a closure that appears on the control to be placed on the stack. This is necessary for higher-order functions which may take closures as arguments.

5.   S E [[F | X] | C] D
     -> (evaluate S E (append (reverse [F | X]) [@ | C]) D)

This rule extends the treatment of applications from 1-place functions to functions of any arity.

A self-evaluating expression is a member of one of the base types, a cons-cell pair (most usually, a list) or a symbol without a binding in the environment. In this implementation, a cons cell pair is represented as a list [cons-pair *head tail*]

```
(define self-evaluating?
  {ob --> environment --> boolean}
   X  E -> (or (string? X) (number? X) (boolean? X)  (empty? X)
           (cons-pair? X) (and (symbol? X) (not (isbound? X E)))))
```

```
(define cons-pair?
  {ob --> boolean}
   [cons-pair _ _] -> true
   _ -> false)
```

The isbound? and lookup functions follow the expected pattern except the global environment is added to the local one during lookup.

```
(define isbound?
  {ob --> (list (ob * ob)) --> boolean}
   X E -> (isbound-h? X (append (value *global*) E)))
```

```
(define isbound-h?
  {A --> (list (A * A)) --> boolean}
   X [(@p X _) | _] -> true
   X [_ | Y] -> (isbound-h? X Y)
   X _ -> false)
```

```
(define lookup
  {ob --> (list (ob * ob)) --> ob}
   X E -> (lookup-h X (append (value *global*) E)))
```

```
(define lookup-h
  {A --> (list (A * A)) --> A}
  X [(@p X Y) | _] -> Y
  X [_ | Y] -> (lookup-h X Y)
  X _ -> X)
```

The apply function sets up a mutual recursion to evaluate. It incorporates the rule for closures taken from the SECD program in figure 22.1, and adds rules for evaluating conditionals. The final line invokes the δ rules for Kλ.

```
(define apply
  {stack --> environment --> control --> dump --> ob}
  [[closure X Y E] Z | S] E' C D
    -> (evaluate [] [(@p X Z) | E] [Y] [(@p S E' C) | D])
  [if true | S] E [Q _ | C] D -> (evaluate S E [Q | C] D)
  [if false | S] E [_ R | C] D -> (evaluate S E [R | C] D)
  S E C D -> (evaluate (execute S) E C D))
```

execute builds a new stack by applying the δ rules for dyadic and monadic primitives. The δ rules are based on the primitives of Kλ. The rules for list processing reflect the conventions of the program representation.

```
(define execute
  {stack --> stack}
  [cons X Y | S] -> [[cons-pair X Y] | S]
  [cons? [cons-pair _ _] | S] -> [true | S]
  [cons? _ | S] -> [false | S]
  [hd [cons-pair X _] | S] -> [X | S]
  [tl [cons-pair _ Y] | S] -> [Y | S]
  [R X Y | S] -> [(reduce2 R X Y) | S]   where (dyadic? R)
  [P X | S] -> [(reduce1 P X) | S]       where (monadic? P))
```

```
(define reduce1
  {(A --> A) --> A --> A}
  P X -> (P X))
```

```
(define reduce2
  {(A --> A --> A) --> A --> A --> A}
  R X Y -> (R X Y))
```

```
(define dyadic?
  {ob --> boolean}
  X -> (element? X [= > < >= <= + - / * pos cn pr set]))
```

```
(define monadic?
  {ob --> boolean}
  X -> (element? X [string->n n->string simple-error number?
                    string? tlstr get-time read-byte value]))
```

22.4 The δ rules for the SECD machine

A quick check shows the program to work.

```
(15+) (secd [defun square [x] [* x x]])
square : ob

(16+) (secd [square 3])
9 : ob

(17+) (secd [defun factorial [x] [if [= x 0] 1 [* x [factorial [- x 1]]]]])
factorial : ob

(18+) (secd [factorial 7])
5040 : ob

(19+) (secd [defun append [x y] [if [= x []] y [cons [hd x] [[append [tl x]] y]]]])
append : ob

(20+) (secd [[append [cons 1 [cons 2 []]]] [cons 3 [cons 4 []]]])
[cons-pair 1 [cons-pair 2 [cons-pair 3 [cons-pair 4 []]]]] : ob
```

The last two examples show that our SECD machine still requires expressions to be curried if they are not listed as dyadic. In the next section we will make the program easier to use and to trace.

22.5 Creating a Repl

Tracing the execution of the SECD machine is illuminating if space consuming. To make this easier we set up a REPL for the SECD.

```
(define repl
  {--> A}
  -> (let Read (do (output "~%> ") (preproc (input+ ob)))
          Eval (trap-error (secd Read) (/. E [error! (error-to-string E)]))
          Print (if (error? Eval) (print-error Eval) (output "~S~%" Eval))
          (repl)))

(define error?
  {ob --> boolean}
  [error! _] -> true
  _ -> false)

(define print-error
  {ob --> ob}
  [error! Message] -> (output "~A~%" Message))
```

22.5 A REPL for the SECD machine

The REPL contains a pre-processor which curries the input and implements certain identities. These identities allow us to reduce certain Kλ constructions such as and, or, cond, let and freeze. Currying allows us to enter formulae in uncurried form.

```
(define preproc
  {ob --> ob}
  X -> (curry (macros X)))

(define macros
  {ob --> ob}
  [and X Y] -> [if X Y false]
  [or X Y] -> [if X true Y]
  [let X Y Z] -> [[lambda X Z] Y]
  [freeze X] -> [lambda (gensym x) X]
  [cond [true X]] -> X
  [cond] -> [simple-error "case failure"]
  [cond [P Q] | R] -> (macros [if P Q [cond | R]])
  [X | Y] -> [(macros X) | (map (function macros) Y)]
  X -> X)

(define curry
  {ob --> ob}
  [defun F Params Body] -> [defun F Params (curry Body)]
  [R | X] -> [R | (map (function curry) X)]  where (primitive? R)
  [R X Y | Z] -> (curry [[R X] Y | Z])
  [X Y] -> [(curry X) (curry Y)]
  X -> X)

(define primitive?
  {ob --> boolean}
  X -> (element? X [= > < >= <= + - / * pos cn number? string? tlstr cons hd tl if
                    simple-error intern str get-time defun lambda read-byte
                    pr string->n n->string set value]))
```

In order to trace the SECD machine, we'll add a flag *track* set to false which if reset to true causes the SECD to trace out its operation.

```
(value *track*) : boolean;

(set *track* false)
```

track will be invoked in first line of evaluate.

```
(define evaluate
  {stack --> environment --> control --> dump --> ob}
  S E C D <- (do (output "S = ~R~%E = ~R~%C = ~R~%D = ~R~%" S E C D)
                 (read-byte (stinput))
                 (fail))   where (value *track*) ......
```

Since SECD state transitions are very long, even for simple computations, we will use only one example to illustrate the operation of the extended SECD. The task is to compute (map (lambda x (+ x 1)) (cons 1 ())) given the conventional definition of map. The focus of the transitions is bolded for each step.

(42+) (set *track* true)
true : boolean

(43+) (repl)

> [defun map [f x] [if [= x []] [] [cons [f [hd x]] [map f [tl x]]]]]
map

We enter the expression to be computed. The first step curries the expression and places it on the control.

```
> [map [lambda x [+ x 1]] [cons 1 []]]
S = ()
E = ()
C = (((map (lambda x (+ x 1))) (cons 1 ()))))
D = ()
```

Steps 2 and 3 systematically flatten the expression towards reverse Polish form.

```
S = ()
E = ()
C = ((cons 1 ()) (map (lambda x (+ x 1))) @)
D = ()
```

```
S = ()
E = ()
C = (() 1 cons @ (map (lambda x (+ x 1))) @)
D = ()
```

Steps 4-6 pop the expressions from the control and place them on the stack.

```
S = (())
E = ()
C = (1 cons @ (map (lambda x (+ x 1))) @)
D = ()
```

```
S = (1 ())
E = ()
C = (cons @ (map (lambda x (+ x 1))) @)
D = ()
```

```
S = (cons 1 ())
E = ()
C = (@ (map (lambda x (+ x 1))) @)
D = ()
```

Step 8 applies the rule for cons forming a cons-cell pair.

S = ((cons-pair 1 ()))
E = ()
C = ((map (lambda x (+ x 1))) @)
D = ()

Step 9 flattens towards reverse Polish form.

S = ((cons-pair 1 ()))
E = ()
C = ((lambda x (+ x 1)) map @ @)
D = ()

Step 10 forms a closure.

S = ((closure x (+ x 1) ()) (cons-pair 1 ()))
E = ()
C = (map @ @)
D = ()

Step 11 expands map by its lambda definition.

S = ((closure x (+ x 1) ()) (cons-pair 1 ()))
E = ()
C = ((lambda f (lambda x (if (= x ()) () (cons (f (hd x)) ((map f) (tl x)))))) @ @)
D = ()

Step 12 converts the lambda definition to a closure and places it on the stack.

S = ((closure f (lambda x (if (= x ()) () (cons (f (hd x)) ((map f) (tl x))))) ()) (closure x
(+ x 1) ()) (cons-pair 1 ()))
E = ()
C = (@ @)
D = ()

Step 13 applies the closure pushing a deferred computation on the dump.

S = ()
E = ((@p f (closure x (+ x 1) ())))
C = ((lambda x (if (= x ()) () (cons (f (hd x)) ((map f) (tl x))))))
D = ((@p ((cons-pair 1 ())) (@p () (@))))

Step 14 converts the lambda *ob* to a closure and places it on the stack.

S = ((closure x (if (= x ()) () (cons (f (hd x)) ((map f) (tl x)))) ((@p f (closure x (+ x 1)
()))))
E = ((@p f (closure x (+ x 1) ())))
C = ()
D = ((@p ((cons-pair 1 ())) (@p () (@))))

Step 15 retrieves the dump contents.

S = ((closure x (if (= x ()) () (cons (f (hd x)) ((map f) (tl x)))) ((@p f (closure x (+ x 1) ()))))) (cons-pair 1 ()))
E = ()
C = (@)
D = ()

The closure is applied to the argument and the result moved to the control.

S = ()
E = (((@p x (cons-pair 1 ())) (@p f (closure x (+ x 1) ()))))
C = ((if (= x ()) () (cons (f (hd x)) ((map f) (tl x)))))
D = (((@p () (@p () ()))))

Steps 17-29 convert the expression on the control to reverse Polish and the result is placed on the stack.

S = ()
E = (((@p x (cons-pair 1 ())) (@p f (closure x (+ x 1) ()))))
C = ((= x ()) if @ () (cons (f (hd x)) ((map f) (tl x))))
D = (((@p () (@p () ()))))

S = ()
E = (((@p x (cons-pair 1 ())) (@p f (closure x (+ x 1) ()))))
C = (() x = @ if @ () (cons (f (hd x)) ((map f) (tl x))))
D = (((@p () (@p () ()))))

S = (())
E = (((@p x (cons-pair 1 ())) (@p f (closure x (+ x 1) ()))))
C = (x = @ if @ () (cons (f (hd x)) ((map f) (tl x))))
D = (((@p () (@p () ()))))

Step 20 replaces the bound x by its value.

S = (())
E = (((@p x (cons-pair 1 ())) (@p f (closure x (+ x 1) ()))))
C = ((cons-pair 1 ()) = @ if @ () (cons (f (hd x)) ((map f) (tl x))))
D = (((@p () (@p () ()))))

S = ((cons-pair 1 ()) ())
E = (((@p x (cons-pair 1 ())) (@p f (closure x (+ x 1) ()))))
C = (= @ if @ () (cons (f (hd x)) ((map f) (tl x))))
D = (((@p () (@p () ()))))

S = (= (cons-pair 1 ()) ())
E = (((@p x (cons-pair 1 ())) (@p f (closure x (+ x 1) ()))))
C = (@ if @ () (cons (f (hd x)) ((map f) (tl x))))
D = (((@p () (@p () ()))))

The identity on the stack is false.

S = **(false)**
E = (((@p x (cons-pair 1 ())) (@p f (closure x (+ x 1) ()))))
C = (**if @ () (cons (f (hd x)) ((map f) (tl x))))**
D = (((@p () (@p () ()))))

Steps 24 and 25 involve a conditional branch. Since the test is false the 'else' part of the branch is chosen.

S = **(if false)**
E = (((@p x (cons-pair 1 ())) (@p f (closure x (+ x 1) ()))))
C = (**@ () (cons (f (hd x)) ((map f) (tl x))))**
D = (((@p () (@p () ()))))

S = **()**
E = (((@p x (cons-pair 1 ())) (@p f (closure x (+ x 1) ()))))
C = (**(cons (f (hd x)) ((map f) (tl x))))**
D = (((@p () (@p () ()))))

Steps 26-28 progressively apply reverse Polish to the control.

S = ()
E = (((@p x (cons-pair 1 ())) (@p f (closure x (+ x 1) ()))))
C = (**((map f) (tl x)) (f (hd x)) cons @)**
D = (((@p () (@p () ()))))

S = ()
E = (((@p x (cons-pair 1 ())) (@p f (closure x (+ x 1) ()))))
C = (**(tl x) (map f) @** (f (hd x)) cons @)
D = (((@p () (@p () ()))))

S = ()
E = (((@p x (cons-pair 1 ())) (@p f (closure x (+ x 1) ()))))
C = (**x tl @** (map f) @ (f (hd x)) cons @)
D = (((@p () (@p () ()))))

Step 29 replaces x by its value in the environment.

S = ()
E = (((@p x (cons-pair 1 ())) (@p f (closure x (+ x 1) ()))))
C = (**(cons-pair 1 ())** tl @ (map f) @ (f (hd x)) cons @)
D = (((@p () (@p () ()))))

Step 30 and step 31 pushes the result on the stack.

S = **((cons-pair 1 ()))**
E = (((@p x (cons-pair 1 ())) (@p f (closure x (+ x 1) ()))))
C = (tl @ (map f) @ (f (hd x)) cons @)
D = (((@p () (@p () ()))))

S = (tl (cons-pair 1 ()))
E = (((@p x (cons-pair 1 ())) (@p f (closure x (+ x 1) ()))))
C = (@ (map f) @ (f (hd x)) cons @)
D = (((@p () (@p () ()))))

Step 32 applies the δ rule for tl and returns the empty list.

S = (())
E = (((@p x (cons-pair 1 ())) (@p f (closure x (+ x 1) ()))))
C = ((map f) @ (f (hd x)) cons @)
D = (((@p () (@p () ()))))

Step 33 flattens the control. f is bound to a closure and is replaced by such in step 34.

S = (())
E = (((@p x (cons-pair 1 ())) (@p f (closure x (+ x 1) ()))))
C = (**f map** @ @ (f (hd x)) cons @)
D = (((@p () (@p () ()))))

S = (())
E = (((@p x (cons-pair 1 ())) (@p f (closure x (+ x 1) ()))))
C = (**(closure x (+ x 1) ())** map @ @ (f (hd x)) cons @)
D = (((@p () (@p () ()))))

Step 35 moves the closure. Step 36 replaces map by its lambda definition.

S = ((closure x (+ x 1) ()) ())
E = (((@p x (cons-pair 1 ())) (@p f (closure x (+ x 1) ()))))
C = (map @ @ (f (hd x)) cons @)
D = (((@p () (@p () ()))))

S = ((closure x (+ x 1) ()) ())
E = (((@p x (cons-pair 1 ())) (@p f (closure x (+ x 1) ()))))
C = ((lambda f (lambda x (if (= x ()) () (cons (f (hd x)) ((map f) (tl x)))))) @ @ (f (hd x)) cons @)
D = (((@p () (@p () ()))))

Step 37 converts the lambda definition to a closure.

S = ((closure f (lambda x (if (= x ()) () (cons (f (hd x)) ((map f) (tl x))))) ((@p x (cons-pair 1 ())) (@p f (closure x (+ x 1) ())))) (closure x (+ x 1) ()) ())
E = (((@p x (cons-pair 1 ())) (@p f (closure x (+ x 1) ()))))
C = (@ @ (f (hd x)) cons @)
D = (((@p () (@p () ()))))

The closure is applied in step 38 and the result placed on the control. Since the result is a lambda expression, step 39 converts it to a closure and places the new closure on the stack.

S = ()
E = (((@p f (closure x (+ x 1) ())) (@p x (cons-pair 1 ())) (@p f (closure x (+ x 1) ()))))
C = ((lambda x (if (= x ()) () (cons (f (hd x)) ((map f) (tl x))))))
D = (((@p (()) (@p ((@p x (cons-pair 1 ())) (@p f (closure x (+ x 1) ())))) (@ (f (hd x)) cons @))) (@p () (@p () ()))))

S = ((closure x (if (= x ()) () (cons (f (hd x)) ((map f) (tl x)))) ((@p f (closure x (+ x 1)
()))) (@p x (cons-pair 1 ())) (@p f (closure x (+ x 1) ())))))
E = (((@p f (closure x (+ x 1) ())) (@p x (cons-pair 1 ())) (@p f (closure x (+ x 1) ()))))
C = ()
D = (((@p (()) (@p (((@p x (cons-pair 1 ())) (@p f (closure x (+ x 1) ())))) (@ (f (hd x))
cons @))) (@p () (@p () ()))))

Step 40 retrieves the deferred computation from the dump. Step 41 applies the
closure placing the result on the control.

S = ((closure x (if (= x ()) () (cons (f (hd x)) ((map f) (tl x)))) ((@p f (closure x (+ x 1)
()))) (@p x (cons-pair 1 ())) (@p f (closure x (+ x 1) ()))))) ())
E = (((@p x (cons-pair 1 ())) (@p f (closure x (+ x 1) ()))))
C = (@ (f (hd x)) cons @)
D = (((@p () (@p () ()))))

S = ()
E = (((@p x ()) (@p f (closure x (+ x 1) ())) (@p x (cons-pair 1 ())) (@p f (closure x
(+ x 1) ()))))
C = ((if (= x ()) () (cons (f (hd x)) ((map f) (tl x)))))
D = (((@p () (@p (((@p x (cons-pair 1 ())) (@p f (closure x (+ x 1) ())))) ((f (hd x))
cons @))) (@p () (@p () ()))))

In steps 42-47 the leading control expression is flattened and the results placed on
the stack. It is assumed by now these operations are familiar.

S = ()
E = (((@p x ()) (@p f (closure x (+ x 1) ())) (@p x (cons-pair 1 ())) (@p f (closure x
(+ x 1) ()))))
C = ((= x ()) if @ () (cons (f (hd x)) ((map f) (tl x))))
D = (((@p () (@p (((@p x (cons-pair 1 ())) (@p f (closure x (+ x 1) ())))) ((f (hd x))
cons @))) (@p () (@p () ()))))

S = ()
E = (((@p x ()) (@p f (closure x (+ x 1) ())) (@p x (cons-pair 1 ())) (@p f (closure x
(+ x 1) ()))))
C = (() x = @ if @ () (cons (f (hd x)) ((map f) (tl x))))
D = (((@p () (@p (((@p x (cons-pair 1 ())) (@p f (closure x (+ x 1) ())))) ((f (hd x))
cons @))) (@p () (@p () ()))))

S = (())
E = (((@p x ()) (@p f (closure x (+ x 1) ())) (@p x (cons-pair 1 ())) (@p f (closure x
(+ x 1) ()))))
C = (x = @ if @ () (cons (f (hd x)) ((map f) (tl x))))
D = (((@p () (@p (((@p x (cons-pair 1 ())) (@p f (closure x (+ x 1) ())))) ((f (hd x))
cons @))) (@p () (@p () ()))))

S = (())
E = (((@p x ()) (@p f (closure x (+ x 1) ())) (@p x (cons-pair 1 ())) (@p f (closure x
(+ x 1) ()))))
C = (() = @ if @ () (cons (f (hd x)) ((map f) (tl x))))
D = (((@p () (@p (((@p x (cons-pair 1 ())) (@p f (closure x (+ x 1) ())))) ((f (hd x))
cons @))) (@p () (@p () ()))))

S = (() ())
E = (((@p x ()) (@p f (closure x (+ x 1) ())) (@p x (cons-pair 1 ())) (@p f (closure x (+ x 1) ()))))
C = (= @ if @ () (cons (f (hd x)) ((map f) (tl x))))
D = (((@p () (@p ((@p x (cons-pair 1 ())) (@p f (closure x (+ x 1) ())))) ((f (hd x)) cons @))) (@p () (@p () ())))

S = (= () ())
E = (((@p x ()) (@p f (closure x (+ x 1) ())) (@p x (cons-pair 1 ())) (@p f (closure x (+ x 1) ()))))
C = (@ if @ () (cons (f (hd x)) ((map f) (tl x))))
D = (((@p () (@p ((@p x (cons-pair 1 ())) (@p f (closure x (+ x 1) ())))) ((f (hd x)) cons @))) (@p () (@p () ())))

Steps 48 to 50 execute the conditional.

S = (true)
E = (((@p x ()) (@p f (closure x (+ x 1) ())) (@p x (cons-pair 1 ())) (@p f (closure x (+ x 1) ()))))
C = (if @ () (cons (f (hd x)) ((map f) (tl x))))
D = (((@p () (@p ((@p x (cons-pair 1 ())) (@p f (closure x (+ x 1) ())))) ((f (hd x)) cons @))) (@p () (@p () ())))

S = (if true)
E = (((@p x ()) (@p f (closure x (+ x 1) ())) (@p x (cons-pair 1 ())) (@p f (closure x (+ x 1) ()))))
C = (@ () (cons (f (hd x)) ((map f) (tl x))))
D = (((@p () (@p ((@p x (cons-pair 1 ())) (@p f (closure x (+ x 1) ())))) ((f (hd x)) cons @))) (@p () (@p () ())))

S = ()
E = (((@p x ()) (@p f (closure x (+ x 1) ())) (@p x (cons-pair 1 ())) (@p f (closure x (+ x 1) ()))))
C = (())
D = (((@p () (@p ((@p x (cons-pair 1 ())) (@p f (closure x (+ x 1) ())))) ((f (hd x)) cons @))) (@p () (@p () ())))

S = (())
E = (((@p x ()) (@p f (closure x (+ x 1) ())) (@p x (cons-pair 1 ())) (@p f (closure x (+ x 1) ()))))
C = ()
D = (((@p () (@p ((@p x (cons-pair 1 ())) (@p f (closure x (+ x 1) ())))) ((f (hd x)) cons @))) (@p () (@p () ())))

Step 51 retrieves the deferred computation from the dump.

S = (())
E = (((@p x (cons-pair 1 ())) (@p f (closure x (+ x 1) ()))))
C = ((f (hd x)) cons @)
D = (((@p () (@p () ()))))

Steps 52-56 unpack the leading control *ob* and the components are placed on the stack.

S = (())
E = ((@p x (cons-pair 1 ())) (@p f (closure x (+ x 1) ())))
C = ((hd x) f @ cons @)
D = ((@p () (@p () ())))

S = (())
E = ((@p x (cons-pair 1 ())) (@p f (closure x (+ x 1) ())))
C = (x hd @ f @ cons @)
D = ((@p () (@p () ())))

S = (())
E = ((@p x (cons-pair 1 ())) (@p f (closure x (+ x 1) ())))
C = ((cons-pair 1 ()) hd @ f @ cons @)
D = ((@p () (@p () ())))

S = ((cons-pair 1 ()) ())
E = ((@p x (cons-pair 1 ())) (@p f (closure x (+ x 1) ())))
C = (hd @ f @ cons @)
D = ((@p () (@p () ())))

S = (hd (cons-pair 1 ()) ())
E = ((@p x (cons-pair 1 ())) (@p f (closure x (+ x 1) ())))
C = (@ f @ cons @)
D = ((@p () (@p () ())))

Step 57 applies the δ rule for hd.

S = (1 ())
E = ((@p x (cons-pair 1 ())) (@p f (closure x (+ x 1) ())))
C = (f @ cons @)
D = ((@p () (@p () ())))

Step 58 replaces f by the closure to which it is bound; this is then pushed onto the stack in step 59. Step 60 reduces this to the computation (+ x 1) with x bound to 1.

S = (1 ())
E = ((@p x (cons-pair 1 ())) (@p f (closure x (+ x 1) ())))
C = ((closure x (+ x 1) ()) @ cons @)
D = ((@p () (@p () ())))

S = ((closure x (+ x 1) ()) 1 ())
E = ((@p x (cons-pair 1 ())) (@p f (closure x (+ x 1) ())))
C = (@ cons @)
D = ((@p () (@p () ())))

S = ()
E = ((@p x 1))
C = ((+ x 1))
D = ((@p (()) (@p ((@p x (cons-pair 1 ())) (@p f (closure x (+ x 1) ())))) (cons @)))
(@p () (@p () ())))

Steps 61-65 effectively compute 1+1.

```
S = ()
E = ((@p x 1))
C = (1 x + @)
D = ((@p (()) (@p ((@p x (cons-pair 1 ())) (@p f (closure x (+ x 1) ())))) (cons @)))
(@p () (@p () ()))))

S = (1)
E = ((@p x 1))
C = (x + @)
D = ((@p (()) (@p ((@p x (cons-pair 1 ())) (@p f (closure x (+ x 1) ())))) (cons @)))
(@p () (@p () ()))))

S = (1)
E = ((@p x 1))
C = (1 + @)
D = ((@p (()) (@p ((@p x (cons-pair 1 ())) (@p f (closure x (+ x 1) ())))) (cons @)))
(@p () (@p () ()))))

S = (1 1)
E = ((@p x 1))
C = (+ @)
D = ((@p (()) (@p ((@p x (cons-pair 1 ())) (@p f (closure x (+ x 1) ())))) (cons @)))
(@p () (@p () ()))))

S = (+ 1 1)
E = ((@p x 1))
C = (@)
D = ((@p (()) (@p ((@p x (cons-pair 1 ())) (@p f (closure x (+ x 1) ())))) (cons @)))
(@p () (@p () ()))))

S = (2)
E = ((@p x 1))
C = ()
D = ((@p (()) (@p ((@p x (cons-pair 1 ())) (@p f (closure x (+ x 1) ())))) (cons @)))
(@p () (@p () ()))))
```

Again the SECD draws upon the dump to continue the computation in step 66. A cons-cell pair is formed and since there are no more deferred computations the SECD exits with the correct answer after 69 transitions.

```
S = (2 ())
E = ((@p x (cons-pair 1 ())) (@p f (closure x (+ x 1) ())))
C = (cons @)
D = ((@p () (@p () ()))))

S = (cons 2 ())
E = ((@p x (cons-pair 1 ())) (@p f (closure x (+ x 1) ())))
C = (@)
D = ((@p () (@p () ()))))
```

```
S = ((cons-pair 2 ()))
E = ((@p x (cons-pair 1 ())) (@p f (closure x (+ x 1) ()))))
C = ()
D = (((@p () (@p () ()))))

S = ((cons-pair 2 ()))
E = ()
C = ()
D = ()
```

(cons-pair 2 ())

22.6 Quotation and Lexical Scope

Consider these two Kλ functions.

```
(defun f (x y) (g x))
(defun g (x) y)
```

Reasoning by λ calculus and by experiment in the Shen REPL, (f *a b*) returns y for any *a* and *b*. However if we compute say, (f 1 2) in our SECD machine, the answer comes out as 2. Here is a trace.

(18+) (repl)

```
> [defun f [x y] [g x]]
f

> [defun g [x] y]
g

> [f 1 2]
S = ()
E = ()
C = (((f 1) 2))
D = ()

S = ()
E = ()
C = (2 (f 1) @)
D = ()

S = (2)
E = ()
C = ((f 1) @)
D = ()

S = (2)
E = ()
C = (1 f @ @)
D = ()
```

S = (1 2)
E = ()
C = (f @ @)
D = ()

S = (1 2)
E = ()
C = ((lambda x (lambda y (g x))) @ @)
D = ()

S = ((closure x (lambda y (g x)) ()) 1 2)
E = ()
C = (@ @)
D = ()

S = ()
E = ((@p x 1))
C = ((lambda y (g x)))
D = ((@p (2) (@p () (@))))

S = ((closure y (g x) ((@p x 1))))
E = ((@p x 1))
C = ()
D = ((@p (2) (@p () (@))))

S = ((closure y (g x) ((@p x 1))) 2)
E = ()
C = (@)
D = ()

S = ()
E = ((@p y 2) (@p x 1))
C = ((g x))
D = ((@p () (@p () ())))

S = ()
E = ((@p y 2) (@p x 1))
C = (x g @)
D = ((@p () (@p () ())))

S = ()
E = ((@p y 2) (@p x 1))
C = (1 g @)
D = ((@p () (@p () ())))

S = (1)
E = ((@p y 2) (@p x 1))
C = (g @)
D = ((@p () (@p () ())))

```
S = (1)
E = ((@p y 2) (@p x 1))
C = ((lambda x y) @)
D = ((@p () (@p () ())))

S = ((closure x y ((@p y 2) (@p x 1))) 1)
E = ((@p y 2) (@p x 1))
C = (@)
D = ((@p () (@p () ())))

S = ()
E = ((@p x 1) (@p y 2) (@p x 1))
C = (y)
D = ((@p () (@p ((@p y 2) (@p x 1)) ())) (@p () (@p () ())))

S = ()
E = ((@p x 1) (@p y 2) (@p x 1))
C = (2)
D = ((@p () (@p ((@p y 2) (@p x 1)) ())) (@p () (@p () ())))

S = (2)
E = ((@p x 1) (@p y 2) (@p x 1))
C = ()
D = ((@p () (@p ((@p y 2) (@p x 1)) ())) (@p () (@p () ())))

S = (2)
E = ((@p y 2) (@p x 1))
C = ()
D = ((@p () (@p () ())))

S = (2)
E = ()
C = ()
D = ()
```

2

The problem arises when the SECD machine evaluates the symbol y which was bound to 2 in the evaluation of the call to f. Reaching into the subconscious memory of its past computation, the SECD retrieves the value 2 and returns it.

The computation is an example of the dangers of **dynamic scope**. The scope of the binding of y in f extends beyond the **lexical scope** of the expression in which it is introduced to include all free occurrences of this symbol within functions called by and subsequent to f; a feature called **dynamic binding**. In contrast, working according to lexical scope, the binding of y only has force within f and the binding is **lexical binding**.

In the history of Lisp, dynamic binding was used in all early implementations and the author's first experience with Lisp, DEC-10 Lisp in 1986, shared this feature.

Dynamic binding can be useful if there is a need to create symbol-value associations which are dynamically made or unmade depending on the state of the computation. Earlier work implementing Prolog in Lisp (Stickel, 1986) used dynamic binding through the PROGV command which survived in Common Lisp as a medium for dynamic binding.

However with the advent of Steele's work (Sussman and Steele, 1974) on Scheme, the vogue for dynamic binding came to an end. It was recognised that dynamic binding made the behaviour of programs hard to fathom and made formal reasoning about them almost unfeasible. Lexical binding reinstated the idea that functional programming should reflect the lambda calculus.

Another wart is that in our model, as soon as a symbol acquires a binding to a lambda expression, then it is evaluated to such. Thus if we define map as before then the expression [john read the map] (suitably rendered in cons form) will not evaluate to itself but will evaluate to a list in which the final element is the lambda definition of map. In languages like Python, this is in fact standard behaviour. As soon as a symbol acquires a definition it is fixed to that definition. However in Kλ, and in Shen, symbols moonlight in various roles and the principle rules that if we want to give a job to a symbol, we have to say exactly what that job is.

A single convention of **quotation** actually solves both of these problems. Quotation was used in the very first Lisp, Lisp 1.5, as a means of allowing the user to manipulate symbols or lists without being obliged to evaluate any binding of the symbol or (in the case of lists) to evaluate their contents. The device occurs in nearly all members of the Lisp family (though not in Shen). A short discursion on quotation in Common Lisp will help to cement understanding.

In Common Lisp, if a symbol is typed into the REPL, say howdy, then unless the symbol is bound an error is raised. In other words, symbols standing on their own (and not bound in definitions or by lambda etc.) are required to denote something.

This behaviour is a nuisance if the intent is to work just with the symbol itself. Since Common Lisp, like Shen, is designed to be a symbolic processing language, Lispers developed the idea of quotation to facilitate symbol and list manipulation. When a symbol S (or indeed any object) is quoted then the evaluation process stops short of evaluating S and what is returned is simply what is quoted. The function that performs this is quote. Hence though howdy will return an error (unless it is assigned a value), (quote howdy) will return howdy. Generally Lispers use a convenient shorthand for quote – the single quote – and (quote howdy) is written as 'howdy. The list [John reads the map] is written in Lisp as '(John reads the map).

Kλ and Shen obviously follow a different convention. Symbols 'do not do anything unless told' and evaluate to themselves unless the programmer specifically shows that they are to be treated otherwise. howdy evaluates to howdy. We can say that in Kλ and Shen, idle symbols are implicitly quoted. Since idle symbols can be determined lexically, it is easy for the compiler to insert the missing quotes.

Syntactically an idle symbol is any symbol that is not lambda bound or used as a function (i.e. placed at the front of a parenthesised expression). Adapting the SECD to processing quoted *ob*s requires two changes. First an extra rule is added to the evaluate function that dictates a 'hands-off' policy to quoted *ob*s.

S E [[quote X] | C] D -> (evaluate [X | S] E C D)

Second, the preproc function is altered to enforce quoting where needed.

```
(define preproc
  {ob --> ob}
  X -> (quote-free-symbols [] (curry (macros X))))

(define quote-free-symbols
  {(list ob) --> ob --> ob}
  Bound [defun F [Param | Params] Body]
  -> [defun F [Param | Params]
       (quote-free-symbols [F | (append [Param | Params] Bound)] Body)]
  Bound [lambda X Y] -> [lambda X (quote-free-symbols [X | Bound] Y)]
  Bound [R | X]
  -> [R | (map (/. Y (quote-free-symbols Bound Y)) X)]  where (symbol? R)
  Bound [X | Y]
  -> [(quote-free-symbols Bound X)
       | (map (/. Z (quote-free-symbols Bound Z)) Y)]
  Bound X -> [quote X]     where (and (symbol? X)
                                       (not (element? X Bound)))
  _ X -> X)
```

22.6 Adding quotation to the SECD

This regime now enforces lexical binding.

```
(3+) (repl)

> [defun f [x y] [g x]]
f

> [defun g [x] y]
g

> [f 1 2]
y
```

There is one proviso. In an expression like (map reverse (cons 1 ()), the reverse is intended to refer to a function. However with implicit quoting, our SECD machine would not compute this expression because (quote reverse) would not be dereferenced to a lambda expression. In such a case one would need to use the lambda expression (lambda x (reverse x)). Hence Shen recommends that (map (function reverse) (cons 1 ()) be used. Changing the code for this case is not difficult and is left as an exercise to this chapter.

22.7 Lisp-1 vs. Lisp-2

There is a conceptual connection between variable assignment and function definition that was touched on in chapter 7. A function definition can be seen as an assignment of a lambda expression to a symbol. Thus (defun f (x) (g x y)) can be seen as syntactic sugar for (set f (lambda x (g x y))).

In some languages like Scheme and Python, this is precisely true. A consequence is that if an expression like (defun f (x) (g x y)) is entered followed by (set f 7), then the assignment overwrites the function definition. In such languages, a symbol may have only meaning and within the Lisp community these are known as **Lisp-1** languages.

In Common Lisp, (set 'f 7) and (defun f (x) (g x y)) coexist without interference marking Common Lisp as a **Lisp-2** language. In a Lisp-2 language a symbol may have more than one denotation.

Theoretically in a *strict* Lisp-1 convention, the use of a function name as a formal parameter would be forbidden; eg. (defun f (map) (g map)) would dynamically create a situation where map would have two bindings. The first binding would be to the global function definition and the second to the local binding made by calling f. The disambiguation of map would depend on the order in which search took place. If the global environment is searched first, then the result would return the lambda definition of map. If the local environment is searched first, then the dynamic binding of map is found.

In our SECD model, the ordering reflects the Kλ convention that the local environment is searched first which is the usual convention in Lisp-1 languages.

In the design of Shen there arose the choice between following Lisp-1 and Lisp-2. Because symbols are inert and 'do nothing unless told', the denotation of the symbol depends on the use made by the programmer. If we want to get at the function denoted by the symbol then function is used; if the intent is to get at the value assigned to it then value is appropriate. Shen effectively chose to follow Common Lisp and Lisp-2.

Exercise 22

1. Augment the SECD machine to
   a. handle trap and error-to-string.
   b. to handle vectors
   c. to handle streams.
   d. to handle higher-order function calls that refer to functions by name within lexical scoping.
   e. Augment the SECD machine to handle zero place functions.

2. In the SECD model of Kλ, it is possible to set up either a Lisp-1 or a Lisp-2 convention with respect to global assignments. Show how to do both.

3. *Our SECD machine is an interpreter that relies on storing every definition d of each user function f. To build a compiler we would need to compile d to a series s of SECD instructions so that when f is invoked then s is executed without consulting d. Build such a compiler and show it works.

4. ** Learn a procedural language like C and link your instruction set in 4. to C so that the SECD instructions emerge as C commands. If you add a garbage collector to this implementation you have a fully fledged low level implementation of Shen.

Further Reading

Landin (1964) is the original paper, but clearer accounts are to be found in Field and Harrison (1988) and Danvy (2003). Quiennec (1996) contains a detailed account of Scheme compilation including actual C code. The standard introduction to C is Kernighan and Richie (1988).

23 Shen Prolog

23.1 A Short History of Prolog

Prolog (short for **pro**gramming in **log**ic) was a programming language developed in 1972 in a collaboration between Colmeraur and Kowalski at the University of Marseille. Prolog introduced a new perspective on programming by which computation was essentially a process of deduction. A Prolog program is a list of assumptions, an input to a Prolog program is a query and the Prolog response is the answer deduced to the question from the assumptions given.

Marseille Prolog was the first Prolog, originally written in Fortran and the performance was poor. Prolog implementations were measured in term of logical inferences per second or **LIPS** and Marseille Prolog executed at a speed of 200 LIPS on the IBM 360/67 mainframe. This was too slow to be practical as a programming language. In 1978 David Warren working at Edinburgh implemented a compiler on the DEC-10 mainframe which compiled Prolog to DEC-10 assembly.

At 40 KLIPS or 40,000 LIPS, **DEC-10 Prolog** fixed the standard notation for Prolog which became known as **Edinburgh notation** and was the first fast Prolog. In 1983 Warren moved to SRI and developed the **Warren Abstract Machine** or **WAM**, a virtual machine that linked Prolog programs to address instructions. The WAM allowed Prolog to run on the Sun 3/50 workstation[67] at 60 KLIPS. Since then, Prolog performance increased due to refinements of the WAM and better hardware so that the commercial Sicstus Prolog is capable of 61,000 KLIPS or 61 MLIPS on a 2.67 GHz machine.

In Shen, Prolog is the language into which type declarations are compiled and it is the Prolog inference engine in Shen that makes the inferences that drive the type checking process. Shen Prolog is, in turn, compiled into Shen and Shen into Kλ. Unlike WAM-based Prologs that compile directly into assembly or microcode, the performance characteristic of an implementation like Sicstus Prolog is absent and under SBCL about 500-1000 KLIPS per GHz would be normal.

---

[67] The 3/50 ran at a clock speed of 15.7 MHz, about 100x slower than a conventional laptop of 2013.

Certain corners were cut in commercial Prologs like Sicstus to boost performance and one of these was the **occurs check** which we will come to later. Without this constraint type checking can fail to produce the correct result and so Shen Prolog reinstated this aspect. Unlike stand-alone Prologs like Sicstus or SWI Prolog, Shen Prolog was designed to integrate with Shen. A grasp of Prolog is essential is we wish to understand the relations between sequent calculus and Prolog and how sequent rules are compiled. We begin with looking at Horn clause logic.

23.2 Horn Clause Logic

The syntax rules of Horn clause logic are rather numerous when stated formally but the underlying idea is simple. Horn clauses are what result from Proplog when we allow Proplog atoms to be replaced by first-order atoms. The syntax rules are laid out in figure 23.1.

1. A Horn clause variable is a member of $V = \{x, y, z, x', y', z' \ldots..\}$.
2. A propositional symbol p is any symbol p where $p \notin V \cup \{\&, \rightarrow\}$.
3. A predicate Φ is any symbol Φ where $\sigma \notin V \cup \{\&, \rightarrow\}$.
4. A name N is a symbol/string/number/boolean where $N \notin V \cup \{\&, \rightarrow\}$.
5. A functional symbol f is any symbol F where $f \notin V \cup \{\&, \rightarrow\}$.
6. A term is either
   a. A name or ...
   b. an element of V or
   c. an expression $(f\ t_1,\ldots,t_n)$ consisting of a function symbol f followed by n $(n \geq 0)$ terms.
7. $\Phi(t_1,..t_n)$ is a Horn clause if Φ is a predicate and $t_1,...,t_n$ $(n \geq 0)$ are terms.
8. A propositional symbol on its own is a Horn clause.

   In cases 7 and 8 the Horn clause is a **Horn clause atom** or **fact**. If an expression is free of Horn clause variables then it is **ground.**

9. If A is an atom then it is a limiting case of a conjunction with only one limb. If A and B are conjunctions then (A & B) is a conjunction.
10. If B is an atom and A is a conjunction then the implication (A → B) is a Horn clause.

Figure 23.1 Horn clause syntax rules

In case 10 the Horn clause is a **Horn clause rule**. B is the **head** of the clause and A is the **body** of the clause.

In a Horn clause proof, the context (i.e. the set of assumptions used in the proof) is a list of rules and facts and the succeedent which is to be proved is a conjunction.

The first three sequent rules for Horn clause logic are almost exactly those of Proplog.

hyp

P >> P;

→-*left*
(P → Q) >> P;
(P → Q) >> Q;

&-*right*
where P *is ground*
P; Q;
(P & Q);

The next two rules relate to variables. Let $P_{t/v}$ be the result of substituting all occurrences of a Horn clause variable v in P by a ground term t.

v-right
$P_{t/v}$;
P;

v-left
$P_{t/v}$, P >> Q;
P >> Q;

The *v*-right and *v*-left rules are very similar to the ∃-*right* and ∀-*right rule* of first-order logic respectively. In fact the Horn clause variables in a sequent are implicitly quantified; a variable in a hypothesis is universally quantified and one occurring in the succeedent is existentially quantified.

Here is an example of a problem in Horn clause logic.

$(\text{mammal}(x) \rightarrow \text{warm-blooded}(x))$,
$\text{mammal}(\text{Socrates})$,
$\text{bipedal}(\text{Socrates}) >> (\text{warm-blooded}(y) \ \& \ \text{bipedal}(y))$.

Read in English

'All mammals are warm-blooded, Socrates is a mammal, also Socrates is bipedal therefore there is something that is warm-blooded and bipedal.'

Here is the proof of the validity of the argument in Horn clause logic.

Applying *v-right* and instantiating y to Socrates derives

(mammal(x) → warm-blooded(x)),
mammal(Socrates),
bipedal(Socrates) >> (warm-blooded(Socrates) & bipedal(Socrates)).

By &-*right,* two sequents are derived.

α   (mammal(x) → warm-blooded(x)),
mammal(Socrates),
bipedal(Socrates) >> warm-blooded(Socrates)

β   (mammal(x) → warm-blooded(x)),
mammal(Socrates),
bipedal(Socrates) >> bipedal(Socrates)

β is solved by *hyp.* By *v-left* applied to α, x is instantiated to 'Socrates'.

(mammal(Socrates) → warm-blooded(Socrates)),
(mammal(x) → warm-blooded(x)),
mammal(Socrates),
bipedal(Socrates) >> warm-blooded(Socrates)

Hence by →–*left.*

(mammal(Socrates) → warm-blooded(Socrates)),
(mammal(x) → warm-blooded(x)),
mammal(Socrates),
bipedal(Socrates) >> mammal(Socrates)

which is solved by *hyp* and the proof is complete.

The importance of the ground restriction on the &-*right* rule is shown by the following 'poof'.[68]

man(Fred), woman(Flora) >> man(x) & woman(x)

Read in English

'Fred is a man, Flora is a woman therefore somebody is a man and a woman.'

By &-*right*, two sequents are derived

α   man(Fred), woman(Flora) >> man(x)
β   man(Fred), woman(Flora) >> woman(x)

---

[68] A term coined by Bundy to describe a purported proof which is not actually a proof at all.

Applying *v-right* to α and instantiating x to Fred gives

man(Fred), woman(Flora) >> man(Fred)

which is solved by *hyp* leaving β. Instantiating x to Flora in β gives

man(Fred), woman(Flora) >> woman(Flora)

which is solved by *hyp*.

The proof goes wrong because the initial *&-right* step does not respect the ground condition.

An important theoretical result is that when Proplog is extended to Horn clause logic then no complete and terminating theorem-prover can be found; that is to say, like first-order logic, Horn clause logic is undecidable.[69]

23.3 Unification

Since the rules for Horn clause logic are virtually identical to those of Proplog apart from the *v-left* and *v-right* rules, it follows that the automation of Horn clause logic will turn on the automating the choice of instances for variables. Once the correct instantiation is found, then a Horn clause problem reduces to a Proplog problem and for that there is already a program to hand.

One solution would be to assemble the set S of ground terms that can be formulated in the vocabulary of the Horn clause proof obligation and systematically test for each possible instantiation. If S is non-empty then S is the **Herbrand universe** H of the problem, and if S is empty then some arbitrary name a is introduced and H = {a}. Theorem-proving in Horn clause logic would then entail working through the Herbrand universe and testing each combination using the Proplog program.

The Davis-Putnam procedure (1961) was a very early work in the area of automated reasoning which used an approach that approximated to this suggestion. It has several disadvantages; the main being that the number of combinations can grow exponentially even if H is finite. If function symbols are introduced then H is infinite. The Herbrand universe of the following problem.

jewish(mother_of(x)) → jewish(x) >> jewish(Albert)

is H = {Albert, mother_of(Albert), mother_of(mother_of(Albert)) ...}. In this case the testing process would not terminate.

---

[69] The easiest way to do this is to encode some standard model of computability in Horn clause logic such as a Turing machine – see http://en.wikipedia.org/wiki/Prolog#Turing_completeness.

Another more promising line is to use pattern-matching as used within Shen. Given

man(x) → mortal(x), man(Socrates) >> mortal(Socrates)

instead of first instantiating the x to 'Socrates', and then applying →-*left* we pattern match the mortal(x) to mortal(Socrates). This works just fine except that there are cases where the matching has to occur not only from the rule to the succeedent, but also from the succeedent to the rule.

likes(Ted, x) >> likes(y, Bill)

Here 'Ted' is matched to y and 'Bill' to x. Unlike Shen pattern matching, pattern matching for Horn clause logic has to work in two directions. This bidirectional pattern matching is called **unification**.

Unification was introduced into computer science by Robinson (1965) who gave an algorithm for the procedure. Two expressions **unify** when there is a uniform substitution for the variables in each expression that makes the two expressions the same.

'likes(Ted, x)' unifies with 'likes(y, Bill)' since the substitution $\sigma = \{x \mapsto$ 'Bill', $y \mapsto$ 'Ted'$\}$ makes the two identical. A set of associations that unifies two expressions e_1 and e_2 is a **unifier** of e_1 and e_2. The **most general unifier** or **MGU** of e_1 and e_2 is the smallest unifier needed to unify the two. Not every unifier is an MGU; 'likes(Ted, x)' unifies with 'likes(Ted, x)' under the unifier $\sigma = \{x \mapsto$ 'Bill'$\}$ which is not the MGU. The MGU here is $\{\}$.

The elements of a unifier are **bindings**, and process of substituting the variables in an expression by their values under a unifier is **dereferencing**. In the case of $\sigma = \{x \mapsto$ 'Bill', $y \mapsto$ 'Ted'$\}$ 'Bill' is said to be the **value** of x under this unification. Conventionally if σ is a unifier of two expressions then the result of dereferencing an expression e by σ is written $\sigma(e)$.

Robinson's algorithm for the unification of e_1 and e_2 begins with the **standardisation apart** of one of the two expressions if the set V_1 of variables in e_1 and the set V_2 of variables in e_2 is such that $V_1 \cap V_2 \neq \{\}$. Standardisation apart involves uniformly replacing the variables in either e_1 or e_2 so that $V_1 \cap V_2 = \{\}$. The motivation is shown in this example.

likes(Ted, x) >> likes(x, Bill)

Here unification cannot occur because the same variable x happens to be used in both the hypothesis and the succeedent. Replacing x by y allows the unification to go through. It is matter of choice which expression is standardised apart, but in logic programming it is always the hypothesis that is treated this way. Standardisation apart having been assumed, Robinson's algorithm takes as inputs two atoms $\Phi(s_1,..s_n)$ and $\Phi(t_1,..t_n)$. The algorithm (figure 23.2) is fairly straightforward, for $i = 1$ to n, each term s_i and t_i is compared using an accumulator M for the MGU.

1. If $s_i = t_i$ then i is incremented.
2. If s_i is a variable which does not occur in t_i then the substitution of t_i for s_i is made throughout both $\Phi(s_1,..s_n)$ and $\Phi(t_1,..t_n)$ and $s_i \mapsto t_i$ is added to M.
3. If t_i is a variable which does not occur in s_i then the substitution of s_i for t_i is made throughout both $\Phi(s_1,..s_n)$ and $\Phi(t_1,..t_n)$ and $t_i \mapsto s_i$ is added to M.
4. If s_i and t_i are complex terms of the form $f(a_1,..., a_m)$ and $f(b_1,...,b_m)$ then unification recurses within the two terms.
5. If none of the above hold then unification fails.

Figure 23.2 Robinson's unification algorithm

In the event of a successful unification, the algorithm has gone from $i = 1$ to n and M is returned as the result. Figure 23.3 gives the Shen code.

```
(define unification
  P P -> []
  [Pred | Ss] [Pred | Ts] -> (unify-loop Ss Ts [])
  _ _ -> (error "unification failure"))

(define unify-loop
  S S Unifier -> Unifier
  [S | Ss] [S | Ts] Unifier -> (unify-loop Ss Ts Unifier)
  [S | Ss] [T | Ts] Unifier -> (unify-loop (deref Ss [[S T] | Unifier])
                                           (deref Ts [[S T] | Unifier])
                                           [[S T] | Unifier])
                          where (and (variable? S) (occurs-check? S T))
  [S | Ss] [T | Ts] Unifier -> (unify-loop (deref Ss [[T S] | Unifier])
                                           (deref Ts [[T S] | Unifier])
                                           [[T S] | Unifier])
                          where (and (variable? T) (occurs-check? T S))
  [[F | S's] | Ss] [[F | T's] | Ts] Unifier
  -> (let NewUnifier (unify-loop [F | S's] [F | T's] Unifier)
        (unify-loop (deref Ss NewUnifier) (deref Ts NewUnifier) NewUnifier))
  _ _ _ -> (error "unification failure"))

(define occurs-check?
  Variable Term -> (= (occurrences Variable Term) 0))

(define deref
  [T | Ts] Unifier -> (map (/. Term (deref Term Unifier)) [T | Ts])
  T Unifier -> (let Binding (assoc T Unifier)
                 (if (empty? Binding) T
                     (deref (hd (tl Binding)) Unifier))))
```

Figure 23.3 Unification in Shen

Figure 23.4 shows some sample inputs to the unification function.

(17-) (unification [f a] [f X])
[[X a]]

(18-) (unification [f [g X]] [f X])
unification failure

(19-) (unification [f [g X] [h Y]] [f Z Z])
unification failure

(20-) (unification [f [g X] [h Y]] [f Z [h Z]])
[[Y [g X]] [Z [g X]]]

Figure 23.4 Running unification

Incorporating unification into the proof theory of Horn clause logic means that the *v-left* and *v-right* rules disappear and →-*left* is interpreted using unification. Since the *v* rules are gone, there is a problem with splitting conjunctions which, as we have seen, is safe only if the leading limb is ground. The solution is to avoid splitting and maintain a succeedent as a sequence of atoms and to dereference this sequence when unification is made. For convenience it is useful to make the body of a Horn clause a sequence of atoms too. Hence instead of

If B is an atom and A is a conjunction then $(A \rightarrow B)$ is a Horn clause.

we have

If B is an atom and A is a sequence of atoms then $(A \rightarrow B)$ is a Horn clause.

This gives us three rules to work with; the first *finish*, simply states when the list of atoms in the succeedent is empty, we can consider the proof finished.

finish

$$\overline{[];}$$

The other two are *hyp* and →-*left* interpreted with unification

hyp
where $\sigma(P, Q_1)$ is defined

$$\frac{P >> \sigma([....Q_n]);}{P >> [Q_1,...,Q_n];}$$

→-*left*
where $\sigma(Q_0, Q_1)$ is defined and $P + [...Qn]$ is the result of appending P to $[...Qn]$

$$\frac{(P \rightarrow Q_0) >> \sigma(P + [...Qn]);}{(P \rightarrow Q_0) >> [Q_1,...,Q_n];}$$

However if we allow that if (A → B) is a Horn clause it is permissible for A to be an empty sequence of atoms, then we can amalgamate facts and rules. A fact then becomes a rule whose body is empty. The significance of this identification is that the *hyp* rule then disappears and our version of Horn clause logic contains only two rules – *finish* (which is only invoked once) and →-*left*. Our →-*left rule* is a thinly disguised and restricted form of what Robinson called **resolution**. His achievement was to show that most inferencing in first-order logic could be reduced to the repeated application of this single rule of resolution. His 1965 work paved the way for the development of logic programming.

23.4 Programming in Horn Clause Logic

Logic programming is based on Horn clause logic. In logic programming the context is a **Prolog program** and the succeedent is a **Prolog query**. The model is that a logic program consists of a series of Horn clauses – rules and facts and the input to a program is a query - that is, a series of Horn clause atoms posed as the succeedent. The response returned by the Horn clause theorem prover to the query is the output of the program.

There is one thing missing with this picture. Logically the only thing that a Horn clause prover can do is return either 'yes' (I can prove that) or 'no' (I cannot prove that). This range of responses is too narrow for general programming and Horn clause logic seems an even more unlikely candidate for a programming language than lambda calculus. There was in fact a missing element required to make Horn clause logic work.

Green (1967) supplied this missing element in the form of an **answer literal**. The answer literal *A* is an atom that is tagged on to the end of the succeedent for the purpose of being able to deliver information. *A* contains all the variables in the succeedent and upon floating to the front of succeedent, the answer literal prints these variables together with their bound values. These values represented the answer to the query.

To illustrate, let's look at the problem we examined before

(mammal(x) → warm-blooded(x)),
mammal(Socrates),
bipedal(Socrates) >> (warm-blooded(y) & bipedal(y)).

Writing the problem in the new format and simplifying the bracketing for clarity this comes out as

mammal(x) → warm-blooded(x),
→ mammal(Socrates),
→ bipedal(Socrates) >> warm-blooded(y), bipedal(y).

The first step suggested by Green, is to add an atom to the succeedent – the so-called answer literal.

mammal(x) → warm-blooded(x),
→ mammal(Socrates),
→ bipedal(Socrates) >> warm-blooded(y), bipedal(y), answer("y", y).

The step of →-*left* unifies 'warm-blooded(x)' with 'warm-blooded(y)'; we can bind x to y or y to x here, but generally logic programming prefers to bind the hypothesis variable – we bind x to y. 'mammal(x)' is added to the succeedent and dereferenced to 'mammal(y)'.

mammal(x) → warm-blooded(x),
→ mammal(Socrates),
→ bipedal(Socrates) >> mammal(y), bipedal(y), answer("y", y).

Here 'mammal(Socrates)' is unified with 'mammal(y)' with y bound to 'Socrates' and the result is

mammal(x) → warm-blooded(x),
→ mammal(Socrates),
→ bipedal(Socrates) >> bipedal(Socrates), answer("y", Socrates).

'bipedal(Socrates)' is eliminated by → bipedal(Socrates) and the answer literal remains.

mammal(x) → warm-blooded(x),
→ mammal(Socrates),
→ bipedal(Socrates) >> answer("y", Socrates).

This is printed out as

y = Socrates

With answer literals, it is possible to do list processing. The following two Horn clauses describe the append relation between lists. [1] is represented as (cons 1 $) with $ being proxy for the empty list.

→ append($, x, x)
append(y,w,z) → append((cons x y), w, (cons x z))

Suppose the query is append((cons 1 $), (cons 2 $), x'). This can be interpreted as a request to append (cons 1 $), and (cons 2 $) i.e. [1] and [2]. The result should be (cons 1 (cons 2 $)). The proof obligation is

$\rightarrow$ append($, x, x$)
append(y,w,z) $\rightarrow$ append((cons x y), w, (cons x z))
>> append((cons 1 $), (cons 2 $), x')

Adding an answer literal we have

$\rightarrow$ append($, x, x$)
append(y,w,z) $\rightarrow$ append((cons x y), w, (cons x z))
>> append((cons 1 $), (cons 2 $), x'), answer("x'''", x')

Resolving by the second rule for append we get

$\rightarrow$ append($, x, x$)
append(y,w,z) $\rightarrow$ append((cons x y), w, (cons x z))
>> append($, (cons 2 $), z$), answer("x'''", (cons 1 z))

Resolving by the fact $\rightarrow$ append($, x, x$)

$\rightarrow$ append($, x, x$)
append(y,w,z) $\rightarrow$ append((cons x y), w, (cons x z))
>> answer("x'''", (cons 1 (cons 2 $)))

$x' = $ (cons 1 (cons 2 $))

23.5 Programming in Prolog

Prolog is essentially a computational embodiment of Horn clause logic with answer-literals, unification and resolution that uses the same search strategy for solving problems that Proplog does. The other additions to Prolog are the equivalent of the δ rules for lambda calculus i.e. provision for the usual arithmetic operations and I/O operations that any language needs. Prolog is almost always written in Edinburgh notation. In this notation variables, as in Shen, are symbols beginning in uppercase. Facts are written in form *predicate(terms)* just as in our version of Horn clause logic except that a full stop is used to terminate the fact.

A rule in Edinburgh notation is not written in the form *body* $\rightarrow$ *head*, but in the form *head :- body.* again terminating with a full stop. Lists are written exactly as they are in Shen using [...] and | plays the same role as it does in Shen. A small note is that commas have to be used in Prolog to separate list items so [1 2 3] in Shen is [1, 2, 3] in Prolog.

SWI Prolog is a free Prolog using standard notation with a good interface and the following shows a session under Windows.

```
Welcome to SWI-Prolog (Multi-threaded, 32 bits, Version 5.10.0)
Copyright (c) 1990-2010 University of Amsterdam, VU Amsterdam
SWI-Prolog comes with ABSOLUTELY NO WARRANTY. This is free
software, and you are welcome to redistribute it under certain conditions.
Please visit http://www.swi-prolog.org for details.

For help, use ?- help(Topic). or ?- apropos(Word)
```

Prolog contains an arithmetic engine. X is (4 + 7) returns 11. Notice the full stop at the end of the query. = compares for equality using unification.

```
1 ?- X is (4 + 7).
X = 11.

2 ? X = a.
X = a
```

It is possible to write programs into Prolog, but it is more civilised to use an editor and load the program here. Here I create a file prologtest.pl and load it into SWI Prolog.

```
4 ? consult(prologtest.pl).
%c:/Users/Mark Tarver/tests.pl compiled 0.00 sec, 1,092 bytes
```

The contents of my file include two simple Prolog programs. One enumerates a list and the other gives the Cartesian product of two lists. As in Shen, an underscore functions as a wildcard.

```
enum(L, E) :- enum_help(L, E, 1).

enum_help([], [], _).
enum_help([X | Y], [[X, N] | E], N) :- M is N+1, enum_help(Y, E, M).
```

Figure 23.4 A simple Prolog program

Here I ask to number the list [a, b ,c]. I then ask to find a value that enumerates to [[a, 1], [b, 2], [c, 3]].

```
3- ? enum([a, b, c], E).
E = [[a, 1], [b, 2], [c, 3]].

4-? enum(L, [[a, 1], [b, 2], [c, 3]]).
L = [a, b, c]
```

append is a system predicate. I query values for X and Y which when appended together give [1, 2, 3], Typing ; to each solution prompts a search for the next.

```
6 ?- append(X,Y,[1,2,3]).
X = [],
Y = [1, 2, 3] ;

X = [1],
Y = [2, 3] ;

X = [1, 2],
Y = [3] ;

X = [1, 2, 3],
Y = [] ;

false
```

This is a brief introduction to Prolog programming in standard Edinburgh notation. For readers interested in becoming proficient in Prolog, the further reading section and the texts by Sterling and Shapiro and Bratko are relevant.

23.6 Shen Prolog

Shen Prolog is a version of Prolog that provides the object code for the sequent calculus rules of Shen. The syntax of Shen Prolog is based on that of Shen itself, with three differences.

1. defprolog is used instead of define.
2. <-- is used instead of -> or <-. In the clause *xxx* <-- *yyy*; the place of *xxx* is taken by a series of terms and *yyy* by a series of literals represented as function calls. Note the semi-colon terminates a clause.
3. Pattern-matching takes place only with respect to lists.

In Edinburgh syntax these facts

```
woman(martha).
woman(joan).
```

are written in Shen Prolog as

```
(defprolog woman
  martha <--;
  joan <--;)
```

To pose a Prolog query, the macro prolog? is used.

```
(3-) (prolog? (woman martha))
true

(4-) (prolog? (woman jean))
false

(5-) (prolog? (woman X))
true

(6-) (prolog? (man martha))
APPLY: undefined function man
```

Figure 23.5 Invoking Prolog

Note that repeated variables in Shen Prolog programs are interpreted using occurs-check unification (in most implementations of Prolog this is not true). (occurs-check -) disables automatic compilation with occurs-check unification. (occurs-check +) restores the default. This declaration also extends to the compilation of data types in Shen Prolog.

The predicate return ends the Prolog computation returning the value of its argument. Here the first value for which (woman X) is true is returned.

```
(7-) (prolog? (woman X) (return X))
martha
```

Figure 23.6 Returning a value from a Prolog call

To find all the values for which (woman X) is true, findall is used. This predicate takes three terms.

1. A variable *x*.
2. An atom *a*.
3. A variable *y*.

and returns bound to *y* all the values of *x* for which *a* is provable.

```
(8-) (prolog? (findall X [woman X] Y) (return Y))
[martha joan]
```

Figure 23.7 Returning a list of values from a Prolog call

The predicate is, as in (is *x* *t*), binds the variable *x* to the result of evaluating *t*.

```
(12-) (prolog? (is X (+ 1 1)) (return X))
2
```

Figure 23.8 Assigning a value to a variable

A very similar predicate bind exists which differs from is only in the respect that the variables in *t* are dereferenced to give a non-variable result – this fast form of dereferencing is called **lazy dereferencing** and is discussed in the next chapter.

The Bible program of chapter 2 can be written in Shen Prolog as follows.

```
(11-) (defprolog lived
   "Adam" 930 <--;
   "Seth" 912 <--;
   "Enos" 905 <--;
   "Ca-i'nan" 910 <--;
   "Mahal'aleel" 895 <--;
   "Jared" 962 <--;
   "Enoch" 365 <--;
   "Methu'selah" 969 <--;
   "Lamech" 777 <--;)
lived

(12-) (defprolog begat
   "Adam" "Seth"  <--;
   "Seth" "Enos" <--;
   "Enos" "Ca-i'nan" <--;
   "Ca-i'nan" "Mahal'aleel" <--;
   "Mahal'aleel" "Jared" <--;
   "Jared" "Enoch" <--;
   "Enoch" "Methu'selah" <--;
   "Methu'selah" "Lamech" <--;)
begat

(13-) (prolog? (findall Age [lived Person Age] Ages)
            (is Total (sum Ages))
            (return Total))
7625
```

Figure 23.9 Computing the total ages of the patriarchs (version 1)

Figure 23.9 uses the Shen system function sum to total the ages. We can also define sum in Shen Prolog.

```
(14-) (defprolog total
      [] 0 <--;
      [X | Y] N <-- (total Y M) (is N (+ M X));)
total

(15-) (prolog? (findall Age [lived Person Age] Ages)
            (total Ages Total)
            (return Total))
7625
```

Figure 23.10 Computing the total ages of the patriarchs (version 2)

The predicate when enables boolean tests to be used; (when *b*) where *b* is a boolean test, succeeds if *b* evaluates to true.

```
(16-) (prolog? (when (> 6 7)))
false

(17-) (prolog? (when (> 16 7)))
true
```

Figure 23.11 Calling a boolean test within Prolog

Shen Prolog allows function expressions to be embedded into the arguments of literals within the tails of clauses. Thus

```
(defprolog f
  X <-- (return (* 2 X));)
```

creates a Horn clause procedure that receives an input and doubles it, passing the result to the top level.

Calling Shen from Prolog is easy. Calling Prolog from Shen is only a little more difficult. The following shows a way *not* to call Prolog from Shen.

```
(1-) (define foo
      X -> (prolog? (is Y (* X X)) (return Y)))
foo

(2-) (foo 9)
The value #(shen.pvar 2) is not of type REAL

(3-) (define foo
      X -> (prolog? (receive X) (is Y (* X X)) (return Y)))
foo

(4-) (foo 9)
81
```

Figure 23.12 Calling Prolog from Shen

Here in the first attempt to call Prolog, the X is treated as a free variable in the Prolog call, and Prolog tries to multiply the variable X by itself which raises an error. The correct approach is to delineate X as a variable whose value is to be received from *outside* the Prolog call using receive.

A basic control mechanism for trimming search space in Prolog is the **cut**. The cut, written as ! in Edinburgh Prolog and Shen Prolog, alters the backtracking behaviour of a Prolog program and occupies the position of an atom in the tail of a Horn clause. When the cut is called it always succeeds; however if control backtracks to a cut, then the effect of the cut is to cut off all consideration of choices after the clause in the Horn clause procedure in which it is invoked. As an example, we will use a case written in Shen Prolog itself.

```
(defprolog woman
  X <-- ! (married-to X john);
  martha <--;)

(defprolog married-to
  joan john <--;)
```

The first clause states that X is a woman if X is married to john. The intrusion of the cut in that clause commits Prolog to solving the query by looking under the married-to predicate. If that search fails, then the cut will block any attempt to look at further clauses in the woman procedure. Hence the query (woman joan) succeeds, but (woman martha) fails.

```
(22-) (prolog? (woman joan))
true

(23-) (prolog? (woman martha))
false
```

Figure 23.13 The cut in operation within Prolog

call functions as a higher-order aspect for Shen Prolog. Given an atom, the atom is turned into a goal by being called. Here it is used to define ~ as negation as failure; where (~ P) is provable (true) just when P is not provable (false).

```
(15-) (defprolog ~
        P <-- (call P) ! (when false);
  ~     _ <--;)

(16-) (prolog? (~ [woman susan]))
true
```

Figure 23.14 Defining negation as failure

Rather than (when false), (prolog-fail) can be used instead.

Mode declarations suspend unification in favour of pattern-matching and are used only in the head of a clause. Mode declarations speed up code and reduce the footprint of the generated Shen code. (mode ... -) enables pattern-matching.

```
(24-) (defprolog f
      (mode a -) <--;)
f

(25-) (prolog? (f X))
false

(26-) (prolog? (f a))
true
```

Figure 23.15 Using mode declarations in Shen Prolog

The default mode is unification signalled by (mode ... +). Mode declarations can be nested as in (mode [f a (mode b +)] -). In this event the innermost declaration has priority. The above expression would thus perform pattern-matching with respect to [f a b] and all its elements save b which would receive unification. In sum, Shen Prolog contains the following extralogical predicates (figure 23.16).

predicate	description
(unify *s t*)	unifies *s* and *t* without an occurs check
(unify! *s t*)	unifies *s* and *t* with an occurs check
(identical *s t*)	succeeds if the terms are identical
(is *x t*)	binds the variable *x* to the result of evaluating *t*. All variables in *t* are completely dereferenced.
(bind *x t*)	as is except all variables in *t* are dereferenced only so far as to derive a non-variable result.
(findall *x a y*)	*x* is a variable, *a* an atom, and *y* a variable; finds all values for *x* in *a* for which *a* is provable and binds the list of these values to *y*.
(when *t*)	*t* is evaluated to true or false and the call succeeds if it is true. All variables in *t* are completely dereferenced.
(fwhen *t*)	as when except all variables in *t* are dereferenced only so far as to derive a non-variable result.
(call *a*)	apply the predicate at the head of *a* to the terms in it. (Prolog apply)
(return *t*)	terminate Prolog returning the dereferenced value of *t*.
!	Prolog cut
(receive *x*)	receives a variable binding to *x* from outside Prolog
(prolog-fail)	Prolog failure

Figure 23.16 The predicates of Shen Prolog

23.7 Implementing a Horn Clause Interpreter

Since this is a book about Shen, let's close this chapter by building a type secure Horn clause interpreter in Shen, designed on the model described in this chapter. A Horn clause atom is a predicate (symbol) followed by terms.
(datatype atom

```
F : symbol; X : (list term);
====================
[F | X] : atom;)
```

A term is a symbol, number, string or boolean or a symbol heading a list of terms.

(datatype term

```
P : symbol;
P : term;

P : number;
P : term;

P : string;
P : term;

P : boolean;
P : term;

F : symbol; X : (list term);
==================
[F | X] : term;)
```

A Horn clause consists of a head followed by a body.

(datatype horn-clause

```
H : atom; B : (list atom);
================
[H <= | B] : horn-clause;)
```

The typed version of the unification algorithm is a little longer than the untyped version but does the same job. Unification failure returns an error.

```
(define unify-atoms
  {atom --> atom --> (list (term * term))}
  P P -> []
  [F | X] [F | Y] -> (unify-terms X Y [ ])
  _ _ -> (error "unification failure!"))
```

```
(define unify-terms
  {(list term) --> (list term) --> (list (term * term)) --> (list (term * term))}
  X X Mgu -> Mgu
  [X | Y] [W | Z] Mgu
  -> (unify-terms Y Z (unify-term (dereference X Mgu)
                                  (dereference W Mgu)
                                  Mgu))
  _ _ _ -> (error "unification failure!"))

(define unify-term
  {term --> term --> (list (term * term)) --> (list (term * term))}
  X X Mgu -> Mgu
  X Y Mgu -> [(@p X Y) | Mgu]   where (occurs-check? X Y)
  X Y Mgu -> [(@p Y X) | Mgu]   where (occurs-check? Y X)
  [F | Y] [F | Z] Mgu -> (unify-terms Y Z Mgu)
  _ _ _ -> (error "unification failure!"))

(define occurs-check?
  {term --> term --> boolean}
  X Y -> (and (variable? X) (not (occurs? X Y))))

(define dereference
  {term --> (list (term * term)) --> term}
  [X | Y] Mgu -> [X | (map (/. Z (dereference Z Mgu)) Y)]
  X Mgu -> (let Val (lookup X Mgu)
                (if (= Val X) X (dereference Val Mgu))))

(define lookup
  {term --> (list (term * term)) --> term}
  X [] -> X
  X [(@p X Y) | _] -> Y
  X [_ | Y] -> (lookup X Y))

(define occurs?
  {term --> term --> boolean}
  X X -> true
  X [Y | Z] -> (or (== X Y) (some (/. W (occurs? X W)) Z))
  _ _ -> false)

(define some
  {(A --> boolean) --> (list A) --> boolean}
  _ [] -> false
  F [X | Y] -> (or (F X) (some F Y)))
```

The Horn clause interpreter top level follows next. The Prolog top level receives a list (stack) of goals and a Horn clause program. We begin by building an answer literal and inserting it onto the end of the goal stack and passing the problem to the prolog-help function which does the heavy lifting. Here the same technique of spreading the input that was used in 6.3 is employed.

```
(define prolog
  {(list atom) --> (list horn-clause) --> boolean}
  Goals Program -> (prolog-help (insert-answer-literal Goals)
                                Program
                                Program))

(define insert-answer-literal
  {(list atom) --> (list atom)}
  Goals -> (append Goals
                   (answer-literal
                     (mapcan (function variables-in-atom) Goals))))
(define answer-literal
  {(list term) --> (list atom)}
  Vs -> [[answer | (answer-terms Vs)]])

(define answer-terms
  {(list term) --> (list term)}
  [] -> []
  [V | Vs] -> [(str V) V | (answer-terms (remove V Vs))])

(define prolog-help
  {(list atom) --> (list horn-clause) --> (list horn-clause) --> boolean}
  [] _ _ -> true
  [[answer | Terms]] _ _ -> (answer Terms)
  [P | Ps] [Clause | Clauses] Program
    -> (let StClause (standardise-apart Clause)
            H (hdcl StClause)
            B (body StClause)
            (or (trap-error
                  (let MGU (unify-atoms P H)
                       Goals (map (/. X (dereference-atom X MGU))
                                  (append B Ps))
                       (prolog-help Goals Program Program)) (/. E false))
                (prolog-help [P | Ps] Clauses Program)))
  _ _ _ -> false)
```

prolog-help returns true if the stack is empty and enters the answer routine if an answer literal pops up. Otherwise the head of the first clause of the program is unified with the leading goal.

1. If the unification fails, the error is trapped and the program recurses on the rest of the Horn clause program.
2. If unification succeeds, then the new goals Goals are assembled and the prolog-help function restores the Horn clause program and attempts to prove Goals. If this attempt fails, then the prolog-help function recurses down the Horn clause program.
3. In the final case, if the list of program clauses is empty then false is returned,

```
(define hdcl
  {horn-clause --> atom}
  [H <= | _] -> H)

(define body
  {horn-clause --> (list atom)}
  [_ <= | Body] -> Body)

(define dereference-atom
  {atom --> (list (term * term)) --> atom}
  [F | Terms] MGU -> [F | (map (/. T (dereference T MGU)) Terms)])
```

The answer routine returns false to an affirmative to computing more solutions.

```
(define answer
  {(list term) --> boolean}
  [ ] -> (not (y-or-n? "~%more? "))
  [String Value | Answer] -> (do (output "~%~A = ~S"  String Value) (answer Answer)))
```

standardise-apart renames all the variables in a program clause.

```
(define standardise-apart
  {horn-clause --> horn-clause}
  Clause -> (st-all (variables-in-clause Clause) Clause))

(define variables-in-clause
  {horn-clause --> (list term)}
  [H <= | B] -> (append (variables-in-atom H) (mapcan (function variables-in-atom) B)))

(define variables-in-atom
  {atom --> (list term)}
  [Predicate | Terms] -> (mapcan (function variables-in-term) Terms))

(define variables-in-term
  {term --> (list term)}
  Term -> [Term]           where (variable? Term)
  [F | Terms] -> (mapcan (function variables-in-term) Terms)
  _ -> [])

(define st-all
  {(list term) --> horn-clause --> horn-clause}
  [] Clause -> Clause
  [V | Vs] Clause -> (st-all (remove V Vs)
                              (replace-term-in-clause V (gensym (protect X)) Clause)))

(define replace-term-in-clause
  {term --> term --> horn-clause --> horn-clause}
  V NewV [H <= | B] -> [(replace-term-in-atom V NewV H) <=
                          | (map (/. A (replace-term-in-atom V NewV A)) B)])

(define replace-term-in-atom
  {term --> term --> atom --> atom}
  V NewV [F | Terms] -> [F | (map (/. T (replace-term V NewV T)) Terms)])
```

```
(define replace-term
  {term --> term --> term --> term}
  V NewV V -> NewV
  V NewV [F | Terms] -> [F | (map (/. T (replace-term V NewV T)) Terms)]
  _ _ Term -> Term)
```

Our implementation of answer literals prints off multiple solutions since typing y to the request for more will cause the value false to be returned. This value will in turn trigger a backtrack in search of new solutions. Here is an example

```
(3+) (prolog [[woman X]]
             [[[woman martha] <=]
              [[woman joan] <=] ])
X = martha
more? y

X = joan
more? y
false : boolean

(4+) (prolog [[append X Y [cons 1 [cons 2 [cons 3 $]]]]]
             [[[append $ X X] <=]
              [[append [cons X Y] W [cons X Z]] <= [append Y W Z]]])

X = $
Y = [cons 1 [cons 2 [cons 3 $]]]
more?  (y/n) y

X = [cons 1 $]
Y = [cons 2 [cons 3 $]]
more?  (y/n) y

X = [cons 1 [cons 2 $]]
Y = [cons 3 $]
more?  (y/n) y

X = [cons 1 [cons 2 [cons 3 $]]]
Y = $
more?  (y/n) y
false : boolean
```

Since our program constitutes an adequate inference engine for Horn clause logic, why not use it as the basis of the Shen Prolog? The short answer is that the performance of our Prolog interpreter is too slow for the requirements of type checking, where it is usual to require thousands of inferences to prove a program type secure. To attain the necessary speed whereby such a proof can be secured in seconds rather than minutes requires the sort of compilation strategies covered in the next chapter.

Exercise 23

1. Write a Prolog program that

     a.   reverses a list l.
     b.   tests if x is an element of list l.
     c.   removes an element x from list l.
     d.   substitutes x for y in z
     e.   tests if every element of l_1 is an element of l_2.
     f.   takes two lists l_1 and l_2 and produces a list l_3 whose elements are all those which are in l_1 but not in l_2.

2. Change the Prolog interpreter in section 23.6 so that it accepts the following Shen Prolog features.

     a.   the cut.
     b.   findall.
     c.   is
     d.   when

3. Build a loop detector into your Prolog so that a rule like [[brother X Y] <= [brother Y X]] does not cause an infinite loop.

4. Reading chapter 18 on propositional and first-order logic, how many of the rules in that chapter can be usefully added to Prolog to increase the expressiveness of the language? Argue your case and implement them

Further Reading

Prolog is discussed in Sterling and Shapiro (1994) and Bratko (2002); Lloyd (1990) provides the theory to Prolog while Hogger (1990) is a rather gentler introduction. Stickel (1984, 1986) describes an extension to Prolog that is complete for first-order logic. Robinson's 1965 unification algorithm remains the standard approach to performing unification. Martelli and Montanari (1973) describe a linear time and space algorithm for performing unification. Knight (1989) provides a good overview of the uses and ramifications of unification.

Web Sites

Roman Bartak (http://kti.ms.mff.cuni.cz/~bartak/constraints) maintains a site devoted to constraint programming. Free implementations of Prolog are easily obtained over the web. Sicstus Prolog (http://www.sics.se/sicstus) is one of the fastest versions of Prolog currently available, but is not freely available. SWI Prolog (http://www.swi.prolog.org) is another widely used implementation and is free. GNU Prolog (http://pauillac.inria.fr/~diaz/gnu-prolog) is a free Prolog implemented by Daniel Diaz that offers extra facilities for constraint satisfaction handling. **Visual Prolog** (http://www.visual-prolog.com) is available from the Prolog Development Centre and includes facilities for building graphical interfaces. A free download version for non-commercial purposes is available from the Web site.

24 The Compilation of Sequent Calculus

24.1 The Architecture of a Sequent Compiler

The compilation of sequent calculus into efficient object code proceeds according to a four step process that begins with sequent calculus and ends with executable code whose exact identity depends on the platform on which Shen is mounted. This chapter is concerned with the strategy of this compilation in all phases except the final compilation of the platform code. In Shen there are 4 stages in the compilation of sequent calculus to Shen (figure 24.1).

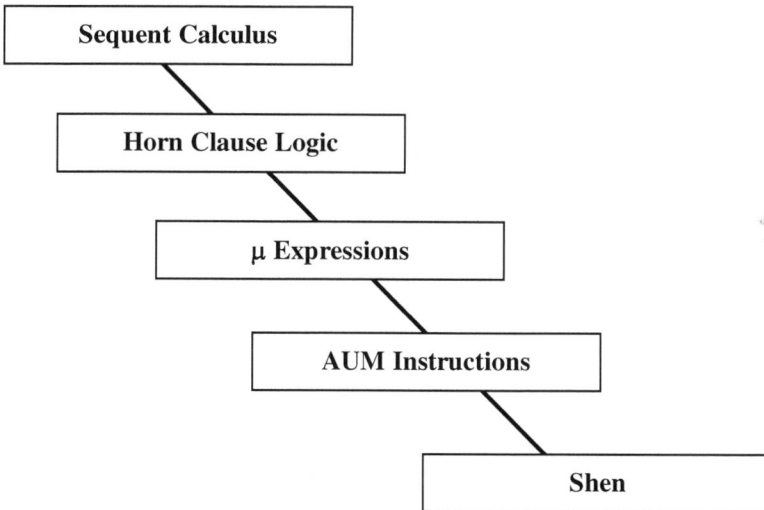

Figure 24.1 The stages in the compilation of sequent calculus to Shen

24.2 From Sequent Rules to Horn Clauses

From chapter 18, we learnt that every sequent rule has three parts; a list of side-conditions (possibly empty), a set of premises[70] (possibly empty) and a concluding sequent which is mandatory (figure 24.2).

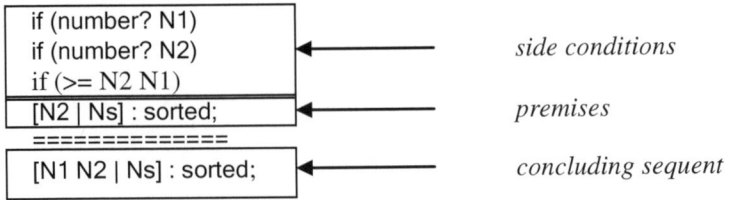

```
if (number? N1)
if (number? N2)          ←————————         side conditions
if (>= N2 N1)
[N2 | Ns] : sorted;      ←————————         premises
===============
[N1 N2 | Ns] : sorted;   ←————————         concluding sequent
```

Figure 24.2 The structure of a derivation rule

When the list of premises is empty and the concluding sequent has an empty assumption list then the rule is an **axiom**.

The compilation of a sequent calculus rule begins with the division of the rule into those three components. The double underline is eliminated, being syntactic sugar for two separate rules.

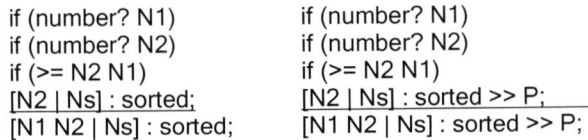

```
if (number? N1)              if (number? N1)
if (number? N2)              if (number? N2)
if (>= N2 N1)                if (>= N2 N1)
[N2 | Ns] : sorted;          [N2 | Ns] : sorted >> P;
[N1 N2 | Ns] : sorted;       [N1 N2 | Ns] : sorted >> P;
```

Figure 24.3 The original rule divided

Each component is compiled in the following order; the concluding sequent, the side conditions and the premises. We shall take as our case study, the compilation of the right-hand rule in figure 24.3.

The conclusion of this sequent becomes the first term of the head of the incipient Horn clause and the predicate is the name of the datatype. The second term is a variable Context representing the list of assumptions currently in play. Thus supposing that the name of the datatype within which our rule is embedded is sorted, then the head of the rule will read

P Context <--;

---

[70] The word 'premises' is also used confusingly for the actual assumptions that form part of a sequent and the word 'conclusion' for what the sequent is attempting to prove from those assumptions. Logic is littered with the unfortunate consequences of overloading words ('soundness' for example, having three distinct though related meanings). There is nothing to be done about this except to accept it and soldier forward, and to be clear at every stage what meaning is intended.

The body of the rule is determined by the rest of the compilation. The creation of the body begins with the isolation of the variables in each of the assumptions. These will become terms in the subsequent body of the clause. Another term which occurs is the **input context variable** V which initially is simply the variable Context.

The second step is to iterate through the assumption list. At each stage, we must be aware of the need to track the values of the variables in the assumption. This dependency is expressed by adding the variables as extra terms to a **search literal**. The job of a search literal is to represent the search for a particular assumption.

A search literal takes n + 2 terms. The last n terms are the variables drawn from the assumption it is representing. The first term is the input context variable and the second term is the **output context variable**. The purpose of these two variables is to (a) receive the current list of working assumptions and (b) output the new list of working assumptions should the search literal succeed. The predicate of the search literal is computer generated. Thus in our sample case, the clause might continue.

P Context <-- (cl55 Context Context1 N1 N2 Ns)
    . . . .

The calls to the search literal must be handled by the corresponding **search procedure**. Each search procedure consists of two **search clauses**; a base case and a recursive case. The base case tests for the assumption, the recursive case recurses on the assumption list. In the case of cl55, these clauses would read as follows.

```
(defprolog cl55
  [[[cons N1 [cons N2 Ns]] : sorted] | In] In N1 N2 Ns <--;
  [Assumption | Assumptions] [Assumption | Out] N1 N2 Ns
    <-- (cl55 Assumptions Out N1 N2 Ns);)
```

The output context variable is now handed to the rest of the compilation process which is relatively easy. Each side condition is either a boolean test or a local assignment. The if side-condition is compiled using the Shen Prolog when predicate thus.

```
Q54, Context <--   (cl55 Context Context1 N1 N2 Ns)
                   (when (number? N1))
                   (when (number? N2))
                   (when (>= N2 N1))
                      . . . . .
```

The final literal feeds control back into the program from which the call to sorted originated. Assuming that this is the type checker (call it t*), then the final literals are calls to t*. These calls will represent the premises of the original rule and the active context will be the final input context variable. Hence the final program is:

```
(defprolog sorted
  P Context <-- (cl55 Context Context1 N1 N2 Ns)
                (when ((number? N1)))
                (when ((number? N2)))
                (when ((>= N2 N1)))
                (t* [[[cons N2 Ns] : sorted] | Context1] P);)

(defprolog cl55
  [[[cons N1 [cons N2 Ns]] : sorted] | In] In N1 N2 Ns <--;
  [Assumption | Assumptions] [Assumption | Out] N1 N2 Ns
    <-- (cl55 Assumptions Out N1 N2 Ns);)
```

Figure 24.4 The generated Horn clause program

The complexity of the Horn clause program compared to the sequent calculus is a good demonstration of the expressive power of the sequent calculus notation.

24.3 From Horn Clauses to μ Expressions

A Horn clause divides into two parts; the head and the tail. In the case of atoms, the tail is empty. If the head $(F\ t_1,...,t_n)$ consists of a predicate F followed by n terms then the clause expects to receive a goal of the form $(F\ t^*_1,...,t^*_n)$. The task of the Shen Prolog engine is to unify each of $t_1,...,t_n$ in turn with $t^*_1,...,t^*_n$, keeping track of the bindings and to call up the tail with the appropriate bindings if the unification succeeds. What kinds of terms can there be? There are 4 important kinds.

1. **Wildcards**; the underscore _. This has precisely the same job as it does it Shen - to indicate a 'don't care' input.
2. **Variables**; signified by uppercase letters.
3. **Constants**; signified by strings, booleans, symbols that are lowercase and numbers.
4. **List Constructions**; like [X | Y].

Let us begin with a concrete case; the most convenient one is the logic programming equivalent of the 'member' function that was used previously.

```
(defprolog member
  X [X | _] <--;
  X [_ | Y] <-- (member X Y);)
```

The first clause is not left-linear. The AUM supposes that all clauses are left-linear, and this assumption considerably simplifies the compilation of the clause. We cope with this requirement by renaming the duplicated variable and pushing a unification test (unify X Y) in Shen Prolog) onto the (empty) tail of the first clause. List expressions are presented in cons form. Wildcards do offer room for optimisation, so these remain.

```
(defprolog member
  X (cons Y _) <-- (unify X Y);
  X (cons _ Y) <-- (member X Y);)
```

Traditionally a functional implementation of logic programming uses functions to model Horn clauses. Each Horn clause is headed by an n-place predicate P (in the above example, a 2-place predicate member holds this position). The predicate P is represented by an $n+1$ place function whose arguments represent the terms of the predicate which are held in the head of the Horn clause. The extra argument, which we will come to later, will hold a **continuation** or the information which directs the processing of the information held in the tail of the Horn clause.

A **Horn clause procedure** F in a logic program L is the set of all clauses in L whose heads share the same predicate. Traditionally it is usual to compile the code from F into a single function with a case for each clause in F. We shall not depart from tradition here in either instance. Hence the function representing the member logic procedure would have the form, member $=_{df}$ (λ A (λ B (λ C ....))) where A and B are the actual inputs to member and C is the continuation.

Having got that far there are now several ways of explaining the process of compilation. It is possible to regard compilation with the AUM in the manner of chapter 16; as a sort of extended β reduction generating a different kind of code than $\mathcal{L}$ expressions. Instead of extended abstractions, we generate μ **expressions** where (μ 1 ...) might represent a term 1 in the head of a Horn clause. A μ **abstraction** is an expression of the form (μ x y) and a μ **application** is one of the form ((μ x y) z). The body of a μ abstraction (μ x y) is y and we say that x is μ **bound** in (μ x y).

A compilation on these lines of the member procedure produces the following code.

```
member =df (λ A (λ B (λ C
            (cases (((μ X (μ (cons Y _)
                    (call the continuation (unify X Y C)))) A) B)
                   (((μ X (μ (cons _ Y)
                    (call the continuation (member X Y C))) A) B))))
```

In chapter 16, the innermost body of an extended abstraction was composed of the expression returned by successfully matching the pattern(s) to the input(s). In the case of logic programming the innermost body is composed of a call to implement the tail of the original Horn clause. This innermost body will be a call to continue the computation using the elements of the tail. Shen writes this as (call the continuation ...) where ... is filled by the tail of the Horn clause with each atom therein carrying an extra argument C, where C is the continuation. Thus the left-linearised logic programming definition of member has two such continuations. (unify is our call to unification).

(call the continuation ((unify X Y C)))
(call the continuation ((member X Y C)))

What are μ expressions? Trivially they are what you get when you run a Horn clause through the Shen compiler, generating expressions that look a little like extended lambda expressions except they have μ rather than λ. More deeply they are, like extended lambda expressions themselves, place-holders for instructions that are eventually realised in lambda calculus (or some enriched version thereof). The task of the AUM is to step through the code and perform **μ-reductions**; that is, to simplify μ applications. The output of a μ-reduction is an abstract unification machine instruction.

24.4 The Abstract Unification Machine

μ reduction issues in AUM instructions, and AUM instructions are legal sentences of a simple context-free language. The choice of a concrete syntax for these commands is a matter of personal taste, but here we arrange for the AUM to return commands in pseudo-code. Figure 24.5 gives the BNF of the AUM.

```
<AUM Instruction> := <Branch> | <Local Assignment> | <Binding>
                      | <Renaming> | <Continuation> | <Failure>
<Branch> := (if <AUM test> then <AUM instruction> else <AUM instruction>)
<Local Assignment> := (let <Symbol> be <Value> in <AUM instruction>)
<Binding> :=  (bind <Symbol> to <Value> in <AUM instruction>)
<Renaming> := (rename the variables in <value> and then <AUM instruction>)
<Continuation> := (call the continuation (<Values>))
<Failure> := FAIL!
<AUM test> := (<Value> is identical to <Value>)
              | (<Value> is a non-empty list) | (<Value is a variable>)
<Value> := <Constant> | <Variable> | (the result of dereferencing <Value>)
           | (the head of <Value>) | (the tail of  <Value>) | (<Values>)
<Values> := <Value> | <Value> <Values>
<Constant> := [ ] | booleans | symbols | strings | numbers
```

Figure 24.5 The BNF of the AUM

There are 4 different rules for μ–reduction corresponding to the different possible cases; namely wildcards, variables, constants and list constructions. We shall consider complex terms as a special case after the section on mode declarations. $\to_\mu$ represents the operation of μ–reduction.

1. Wildcards

$((\mu \_ y) z) \rightarrow_\mu y$

The simplest μ–reduction; the μ application of a wildcard returns the body y of the μ–abstraction.

2. Variables

Variables are almost as simple.

Where x is a variable; $((\mu x y) z) \rightarrow_\mu$ (let x be z in y)

A μ–reduction generates a local assignment if the μ-bound expression is a variable.

There is an optimisation to be gained here however. If x is a variable and z is a **formal parameter** (i.e. a variable standing for a term of the original predicate) then the local assignment can be eliminated. In such a case x is an **ephemeral variable** and can be replaced by the formal parameter itself.

Example: in the Horn clauses

```
(defprolog member
   X [X | _] <--;
   X,[_ | Y] <-- (member X Y))
```

the first term of the head of each clause is an ephemeral variable.

The optimised rules are therefore

Where x is <u>not</u> an ephemeral variable; $((\mu x y) z) \rightarrow_\mu$ (let x be z in y)
Where x is an ephemeral variable; $((\mu x y) z) \rightarrow_\mu$ substitute z for x in y

3. Constants

Where c is a constant and z^* is fresh;
$((\mu c y) z) \rightarrow_\mu$ (let z^* be (the result of dereferencing z)
                          in (if (z^* is identical to c)
                              then y
                              else   (if (z^* is a variable)
                                  then (bind c to z^* in y)
                                  else FAIL!)))

The pseudo-code for a constant is more complex. The corresponding goal term is dereferenced and the result stored in a local assignment z^* and used in the rest of the instruction. The rest of this instruction says that z^* is to be compared for identity with c and if this test is met, then y is returned. If not, then if z^* is a variable then c is to be bound to z^* in the context of evaluating y. In all other cases, FAIL! is returned.

4. **List Structures**

where z^* is fresh and V is the list of variables in x and y

```
((μ (cons x y) w) z)
 →μ (let z* be (the result of dereferencing z)
        in (if (z* is a non-empty list)
            then
                ((μ x ((μ y w) (the tail of z*))) (the head of z*)))
            else (if (z* is a variable)
                    then   (rename the variables in V
                    and then (bind (cons x y) to z* in w))
                    else FAIL!))))
```

The code for the fourth case is more complex than any of the preceding three. The AUM uses some fresh symbol z^*. The instruction says that z^* is to be bound to the result of dereferencing z (part of the actual input to the Horn clause) and the following branching instruction is to be performed. If z^* is a non-empty list then the μ reduction of the μ application ((μ x ((μ y w) (the tail of z^*))) (the head of z^*))) is to be returned.

If the non-empty list test fails then z^* is tested to see if it is a variable. If it is then the variables in x and y are to be extracted and the command issued for them to be renamed (i.e. standardised apart in logical parlance) and the expression (cons x y) is bound to z^* in the evaluation of w. If the variable test fails, then FAIL! is returned.

The preceding cases really describe the heart of the AUM. There is only one extra complexity concerning the AUM representation of the tail of the Horn clause. The tail gets converted, of course, into a continuation. In the member case the continuations were represented as

```
(call the continuation ((unify X Y C)))
(call the continuation ((member X Y C)))
```

The BNF for continuation allows for a local assignment in calling a continuation. The reason for this is that logic programming, unlike functional programming, allows for the continuation to contain bindable free variables that are not found in the head of the clause. An example is to be found in the second clause of this procedure.

```
(defprolog reverse
 [] [] <--;
 [X | Y] Z <-- (reverse Y W)  (append W [X] Z);)
```

The variable W is not bound in the head of the clause, and therefore the AUM will compile the tail into an AUM instruction in which the variable is renamed.

```
(rename the variables in (W) and then
    (call the continuation
        ((reverse Y W) (append W (cons X [ ]) Z))))
```

Figure 24.6 gives a translation of a Horn clause into the AUM .

clause	AUM Code
[X | Y] Z <-- (reverse Y W) (append W [X] Z);	(let X9323 be (the result of dereferencing A) in (if (X9323 is a non-empty list) then (let X be (the head of X9323) in (let Y be (the tail of X9323) in (rename the variables in (W) and then (call the continuation ((reverse Y W) (append W (X) B)))))) else (if (X9323 is a variable) then (rename the variables in (X Y) and then (bind (cons X Y) to X9323 in (rename the variables in (W) and then (call the continuation ((reverse Y W) (append W (X) B)))))) else FAIL!)))

Figure 24.6 A Horn clause and its translation into AUM instructions

24.5 Mode Declarations

Shen Prolog, and by extension Shen in its treatment of sequents, gives the option of mode declarations. Mode declarations allow the user to stipulate that pattern-matching rather than unification is to be employed in respect to any term. In performance terms, mode declarations do not give a large speed increase, since only a simple variable test is avoided by using them. However they do reduce the size of the AUM code and can perform useful service in avoiding unwanted unifications with free variables in the input.

The following outputs represent AUM outputs for pattern-matching only; in all other cases the instructions are as before.

Where c is a constant and z^* is fresh

```
((μ c y) z) →μ (let z* be (the result of dereferencing z)
                    in (if (z* is identical to c)
                    then y
                    else
                    FAIL!))
```

Where z* is fresh

$((\mu\ (cons\ x\ y)\ w)\ z)$
$\rightarrow\mu$ (let z* be (the result of dereferencing z)
          in (if (z* is a non-empty list)
             then $((\mu\ x\ ((\mu\ y\ w)\ (the\ tail\ of\ z^*)))(the\ head\ of\ z^*)))$
             else FAIL!))

24.6 Compiling the AUM to Shen

The AUM is designed to compile out into object code in a functional language but the nature of that compilation, and the way that AUM instructions are interpreted, is not fixed.[71] The following gives the interpretation within Shen; by which Horn clauses are compiled into Shen functions.

Every n-place Horn clause procedure is compiled into an $n+2$ place Shen function. The extra two places are reserved for

1.   The **Prolog process number**.
2.   The **continuation**

The Prolog process number is a unique positive integer which is assigned to a Prolog process when it is invoked. A Prolog process number n indexes into a ragged two-dimensional **Prolog process array** which contains in its nth place, vector V_n of bindings. Since the Prolog processes are maintained in an array, it is possible to maintain many concurrent Prolog computations in Shen. The limits are determined only by the practicalities of memory and the size of the Prolog process array which by default can run up to 1,000 Prolog processes.

The continuation represents the unsolved part of the computation, or in our original interpreter-based model, the goal stack. However computationally it is more efficient to represent the continuation, not as a list, but as a lazy object which can be thawed when needed (the equivalent of popping the goal stack). The continuation, when thawed will eventually evaluate to an object which is the result of the computation. If this object is false, then the computation has failed and our Prolog backtracks. If not, then the object found is returned as the result of the Prolog computation.

The **binding vector** V_n contains all the needed information to maintain the bindings for the Prolog variables. Every Prolog variable v_i generated during the computation is generated as a print vector composed of

---

[71] In Qi, the predecessor to Shen, the AUM was compiled out into Common Lisp using an interpretation then called CLI ('Current Lisp Interpretation') which gave good performance but was highly platform specific. Part of the development of Shen required that the instruction set of the Prolog be kept within the set of functions definable within Shen on the basis of the Kλ instruction set.

a. A tag in the zeroth place indicating that the non-standard vector is standing for a Prolog variable.
b. A unique positive integer i in the first place that determines the identity of the variable; (figure 24.7).

pvar	713735

Figure 24.7 The vector anatomy of a Prolog variable Var713735

The binding for v_i is found in the ith address of V_n. With this background, let us now examine the interpretation of AUM instructions into Shen. An AUM instruction has the syntax.

<AUM Instruction> := <Branch> | <Local Assignment> |
                         <Binding> | <Renaming> | <Continuation> | <Failure>

This gives six different cases to interpret. The function σ, defined as follows, maps AUM instructions into Shen.

1. Branch

Syntax: <Branch> := (if <AUM test> then <AUM instruction> else <AUM instruction>)

This is interpreted straightforwardly as a conditional in Shen.

σ (if <AUM test> then <AUM instruction> else <AUM instruction>)
= (**if** σ(<AUM test>) σ(<AUM instruction>) σ(<AUM instruction>))

2. Local Assignment

Syntax: <Local Assignment> := (let <Symbol> be <Value> in <AUM instruction>)

This is interpreted straightforwardly as a local assignment in Shen.

σ(let <Symbol> be <Value> in <AUM instruction>)
= (**let** <Symbol> ϖ(<Value>) σ(<AUM instruction>))

where

a. ϖ(cons x y) = (**cons** ϖ(x) ϖ(y))
b. ϖ(the head of x) = (**hd** ϖ(x))
c. ϖ(the tail of x) = (**tl** ϖ(x))
d. ϖ(the result of dereferencing <value>)
    = (**lazyderef** ϖ(<value>) **ProcessNumber**)
e. ϖ(f x_1 ... x_n) = (**cons** ϖ(f) ϖ(x_1 ... x_n))
f. ϖ(_) = (**newprologvariable**)
g. ϖ(x) = x   in all other cases

We have seen that dereferencing is a process by which the value δ of any variable V is found by following a chain of pointers from that variable and replacing V by δ.   In **eager dereferencing**, the actual value is found, whereas in **lazy dereferencing** the chain of pointers is followed only as far as is needed to find an object that is not a bound variable.

To see the difference, consider a binding vector in which the variable V3 is bound to [V5 V6]. In binding vector terms this means that the third index is occupied by the list [V5 V6] (figure 24.7). V5 is in turn bound to a and V6 to b as signified by the presence of these elements in the fifth and sixth positions.

	...	[V5 V6]	...	a	b	...	...
1	2	3	4	5	6	7	8

Figure 24.8 A binding vector illustrating eager and lazy dereferencing

Using lazy dereferencing, V3 is dereferenced to [V5 V6] and the process ends because the result is not a variable.   Using eager dereferencing, V3 is dereferenced to [a b]. Lazy dereferencing is obviously faster than eager, and since the structure of the computation only requires that a non-variable result be used, lazy deferencing is used in Shen Prolog.

3. Binding

Syntax:

<Binding Assignment> := (bind <Symbol> to <Value> in <AUM instruction>)

σ (bind <Symbol> to <Value> in <AUM instruction>)
= (let Binding (bindv <Symbol> <Value> **Process-Number**)
        Continue σ<AUM instruction>
        (if (= false Continue)
        (do (unbindv <Symbol> Process-Number) Continue)
        Continue))

The code here is a little more complex. If a symbol (variable) is to be bound to a value then the first action is to destructively update the binding vector by binding the symbol to the value using the process number to access the appropriate vector. Binding a variable means, of course, using the number embedded in that variable to access the appropriate index in the vector.

The computation continues with the translation of the AUM instruction. If that computation should fail by returning **false,** (Prolog does not find a solution), then we unbind the variable from its value returning **false** or else, if the computation has succeeded, we return that result whatever it is.

4. Renaming

Syntax: <Renaming> := (rename the variables in <value>
                                and then <AUM instruction>)

Here two possibilities arise; that <value> has no variables in it or that it has. Let ς be the set of all variables in <value> then

σ(rename the variables in <value> and then <AUM instruction>)
        = σ(rename the variable set ς and then <AUM instruction>)

if $\varsigma = \{\}$
then
σ(rename the variable set ς and then <AUM instruction>)
        = σ(<AUM instruction>)
else if $\varsigma = \{V\} \cup \varsigma'$
σ(rename the variable set ς and then <AUM instruction>)
    = **(let V (newprologvariable)**
            σ(rename the variable set ς' and then <AUM instruction>))

Here **newprologvariable** generates a new Prolog variable.

5. Continuations

σ(call the continuation []) = **(thaw Continuation)**
σ(call the continuation [[F x_1 ... x_n]])
    = **(F** x_1 ... x_n **Process-Number Continuation)**
σ(call the continuation [[F x_1 ... x_n] L_2 ...L_m])
    = **(F** x_1 ... x_n **Process-Number** $\pi([L_2 ...L_m])$**)**

In processing the continuation there are three cases. The first corresponds to where the tail of the Horn clause is empty and the goal stack is popped; the appropriate call is to thus thaw the continuation. In the second case the tail of the Horn clause contains exactly one literal. In that event the computation must call directly the function cited by the predicate symbol in the literal; this function will of course need both the process number and continuation as extra arguments.

In the last case the Horn clause has more than one literal; again we must call directly the function cited by the predicate symbol F in the literal. However this time the continuation must be augmented by our representation π of the literals L_2 ...L_m that occur after the first literal. The equations for π are:

$\pi([]) =$ **Continuation**
$\pi(G \ y_1 \ ... \ y_k] \ ... \ L_m) =$ **(freeze (G** y_1 ... $y_m \pi(\ ... \ L_m])$**))**

What π does is to systematically recurse through the list of literals, turning them into frozen computations that will, if the computation is successful, be thawed.

6. Failure

σ(FAIL!) = **false**

The AUM tests are translated as follows.

σ(<Value₁> is identical to <Value₂>)
= (= ϖ(<Value₁>) ϖ(<Value₂>))
σ(<Value> is a non-empty list) = **(cons?** ϖ(<Value>))
σ(<Value> is a variable) = **(prologvar?** ϖ(<Value>))

24.7 Compiling the Cut

In Shen, the cut literal !, which appears as a zero-place predicate is actually compiled as a 1-place predicate cut. Since the compilation process always generates an n+2 place function from an n-place predicate, cut issues in a 3-place function.

```
(define cut
    Throw ProcessNumber Continuation
    -> (let Compute (thaw Continuation)
          (if (= Compute false)
              (simple-error Throw)
              Compute)))
```

The significant parameter here is Throw, which is taken by a string. If the continuation succeeds then the result is returned, but if it fails then cut throws out an exception E using Throw.

The exception is caught by the Horn clause procedure (Shen function) *f* which called the cut. It is the responsibility of *f* to handle the unique dynamically generated string value S for Throw and using trap-error, to trap the exception that the cut produces. Any exception E is trapped by *f* and mapped back to a string S' which is compared to S. If S = S', then this must have been raised by the cut and hence the exception is trapped and false is returned curtailing any further search within *f*. If S <> S', then the exception is not the responsibility of *f* and it is simply passed on for another clause invocation to deal with.

24.8 Head Abstraction

Although the AUM instructions are efficient, the branching nature of the AUM can lead to slow compilation speeds when dealing with clauses with large heads. The exponential growth is clearly illustrated in the following progression (figure 24.9).

Clause	Lines of Shen Generated
(defprolog f [a] <--;)	21
(defprolog g [a b] <--;)	48
(defprolog h [a b c] <--;)	103
(defprolog i [a b c d] <--;)	217

Figure 24.9 Exponential code generation in the AUM

The AUM will generate instructions in space proportional to 2^n, where n is the number of non-variable subterms in the head of the Horn clause. This behaviour arises from the fact that the AUM generates what is effectively a binary tree. Pattern-matching mode declarations effectively lop branches reducing the tree to a straight line in which space utilisation becomes linear.

The solution adopted within the AUM is to place a cap on the complexity of the head of the clause and to use a technique here called **head abstraction** if the cap is exceeded.

The trick of head abstraction is to replace non-variable terms in the head by variables which reduce the complexity of the head of the clause. The displaced non-variable terms are then pushed onto the tail of the Horn clause. This can be done in two ways.

The simplest method, **naïve head abstraction**, places a unification test at front of the body which simply unifies the head of the clause with a variable. Using this technique on the clause (defprolog i [a b c d] <--;) by abstracting [a b c d] gives (defprolog i X <-- (= X [a b c d]);). This simple technique reduces code generation from 217 lines to 4 lines! Its downside is that it loses computational speed since run-time unification is employed and some of the benefits of partial evaluation are lost.

Head abstraction in its full or sophisticated form generates code that is both time and space efficient. Instead of simply inserting a full unification test, the head abstraction algorithm cycles through the head of the Horn clause, abstracting non-variable terms and replacing them with variables. The algorithm then generates **prosthetic literals** which are placed on the body of the optimised clause.

```
(defprolog i [a b c d] <--;)
```

might be optimised to.

```
(defprolog i [a b c d] <-- (i₁ W), (i₂ X), (i₃ Y), (i₄ Z);)
```

Prosthetic clauses are generated to handle these calls.

```
(defprolog i₁ a <--;)
(defprolog i₂ b <--;)
(defprolog i₃ c <--;)
(defprolog i₄ d <--;)
```

This style of head abstraction reduces the code generation from 217 to 91 lines.

Though head abstraction is essentially a simple algorithm there are some important features to grasp about it. The first is that head abstraction is a recursive algorithm; whether working top down (abstracting from the most complex terms) or bottom up (from the least complex non-variable terms), the algorithm may be applied to its own output in order to reduce the complexity to the required level. The measure of complexity is defined by the following equations which define the number of control paths.

For any head $(f\ t_1,....t_n)$, the complexity χ of $f(t_1,....t_n)$ is defined as $\Sigma(\chi(t_i))$ for all $i \leq n$ and $i \geq 1$; such that where t is a term;

if t is a variable then $\chi(t) = 1$;
if t is a constant then $\chi(t) = 2$;
if t has the form $[t_1 \mid t_2]$ then $\chi(t) = 2 * \chi(t_1) * \chi(t_2)$.

The choice of a threshold for invoking head abstraction is a matter of taste. In Shen the level is set at 128 and can be reconfigured by the maxcomplexity function. The absolutely lowest value that can sensibly be set is 2. Any figure below this will cause an infinite regress.

The second point to grasp is that variable dependencies must be preserved in the generation of the prosthetic literals. These variable dependencies may exist when the original clause has a non-empty body (i.e. the clause is a rule).

For example suppose that the clause is

```
(defprolog j
  [X | Y] X [Y Z]) <-- (k X Y) (l Y Z);)
```

The complexity of the head of this clause is 16. [X | Y] is 2. X is 1. [Y Z] is really [Y | [Z | [ ]]] which is 8. There are thus 16 possible control paths in this head.

Suppose then we set out to reduce this to 1 by head abstraction. First we left-linearise the clause.

```
(defprolog j
  [X | Y] X1 [Y1 Z] <-- (= X X1) (= Y Y1) (k X Y) (l Y Z);)
```

An initial erroneous attempt just replaces the top level non-variable terms by variables generating this code.

```
(defprolog j
  V1 X1 V2 <-- (pr1 V1) (pr2 V2) (= X X1) (= Y Y1)  (k X Y) (l Y Z);)

(defprolog pr1
  [X | Y] <--;)

(defprolog pr2
  Y1 Z <--;).
```

But this is wrong, because in the top clause the variables X, Y and Z are no longer bound by the head of the clause. In order for these bindings to be remembered, the prosthetic literals need to carry extra **prosthetic variables**. These variables represent the intersection of the variables cited in the prosthetic clauses with those variables that occurred in the body of the original clause.

```
(defprolog j
  V1 X1 V2 <-- (pr1 V1 X Y) (pr2 V2 Y1 Z) (= X X1) (= Y Y1) (k XY) (l Y Z);)

(defprolog pr1   [X | Y] X Y <--;)

(defprolog pr2   [Y1 Z] Y1 Z <--;)
```

Further optimisation is possible because the prosthetic variables are always passed to the prosthetic clauses as free variables. Hence instead of a generalised and inefficient unification test in the prosthetic clauses, the faster Shen Prolog bind can be inserted.

```
(defprolog pr1 [X | Y] V W  <-- (bind V X) (bind W Y);)
(defprolog pr2 [Y1, Z], V, W <-- (bind V Y1) (bind W Z);)
```

Now the code is correct since the proper bindings for X, Y and Z are transmitted through the prosthetic literals. The most complex clause, pr2, has a complexity of 8 - half that of the original and the total complexity of this group is 10.

Exercise 24

1. What sort of Horn clause programs would be produced by the following sequent rules?

    $$\frac{X : zero\text{-}or\text{-}one, \ [Y \mid Z] : binary >> P;}{[X \ Y \mid Z] : binary >> P;}$$

    $$\frac{X : variable; \ Y : lambda\_expr;}{[/. \ X \ Y] : lambda\_expr;}$$

    $$\frac{if \ (prime? \ X)}{X : prime;}$$

2. Generate μ applications from the following Horn clause procedures.

    ```
    (defprolog app
     [ ] X X <--;
     [X | Y] Z [X | W] <-- (app Y Z W);)
    ```

    ```
    (defprolog sub
     X Y Y X <--;
     X Y [W | Z] [W1 | Z1] <-- (sub X Y W W1) (sub X Y Z Z1);)
    ```

3. From your answers to 3, perform mu reduction and generate AUM instructions.

4. Define the class of AUM instructions as a datatype.

5. Define the class of Shen Prolog expressions as a datatype.

6. Define the class of mu expressions as a datatype.

7. Construct a type secure Shen Prolog to mu expression compiler.

8. Construct a type secure mu-expression to AUM compiler.

9. ** How would you type check Shen Prolog?

10. Perform head abstraction on the following clause,

    ```
    (defprolog k
     X [X Y a] [a b] Z Z <-- (l X Y) (m Y Z);)
    ```

    repeating where necessary so that every resulting clause has a complexity of no more than 2.

11. How might you apply the factorisation techniques discussed in 15.3 to optimise the output of the AUM?

Further Reading

The first high performance compiler for Prolog was written for the DEC-10 by David Warren. He later generalised this to produce the Warren Abstract Machine (Warren 1983). A good account of Prolog compilation techniques is found in Maier and Warren (1988).

Web Sites

Ait-Kaci http://www.vanx.org/archive/wam/wambook.pdf gives a free online tutorial in pdf on the Warren Abstract Machine.

25 System ᘐ

We know that sequent calculus is a powerful notation for expressing rules of deduction. We've also learnt that type theories for our programs can be expressed in terms of sequent calculus rules. Unsurprisingly, the type theory underlying Shen itself is expressible as a set of sequent calculus rules called system ᘐ and the goal of this chapter is to present this system. In the next chapter we will prove that our proof procedure for ᘐ has some desirable properties including termination.

25.1 Type Checking Applications

Our first set of rules (figure 25.1) enables applications to be type checked.

Sequents	*Application*	*Primitive*
$\dfrac{}{X : A >> X : A;}$	$\dfrac{F : (A \rightarrow B); X : A;}{(F\ X) : B;}$	$\dfrac{\text{if X is base and A} \in \tau(X)}{X : A;}$

Figure 25.1 The rules for type checking applications

The *Sequents Rule* is obvious. The *Rule of Application* states that an application (F X) has the type B provided F has the type A $\rightarrow$ B for some A and X has the type A. The *Primitive Rule* assumes that there is a function τ from the set of all base expressions of Shen (i.e. numbers, symbols, function symbols and the rest) into the powerset of all types such that A $\in \tau(e)$ when A is a type of e; thus $\tau(1) =$ {number}, $\tau("1") =$ {string}, $\tau(+) =$ {number $\rightarrow$ (number $\rightarrow$ number), symbol}. The *Primitive Rule* states that given a typing $e : A$ to prove, we may prove it if e is a base object where A $\in \tau(e)$.

From these rules, we can establish the types of applications. Here is an example; the goal is to prove that (* 1 0) : number. To adopt the curried form required by the *Rule of Application* we write (* 1 0) as ((* 1) 0).

Proof: by the *Rule of Application* ((* 1) 0) : number is proved if there is a type A such that (* 1) : A · number and 0 : A. Let A be the type number. Then we need to prove (* 1) : number $\rightarrow$ number and 0 : number. 0 : number follows by the

Primitive Rule. By the *Rule of Application* (* 1) : number if there is some type B such that * : B → (number → number) and 1 : B. Let B be the type number; * : number → (number → number) and 1 : number are proved by the *Primitive Rule.*

The preceding proof could be easily mechanised on a computer except for the problem of choosing values for variables. Consider the case in the preceding proof where it was necessary to decide a value for 'B' such that '* : B → (number → number)' was solvable. The *Primitive Rule* can show that * : number → (number · number). The problem is to match '* : number → (number → number)' to the conclusion '* : B → (number → number)'. These two typings match completely except where 'B' is matched to 'number'.

In order to agree that the two typings match, an extended notion of "match" must be used and unification provides this notion. Unification is used within type checking to perform the needed substitutions. The typings * : B → (number → number) and * : number → (number → number) are unified to find their MGU σ and the instantiation is given by σ(B). Here σ(B) = number.

In Shen, all the rules of its type system (including those entered by the user) are interpreted *modulo* unification with respect to types. We shall adopt this approach in all the subsequent proofs in this chapter.

25.2 Type Checking Abstractions

The *Rule of Abstraction* says that (λ V X) has the type A → B if, where *c* is arbitrary object of type A, $[X]_{c/v}$ (the result of replacing all free occurrences of V by *c* throughout X) is of the type B (figure 25.2).

Abstraction

where c is fresh
$c : A \gg [X]_{c/v} : B;$
(λ V X) : (A → B);

Figure 25.2 The rule for type checking abstractions

Here is a proof of (λ x ((* 3) x)) : number → number, demonstrating the use of the *Abstraction* and *Sequents Rules*

Proof: by the *Abstraction Rule*, (λ x ((* 3) x)) : number → number is provable if *a* : number >> ((* 3) *a*) : number is provable (*a* is our fresh symbol). By the *Rule of Application*, *a* : number >> ((* 3) *a*) : number is provable if both

a : number >> (* 3) : A → number
a : number >> *a* : A

are provable for some type A. The second sequent is solved using the *Sequents Rule* with unifier $\{A \mapsto \text{number}\}$. The first sequent now becomes

a : number >> (* 3) : number $\rightarrow$ number.

By the *Rule of Application* again, this splits into two subproblems

a : number >> * : B $\rightarrow$ (number $\rightarrow$ number).
a : number >> 3 : B

Both these problems are solved by the *Primitive Rule* using the unifier $\{B \mapsto \text{number}\}$.

These three rules define the type theory of the **simply typed lambda calculus** (STL) and are implicit in all typed functional languages. This type theory is extremely basic; in fact it is provable that expressions that are well-typed according to STL are guaranteed to have terminating evaluations; a property called **strong normalisation**. The price for this property is that certain expressions like the Y-combinator cannot be type checked within the STL. Shen requires additional rules to operate as a practical language for programming. We next look at the rules for polymorphic types.

25.3 Polymorphic Functions

When we say that the polymorphic function $(\lambda x\ x)$ has the type A $\rightarrow$ A, this is a shorthand for asserting that for *all* values of A, $(\lambda x\ x)$ inhabits A $\rightarrow$ A, or in logical notation $(\forall A\ (A \rightarrow A))$. The *Rule of Generalisation* enables proofs of the types of polymorphic functions. To prove that X : $(\forall A\ B)$, we must prove that, where t is any arbitrary type, X : $B_{C/A}$ (where $B_{C/A}$ is the result of substituting all occurrences of A by C). The concept of arbitrary is defined in the same way as previously - by the introduction of a fresh symbol.

Where t is fresh   and c is any type.

Generalisation	Specialisation
$\dfrac{X : [B]_{t/v;}}{X : (\forall v\ B);}$	$\dfrac{X : [B]_{c/v},\ X : (\forall v\ B)\ >> P;}{X : (\forall v\ B)\ >> P;}$

Figure 25.3 The rules for type checking with polytypes

Here is a proof that $(\lambda x\ x) : (\forall A\ (A \rightarrow A))$.

Proof: Applying the *Rule of Generalisation* to the problem derives $(\lambda\ x\ x) : a \rightarrow a$, ($a$ is our fresh symbol). Applying the *Rule of Abstraction* to $(\lambda\ x\ x) : a \rightarrow a$ derives $b : a \gg b : a$ (b is our fresh symbol) which is solved by the *Sequents Rule*.

The *Rule of Specialisation* is obvious; if we have shown that $X : (\forall v\ B)$, then we can conclude that $X : B_{c/v}$ for any type C we care to choose. Here is a proof of that [ ] : $(\forall A$ (list A)), remove : $(\forall A$ (A $\rightarrow$ ((list A) $\rightarrow$ (list A)))) $\gg$ ((remove 1) [ ]) : (list number).

Proof: By the *Rule of Specialisation* applied twice, we derive

[ ] : $\forall A$ (list A), [ ] : (list number),
remove : (number $\rightarrow$ ((list number) $\rightarrow$ (list number))),
remove : $\forall A$(A $\rightarrow$ ((list A) $\rightarrow$ (list A))) $\gg$ ((remove 1) [ ]) : (list number).

Let Δ be the assumptions in this sequent. We have to prove

$\Delta \gg$ ((remove 1) [ ]) : (list number).

By the *Rule of Applications* we have two sequents to prove; $\Delta \gg$ (remove 1) : (B $\rightarrow$ (list number)) and [ ] : B. Applying the *Rule of Applications* to the first sequent we derive a total of three sequents;

1. $\Delta \gg$ remove : (C $\rightarrow$ (B $\rightarrow$ (list number)))
2. $\Delta \gg 1 : C$.
3. $\Delta \gg$ [ ] : B

The first is solved by unification using the *Sequents Rule* ($\{C \mapsto$ number, B $\mapsto$ (list number)$\}$). The second (1 : C, with C $\mapsto$ number) is solved by *Primitive* and [ ] : B is solved by the *Sequents Rule* with B $\mapsto$ (list number).

In the implementation of Shen, the *Specialisation Rule* is not used, since its purpose is only to allow us to specialise the $\forall$-bound symbols. Instead, unification is used. The objects $\perp$ and $\otimes$ have the type ($\forall$ A A).

$$\frac{\rule{3cm}{0.4pt}}{\perp : (\forall\ A\ A);} \qquad \frac{\rule{3cm}{0.4pt}}{\otimes : (\forall\ A\ A);}$$

Figure 25.4 The rules for error objects

25.4 Special Forms

Certain expressions of Shen are special forms - they cannot be curried and they have their own typing rules (figure 14.6).[72]

Cons Rule (left)
X : A, Y : (list A) >> P;
(**cons** X Y) : (list A) >> P;

Cons Rule (right)
X : A; Y : (list A);
(**cons** X Y) : (list A)

@p Rule (left)
X : A, Y : B >> P;
(**@p** X Y) : (A * B) >> P;

@p Rule (right)
X : A; Y : B;
(**@p** X Y) : (A * B)

Local Rule
where c is fresh
Y : B; c : B >> [Z]c/X : A;
(let X Y Z) : A;

Figure 25.5 The rules for special forms

Here is a proof that (let X 6 (if (= X 5) 0 1)) : number. By the *Local Rule*, (let X 6 (if (= X 5) 0 1)) : number if both 6 : A and x : A >> (if (= x 5) 0 1) : number. The first problem is solved by the *Primitive Rule* with A $\mapsto$ number. The second problem dereferences to

$$x : \text{number} >> (\text{if } (= x \ 5) \ 0 \ 1) : \text{number}$$

By the type for *if*, this problem is solvable if the following are solvable.

1. x : number >> (= x 5) : boolean;
2. x : number >> 0 : number
3. x : number >> 1 : number

2. and 3. are solvable by the *Primitive Rule* and 1. decomposes to

4. x : number >> x : B
5. x : number >> 5 : B

4. is solved by the *Sequents Rule* with B $\mapsto$ number and 5. by the *Primitive Rule*.

---

[72] Other expressions which have their own typing rules are @s, @v, error, input+, make-string and output.

25.5 Recursion, Cases, Patterns and Guards

The rules in this section deal with two important aspects - recursion and patterns
The first rule deals with the Y combinator.

Combinator Rule
where c is fresh

$$\frac{c : A >> [Y]_{c/v} : A}{(Y \; (\lambda \; v \; Y)) : A}$$

Figure 25.6 The rule for type checking recursive functions

In chapter 16 we saw that that the combinator Y could be used to define recursive functions. The combinator rule allows us to type check the types of such functions. We define factorial as $(\lambda \; x \; (\text{if} \; (= x \; 0) \; 1) \; ((* \; x) \; (factorial \; ((- \; x) \; 1)))))$; or expressed with Y - $(Y \; (\lambda \; y \; (\lambda \; x \; (\text{if} \; (= x \; 0) \; 1 \; ((* \; x) \; (y \; ((- \; x) \; 1)))))))$. We prove that this expression has the type number $\rightarrow$ number.

Proof Sketch:

We want to prove $(Y \; (\lambda \; f \; (\lambda \; x \; (\text{if} \; (= x \; 0) \; 1 \; ((* \; x) \; (f \; ((- \; x) \; 1))))))) :$ number $\rightarrow$ number. By the *Combinator Rule*, this is provable if

$f :$ number $\rightarrow$ number $>> (\lambda \; x \; (\text{if} \; (= x \; 0) \; 1 \; ((* \; x) \; (f \; ((- \; x) \; 1))))) :$ number $\rightarrow$ number

The reader can complete the proof. The next two rules deal with case statements and guards.

Cases Rule
For each i, $1 \leq i \leq n$
$\underline{\text{Case}_i : A;}$
$(\textbf{cases} \; \text{Case}_1 \; ... \; \text{Case}_n) : A$

Guard Rule
Guard : boolean;
$\underline{\text{Guard : verified} >> X : A;}$
$(\textbf{where} \; \text{Guard} \; X) : A$

Figure 25.7 The rules for type checking cases and guards

The first rule says that the body of a function definition (consisting of a series of cases) has the type A if every case in the body of the function has the type A. The second rule applies to guards and says that a guarded expression X has the type A if the guard has the type boolean and X has the type A under the assumption that the guard is verified. These rules are fairly straightforward.

The Patterns Rule is used to type check extended abstractions. We assume that V_1 ....V_n are all the variables occurring in P, and ϕ_1 , ..., ϕ_n are fresh symbols, and C_1, ...C_n are fresh variables. For any κ, the expression $[\kappa]_{<\phi_1... \phi_n>/<V_1,...,V_n>}$ indicates the replacement of the free occurrences of the variables V_1 ....V_n in κ by ϕ_1 , ..., ϕ_n.

Patterns Rule

$\phi_1 : C_1, ..., \phi_n : C_n \gg [P]_{<\phi_1... \phi_n>/<V_1,...,V_n>} : A;$

$\dfrac{[P]_{<\phi_1...-\phi_n>/<V_1...V_n>} : A \gg [X]_{<\phi_1...-\phi_n>/<V_1...V_n>} : B;}{(\lambda\ P\ X) : (A \to B);}$

Figure 25.8 The rule for type checking extended abstractions

The *Patterns Rule* subsumes the *Abstractions Rule* as a special case. Thus given P is a variable then the sequent $\phi_1 : C_1, ..., \phi_n : C_n \gg [P]_{<\phi_1... \phi_n>/<V_1,...,V_n>} : A;$ collapses into a problem equivalent to the trivial P : C $\gg$ P : A (where C is a fresh variable). The second sequent is just the same as the problem posed by the *Abstractions Rule*.

We illustrate the action of these rules by reference to the example of chapter 15, which in the language of $\mathcal{L}$ with fixpoints is.

$(Y$ $(\lambda$ M $(\lambda$ A $(\lambda$ B (cases $(((\lambda$ V $(\lambda$ [ ] false)) A) B)
$(((\lambda$ X $(\lambda$ (cons U W) (where (= U X) true)) A) B)
$(((\lambda$ X $(\lambda$ (cons Z Y) ((M X) Y))) A) B))))))

Here is a proof that the function defined has the type $(\forall A\ (A \to ((\text{list A}) \to \text{boolean})))$.

Proof: $(Y$ $(\lambda$ M $(\lambda$ A $(\lambda$ B (cases $(((\lambda$ V $(\lambda$ [ ] false)) A) B)
$(((\lambda$ X $(\lambda$ (cons U W) (where (= U X) true)) A) B)
$(((\lambda$ X $(\lambda$ (cons Z Y) ((M X) Y))) A) B))))))
$: (\forall A\ (A \to ((\text{list A}) \to \text{boolean})))$

By the *Generalisation Rule* this is provable if

$(Y$ $(\lambda$ M $(\lambda$ A $(\lambda$ B (cases $(((\lambda$ V $(\lambda$ [ ] false)) A) B)
$(((\lambda$ X $(\lambda$ (cons U W) (where (= U X) true)) A) B)
$(((\lambda$ X $(\lambda$ (cons Z Y) ((M X) Y))) A) B))))))
$: (c \to ((\text{list } c) \to \text{boolean}))$

By the *Combinator Rule* this is provable if

$m : (c \rightarrow ((\text{list } c) \rightarrow \text{boolean}))$
$\gg (\lambda \text{ A } (\lambda \text{ B } (\text{cases } (((\lambda \text{ V } (\lambda \text{ [ ] false}))\text{ A}) \text{ B})$
$\qquad\qquad\qquad (((\lambda \text{ X } (\lambda \text{ (cons U W) (where (= U X) true))}) \text{ A}) \text{ B})$
$\qquad\qquad\qquad (((\lambda \text{ X } (\lambda \text{ (cons Z Y) } ((m \text{ X}) \text{ Y}))) \text{ A}) \text{ B}))))$
$\qquad\qquad\qquad\qquad\qquad\qquad : (c \rightarrow ((\text{list } c) \rightarrow \text{boolean}))$

By the *Abstractions Rule* this is provable if

$a : c, m : c \rightarrow ((\text{list } c) \rightarrow \text{boolean})$
$\gg (\lambda \text{ B } (\text{cases } (((\lambda \text{ V } (\lambda \text{ [ ] false}))\text{ } a) \text{ B})$
$\qquad\qquad (((\lambda \text{ X } (\lambda \text{ (cons U W) (where (= U X) true))}) \text{ } a) \text{ B})$
$\qquad\qquad (((\lambda \text{ X } (\lambda \text{ (cons Z Y) } ((m \text{ X}) \text{ Y}))) \text{ } a) \text{ B}))) : ((\text{list } c) \rightarrow \text{boolean})$

By the *Abstractions Rule* this is provable if

$b : (\text{list } c), a : c, m : c \rightarrow ((\text{list } c) \rightarrow \text{boolean})$
$\gg (\text{cases } (((\lambda \text{ V } (\lambda \text{ [ ] false}))\text{ } a) \text{ } b)$
$\qquad\quad (((\lambda \text{ X } (\lambda \text{ (cons U W) (where (= U X) true))}) \text{ } a) \text{ } b)$
$\qquad\quad (((\lambda \text{ X } (\lambda \text{ (cons Z Y) } ((m \text{ X}) \text{ Y}))) \text{ } a) \text{ } b)) : \text{boolean}$

Let $\Delta = \{ b : (\text{list } c), a : c, m : c \rightarrow ((\text{list } c) \rightarrow \text{boolean})\}$, then by the *Cases Rule*, three cases remain to be proved.

1. $\Delta \gg (((\lambda \text{ V } (\lambda \text{ [ ] false}))\text{ } a) \text{ } b) : \text{boolean}$
2. $\Delta \gg (((\lambda \text{ X } (\lambda \text{ (cons U W) (where (= U X) true))}) \text{ } a) \text{ } b) : \text{boolean}$
3. $\Delta \gg (((\lambda \text{ X } (\lambda \text{ (cons Z Y) } ((m \text{ X}) \text{ Y}))) \text{ } a) \text{ } b) : \text{boolean}$

Case 1 $\Delta \gg (((\lambda \text{ V } (\lambda \text{ [ ] false}))\text{ } a) \text{ } b) : \text{boolean}$

By the *Applications Rule* this is provable if

$\Delta \gg ((\lambda \text{ V } (\lambda \text{ [ ] false}))\text{ } a) : \text{D} \rightarrow \text{boolean}$
$\Delta \gg b : \text{D}$

The second problem is solved by *Sequents* with $\text{D} \mapsto (\text{list } c)$. We are left with

$\Delta \gg ((\lambda \text{ V } (\lambda \text{ [ ] false}))\text{ } a) : (\text{list } c) \rightarrow \text{boolean}$

By the *Applications Rule* this is provable if

$\Delta \gg (\lambda \text{ V } (\lambda \text{ [ ] false})) : \text{E} \rightarrow ((\text{list } c) \rightarrow \text{boolean}))$
$\Delta \gg a : \text{E}$

The second problem is solved by *Sequents* with $E \mapsto c$. We are left with

$\Delta \gg (\lambda\ V\ (\lambda\ [\ ]\ \text{false})) : c \rightarrow ((\text{list}\ c) \rightarrow \text{boolean})$

By the *Abstractions Rule* this is provable if

$v : c, \Delta \gg (\lambda\ [\ ]\ \text{false}) : (\text{list}\ c) \rightarrow \text{boolean}$

By the *Patterns Rule* this is provable if

$v : c, \Delta \gg [\ ] : (\text{list}\ c)$
$v : c, [\ ] : (\text{list}\ c), \Delta \gg \text{false} : \text{boolean}$

which are both solved by the *Primitive Rule*. The proof of the remaining cases is left to the reader.

Internal forms are all ephemeral objects that exist during the compilation of Shen functions and do not appear in the resulting object code. Consequently it is not possible to execute some of these internal forms as actual procedures.

25.6 Global Variables

The *Global Rule* states that an assignment of X to a global variable G has the type A just when G is a symbol and it is provable that both the current value of G has the type A and so does X. Since Shen contains no rules to enable the conclusion (value G) : A to be proved, it is left to the user to enrich the type system by a rule stating the kind of object assigned to G in the way explained in chapter 19. set is also a special form.

where g is a symbol

(value G) : A; X : A;
(set G X) : A;

Figure 25.9 The rule for type checking global assignments

Exercise 25

1. Prove that the following functions have the following types:

   a. plus of chapter 3 has the type number $\rightarrow$ (number $\rightarrow$ number).
   b. fibonacchi of chapter 3 has the type number $\rightarrow$ number.
   c. join of chapter 4 has the type $\forall A$ (list A) $\rightarrow$ ((list A) $\rightarrow$ (list A))
   d. rev of chapter 4 has the type $\forall A$ (list A) $\rightarrow$ (list A).
   e. powerset of chapter 4 has the type $\forall A$ (list A) $\rightarrow$ (list (list A))
   f. converge of chapter 6 has the type $\forall A$ (A $\rightarrow$ A) $\rightarrow$ (A $\rightarrow$ A).

2. Suggest sequent rules for & and ∨, where $x : (\alpha \vee \beta)$ just when $x : \alpha$ or $x : \beta$; and $x : (\alpha \ \& \ \beta)$ just when $x : \alpha$ and $x : \beta$.

3. What happens when you try to implement your answer to 4 in Shen and why?

4. *Implement a type secure program that allows you to interactively do proofs in ℑ. This is called a **proof assistant**.

5. Extend your proof assistant to allow the system to receive new sequent rules which can be named. Add to the system your answers to 2.

6. Read Barendregt's article on the lambda cube and implement the vertices of the cube within the proof assistant.

7. *Read Thompson on Martin-Lof type theory and implement that system. Show that any two natural numbers have a sum and synthesise a program that adds them together.

8. Why cannot the Y-combinator be given a type in simply typed lambda calculus?

Further Reading

An axiomatisation for a typed functional language was described by Cardelli (1984); our system is closely modelled around Cardelli's axiomatisation. Discussions of alternative type systems can be found in Diller (1988), Girard (1989), Odifreddi ed. (1990), Turner (1991), Thompson (1991), Barendregt (1992), Gunter (1992) and Peirce (2002). Cerrito and Kesner (1999) describe a type system for an extended lambda calculus based on pattern-matching.

26 The Correctness of $\mathbf{S}$

The goal of this chapter is to prove that $\mathbf{S}$ is correct. In order to do that it is necessary to give some account of what 'correct' means in this context. More formally we shall prove for any virgin Shen image

1. If Shen assigns a type τ to an expression x, and x evaluates to y then Shen assigns τ to y. This is called the **subject reduction** property.
2. That if Shen assigns a type τ to an expression x which is a normal form then x really does have the type τ.
3. That in the absence of user defined derivation rules using datatype and synonym, Shen terminates for all inputs.

In order to achieve these results, some model of Shen execution has to be supplied. We do this by supplying an operational semantics for the enriched lambda calculus $\mathcal{L}$ of chapter 15. This calculus is directly transposable into a Shen program and has the advantage of being easily parsed. To save needless repetition, we shall not look at string and vector pattern matching in $\mathcal{L}$ because the logic of these operations is very much reflected in list pattern matching.

Using this operational semantics, we then prove the above theorems for a proof procedure $\mathcal{T}$ which is essentially an application of an ordering of the rules of $\mathbf{S}$. Then we shall describe a more efficient procedure $\mathcal{T}^*$. Finally we show that $\mathcal{T}^*$ reaches the same results as $\mathcal{T}$.

26.1 An Operational Semantics for $\mathcal{L}$

We assume as $\mathcal{L}$ system functions, ++ (the successor function), -- (the predecessor function), @p, **if**, **let**, **cases**, **where** and **cons**. $\mathcal{L}$ contains two special symbols; $\perp$ designates the error condition and $\otimes$ the special error condition generated from unsuccessfully matching an extended abstraction to an input. A **primitive object** of $\mathcal{L}$ is a string, number, character, boolean or symbol which is not used as a system function. For simplicity, string and vector pattern matching is omitted in this semantics though these extensions are not difficult and are left as an exercise for the reader to complete. $\mathcal{L}$ is nevertheless Turing complete.

The syntax rules for $\mathcal{L}$ are given in figure 26.1.

1. A primitive object is a formula of $\mathcal{L}$.
2. ( ) is a formula of $\mathcal{L}$.
3. $\perp$ and $\otimes$ are formulae of $\mathcal{L}$.
4. If x, y and z are formulae of $\mathcal{L}$, so is (if x y z), (cons x y), (@p x y), (where x y), (= x y), (x y).
5. If x is a variable and y and z are formulae of $\mathcal{L}$, then (let x y z) is a formula of $\mathcal{L}$.
6. If $x_i,\ldots,x_n$ ($0 \le i \le n$) are formulae of $\mathcal{L}$, so is (cases $x_i\ldots x_n$).
7. A primitive object is a pattern.
8. A variable is a pattern.
9. ( ) is a pattern.
10. If p_1 and p_2 are patterns then so is (cons p_1 p_2) and (@p p_1 p_2).
11. If p is a pattern and x is a formula of $\mathcal{L}$ then the abstraction (λ p x) is a formula of $\mathcal{L}$.
12. If v is a variable and the abstraction (λ v x) is a formula of $\mathcal{L}$ then ($\mathbf{Y}$ (λ v x)) is a formula of $\mathcal{L}$.

Figure 26.1 The syntax rules of $\mathcal{L}$

We assume that all patterns are linear; i.e. there are no repeated variables in a pattern. Next the rules giving the operational semantics of $\mathcal{L}$. The symbol $\Rightarrow$ means "rewrites to" and $\Downarrow$ indicates the normal form of an expression under rewriting; error(x) indicates x evaluates to $\otimes$ or $\perp$. Rules are applied in order of appearance.

Rule #1. (= x y) $\Rightarrow$ true if $\Downarrow x = \Downarrow y$ and not error($\Downarrow x$)
Rule #2. (= x y) $\Rightarrow$ false if $\Downarrow x \ne \Downarrow y$ and not error($\Downarrow x$) and not error($\Downarrow y$)
Rule #3. (= x y) $\Rightarrow \perp$ if error($\Downarrow x$) or error($\Downarrow y$)
Rule #4. ((λ p x) y) $\Rightarrow$ let σ be *match*(p, $\Downarrow y$); if $\sigma = \otimes$ then $\otimes$ else *sub*(σ, x)
Rule #5. (if x y z) $\Rightarrow$ if $\Downarrow x =$ true then y else if $\Downarrow x =$ false then z else $\perp$
Rule #6. (let x y z) $\Rightarrow$ ((λ x z) y)
Rule #7. (cons x y) $\Rightarrow$ if error($\Downarrow x$) or error($\Downarrow y$) then $\perp$ else (cons $\Downarrow x$ $\Downarrow y$)
Rule #8. (@p x y) $\Rightarrow$ if error($\Downarrow x$) or error($\Downarrow y$) then $\perp$ else (@p $\Downarrow x$ $\Downarrow y$)
Rule #9. (++ x) $\Rightarrow$ if $\Downarrow x$ is a number then $1 + \Downarrow x$ else $\perp$
Rule #10. (-- x) $\Rightarrow$ if $\Downarrow x$ is a number then $\Downarrow x$ - 1 else $\perp$
Rule #11. (cases $x_1 \ldots x_n$) $\Rightarrow$ if $\Downarrow x_1 = \otimes$ then (cases $\ldots x_n$) else $\Downarrow x_1$.
Rule #12. (cases) $\Rightarrow \perp$
Rule #13. (where x y) $\Rightarrow$ (if x y $\otimes$)
Rule #14. ($\mathbf{Y}$ (λ v x)) $\Rightarrow [x]_{v/(\mathbf{Y}\ (\lambda\ v\ x))}$
Rule #15. (x y) $\Rightarrow$ if error($\Downarrow x$) or error($\Downarrow y$) then $\perp$ else ($\Downarrow x$ $\Downarrow y$)
Rule #16. $x \Rightarrow x$ for any primitive

The equations for *match* and *sub* are as follows.

Match #1. $match(x, x) = \{\}$
Match #2. where x is a variable; $match(x, y) = \{<x, y>\}$
Match #3. $match((\text{cons } x \ y), (\text{cons } w \ z))$
　　　　　$= \text{let } \sigma_1 \text{ be } match(x, w), \text{ let } \sigma_2 \text{ be } match(y, z);$
　　　　　　　$\text{if } \sigma_1 = \otimes \text{ or } \sigma_2 = \otimes \text{ then } \otimes \text{ else } \sigma_1 \cup \sigma_2$
Match #4. $match((@\text{p } x \ y), (@\text{p } w \ z))$
　　　　　$= \text{let } \sigma_1 \text{ be } match(x, w), \text{ let } \sigma_2 \text{ be } match(y, z);$
　　　　　　　$\text{if } \sigma_1 = \otimes \text{ or } \sigma_2 = \otimes \text{ then } \otimes \text{ else } \sigma_1 \cup \sigma_2$
Match #5. $match(x, y) = \otimes$ in all cases not covered by Match #1-#4

Sub#1 $sub(\{\}, x) = x$
Sub#2 $sub(\{<x, y>\} \cup S, z) = sub(S, [z]_{y/x})$

We can use the rules of an operational semantics to hand-simulate an evaluation of a $\mathcal{I}$ expression. Figure 13.12 shows an example.

(let x 3 (if (= x 5) x (++ x)))
$\Rightarrow$ ((λ x (if (= x 5) x (++ x))) 3)
$\Rightarrow$ (if (= 3 5) 3 (++ 3))
$\Rightarrow$ (if false 3 (++ 3))
$\Rightarrow$ (++ 3)
$\Rightarrow$ 4

26.2 An Interpreter for $\mathcal{I}$

To show that our rules actually work, here is a complete interpreter for $\mathcal{I}$ written in Shen and based on our operational semantics. We begin by defining the datatypes of $\mathcal{I}$.

(datatype number

(number? X) : verified >> X : number;)

(datatype primitive_object

　　X : symbol;
　　X : primitive_object;

　　X : string;
　　X : primitive_object;

　　X : boolean;
　　X : primitive_object;

X : number;
X : primitive_object;
_____
[ ] : primitive_object;)

(datatype pattern

X : primitive_object;
X : pattern;

P1 : pattern; P2 : pattern;
==================
[cons P1 P2] : pattern;

P1 : pattern; P2 : pattern;
==================
[@p P1 P2] : pattern;)

(datatype number

_____
(number? X) : verified >> X : number;)

(datatype l_formula

X : pattern;
X : l_formula;

X : l_formula; Y : l_formula; Z : l_formula;
=================================
[if X Y Z] : l_formula;

X : variable; Y : l_formula; Z : l_formula;
=================================
[let X Y Z] : l_formula;

X : l_formula; Y : l_formula;
====================
[cons X Y] : l_formula;

X : l_formula; Y : l_formula;
====================
[@p X Y] : l_formula;

X : l_formula; Y : l_formula;
====================
[where X Y] : l_formula;

X : l_formula; Y : l_formula;
====================
[= X Y] : l_formula;

```
X : I_formula; Y : I_formula;
=====================
[X Y] : I_formula;

Xn : (list I_formula);
================
[cases | Xn] : I_formula;

P : pattern; X : I_formula;
====================
[/. P X] : I_formula;)
```

The code for the $\mathcal{I}$ interpreter now follows.

```
(define I_interpreter
  {A --> B}
  _ -> (read_eval_print_loop
         (output "~%L interpreter ~%~%~%~%I-interp --> ")
         (output "~A~%" (normal_form (input+ : I_formula)))))

(define read_eval_print_loop
  {string --> string --> A}
  _ _ -> (read_eval_print_loop
            (output "I-interp --> ")
            (output "~A~%" (normal_form (input+ : I_formula)))))

(define ==>
  {I_formula --> I_formula}
  [= X Y] -> (let X* (normal_form X) Y* (normal_form Y)
                 (cases (or (eval_error? X*) (eval_error? Y*)) "error!"
                        (= X* Y*) true
                        true false))
  [[/. P X] Y] -> (let Match (match P (normal_form Y))
                      (if (no_match? Match)
                          "no match" (sub Match X)))
  [if X Y Z] -> (let X* (normal_form X)
                    (cases (= X* true)  Y
                           (= X* false) Z
                           true  "error!"))
  [let X Y Z] -> [[/. X Z] Y]
  [@p X Y] -> (let X* (normal_form X) Y* (normal_form Y)
                  (if (or (eval_error? X*) (eval_error? Y*))
                      "error!" [@p X* Y*]))
  [cons X Y] -> (let X* (normal_form X)  Y* (normal_form Y)
                    (if (or (eval_error? X*) (eval_error? Y*))
                        "error!"
                        [cons X* Y*]))
  [++ X] -> (successor (normal_form X))
  [- - X] -> (predecessor (normal_form X))
  [cases X1 | Xn]
   -> (let Case1 (normal_form X1)
          (if (= Case1 "no match") [cases | Xn] Case1))
```

```
    [cases] -> "error!"
    [where X Y] -> [if X Y "no match"]
    [y-combinator [/. X Y]] -> (replace X [y-combinator [/. X Y]] Y)
    [X Y] -> (let X* (normal_form X)
                  Y* (normal_form Y)
                  (if (or (eval_error? X*) (eval_error? Y*))
                    "error!"
                    [X* Y*]))
  X -> X)

(define eval_error?
 {l_formula --> boolean}
  "error!" -> true
  "no match" -> true
  _ -> false)

(define normal_form
 {l_formula --> l_formula}
  X -> (fix ==> X))

(define successor
 {A --> l_formula}
  X -> (+ X 1) where (number? X)
  _ -> "error!")

(define predecessor
 {A --> l_formula}
  X -> (- X 1) where (number? X)
  _ -> "error!")

(define sub
 {[(pattern * l_formula)] --> l_formula --> l_formula}
  [] X -> X
  [(@p Var Val) | Assoc] X -> (sub Assoc (replace Var Val X)))

(define match
 {pattern --> l_formula --> [(pattern * l_formula)]}
  P X -> []                 where (== P X)
  P X -> [(@p P X)]     where (variable? P)
  [cons P1 P2] [cons X Y]
         -> (let Match1 (match P1 X)
              (if (no_match? Match1)
                 Match1
                 (let Match2 (match P2 Y)
                    (if (no_match? Match2)
                       Match2
                       (append Match1 Match2)))))
  [@p P1 P2] [@p X Y] -> (let Match1 (match P1 X)
                            (if (no_match? Match1)
                               Match1
                               (let Match2 (match P2 Y)
                                  (if (no_match? Match2)
```

```
                              Match2
                              (append Match1 Match2)))))
  _ _ -> [(@p no matching)])

(define no_match?
  {[(pattern * l_formula)] --> boolean}
  [(@p no matching)] -> true
  _ -> false)

(define replace
  {pattern --> l_formula --> l_formula --> l_formula}
  V W [let V X Y] -> [let V X Y]
  X Y X -> Y
  V W [= X Y] -> [= (replace V W X) (replace V W Y)]
  V W [/. P X] -> [/. P (replace V W X)]  where (free? V P)
  V W [if X Y Z] -> [if (replace V W X) (replace V W Y) (replace V W Z)]
  V W [let X Y Z] -> [let X (replace V W Y) (replace V W Z)]
  V W [@p X Y] -> [@p (replace V W X) (replace V W Y)]
  V W [cons X Y] -> [cons (replace V W X) (replace V W Y)]
  V W [cases | Xn] -> [cases | (map (/. Xi (replace V W Xi)) Xn)]
  V W [where X Y] -> [where (replace V W X) (replace V W Y)]
  V W [X Y] -> [(replace V W X) (replace V W Y)]
  _ _ X -> X)

(define free?
  {pattern --> pattern --> boolean}
  P P -> false
  P [cons P1 P2] -> (and (free? P P1) (free? P P2))
  P [@p P1 P2] -> (and (free? P P1) (free? P P2))
  _ _ -> true)
```

Figure 26.2 gives a short sample of our working interpreter.

```
(2+) (l_interpreter start)
L interpreter

l-interp --> [[/. 3 5] 3]
5

l-interp --> [[[y-combinator
             [/. ADD [/. X [/. Y [if [= X 0] Y [[ADD [++ X]] [-- Y]]]]]]  3] 4]
7

l-interp  --> [[[y-combinator [/. APPEND [/. X [/. Y
       [if [= X [ ]] Y  [cons [[/. [cons A B] A] X]
       [[APPEND [[/. [cons A B] B] X]] Y]]]]]]] [cons 1 [ ]]] [cons 2 [ ]]]
[cons 1 [cons 2 [ ]]]
```

Figure 26.2 The interpreter on some sample inputs

26.3 The Correctness of 𝕵

We define a **primitive data structure** (p.d.) as a symbol, boolean, number, string, list or tuple of p.d.s. The expression '$>> e : A$' is taken to mean '$e : A$ is provable in 𝕵'.

Our proof of the correctness of 𝕵 is covered in 3 theorems. In the first theorem, we demonstrate that if e is an p.d. of $\mathcal{I}$ and $>> e : A$, then $e : A$. In the second theorem, we demonstrate the **subject reduction property**, namely;

$$\text{if} >> e : A \text{ and } e \Rightarrow e^* \text{ then} >> e^* : A.$$

The third theorem is a consequence of both these theorems; namely that if $>> e : A$, then the evaluation of e to a p.d. e^* will produce an expression of type A.

Notice that it is not true that if $e \Rightarrow e^*$ and $>> e^* : A$ then $>> e : A$. The expression (if (= 1 0) a "a") evaluates to "a", but although $>>$ "a" : string, it is not a theorem that (if (= 1 0) a "a") : string.

Theorem 1: if e is a p.d. and $>> e : A$ then $e : A$.

Proof: Suppose e is a p.d. and $>> e : A$; then e is either

(a) a primitive expression (symbol, boolean, number or string), or
(b) a list of p.d.s, or
(c) a tuple of p.d.s.

Suppose (a), then the type of e is determined by τ, so that $e :$ string iff string $\in \tau(e)$ etc. The only type rule in $\mathcal{I}$ for proving the type of e is the *Primitive Rule* which establishes e : A only if $A \in \tau(e)$. Hence if $>> e : A$ then $A \in \tau(e)$ and so $e : A$.

Suppose (b), then e is a list and the proof proceeds by induction. Let the **ultimate length** (υ) be defined as follows.

$\upsilon(x) = 1$ where x is a primitive object.
for any list l, $\upsilon(l) = \Sigma(\upsilon(i))$ where i is an element in l.

Base Case: $\upsilon(e) = 0$

then $e = []$; according to the *Primitive Rule*, which is the only applicable rule, $>> e : \forall A$ (list A). By the inhabitation rule for lists (chapter 13);

$$\forall A(e : (\text{list } A) \leftrightarrow (\forall x \ \text{element} \ (x,e) \supset x : A))^{73}$$

Since $\sim\exists x$ element(x,e) then $e : \forall A: (\text{list } A)$.

Inductive Case: the theorem holds for all lists l where $\upsilon(l) \leq n$.

Let $e = [X \mid Y]$ be a list expression of ultimate length $n + 1$. Then if e has a type under Shen, it has the type (list A) for some A and so $>> e : (\text{list } A)$. This can only be established by the *Cons (right) Rule* and so $>> X : A$ and $>> Y : (\text{list } A)$. By the inductive hypothesis we conclude that $X : A$ and $Y : (\text{list } A)$. In which case $[X \mid Y] : (\text{list } A)$ and so $e : (\text{list } A)$.

Suppose (c), then e is a tuple $(@p \ x \ y)$. Let the **tuple size** (σ) be defined as follows.

$$\sigma(x) = 0 \text{ if } x \text{ is not a tuple.}$$
$$\sigma(@p \ x \ y) = 1 + \sigma(x) + \sigma(y).$$

The proof is by induction on the size of $\sigma(e)$.

Base Case: $\sigma(e) = 1$

Suppose $>> e : A$; then for some B, C, $A = (B * C)$ and $>> (@p \ x \ y) : (B * C)$. But if $>> (@p \ x \ y) : (B * C)$ then $>> x : A$ and $>> y : B$. But since $\sigma(x) = \sigma(y) = 0$, x and y are not tuples and are primitive, $x : B$ and $y : C$. By the inhabitation rule for tuples:

$$((@p \ x \ y) : (B * C)) \leftrightarrow ((x : B) \ \& \ (y : C))$$

Since the RHS of this equivalence is true, then $(@p \ x \ y) : (B * C)$ and so $e : A$.

Inductive Case: the theorem holds for all tuples t where $\sigma(t) \leq n$.

Suppose $\sigma(e) = n + 1$ and $>> e : A$; then for some B, C, $A = (B * C)$ and $>> (@p \ x \ y) : (B * C)$. But if $>> (@p \ x \ y) : (B * C)$ then $>> x : A$ and $>> y : B$. Also $\sigma(x) \leq n$ and $\sigma(y) \leq n$ and so by the inductive hypothesis, $x : B$ and $y : C$. By the inhabitation rule for tuples:

$$((@p \ x \ y) : (B * C)) \leftrightarrow ((x : B) \ \& \ (y : C))$$

---

[73] A potential for confusion exists between the use of $\rightarrow$ for logical implication and $\rightarrow$ for the function space type operator. Rather than relying on context alone to disambiguate the intended meaning, the proof uses the older $\supset$ for logical implication and $\rightarrow$ for the type operator.

Since the RHS of this equivalence is true, then $(@p \ x \ y) : (B * C)$ and so $e : A$.

Theorem 2: if $|\text{-} \ e : A$ and $e \Rightarrow e^*$ then $|\text{-} \ e^* : A$.

The proof proceeds by cases. The reduction of e to e^* must be one of the rules #1-16 in the semantics for $\mathcal{L}$.

By rule #1; then $e = (= x \ y)$, by the signature for $=$, $>> e$: boolean and since $e^* =$ true then $>> e^*$: boolean.

By rule #2, then $e = (= x \ y)$, by the signature for $=$, $>> e$: boolean and since $e^* =$ false then $>> e^*$: boolean.

By rule #3; then $e = (= x \ y)$ and suppose $>> e : A$. By rule #3, $e^* = \bot$ or $e^* = \otimes$ and by the rules for error conditions, $e^* : A$.

By rule #4; then $e = ((\lambda \ p \ x) \ y)$. Assume $>> e : A$, then by the *Applications Rule* for some B

$$>> (\lambda \ p \ x) : B \to A$$
$$>> y : B$$

Either $match(p, \ y) = \otimes$ or $match(p, \ y) \neq \otimes$. Assume $match(p, \ y) = \otimes$, then $e^* = \otimes$ and $>> e^* : A$ (since $>> \otimes : (\forall \ A \ A)$).

Assume $match(p, \ y) \neq \otimes$, then either

(a) p is a constant and $p = y$ and so $e^* = x$. We have $>> (\lambda \ p \ x) : B \to A$ which by the *Patterns Rule* is provable only if $>> p : B$ and $p : B >> x : A$. But if $>> p : B$ then $p : B >> x : A$ iff $>> x : A$. Hence $>> e^* : A$.

(b) p is a variable; then $e^* = [x]_{y/p}$. We have $>> (\lambda \ p \ x) : B \to A$ which by the *Patterns Rule* is provable only if

$z : C >> z : B$ where z is any arbitrary name and C is a fresh type variable.
$z : B >> [x]_{z/p} : A$

Note: the sequent $z : C >> z : B$ is trivially soluble by unification of B with the fresh C. In this case the *Patterns Rule* just acts like the *Abstractions Rule* in Simply Typed Lambda calculus.

But if $z : B >> [x]_{z/p} : A$ for any arbitrary z, then certainly $y : B >> [x]_{y/p} : A$ and given $>> y : B$ then $>> [x]_{y/p} : A$ and so $>> e^* : A$.

(c) p is a pattern of the form (cons $v \ w$) or $(@p \ v \ w)$; then since $match(p, \ y) \neq \otimes$ then $match(p, \ y)$ is a set σ of bindings. Each element $<v, \ b>$ of σ is an association of a variable v with a value b. We know from the *Patterns Rule* that $(\lambda\ p\ x) : B \rightarrow A$ is provable only if

1. $N_1 : A_1, ... N_n : A_n >> p^* : B$;
2. $p^* : B >> x^* : A$;

where $N_1...N_n$ are fresh names and $A_1...A_n$ are fresh type variables, p^* results from p by replacing all the variables $x_1,..,x_n$ in p by $N_1...N_n$ and x^* results from x by replacing all the free variables from $x_1,..,x_n$ by $N_1...N_n$.

$p^* : B >> x^* : A$ states that assuming an arbitrary substitution instance of the variables in p (i.e. p^*) to be of type B, that same substitution applied to the free variables in x produces an object (i.e. x^*) that can be proved to be of type A. Since *match*(p, y) succeeds y is a substitution instance of p.

So we have

$\sigma(p) : B >> \sigma(x) : A$

But $\sigma(p) = y$ and $\sigma(x) = e^*$. So we have

$y : B >> e^* : A$

But given $>> y : B$ then $>> e^* : A$

By rule #5; then $e = (\text{if } x\ y\ z)$; and $e^* = y$ or $e^* = z$ or $e^* = \bot$. Assume that $>> e : A$, then this is provable by the type of *if* and so $>> y : A$ and $>> z : A$. Since $>> \bot : A$, then $>> e^* : A$.

By rule #6; then $e = (\text{let } x\ y\ z)$, suppose $>> e : A$. Then by the *Local Rule* for some B, where x^* is fresh; $>> y : B$ and $x^* : B >> z_{x^*/x} : A$

Here $e^* = ((\lambda\ x\ z)\ y)$; by the *Applications Rule* $e^* : A$ if for some B;

$>> y : B$ and
$>> (\lambda\ x\ z) : (B \rightarrow A)$

By the *Patterns Rule*, $>> (\lambda\ x\ z) : (B \rightarrow A)$ just when, where x^* is fresh and C is a fresh type variable.

$x^* : C >> x^* : B$ and
$x^* : B >> z_{x^*/x} : A$

Since x is a variable the first sequent is easily soluble (unify C with B). So $>> e^* : A$ if both the following are provable.

$>> y : B$ and
$x^* : B >> z_{x^*/x} : A$

By hypothesis these are both provable, hence $>> e^* : A$.

By rule #7; then $e = $ (cons x y) and $>> e : A$ and either $e^* = \perp$ or $e^* = $ (cons $\Downarrow x$ $\Downarrow y$). If $e^* = \perp$ then $>> e^* : A$. Suppose $e^* = $ (cons $\Downarrow x$ $\Downarrow y$). We write '$e \Rightarrow_n e^*$' when e can be normalised to e^* using n rewrite rules. The proof of subject reduction is by induction on n. Suppose $n = 0$; then $e = e^*$ and the proof is immediate. Suppose that subject reduction holds when n rules are used; i.e. we assume if $>> e : A$ and $e \Rightarrow_n e_n$, then $>> e_n : A$ as an inductive hypothesis. We wish to show $>> e : A$ and $e \Rightarrow_{n+1} e_{n+1}$, then $>> e_{n+1} : A$. In this case we need to show only that each individual rule of our semantics preserves subject reduction where no further normalisation is needed above what is performed in the rule itself. Such a proof is essentially nothing more than a reiteration of the cases already cited. In the case of rule #7, if no normalisation of x or y is required, then again $e = e^*$ and the proof is immediate.

What our reasoning establishes is that the presence of the $\Downarrow$ symbol is irrelevant to the subject reduction property. Provided *every* rule preserves subject reduction in *every* case where no further normalisation is needed above what is performed in the rule itself, then subject reduction will obtain for the system overall. In future we will invoke this argument to banish the $\Downarrow$ by the phrase "by induction on the order of rewriting".

By rule #8; then $e = $ (@p x y) and $>> e : A$ and either $e^* = \perp$ or $e^* = $ (@p $\Downarrow x$ $\Downarrow y$). By induction on the order of rewriting, we drop the $\Downarrow$ and consider only $e^* = \perp$ or $e^* = $ (@p x y). If $e^* = \perp$ then $>> e^* : A$. If $e^* = $ (@p x y) then the proof is immediate.

By rule #9; then $e = (++ x)$ and $>> e : $ number. Either $e^* = \perp$ or $e^* = (1 + \Downarrow x)$. If $e^* = \perp$ then certainly $>> e : $ number. If $\Downarrow x$ is a number then $1 + \Downarrow x$ is a number and by the *Primitive Rule*, $>> 1 + \Downarrow x : $ number and so $>> e^* : $ number.

By rule #10; then $e = (- - x)$ and $>> e : $ number. Either $e^* = \perp$ or $e^* = (\Downarrow x - 1)$. If $e^* = \perp$ then certainly $>> e : $ number. If $\Downarrow x$ is a number then $\Downarrow x - 1$ is a number and by the *Primitive Rule*, $>> \Downarrow x - 1 : $ number and so $>> e^* : $ number.

By rule #11; then $e = $ (cases $x_1 \ldots x_n$) and $>> e : A$. Either $\Downarrow x_1 = \otimes$ or $\Downarrow x_1 \neq \otimes$. By induction on the order of rewriting, we drop the $\Downarrow$ and consider only the cases $x_1 = \otimes$ or not $x_1 = \otimes$.

If $x_1 = \otimes$ then $e^* = $ (cases $\ldots x_n$). By the *Cases Rule*, $>> e : A$ just when each x_i in (cases $x_1 \ldots x_n$) is such that $>> x_i : A$. So certainly it must be true that $>> $ (cases $\ldots x_n$) : A and therefore $>> e^* : A$.

If $x_1 \neq \otimes$, then $e^* = x_1$ and since by the *Cases Rule* for each x_i in (cases $x_1 \ldots x_n$), $>> x_i : A$ then $>> x_1 : A$ and so $>> e^* : A$.

By rule #12; then $e^* = \otimes$ and since $>> \otimes : (\forall A \, A))$, subject reduction holds.

By rule #13; then $e =$ (where $x \, y$) and $e^* =$ (if $x \, y \, \otimes$). Suppose $>> e : A$, then by the *Guard Rule*, $>> x :$ boolean and $>> y : A$. By the type of *if* to prove $>> e^* : A$, it suffices to prove $>> x :$ boolean and $>> y : A$ and $>> \otimes : A$. By hypothesis, the first two are provable and the third follows from $>> \otimes : (\forall A \, A))$.

By rule #14; in that case e is a combinator expression, $(Y \, (\lambda \, v \, x))$ and $e^* = [x]_{v/(Y \, (\lambda \, v \, x))}$. Assume $e : A$, then $(Y \, (\lambda \, v \, x)) : A$ and this is provable only if $v : A >> x : A$. Consider the proof tree for $v : A >> x : A$. For every subgoal of the form $v : A$, the assumption $v : A$ will be used to solve it. Now replace this subgoal by $(Y \, (\lambda \, v \, x))$ and drop the assumption $v : A$. By the *Combinator Rule*, this is provable if $v : A >> x : A$, which by hypothesis *is* provable. Hence if there is a proof of $v : A >> x : A$ then there is a proof of $[x]_{v/(Y \, (\lambda \, v \, x))} : A$ and so $>> e^* : A$.

By rule #15; in that case e is an application $(x \, y)$. Suppose $>> e : A$ and $e^* = \perp$ then $>> e^* : A$. Suppose $e^* = (\Downarrow x \, \Downarrow y)$. By induction on the order of rewriting, we drop the $\Downarrow$ and consider only the case $(x \, y)$ and the proof is trivial.

By rule #16; then $e = e^*$ and the proof is immediate.

Theorem 3: if $>> e : A$ then, if $\Downarrow e$ is a p.d., then $\Downarrow e : A$.

Assume $>> e : A$ and $\Downarrow e$ is a p.d.. We write '$e \Rightarrow_m e^*$' when e can be normalised to e^* using m rewrite rules. The proof is by induction on m. If $e \Rightarrow_0 \Downarrow e$, then e is a normal form and by theorem 1, $\Downarrow e : A$.. Assume the theorem holds for n rewrites. Assume $e \Rightarrow_{n+1} \Downarrow e$; then for some e^*, $e \Rightarrow e^* \Rightarrow_n \Downarrow e$. By theorem 2 we know that if $>> e : A$ then $>> e^* : A$, and by the inductive hypothesis, we have if $>> e^* : A$ then $\Downarrow e : A$. So $>> e : A$ implies $\Downarrow e : A$.

26.4 The Termination of $\mathcal{T}$

One desirable property of a type checking procedure is that it is terminating, sound and complete; that is to say, the procedure constitutes a decision procedure for the type system in question. Fairly obviously, $\mathcal{T}$ is sound (since it uses only the type rules for $\mathcal{L}$). Moreover the previous section established the type security of the system itself. We will prove $\mathcal{T}$ is terminating.

We first have to prove a theorem based on the nature of the type rules that $\mathcal{T}$ uses. The type rules are of two kinds.

A. Type rules that eliminate goals without producing subgoals.
B. Type rules that generate subgoals but reduce the bracketing of an expression in the original goal.

We will call these 'A-rules' and 'B-rules' respectively. Let us say that a sequent system is an **AB system** if every rule in it is an A-rule or a B-rule. Intuitively, any proof procedure which uses an AB system by applying all the rules in it will eventually generate a fixpoint. In other words, it needs to be proved that there is no infinite chain of rule applications R_1, R_2, R_3, ... which can be successively applied to a series of goals G such that for all n, $R_n(...(R_1(G))) \neq R_{n+1}(...(R_n(R_1(G))))$. The theorem that states this is the **AB theorem**.

To prove this formally, we need a function, β, which returns a value based on the bracketing found in the expressions used in the proof procedure. We begin by inductively defining β for typings. A typing is an expression of the form $x : \tau$, where x is an expression of $\mathcal{I}$ and τ is a type expression. Typings are effectively the well-formed formulae of a proof conducted by $\mathcal{T}$. Type expressions are defined inductively.

1. A symbol is a type expression.
2. If a is a type expression and b is a type expression and v is a variable, then $(a \to b)$, $(a * b)$, (list a), $(\forall v\ a)$ are type expressions.

The function β is defined inductively over typings as follows.

$$\beta(x : \tau) = \beta(x) + 1$$

For $\mathcal{I}$ expressions, β is defined as follows.

$$\beta(x) = 0 \text{ if x is a primitive object}$$
$$\beta(x_1 ....x_n) = \Sigma(x_i) + 1 \text{ for i} = 1 \text{ to i} = n.$$

If $\beta(x) = n$ we say that the **B-value** of x is n. Given a sequent $\Delta \gg C$, we associate it to the B-value of this sequent by the following equation.

$$\beta(\Delta \gg C) = \Sigma(\beta(x_i)) + \beta(C) \text{ for all } x_i \text{ in } \Delta.$$

In other words to calculate the B-value of a sequent we simply total the B-values of its constituent wffs. We can now define a B-rule precisely.

A rule R is a B-rule just if whenever R is successfully applied to a tuple of goals $<G_0, G_1,..., G_n>$, the resulting tuple of goals $<G^*_1,...,G^*_m, G_1, ..., G_n>$ is such that $\beta(G^*_i) < \beta(G_0)$ for all i, where $1 \leq i \leq m$.

Theorem: all the rules of the type system for $\mathcal{L}$ are B-type rules with the exception of the Primitive, Sequents, Generalisation and Specialisation Rules.

Proof: the proof is long but straightforward. We will cover one case and leave it to the reader to complete the other cases.

The type rule for *if* states

X : boolean; Y : A; Z : A;
(if X Y Z) : A;

Let $<G_0, G_1, ..., .G_n>$ be a tuple of goals. Assume $\beta(G_0) = m$. Assume the Conditional Rule is successfully applied to $<G_0, G_1, ..., .G_n>$. If so, then G_0 is of the form $\Delta >>$ (if X Y Z) : A, and the output of the rule application is $<G_x, G_y, G_z, G_1, ..., .G_n>$ where G_x, G_y, and G_z are defined as follows.

$G_x = \Delta >> X :$ boolean
$G_y = \Delta >> Y : A$
$G_z = \Delta >> Z : A$

We have the following equalities

$\beta(G_0) = m = \beta(\Delta) + \beta((\text{if } X\ Y\ Z) : A)$
$\beta(G_x) = \beta(\Delta) + \beta(X : \text{boolean})$
$\beta(G_y) = \beta(\Delta) + \beta(Y : A)$
$\beta(G_z) = \beta(\Delta) + \beta(Z : A)$

But by the definition of β, the following inequalities hold.

$\beta(X : \text{boolean}) < \beta((\text{if } X\ Y\ Z) : A)$
$\beta(Y : A) < \beta((\text{if } X\ Y\ Z) : A)$
$\beta(Z : A) < \beta((\text{if } X\ Y\ Z) : A)$

Abbreviating $\beta(\Delta)$ by d and $\beta((\text{if } X\ Y\ Z) : A)$ by i, and $\beta(X : \text{boolean})$, $\beta(Y : A)$ and $\beta(Z : A)$ by x, y and z respectively, we have the following equalities.

$\beta(G_0) = m = d + i$
$\beta(G_x) = d + x$ where $x < i$
$\beta(G_y) = d + y$ where $y < i$
$\beta(G_z) = d + z$ where $z < i$

Hence $\beta(G_x) < \beta(G_0)$ and $\beta(G_y) < \beta(G_0)$ and $\beta(G_z) < \beta(G_0)$ and the Conditional Rule is a B-rule.

Theorem: the Primitive and Sequents Rules are A-rules.

Proof: by inspection of the rules.

Corollary: the type system for $\mathcal{L}$, excepting the Specialisation Rule, is an AB system.

The omission of the *Specialisation Rule* is generally not important in $\mathcal{T}$, since unification is used to bind variables. The omission of this rule and the *Generalisation Rule* will be discussed later.

An **AB series** is a series of lists of goals where (a) the first list contains a single goal (b) for any element G_n in the series, the immediate successor G_{n+1} is generated from G_n by the successful application of an A-rule or a B-rule. To prove the termination of $\mathcal{T}$, we have to prove that there is no infinite AB series.

Since the β function maps every sequent to its B-value, we can associate each element in an AB series with a list of numbers. Each number is the B-value of the sequent in the goal. Therefore we extend the concept of a B-value (and hence the domain of β) to embrace goals and AB series.

Let G be a goal, where $G = [s_1,...,s_m]$ and let $\beta(s_1) = n_1,....,\beta(s_m) = n_m$. The B-value of the goal G is the list of numbers $[n_1,...,n_m]$. Let $G_0, ...,G_n$ be any series of goals. The B-value of this series is just the series $\beta(G_0),...,\beta(G_n)$.

The B-value of an AB series is therefore a numeric representation of that series; it consists of a series of lists of numbers. Let us call such a series, an **AB_n series**. Since this series is derived by a mapping from an AB series, it has the following property.

Let L_n and L_{n+1} be elements of an AB_n series and let a be the number at the head of L_n. Then either

(a) L_{n+1} is the tail of L_n ($L_{n+1} = \text{tail}(L_n)$) or
(b) L_{n+1} is identical to the result of appending a list $[b_1,...,b_k]$ to $\text{tail}(L_n)$ such that for each b_i, $b_i < a$.

In case (a) the inverse of L_{n+1} under β is derived from its predecessor by an A-operation. In the case of (b), the inverse of L_{n+1} under β is derived from its predecessor by a B-operation.

We will call the operation on L_n that corresponds to case (a) **the A_n operation**, and an operation that corresponds to case (b) **a B_n operation**. AB_n series are thus built up from a list containing a single number, by successively iterating A_n and B_n operations. Since the elements of an AB series are correlated 1-1 with elements of the corresponding AB_n series, we can show that there is no infinite AB series by proving the following theorem.

Theorem: There is no infinite AB_n series.

Let us say that an AB_n series is **protracted**, if there is no element L in the series that lacks a successor when an A_n or B_n operation could be successfully applied to L. We shall prove that there is no infinite AB_n series by proving the following result.

Theorem: If L_n is a non-empty list of numbers in a protracted AB_n series, then $tail(L_n)$ occurs in the series.

Proof: the proof proceeds by use of strong induction over the value of the first number a in L_n.

Base Case: $a = 0$. Then the only admissible AB_n operation that can be carried out on L_n is the A_n operation, and so $L_{n+1} = tail(L_n)$ and the theorem is proved.

Inductive Case: the theorem holds for all values for a less than m. Let $L_n = [m,....]$. Consider L_{n+1}. Either

    (a) L_{n+1} is derived from L_n by the A_n operation. If so, $L_{n+1} = tail(L_n)$ and the theorem is proved.

    (b) L_{n+1} is derived from L_n by a B_n operation. In which case $L_{n+1} = [b_1,...,b_k \mid tail(L_n)]$. Since each of the $b_1,...,b_k$ is less than m, the inductive hypothesis applies to each of $[b_1,...,b_k \mid tail(L_n)]$, $[b_2,...,b_k \mid tail(L_n)]$ ..... and so on to $[b_k \mid tail(L_n)]$. But if the inductive hypothesis applies to $[b_k \mid tail(L_n)]$, then $tail(L_n)$ occurs in the series and the theorem is proved.

Theorem: every protracted AB_n series is terminated by the empty list.

Proof: every AB_n series begins with a list containing a single number and the tail of that list is the empty list. Since no AB_n operation can be applied to the empty list, any protracted AB_n series terminates with the empty list.

Theorem: there is no infinite AB_n series.

Proof: assume X is an infinite AB_n series. Every infinite AB_n series must be protracted, since if it were not, it would terminate with a list to which an AB_n operation could be applied. So X is protracted and since every protracted AB_n series terminates with [ ], X is a terminating infinite series. By *reductio*, X does not exist.

The AB Theorem: there is no infinite AB series.

Proof: since the elements of every AB series are correlated 1-1 with every AB_n series, since there is no infinite AB_n series, there is no infinite AB series.

Hence we can finally assert.

Theorem: $\mathcal{T}$ is terminating.

Proof: If $\mathcal{T}$ failed to terminate, then an infinitely long AB series would exist.

26.5 Procedure $\mathcal{T}^*$

In the absence of any user axioms, the proof procedure $\mathcal{T}$ for type checking is depth-first search with chronological backtracking. From the previous two sections we know that $\mathcal{T}$ is terminating in respect of the type rules we have stated. Another piece of good news is $\mathcal{T}$ is accurate, in the sense that if $\mathcal{T}$ says that an expression has a type, then it really does have that type.

The downside is that $\mathcal{T}$ is not particularly efficient. The *Cases Rule*, for instance, splits a proof of (cases $Case_1$ ... $Case_n$) : A into a number of subproofs that work on each $Case_i$. Since the type A is known and is variable-free, each $Case_i$ can be treated independently and there is really no need for backtracking between these subproofs of $Case_i$: A. Other rules offer opportunities for the elimination of choice points. The *Combinator Rule* is the only rule for checking combinators and so is a **committed choice** in the sense that if it can be applied, it should be and there should be no backtracking to reconsider this decision.

Another problem with $\mathcal{T}$ is that the procedure targets $\mathcal{L}$ expressions rather than Shen expressions, and this creates two problems. First, $\mathcal{L}$ expressions are generally larger and more deeply nested than Shen expressions, so the time spent on inferencing is proportionately greater. Second, any type errors detected are detected in $\mathcal{L}$ expressions and not in the Shen source, which makes it hard to raise a clear type error report.

The $\mathcal{T}^*$ procedure eliminates these disadvantages by type checking Shen source, and procedurally implements the role of many of the type rules used in $\mathcal{T}$. The Y-combinator, Pattern, Cases, Generalisation and Guard rules are redundant in $\mathcal{T}^*$. The bogus choice points are omitted. The $\mathcal{T}^*$ procedure operates on a typed Shen function definition. Such a definition generally has the form.

```
(define <function>
  {A₁ --> ... Aₙ --> B}
  ₐp₁ ... ₐpₙ -> rₐ
  ..................
  ₘp₁ ... ₘpₙ -> rₘ)
```

Each rule $_ip_1$ ... $_ip_n$ -> r_i can be thought of as defining a sort of mini-function whose type is intended to be identical with the host function. Therefore to type check the entire function, it is enough to show that each rewrite rule obeys the type associated with its host function.

Under $\mathcal{T}^*$, the process of type checking a rewrite rule has two parts, corresponding to the two structural components of a rule. The first structural component is a sequence of patterns and the second is the result returned if the patterns match the inputs. The first job of the type checker is to show that each pattern p fits the type assigned to it. This we call **the integrity condition**. The second job is to show that, assuming the integrity conditions are met, that the result has the type expected of it. This we call the **correctness condition**. The two principles are defined below.

The Integrity Condition

An assignment of a type B to pattern p meets the integrity condition just when the sequent $\Delta \gg p : B$ is provable; where $\Delta = \{V, A \mid V : A\}$ where V is a variable in p and A is a fresh type variable.

The Correctness Condition

Assume a rule $p_1 \ldots p_n \rightarrow r$ is assigned the type $A_1 \rightarrow \ldots A_n \rightarrow B$. Then this assignment meets the correctness condition just when the sequent $p_1 : A_1 \ldots p_n : A_n \gg r : B$ is provable.

$\mathcal{T}^*$ verifies the type security of a function through establishing these two properties. Let's see what this means in concrete terms through an example. Here is a definition of a datatype details which represents the details about a person – her name, address and telephone number.

```
(datatype details

  \\ details right
  Name : string; Address : string; Telephone : number;
  [Name Address Telephone] : details;

  \\ details left
  Name : string, Address : string, Telephone : number >> P;
  [Name Address Telephone] : details >> P;)
```

The function address returns the address of a person given their details.

```
(define address
  {details --> string}
  [Name Address Telephone] -> Address)
```

Represented in cons form; this definition appears as:

```
(define address
  {details --> string}
  (cons Name (cons Address (cons Telephone []))) -> Address)
```

To establish the type details --> string, we have to satisfy the Integrity and Correctness Principles. The Integrity Principle requires that the following sequent be proved.

```
Name : A, Address : B, Telephone : C
  >> (cons Name (cons Address (cons Telephone []))) : details
```

The details right rule maps this sequent to three subgoals.

```
Name : A, Address : B, Telephone : C  >> Name : string;
Name : A, Address : B, Telephone : C  >> Address : string;
Name : A, Address : B, Telephone : C  >> Telephone : number;
```

These sequents are solvable under the assignments $A \mapsto$ string, $B \mapsto$ string, and $C \mapsto$ number. The Correctness Condition then requires that that the following sequent be proved.

```
(cons Name (cons Address (cons Telephone []))) : details >> Address : string
```

The details left rule maps this sequent to an immediately soluble goal.

```
Name : string, Address : string, Telephone : number >> Address : string
```

The Correctness Condition in its current form is adequate only for non-recursive functions. We define the expression 'r is recursive w.r.t. f' to mean that r occurs in a recursive definition of f and a recursive call to f occurs within r. The first revision to the Correctness Condition caters for such recursive calls.

The Correctness Condition (Revised)

Assume a rule $p_1 \ldots p_n \rightarrow r$ is assigned the type $A_1 \rightarrow \ldots A_n \rightarrow B$ and r is recursive w.r.t. f. Then this assignment meets the correctness condition just when the sequent $f : A_1 \rightarrow \ldots A_n \rightarrow B, p_1 : A_1 \ldots p_n : A_n >> r : B$ is provable.

Thus using the linear recursive definition of the factorial function.

```
(define factorial
  {number --> number}
  0 -> 1
  X -> (* X (factorial (- X 1))))
```

After currying, the proof obligations that the type checker generates are:

1. >> 0 : number;
2. 0 : number >> 1 : number;
3. X : A >> X : number;
4. X : number, factorial : (number --> number) >> ((* X) (factorial ((- X) 1)))) : number

Sequent 1. is generated by applying the Integrity Condition to the first rewrite rule and sequent 3. by applying the same condition to the second rewrite rule. Sequents 2. and 3. come from applying the Correctness Condition to the first and second rewrite rules respectively. Since the expression (* X (factorial (- X 1))) is recursive with respect to factorial, an extra assumption factorial : (number --> number) is required.

The Correctness Condition does not deal with guards or constructions using <-. The latter do not pose any special problem because they can be eliminated in favour of the forward arrow using the equivalences of chapter 10. The use of guards is also straightforward to type check. The rule

$$p_1 \dots p_n \to r \qquad \text{where } g$$

has the type $A_1 \to \dots A_n \to B$ just when the Integrity Condition and Correctness Conditions are met and g can be proved to be a boolean. In other words that is, all of the following conditions are met; for each p_i let Δ_i be the set of typings $\{V, A \mid V : A\}$ where V is a variable in p_i and A is a fresh type variable.

1. $\Delta_i \gg p_i : A_i$ is provable for each i of $1,\dots,n$.   (Integrity)
2. g : verified, $p_1 : A_1 \dots p_n : A_n \gg r : B$ is provable.   (Correctness)
3. $p_1 : A_1 \dots p_n : A_n \gg g$: boolean is provable.   (Guard)

Here is an example using these conditions.

```
(define find_address
    {string --> (list details) --> string}
    Name [[Name Address Telephone] | _] -> Address
    Name [_ | Details] -> (find_address Name Details))
```

The function contains no explicit guard, but it also contains a non-left linear rewrite rule in the first position. To render it left-linear for the purposes of type checking, we need to insert a guard. After doing this, the definition appears as below.

```
(define find_address
    {string --> (list details) --> string}
    Name1 [[Name2 Address Telephone] | _] -> Address
                              where (= Name_1 Name_2)
    Name [_ | Details] -> (find_address Name Details))
```

There are 8 proof obligations for type checking find_address (figure 26.3). The proof obligation Name_1 : A >> Name_1 : string is trivially solvable. Problems of this kind are always generated from patterns that are simply variables, and so $\mathcal{T}^*$ may omit these proof obligations because they are always solvable.

Rewrite Rule 1

Integrity Requirements

1. Name1 : A >> Name1 : string
2. Name2 : B, Address : C, Telephone : D, Whatever : E
    >> [[Name2 Address Telephone] | X] : (list details)

Correctness Requirements

3. Name1 : string, [[Name2 Address Telephone] | X] : (list details),
    (= Name1 Name2) : verified >> Address : string

Guard

4. Name : string, [[Name2 Address Telephone] | X] : (list details)
    >> (= Name1 Name2) : boolean

Rewrite Rule 2

Integrity Requirements

5. Name : string, [[Name2 Address Telephone] | Whatever] : (list details)
        >> (= Name1 Name2) : boolean
6. Name : F >> Name : string
7. Detail : G, Details : H >> [Detail | Details] : (list details)

Correctness Requirements

8. Name : string, [Detail | Details] : (list details),
    find_address : string --> ((list details) --> string)
    >> ((find_address Name) Details) : string

Figure 26.3 The proof obligations from the find_address *function*

Finally only mutual recursion remains to be dealt with. The technique of handling a mutual recursion like

```
(define even?
  {number --> boolean}
  1 -> false
  X -> (odd? (- X 1)))

(define odd?
  {number --> boolean}
  1 -> true
  X -> (even? (- X 1)))
```

is to assume the typings odd? : number $\rightarrow$ boolean and even? : number $\rightarrow$ boolean in type checking the recursive calls. There are eight proof obligations generated by these two functions, but two are trivial and so we omit them. The remaining six are shown in figure 26.4.

---

even?

    1.   >> 1 : number;
    2.   1 : number >> true : boolean;
    3.   X : number, odd? : (number --> boolean)
                >> (odd? ((- X) 1)) : boolean

odd?

    4.   >> 1 : number;
    5.   1 : number >> false : boolean;
    6.   X : number, even? : (number --> boolean)
      >> (even? ((- X) 1)) : boolean

Figure 26.4 The proof obligations from the odd? and even? functions

The technique of $\mathscr{T}^*$ is to prove Integrity and Correctness for each rule of the function. There is no need for the Y-combinator, Pattern, Cases and Guard rules and these rules are no longer retained. Type variables in the type of a function are replaced by fresh terms at the start of the proof and so the Generalisation Rule is not required. $\mathscr{T}^*$ trades declarative purity for a reduction in the size of the type theory, and the elimination of bogus choice points, but delivers the same result in less time.[74]

We shall prove the procedural equivalence[75] of $\mathscr{T}$ and $\mathscr{T}^*$ by showing how the rules not used by $\mathscr{T}$ are implemented procedurally within $\mathscr{T}^*$. The procedural equivalence is quite simple to show, except in the case of the Patterns Rule.

The efficiency gain in $\mathscr{T}^*$ comes from two sources.

1. The elimination of rules that are used only once in the proof. Instead these rules are procedurally invoked early in the procedure and then not used again.

2. The elimination of long stretches of proof that are purely mechanical and add to the search space without changing the result.

The easiest way to demonstrate the procedural equivalence of $\mathscr{T}$ and $\mathscr{T}*$ is to work through the rules that $\mathscr{T}^*$ does not use and see why $\mathscr{T}^*$ does not use them.

---

[74] The improvement in performance is significant; using $\mathscr{T}$ to type check and compile one program took 77,453 inferences. Under $\mathscr{T}^*$, the same program was checked and compiled using 10,187 inferences. In cases where there are type errors, $\mathscr{T}^*$ is less likely than $\mathscr{T}$ to lose itself in combinatorial complexities.

[75] i.e.; that they both produce the same result for the same input.

First, the Generalisation Rule needs only to be used once in $\mathcal{T}$, at the beginning of a proof to remove the universal quantifiers binding the type variables. Since all types are shallow types, the Generalisation Rule is not needed after these quantifiers are removed. This is done automatically in $\mathcal{T}^*$, so the Generalisation Rule is not needed.

The Cases Rule requires that each case in the body of a definition obeys the type constraints of the whole function. The type constraints are free of shared variables, so that in effect, any proof using Cases can be split into n independent subproofs. In $\mathcal{T}^*$, this is exactly what happens, each rewrite rule is checked separately to ensure that it meets the type constraints. This means that the Cases Rule is not needed in $\mathcal{T}^*$.

The Y-combinator Rule is used in $\mathcal{T}$ to type check recursive functions. Effectively any abstraction $(\lambda\ x\ y)$ which amounts to the recursive definition of a function f is written as $(Y\ f(\lambda\ x\ y))$. The Y-combinator Rule, when applied to a problem of the form $(Y\ f(\lambda\ x\ y)) : A$, gives $f : A \gg (\lambda\ x\ y) : A$. Thereafter the Y-combinator Rule plays no further part in the proof. A procedural optimisation generates the problem $f : A \gg (\lambda\ x\ y) : A$ directly from the recursive definition, and dispenses with the Y-combinator Rule which is not needed in $\mathcal{T}^*$.

The optimisation of dispensing with the Patterns and Guard Rules is more delicate. Recall that in $\mathcal{T}$, the task of type checking a function begins with a problem of the form $(\lambda\ x_1\ ...(\lambda\ x_n\ y)) : A_1 \rightarrow ... A_n \rightarrow A_{n+1}$. Each x_i is a variable, and by repeated applications of the Abstractions Rule, we generate a problem $x_1 : A_1,..., x_n : A_n \gg y : A_{n+1}$. The body y of the former abstraction will consist of a series of cases $c_1, ..., c_m$ each of which must be proved to be of type A_{n+1}. That is, our proof obligation breaks down into the following series.

$$x_1 : A_1,..., x_n : A_n \gg c_1 : A_{n+1}$$
....
$$x_1 : A_1,..., x_n : A_n \gg c_m : A_{n+1}$$

Each c_i is an application composed of an n-place abstraction $(\lambda\ p_1\ ...\ (\lambda\ p_n\ z))$ applied to $x_1 ,..., x_n$ taking the form $(((\lambda\ p_1\ ...\ (\lambda\ p_n\ z))\ x_1)...\ x_n)$. Each p_i is a pattern. Thus the proof obligation for c_i is:

$$x_1 : A_1,..., x_n : A_n \gg (((\lambda\ p_1\ ...\ (\lambda\ p_n\ z))\ x_1)...\ x_n) : A_{n+1}$$

Repeated use of the Applications Rule gives the following proof obligations; where $B_1\ ...\ B_n$ are free type variables

$$x_1 : A_1,..., x_n : A_n \gg x_1 : B_1$$
....
$$x_1 : A_1,..., x_n : A_n \gg x_n : B_n$$
$$x_1 : A_1,..., x_n : A_n \gg (\lambda\ p_1\ ...\ (\lambda\ p_n\ z)) : B_1 \rightarrow ... B_n \rightarrow A_{n+1}$$

The proof obligation is

$$x_1 : A_1,\ldots, x_n : A_n \gg x_1 : B_1$$
$$\cdots\cdots\cdots\cdots\cdots\cdots\cdots$$
$$x_1 : A_1,\ldots, x_n : A_n \gg x_n : B_n$$

are trivially solvable by unifying each $x_i : B_i$ with the assumption $x_i : A_i$.
The final proof obligation is therefore

$$x_1 : A_1,\ldots, x_n : A_n \gg (\lambda\, p_1 \ldots (\lambda\, p_n\ z)) : A_1 \to \ldots A_n \to A_{n+1}$$

The expressions $x_1,\ldots, x_n$ do not occur anywhere within the conclusion of this sequent. Consequently they play no further part in the proof and may be thinned away. The proof obligation can now be simplified to

$$\gg (\lambda\, p_1 \ldots (\lambda\, p_n\ z)) : A_1 \to \ldots A_n \to A_{n+1}$$

n repeated applications of the Patterns Rule gives the following proof obligations. Each Δ_i is a series of typings of the form $v : C$, where v is a variable in p_i and C is a fresh type variable.

$$\Delta_1 \gg p_1 : A_1$$
$$\cdots\cdots\cdots\cdots$$
$$\Delta_n \gg p_n : A_n$$
$$p_1 : A_1 \ldots p_n : A_n \gg z : A_{n+1}$$

Let us pause at this point and observe that the proof process so far is not only entirely mechanical, but is guaranteed to succeed merely by virtue of the syntactic structure of the language $\mathcal{L}$. In other words, type failure can only occur past this point, and reconsideration of the previous steps is a waste of time.

The second observation is that the proof obligations now facing us correspond precisely to the integrity and correctness checks required by $\mathcal{T}^*$. The integrity checks are contained exactly by the proof obligations

$$\Delta_1 \gg p_1 : A_1$$
$$\cdots\cdots\cdots\cdots$$
$$\Delta_n \gg p_n : A_n$$

while the correctness check is contained by the proof obligation

$$p_1 : A_1 \ldots p_n : A_n \gg z : A_{n+1}$$

The advantage of $\mathcal{T}^*$ is that the mechanical and time-wasting steps required in $\mathcal{T}$ to get to this point are eliminated.

Exercise 26

1. **Implement $\mathcal{T}$. Your program should type check a Shen program from a text file.

2. **Using your answer to 2., implement $\mathcal{T}^*$.

3. Melvin Micro types in the rules for binary from chapter 14 into Shen and then types [(+ 1 0)] : binary and gets a type error. He is puzzled because (+ 1 0) is just 1 and [1] is a binary number. Explain why Melvin gets this error.

4. Melvin continues to experiment. He types in the definition of a function that removes all the internal [...]s from within a list.

```
(define flat
  {(list (list A)) --> (list A)}
  [ ] -> []
  [[X | Y] | Z] -> (append (flat [X | Y]) (flat Z))
  [X | Y] -> [X | (flat Y)])
```

and gets another type error. Why?

5. Melvin argues that the definition of complement in chapter 14 is too long. He redefines it as

```
(define my_complement
  {binary --> binary}
  [X] -> (if (= X 1) [0] [1])
  [X | Y] -> (if (= X 0) [1 | (my_complement Y)] [0 | (my_complement Y)]))
```

He finds that with type checking disabled, this function works on binary numbers just like the old complement function does. However my_complement does not type check. Explain why.

Further Reading

The first practical type checking algorithm was incorporated into Edinburgh ML and is described in Milner (1975) and Field and Harrison (1988).

Appendix A

System Functions and their Types in Shen

- **absvector**

  _

  Given a non-negative integer returns a vector in the native platform.

- **absvector?**

  A → boolean

  Recognisor for native vectors.

- **address->**

  _

  Given an absolute vector A, a positive integer i and a value V places V in the A[i]th position.

- **<-address**

  _

  Given an absolute vector A, a positive integer i retrieves V from the A[i]th position.

- **adjoin**

  A → (list A) → (list A)

  Conses an object to a list if it is not already an element..

- **and**

  boolean → boolean → boolean

  Boolean and.

- **append**

  (list A) → (list A) → (list A)

  Appends two lists into one list.

- **arity**

  A → number

  Given a Shen function, returns its arity otherwise -1.

- **boolean?**

  A → boolean

  Recognisor for booleans.

- **bound?**
  symbol → boolean
  Returns true if the variable is globally bound.

- **cd**
  string → string
  Changes the home directory. (cd "Prog") causes (load "hello_world.txt") to load Prog/hello_world.txt. (cd "") is the default.

- **close**
  (stream A) → (list B)
  Closes a stream returning the empty list.

- **cn**
  string → string → string
  Concatenates two strings.

- **concat**

  —
  Concatenates two symbols or booleans.

- **cons**

  —
  A special form that takes an object e of type A and a list l of type (list A) and produces a list of type (list A) by adding e to the front of l.

- **cons?**
  A → boolean
  Returns true iff the input is a non-empty list.

- **declare**

  —
  Takes a function name f and a type t expressed as a list and gives f the type t.

- **define**

  —
  Top level form for Shen definitions.

- **defmacro**

  —
  Top level form for Shen macros.

- **defprolog**

  —
  Top level form for Shen Prolog definitions.

- **destroy**
  (A → B) → symbol
  Receives the name of a function and removes it and its type from the environment.

- **difference**
  (list A) → (list A) → (list A)
  Subtracts the elements of the second list from the first.

- **do**
  A → (B → B)
  Returns its last argument; polyadic courtesy of the reader.

- **element?**
  A → (list A) → boolean
  Returns true iff the first input is an element in the second.

- **empty?**
  A → boolean
  Returns true iff the input is [ ].

- **error**

  —
  A special form: takes a string followed by n ($n \geq 0$) expressions. Prints error string.

- **error-to-string**
  exception → string
  Maps an error message to the corresponding string.

- **eval**

  —
  Evaluates the input.

- **eval-kl**

  —
  Evaluates the input as a Kλ expression.

- **explode**
  A → (list string)
  Explodes an object to a list of strings.

- **external**
  symbol → (list symbol)
  Given a package name, returns the list of symbols external to that package.

- **fail**

  → symbol

  Returns the failure object – a symbol internal to the Shen package printed as **....**

- **fix**

  $(A \rightarrow A) \rightarrow (A \rightarrow A)$

  Applies a function to generate a fixpoint.

- **freeze**

  $A \rightarrow (lazy\ A)$

  Returns a frozen version of its input.

- **fst**

  $(A * B) \rightarrow A$

  Returns the first element of a tuple.

- **function**

  $(A \rightarrow B) \rightarrow (A \rightarrow B)$

  Maps a symbol to the function which it denotes.

- **gensym**

  symbol → symbol

  Generates a fresh symbol or variable from a symbol.

- **get-time**

  symbol → number

  For the argument *run* or *real* returns a number representing the real or run time elapsed since the last call. One of these options must be supported. For the argument *unix* returns the Unix time.

- **get**

  –

  takes a symbol S, a pointer P and optionally a vector V and returns the value in V pointed by P from S (if one exists) or an error otherwise. If V is omitted the global property vector is used.

- **hash**

  $A \rightarrow number \rightarrow number$

  Returns a hashing of the first argument subject to the restriction that the encoding must not be greater than the second argument.

- **head**

  $(list\ A) \rightarrow A$

  Returns the first element of a list; if the list is empty returns an error

- **hd**

  (list A) → A

  Returns the first element of a list; if the list is empty returns an unspecified object

- **hdstr**

  string → string

  Returns the first element of a string.

- **hdv**

  (vector A) → A

  Returns the first element of a standard vector.

- **if**

  boolean → A → A → A

  takes a boolean *b* and two expressions *x* and *y* and evaluates *x* if *b* evaluates to true and evaluates *y* if *b* evaluates to false.

- **implementation**

  → string

  Returns a string denoting the implementation on which Shen is running.

- **include**

  (list symbol) → (list symbol)

  Includes the datatype theories or synonyms for use in type checking.

- **include-all-but**

  (list symbol) → (list symbol)

  Includes all loaded datatype theories and synonyms for use in type checking apart from those entered.

- **inferences**

  → number

  Returns the number of logical inferences executed since the last call to the top level.

- **input**

  ‾

  0-place function. Takes a user input *i* and returns the normal form of *i*.

- **input+**

  ‾

  Special form. Takes inputs of the form **<expr> <stream>**. If **<stream>** is not specified then defaults to standard input. *d*(**<expr>**) is the type denoted by the choice of expression (e.g. 'number' denotes the type number). Takes a user input *i* and returns the normal form of *i* given *i* is of the type *d*(**<expr>**).

- **integer?**
  A → boolean
  Recognisor for integers.

- **intern**

  ‾
  Maps a string to a symbol.

- **internal**
  symbol → (list symbol)
  Maps a package name to the symbols internal to it.

- **intersection**
  (list A) → (list A) → (list A)
  Computes the intersection of two lists.

- **it**
  → string
  Returns the last input to standard input embedded in a string.

- **lambda**

  ‾
  Builds a lambda expression from a variable and an expression.

- **language**
  → string
  Returns a string denoting the language on which Shen is running.

- **length**
  (list A) → number
  Returns the number of elements in a list.

- **limit**
  (vector A) → number
  Returns the maximum index of a vector.

- **lineread**
  (stream in) → (list unit)
  Top level reader of read-evaluate-print loop. Reads elements into a list.
  lineread terminates with carriage return when brackets are balanced. ^ aborts
  lineread.

- **load**
  string → symbol
  Takes a file name and loads the file, returning **loaded** as a symbol.

- **macroexpand**

  Expand an expression by the available macros.

- **map**
  $(A \rightarrow B) \rightarrow (\text{list } A) \rightarrow (\text{list } B)$
  The first input is applied to each member of the second input and the results consed into one list.

- **mapcan**
  $(A \rightarrow (\text{list } B)) \rightarrow (\text{list } A) \rightarrow (\text{list } B)$
  The first input is applied to each member of the second input and the results appended into one list.

- **make-string**

  A special form: takes a string followed by n ($n \geq 0$) well-typed expressions; assembles and returns a string.

- **maxinferences**
  number $\rightarrow$ number
  Returns the input and as a side-effect, sets a global variable to a number that limits the maximum number of inferences that can be expended on attempting to type check a program. The default is 10^6.

- **nl**
  number $\rightarrow$ number
  Prints n new lines.

- **not**
  boolean $\rightarrow$ boolean
  Boolean not.

- **nth**
  number $\rightarrow$ (list A) $\rightarrow$ A
  Gets the nth element of a list numbered from 1.

- **number?**
  A $\rightarrow$ boolean
  Recognisor for numbers.

- **n->string**
  number $\rightarrow$ string
  Given a number n returns a unit string whose ASCII number is n.

- **occurrences**
  A → B → number
  Returns the number of times the first argument occurs in the second.

- **occurs-check**
  symbol → boolean
  Receives either + or - and enables/disables occur checking in Prolog,
  datatype definitions and rule closures.   The default is +.

- **open**
  —
  Takes two arguments; the location from which it is drawn and the direction (*in*
  or *out*) and creates either a source or a sink stream.

- **optimise**
  symbol → boolean
  Takes either + or -.   If + then Kλ code may be optimised to take advantage of
  type information.

- **or**
  boolean → (boolean → boolean)
  Boolean or.

- **os**
  → string
  Returns a string denoting the operating system on which Shen is running.

- **output**
  —
  A special form: takes a string followed by n ($n \geq 0$) well-typed expressions;
  prints a message to the screen and returns an object of type string (the string
  "done").

- **package**
  —
  Takes a symbol, a list of symbols and any number of expressions and places
  them in a package.

- **package?**
  symbol → boolean
  Returns **true** if the symbol names a package else returns **false**.

- **pos**

  string → number → string

  Given a string and a natural number *n* returns the *n*th unit string numbering from zero.

- **pr**

  string → (stream out) → string

  Takes a string, a sink object and prints the string to the sink, returning the string as a result. If no stream is supplied defaults to the standard output.

- **preclude**

  (list symbol) → (list symbol)

  Removes the mentioned datatype theories and synonyms from use in type checking.

- **preclude-all-but**

  (list symbol) → (list symbol)

  Removes all the datatype theories and synonyms from use in type checking apart from the ones given.

- **print**

  A → A

  Takes an object and prints it, returning it as a result.

- **profile**

  (A → B) → (A → B)

  Takes a function represented by a function name and inserts profiling code returning the function as an output.

- **profile-results**

  (A → B) → ((A → B) * number)

  Takes a profiled function f and returns the total run time expended on f since profile-results was last invoked..

- **ps**

  symbol → (list unit)

  Receives a symbol denoting a Shen function and prints the Kλ source code associated with the function.

- **put**

  —

  3-place function that takes a symbol S, a pointer P (a string symbol or number), and an expression E. The pointer P is set to point from S to the normal form of E which is then returned.

- **read**

  (stream in) → unit

  Takes a stream and reads off the first Shen token; defaults with zero arguments to standard input.

- **read-byte**

  (stream in) → number

  Takes a source and reads the first byte off it; defaults with zero arguments to standard input.

- **read-file**

  string → (list unit)

  Returns the contents of an ASCII file designated by a string. Returns a list of units, where unit is an unspecified type.

- **read-file-as-bytelist**

  string → (list number)

  Returns the contents of an ASCII file designated by a string as a list of bytes.

- **read-file-as-string**

  string → string

  Returns the string contents of an ASCII file designated by a string.

- **read-from-string**

  string → (list unit)

  Reads a list of expressions from a string.

- **remove**

  A → (list A) → (list A)

  Removes all occurrences of an element from a list.

- **reverse**

  (list A) → (list A)

  Reverses a list.

- **simple-error**

  string → A

  Given a string, raises it as an error message.

- **snd**

  (A * B) → B

  Returns the second element of a tuple.

- **specialise**

  symbol → symbol

  Receives the name of a function and turns it into a special form. Special forms are not curried during evaluation or compilation.

- **spy**

  symbol → boolean

  Receives either + or − and respectively enables/disables tracing the operation of $\mathcal{T}^*$.

- **step**

  symbol → boolean

  Receives either + or − and enables/disables stepping in the trace.

- **stinput**

  → (stream in)

  Returns the standard input stream.

- **stoutput**

  → (stream out)

  Returns the standard output stream.

- **str**

  A → string

  Given an atom (boolean, symbol, string, number) flanks it in quotes. For other inputs an error may be returned.

- **string?**

  A → boolean

  Recognisor for strings.

- **string->n**

  string → number

  Maps a unti string to its code point.

- **subst**

  —

  Given (*subst x y z*) replaces *y* by *x* in *z* where *z* is a list or an atom.

- **sum**

  (list number) → number

  Sums a list of numbers.

- **symbol?**

  A → boolean

  Recognisor for symbols.

- **systemf**

  symbol → symbol
  Gives the symbol the status of an identifier for a system function; its definition may not be overwritten'. Returns the symbol itself.

- **tail**

  (list A) → (list A)
  Returns all but the first element of a non-empty list.

- **tc**

  symbol → boolean
  Receives either + or – and respectively enables/disables static typing.

- **tc?**

  A → boolean
  Returns true iff typechecking is enabled.

- **thaw**

  (lazy A) → A
  Receives a frozen input and evaluates it to get the unthawed result..

- **time**

  _
  Prints the run time for the evaluation of its input and returns its normal form.

- **tl**

  _
  Returns the tail of a list; for [] the result is platform dependent.

- **tlstr**

  string → string
  Returns the tail of a string.

- **tlv**

  (vector A) → (vector A)
  Returns the tail of a non-empty vector.

- **track**

  symbol → symbol
  Tracks the I/O behaviour of a function.

- **trap-error**

  A → (exception → A) → A
  Tracks the I/O behaviour of a function.

- **tuple?**
  A → boolean
  Recognisor for tuples.

- **type**

  _

  Used under type checking; takes an expression *e* and a type A; *e* is
  evaluated only if *e* inhabits A.

- **undefmacro**
  symbol → symbol
  Removes a macro.

- **union**
  (list A) → (list A) → (list A)
  Forms the union of two lists.

- **unprofile**
  (A → B) → (A → B)
  Unprofiles a function.

- **unput**

  _

  Given arguments *x* and *y* removes (put *x y z*) for any *z*.

- **unspecialise**
  symbol → symbol
  Receives the name of a function and deletes its special form status.

- **untrack**
  symbol → symbol
  Untracks a function.

- **value**

  _

  Applied to a symbol, returns the global value assigned to it.

- **variable?**
  A → boolean
  Applied to a variable, returns true.

- **version**
  string → string
  Changes the version string displayed on startup.

- **vector**

  number → (vector A)

  Creates a vector of size *n*.

- **vector?**

  A → boolean

  Recognises a standard vector.

- **vector->**

  (vector A) → number → A → (vector A)

  Given a vector V and an index *i* and object *o*, assigns *o* to V[*i*].

- **<-vector**

  (vector A) → number → A

  Given a vector V and an index *i* and object *o*, assigns *o* to V[*i*].

- **write-byte**

  number → (stream out) → number

  Takes a byte as an integer *n* between 0 and 255 and writes the corresponding byte to the stream returning *n*.

- **write-to-file**

  string → A → A

  Writes the second input into a file named in the first input. If the file does not exist, it is created, else it is overwritten. If the second input is a string then it is written to the file without the enclosing quotes. The second input is returned.

- **y-or-n?**

  string → boolean

  Prints the string as a question and returns true for y and false for n.

- **@p**

  $\overline{}$

  Takes *n* (*n* > 1) inputs and forms the tuple.

- **@s**

  $\overline{}$

  Takes *n* (*n* > 1) strings and forms their concatenation

- **@v**

  $\overline{}$

  Takes *n* inputs, the last being a vector V and forms a vector of these elements appended to the front of V.

- **<e>**

  Used by Shen-YACC – indicates the ε (empty) expansion in a grammar..

- **<!>**

  Used by Shen-YACC – consumes the remaining input and returns it.

- **<end>**

  Used by Shen-YACC – succeeds and acts as the identity function if the parse object is consumed or else fails.

- **$**

  Used by the reader; the argument is read in as an exploded list of unit strings.

- **+**

  number → number → number
  Number addition.

- **–**

  number → number → number
  Number subtraction.

- *****

  number → number → number
  Number multiplication.

- **/**

  number → number → number
  Number division.

- **/.**

  Abstraction builder, receives n variables and an expression; does the job of a (nested) λ in the lambda calculus.

- **>**

  number → number → boolean
  Greater than.

- <

  number → number → boolean
  Less than.

- =

  A → A → boolean
  Equal to.

- ==

  A → B → boolean
  Equal to.

- >=

  number → number → boolean
  Greater than or equal to.

- <=

  number → number → boolean
  Less than or equal to.

Appendix B

The Syntax of Shen

The syntax of Shen is presented as a context-free grammar in BNF notation annotated where necessary to explain certain context-sensitive restrictions. Terminals which represent parts of the Shen language are bolded, and in particular the bar | in Shen is bolded to **|** to distinguish it from the | used in the BNF to separate alternatives. For all X, the expansion $<X> ::= \varepsilon \mid \ldots$ indicates that $<X>$ may be expanded to an empty series of expressions.

Syntax Rules for Shen Definitions

```
<Shen def> ::= (define < lowercase > {<types>} <rules>)
             | (define <lowercase> <rules>)
             | (defmacro <lowercase> <rules>)
<lowercase> ::= any <symbol> not beginning in uppercase
<rules> ::= <rule> |  <rule> <rules>
<rule> ::= <patterns> -> <item> | <patterns> <- <item>
         | <patterns> -> <item> where <item>
         | <patterns> <- <item> where <item>
<patterns> ::= ε |  <pattern> <patterns>
<pattern> ::= <base> (except -> and <-)
            | [<pattern> <patterns> | <pattern>]
            | [<patterns>] | (cons <pattern> <pattern>)
            | (@p <pattern> <pattern> <patterns>)
            | (@s <pattern> <pattern> <patterns>)
            | (@v <pattern> <pattern> <patterns>)
<item> ::= <base> | [<items> | <item>]  | [<items>]
         | <application> | <abstraction>
<items> ::= <item> | <item> <items>
<base> ::= <symbol> (except |) | <string> | <boolean> | <number> | ( ) | [ ]
<application> ::= (<items>)
<abstraction> ::= (/. <variables> <item>)
<variables> ::= <variable> | <variable> <variables>
<variable> ::= any <symbol> beginning in uppercase
<types> ::= ε |  (<types>) | <types> --> <types> | <symbol>

<symbol> := <alpha> <symbolchars> |  <alpha>
<symbolchars> := <alpha> <symbolchars>
              | <digit> <symbolchars>
              | <alpha>
              | <digit>
```

```
<alpha> ::= a | b | c | d | e | f | g | h | i | j | k | l | m |
            n | o | p | q | r | s | t | u | v | w | x | y | z
            A | B | C | D | E | F | G | H | I | J | K | L |
            M | N | O | P | Q | R | S | T | U | V | W | X | Y | Z | .
            = | - | * | / | + | _ | ? | $ | ! | @ | ~ | > | < | & | % | ' | # | ` | ; | : | { | }
```

```
<digit> ::= 0 | 1 | 2 | 3 | 4 | 5 | 6 | 7 | 8 | 9
```

```
<number> ::= <signs> <float> | <signs> <integer> | <signs> <e-number>
<signs> ::= ε | + <signs> | - <signs>
<float> ::= <digits> . <digits> | . <digits>
<integer> ::= <digits>
<digits> ::= <digit> | <digit> <digits>
<e-number> ::= <integer> e - <integer> | <integer> e <integer>
              | <float> e - <integer> | <float> e < integer>
```

Syntax Rules for Shen Datatype Definitions

```
<datatype_definition> ::= (datatype <lowercase> <datatype-rules>)
<datatype-rules> ::= <datatype-rule> | <datatype-rule> <datatype-rules>
<datatype-rule> :: = <side-conditions> <schemes> <underline> <scheme>;
   | <side-conditions> <simple schemes> <double underline> <formula>;
<side-conditions> ::= ε | <side-condition> | <side-condition> <side-conditions>
<side-condition> | if <item> | let <variable> <item>
<underline> ::= _ | one or more concatenations of the underscore _
<double underline> ::= = | one or more concatenations of =
<simple schemes> ::= <formula> ; | <formula> ; <simple schemes>
<formula> := <item> : <item> | <item>

<schemes> ::= ε | <scheme> ; <schemes>
<scheme> ::= <assumptions> >> <formula> | <formula>
<assumptions> ::= <formula> | <formula>, <assumptions>
```

Syntax Rules for Shen Prolog Definitions

```
<prolog_definition> ::= (defprolog <lowercase> <clauses>)
<clauses> ::= <clause> | <clause> <clauses>
<clause> ::= <head> <-- <tail>;
<head> ::= <prolog-patterns>

<prolog-patterns> ::= ε | <prolog-pattern> <prolog-patterns>
<prolog-pattern> ::= <base>
                  | [<prolog-pattern> <prolog-patterns> | <prolog-pattern>]
                  | [<prolog-patterns>]
                  | (cons <prolog-pattern> <prolog-pattern>)
<tail> := ε | <application> <tail>
```

Appendix C

The Next Lisp: Back to the Future

This talk was delivered in Milan in May 2009 to the European Symposium on Lisp and it was the first talk in which Shen was mentioned. It lays out fairly clearly the motivation for Shen and how the project was to be carried out. The criticisms of Common Lisp in this talk were not well received by the audience.

OK; from the title we're obviously going to talk about Lisp. It might seem tricky if I start off by debating exactly what we mean by 'Lisp'. But I'm going to do just that because it will shed a light on what I'm going to say. And I'm going to start off with a biological metaphor, and there will be a few of them in this talk. I hope any biologists out there will forgive me.

In biology there is a distinction between *genotype* and *phenotype*. The genotype of a person is the genetic legacy that the person carries. The phenotype is the way that genetic legacy expresses itself. So, for example, you might find that you carry a gene from your father for blue eyes and one from your mother for brown eyes. Your genotype is blue-brown, but your phenotype is the way your eyes appear which is brown.

Applied to languages the genotype of the language is the DNA of the language. It incorporates the essential ideas of the language. The phenotype is the actualisation of those ideas on a platform.

If we ask ourselves, 'What is the genotype of Lisp?', what is its DNA, its genetic legacy, I'd suggest that it is composed of the following five ideas.

1. Recursion as the primary mean of expressing procedure calling.
2. Heterogeneous lists for composing and dissecting complex data.
3. Programming by defining functions.
4. Garbage collection.
5. Programs as data.

So having defined Lisp as a genotype, we can now ask what we mean by 'Lisp'. Are we talking about a genotype - a particular set of ideas, or a phenotype, the way those ideas are represented on the computer? If we're talking about a genotype then Lisp is doing very well. Python, Ruby, NewLisp, Clojure and even TCL/tk are all inheritors of this genetic legacy. But I guess if I stood here and talked about Python for an hour nobody would be too pleased. So I have to talk about phenotypes, and the main one is Common Lisp and that is not doing so well.

What Went Wrong with Common Lisp?

To understand Common Lisp and what has gone wrong with it, we have to begin with Lisp 1.5. Lisp 1.5 was the brainchild of John McCarthy and his group and it was the first practical Lisp to incorporate all the ideas of the Lisp genotype. Lisp 1.5 was maybe 30 years ahead of the game in terms of programming language design. A lot of very bright guys ran with the idea and it mutated into a polyphony of Lisp dialects - Zeta Lisp, DEC-10 Lisp, InterLisp-D and so on. So Common Lisp was devised as an acceptable political solution for unifying the many tongues of Lisp. But now, 25 years on, it is not the dominant phenotype of the Lisp genotype. Why?

The answer is that quite a few mistakes were made with Common Lisp. The first was that it was too big. The drive was to make the language compatible with the previous dialects and the easiest way was to union these features together. This is generally what happens when you get a committee of guys each with their own input. The language specification explodes.

But for all the size of the CL spec, there are things that are missing from it. The foreign language interface is not defined. Calling the OS is possible in CL but every platform does it differently. Threads and concurrency are nowhere in sight (remember this is 1984).

The Common Lisp community has tried to deal with this through libraries. But these libraries are unsupported, and either undocumented or poorly so. I regard this as partly a weakness of the open source model, but of this another time. But the result is that CL has become unpopular with developers who want a good solution which is free and well supported. For that they turn to Python.

On the academic front CL is not popular as an introduction to functional programming and is the victim of early standardisation. To a degree, CL is a snapshot of functional programming in the '70s. Pattern-matching and static typing are not there. There is much in CL that is heavily procedural, too much so for teachers trying to convey the art of functional programming. The syntax is viewed as unattractive, Larry Wall's comment that 'Lisp has the visual appeal of oatmeal with finger nail clippings mixed in.' is funny and irreverent, but largely true. It's a great language but it doesn't look great.

I guess a review of past mistakes would be incomplete without a look at Lisp machines. In 'The Bipolar Lisp Programmer' I talked about brilliant failures and the Lisp machines were exactly that. The basic idea was simple: make Lisp run fast by making it run on special hardware. The problem was that in the mid-80s standard hardware was doubling in performance every 18 months. So a Lisp machine that promised at the design stage to be 10x faster than conventional hardware might be 5x faster by the time it appeared and that advantage would last only 2 years or so.

Symbolics woke up far too late that the real strength of the company lay in its ideas - in Genera. In our biological terms, they had got stuck on obsessing over the phenotype, and missed the significance of the genotype. So the DNA of Genera got trapped on a dying phenotype and today all that work is a lost investment. Imagine what the Lisp community would be like today if Symbolics had done what Torvalds did later and moved their ideas onto a PC!

When the CL community is exposed to criticism of CL their attitude is confrontational and conservative. For example, nearly every other newbie who hits CL for the first time complains about the brackets. And when they do they are told to shut up because they don't understand Lisp. Actually that response shows that the shushers don't understand Lisp, because the Lisp genotype is not hung on the idea of brackets. Guido van Rossum realised that in creating Python. Python is not new; it's just a sugaring on the Lisp genotype in favour of a syntax that people feel comfortable with. And look how far that idea went.

Along with all these ills went another - **macro laziness**. CL programmers think that macros are absolutely central whereas they are not. In Qi, the defmacro construction could be eliminated from the source without remainder by using the programmable reader. I've left them in because of laziness. But macro laziness arises when a challenge to CL is met by 'I could always write a macro to do that'. It's the same response of the slob on the sofa watching TV and saying 'I can always get into shape'. Actually being in shape and being able to get in shape are not the same. And since CL has stayed on the same sofa for 25 years, getting this fat specification from the supine position and into shape is not easy.

So what lessons do we learn from all this? I make about 7, which is a nice magical number.

1. Don't bet the farm on a cumbersome language standard that is difficult to change and replace.
2. Create a standard approach to common problems like concurrency, threads and OS calling.
3. Hive off stuff into libraries.
4. Absorb the lessons of programming development going on around you.
5. Don't get trapped in a phenotype - whether machine or language.
6. Listen to your critics - particularly newbies.
7. Learn to communicate.

Qi

Now I want to talk a bit about my own work on Qi. By the way, I have pronounced it as 'Q Eye' for years which is wrong. I got the habit from my students. It really should be 'chee' which is the Taoist concept of life force. I'm a Taoist and hope to return to the mountains one day. But right now I'm here in the world of men and so I'll continue talking for a while.

Qi began life in the Laboratory for the Foundations of Computer Science in 1989. It owes its character from observing the activity with Standard ML, since the LFCS was the origin of that particular language. Essentially Qi is a harmonious fusion of three different paradigms; a functional one based on pattern-directed list handling and using sequent calculus to define types; a logic programming component based on Prolog and a language-oriented component based on compiler-compiler technology.

It's a powerful combination and it's not an accidental one. Each component has an important part to play in the coding of Qi. The compiler-compiler is used to frame the reader and writer, the Prolog compiles the sequent calculus to code and the functional language does nearly everything else. The result is that the source is amazingly small - about 2000 lines, but packs a punch like Bruce Lee who was built on the same scale.

The idea of Qi was to provide a programming environment based on CL but with the features of a modern functional programming environment. In fact, Qi is ahead of functional programming design in many of its features. Its generally efficient, being faster in execution than hand-coded native CL and has all the features of the Lisp genotype while being about 3x more compact for programming purposes than CL. It comes with a book and a collection of correctness proofs that nobody reads.

Qi is very powerful, but it is not computationally adequate as it stands. 'Computational adequacy' is a term I've coined to describe the characteristics that a language has when it is adequate for the needs of the programmers of the day. CL was computationally adequate in 1984 but is not today. Computational adequacy today means finding good answers to questions of how to provide threads, concurrency, FFI, GUI support and so on. Qi is not computationally adequate because it is written in CL which is itself not computationally adequate. I'm going to talk about what I've been doing to fix that, because it reflects back on the way that Lisp itself should go.

The general strategy of Qi development can be summed up in 6 aphorisms.

1. Grab the easy stuff.
2. Featurise out differences.
3. Infiltrate don't confront.
4. Isolate the core.
5. The genotype is always more important than the phenotype.
6. Educate people.

Since Qi is written in CL, grabbing the easy stuff meant grabbing the CL libraries and bits of the CL specification. **CLStrings**, **CLMaths** and **CLErrors** are all part of the Qi library and they bring type security to CL maths, string and error handling. CLHash and ClStreams are on the way. They are easy pickings. The combined sum is a lazy week's work.

Parts of the Qi library are not part of CL. **Qi/tk** is the biggest. The type theory of Qi/tk is 511 lines of Qi that generates over 200 rules and axioms of sequent calculus. This in turn generates over 27,000 lines of Common Lisp. But it's quick. A game program of 561 lines type checks and compiles in 5 seconds under CLisp (1-2 seconds under SBCL). It includes constraint propagation that allows you to dynamically link the properties of widgets to each other.

I've begun to featurise out the differences between CL implementations; there is one way to quit, one way to save an image and hopefully one day, one way to call the OS. Our goal is to make the Lisp platform invisible; and by 'Lisp' I'm talking about the Lisp genotype not the phenotype.

'CL is great and Blub is crap' has not worked as a strategy for selling Common Lisp. People invest years of their life learning Blub and don't want to hear this message. A strategy of infiltration is better. The **Q machines** are intended as a collection of machines that cross-compile Qi into any member of the Lisp genotype. Qi compiles into CL, but **Quip** compiles Qi into Python and that already exists. Clojure, Ruby, Perl are later targets. Qi can be used to provide optional type security for untyped languages like Python. The proper destination for Qi is as a universal metalanguage. Write once, run anywhere.

The Kernel Lisp Project: Back to the Future

When I started thinking of porting Qi to other members of the Lisp genotype I looked at the CL sources for Qi. They are amazingly small. About 8,500 lines from 2,000 lines of Qi. Because I'm a conservative coder nearly all of Qi is running on the Lisp 1.5 core. In all there are about 68 primitive functions in Qi and many of them like CADR are not really primitive. If we talk about 'kernel functions' meaning the stuff that is really primitive then we're down to about 50, if that.

This kernel defines a Lisp, call it **Kλ**, that is the kernel necessary to run Qi. Now the interesting bit is that Qi is mapped to Python etc. through a mapping from the Qi-generated Lisp source to the Python language. So by mapping Kλ to Blub, you get a version of Qi that runs under Blub.

Based on this idea, this opens the prospect of a new Lisp that would be effectively a virtual machine for the entire Lisp genotype. Kλ would and should be an enhanced version of Lisp 1.5, getting back to the roots of Lisp. By defining Kλ and running Qi and the Q machine cross-compilers on Kλ, we get a unified platform for the entire Lisp genotype with Qi functionality; state of the art thinking in functional programming across the genotype spectrum.

This process I call **kernelisation** is going to change the shape of a lot of computing in the next decade, in the way that RISC changed hardware in the '80s. In particular the profusion of different languages we have at the moment will be tamed through this technique. Kernelisation is really the computing analogue of **formalisation** - that expression of the mathematician's hunger for simplicity in the expression of formal systems; the fewest primitives and the fewest axioms needed to derive what we take as true. Formalisation issued in a rich developments of mathematical logic like Zermelo-Frankel set theory and it was used to tame the wildness of C19 mathematics. Today I see us as poised to tame computing in the C21 in the same way.

Back to Lisp. What should Kλ look like? I've already given one answer relative to Qi; that it should incorporate all the functions necessary to run Qi. But Qi is itself not complete as a language specification. For example in *Functional Programming in Qi* I don't deal with how to interact with streams. The reason I don't deal with this and other such issues is that CL already deals with them and I assumed those people who wanted to learn how to do this would learn CL. But if Qi becomes portable across the Lisp genotype then that aspect will have to be addressed.

Hence the shape and the form of Kλ is not determined by Qi even though it should support Qi. But the general shape and form are, I think, reasonably clear. There has to be several components of Kλ.

1. **A Turing-equivalent subset based on classical functional programming.** This subset should be *really really* small. For instance you can build a decent functional model using if, = (generic equality), basic arithmetic and λ (for abstractions). Cons, car and cdr are all λ definable. All the utility functions go into a standard library.

2. **It should be dynamically typed but support detailed type annotations.** Qi can provide a wealth of detail about the types of Lisp

expressions which compilers can eat up. Kernel Lisp needs to be able to use this.

3. **It should support arrays, streams, concurrency, error handling in a straightforward way.** CLErrors is tiny but does what I need. One objection is that we still don't know how best to handle concurrency. But that does not matter, we can decide conventions on calling concurrency and leave it to developers to decide how to implement it.

4. **There should be an open source, freely available Kλ library for CL.** CL survives in library form. CL developers can load this library. Kλ would be an enormous help for implementers of CL. Right now there is too much reduplicated effort going on in a small community for CL to prosper. Putting all the stuff in a library would leave developers free to optimize Kλ and would improve Lisp performance no end.

To continue with the biological metaphor, Qi has wonderful viral characteristics; it is small and easy to move and because of its conservative encoding it will fit comfortably into Kλ. Once established on top of any instance of the Lisp genotype it forms a symbiotic relation with the host language improving the general well-being of the language it symbiotes. I hope with the help of the functional community we can make this dream happen.

(The Shen project was sponsored 18 months after this talk of May 2009 and the first version of Shen appeared in September 2011)

Bibliography

Abelson H. and Sussman G.J.
Structure and Interpretation of Computer Programs, 2nd edition, MIT Press, 1996.

Abramsky S., Gabbay D.M. and Maibaum T.S.
Handbook of Logic in Computer Science, vols. 1-6, Clarendon Press, Oxford, 1993-5.

Adams A. A.
"INDUCT: A Logical Framework for Induction over Natural Numbers and Lists built in SEQUEL", M.Sc. thesis, Leeds Computer Studies 1994.

Aho A.V. and Ullman J.D.
The Theory of Parsing, Translation and Compiling. Vol. 1 Englewood Cliffs, NJ: Prentice Hall, 1972.

Aiken A. and Murphy B.
"Static type inference in a dynamically typed language" In Proc. 18th ACM Symposium on Principles of Programming Languages, 1991.

Aiken A. et al.
"Soft typing with Dependent Types", In Proc. 18th *ACM Symposium on Principles of Programming Languages*, 1994.

Ait-Kaci H. and Podelski A.
"Towards a meaning of LIFE", *Journal of Logic Programming*, 1993.

Allen J.
The Anatomy of Lisp, McGraw-Hill, 1978.

Andrews P.B.
"Theorem Proving via General Matings", JACM 28, 2, 1981.

Aubin R.
"Mechanising Structural Induction", Theoretical Computer Science, 1979.

Baber R.L.
The Spine of Software: Designing Provably Correct Software, Theory and Practice, Chichester: Wiley, 1987.

Backhouse R.
"Constructive Type Theory: a perspective from computing science" in Dijkstra (ed.) 1990.

Backus J.
"Can Programming be liberated from the von Neumann style? A functional style and its algebra of programs", *CACM*, 1978.

Baeten J. and J. Bergstra
"Term Rewriting Systems with Priorities", in *Rewriting Techniques and Applications*, LNCS 256, Springer-Verlag, 1986.

Barendregt H.P.
The Lambda Calculus: its syntax and semantics, North Holland, 1984.

Barendregt H.P.
"Lambda Calculus with Types", in Abramsky, Gabbay and Maibaum, vol. 2, 1993.

Bartree T.
Digital computer Fundamentals, Tata-McGraw-Hill, 2004

Basin D.A. & Kaufmann M.
"The Boyer-Moore Prover and NuPrl: An Experimental Comparison", *Logical Frameworks*, CUP, 1991.

Beckert B. and Posegga J.
"leanT^{A}P: Lean Tableau-based Deduction", JAR 1997.

Bibel W.
"On matrices with connections", J. ACM 1981.

Bibel W. and Jorrand P.
Fundamentals of Artificial Intelligence: an advanced course, Springer-Verlag, 1986.

Bird R.S.
"The Promotion and Accumulation Strategies in Transformational Programming", *ACM Transactions on Programming Languages and Systems* 6, 1984.

Bird R. and Wadler P.
Introduction to Functional Programming, Prentice-Hall, 1998.

Blasius K.H. and Burckert H.J.
Deduction Systems in Artificial Intelligence, Ellis Horwood, 1989.

Bobrow D.G. and Winograd T.
"An Overview of KRL", *Cognitive Science* I, 1977.

Boolos G.S., Burgess J.P. and Jeffrey R.C.
Computability and Logic, 4th edition, Cambridge University Press, 2002.

Boyer R. S. and Moore J. S.
A Computational Logic, Academic Press, 1979.

Boyer R. S. and Moore J. S.
A Computational Logic Handbook, Academic Press, 1997.

Baier C. and Katoen J.
Principles of Model Checking, MIT Press, 2008.

Bratko I.
Prolog Programming for Artificial Intelligence, Addison-Wesley, 2000.

de Bruijn N.G.
"Lambda Calculus Notation with Nameless Dummies, a tool for automatic formula manipulation, with application to the Church-Rosser theorem", Indag. Math., 1972.

Bundy A.
The Mechanisation of Mathematical Reasoning, Academic Press, 1983.

Bundy A., Stevens A., Harmelen F., Ireland A., & Smaill A.
"Rippling: A heuristic for guiding inductive proofs", *Artificial Intelligence* 1993.

Burstall R. A and Darlington J.
"A Transformation Program for Developing Recursive Programs", *Journal of the ACM*, 24, 1977.

Burstall R.., MacQueen D., Sannella D.: HOPE: An Experimental Applicative Language. LISP Conference 1980:

Cardelli L.
"The Functional Abstract Machine", *Polymorphism*, vol. 1., #1, 1983.

Cartwright R. and Fagan M.
"Soft typing". In *Proc. SIGPLAN '91 Conference on Programming Language Design and Implementation*, 1991, 278--292.

Cerrito S. and Kesner D.
"Pattern Matching as Cut Elimination", *Logic in Computer Science*, 1999.

Chang C. and Lee R.
Symbolic Logic and Mechanical Theorem Proving, Academic Press, 1973.

Charniak E. and McDermott D.
Introduction to Artificial Intelligence, Addison Wesley, 1985.

Church A.
"A Note on the Entscheidungsproblem", *Journal of Symbolic Logic*, 1936.

Church A.
The Calculi of Lambda Conversion, Princeton University Press, 1941.

Codd E.
"Relational Completeness of Data Base Sublanguages". Database Systems: 65–98

Colby K.
Artificial Paranoia, New York: Pergamon Press, 1975.

Constable R.
Implementing Mathematics with the Nuprl Proof Development System, Createspace, 2012.

Cooke D.J. and Bez H.E.
Computer Mathematics, Cambridge University Press, 1984.

Date C. J. and Darwen H.
The SQL Standard, 4th edition, Addison-Wesley, 1996.

Darlington J., Henderson P., and Turner D.A.
Functional Programming and its Applications, an advanced course, Cambridge University Press, 1982.

Davis M. and Putnam H.
"A Computing Procedure for Quantification Theory", *Journal of the Association of Computing Machinery*, 1960.

DeMillo R., Lipton R., and Perlis A.
"Social Processes and Proofs of Theorems and Programs", *Communications of the ACM* 22, 1979.

Dijkstra E.W.
Formal Development of Programs and Proofs, Addison-Wesley, 1990.

Diller A.
Compiling Functional Languages, John Wiley, 1988.

Diller A.
Z: an Introduction to Formal Methods, John Wiley, 1990.

Dreyfus, H. L.
What computers can't do : a critique of artificial reason, New York: Harper & Row, 1972.

Dreyfus, H. L.
What computers still can't do: a critique of artificial reason Cambridge, Mass. London: MIT Press, 1992.

Duffy D.
Principles of Automated Theorem Proving, Wiley, 1991.

Eder E.
"An Implementation of a Theorem Prover Based on the Connection Method", *Artificial Intelligence*, ed. Bible and Petkoff, North-Holland, 1985.

Eisinger N. and Nonnengart A.
"Term Rewriting Systems", in Blasius and Burckert, 1989.

Emmer, M..
SNOBOL4+: The SNOBOL4 Language for the Personal Computer User. Englewood Cliffs, NJ: Prentice Hall, 1985

Faé M. I. and Tarver M.
"Wardrop's Principle Revisited: a multiagent approach", *ANPET 2002*.

Ferber J.
Multi-Agent Systems: An Introduction to Distributed Artificial Intelligence, Addison Wesley, 1999

Fetzer J.H.
Communications of the ACM 31, 1988.
Artificial Intelligence: its Scope and Limits, Kluwer Academic Publishers, 1990.

Field A. J. and Harrison P. G.
Functional Programming, Addison-Wesley, 1988.

Fitting M.
Proof Methods for Modal and Intuitionistic Logics, Synthese library, 1983.

Frost R.A.
Introduction to Knowledge Based Systems, Collins, 1986.

Futumara Y.
"Partial Computation of Programs", in Goto ed. *RIMS Symposia on Software Engineering and Science*, LNCS, Springer-Verlag 1983.

Gabbay D.M. and Robinson J.A.
Handbook of Logic in Artificial Intelligence and Logic Programming Hogger C.J. Vols 1-6, Clarendon Press, Oxford, 1993.

Gallier J.N., Plaisted D., Ecqstz S. and Snyder W.
"An algorithm for finding canonical sets of ground rewrite rules in polynomial time", *Journal of the ACM*, 1993.

Gabrial R.P.
"Lisp: Good News, Bad News, How to Win Big", *European Conference on Practical Applications of Lisp*, 1990.

Gardner M.
Logic Machines and Diagrams, University of Chicago Press, 1983.

Gentzen G.
Investigations into logical deduction (first published 1934) in *The Collected Papers of Gerhard Gentzen* (Szabo, ed.), Amsterdam, North Holland 1969.

Giarratano J.C. and Riley G. D.
Expert Systems: Principles and Programming (3rd edition), PWS, 1998.

Girard J.Y., Lafont Y. and Taylor P.
Proofs and Types, Cambridge University Press, 1989.

Gordon M.J.
Programming Language Theory and its Implementation, Prentice Hall, 1988.

Gordon M.J., Milner R. and Wadsworth P.
Programming in the Edinburgh LCF, Springer-Verlag, 1979

Gray P.
Logic, Algebra and Databases, Ellis-Horwood, 1984.

Green J. A.
Sets and Groups, Library of Mathematics, Routledge and Kegan Paul, 1965.

Green C.
Theorem-proving by resolution as a basis for question-answering systems, Machine Intelligence 4, 1969.

Grune D. and Jacobs C.J.H.
Parsing Techniques: a practical guide, Ellis Horwood, 1991.

Gunter C.
The Semantics of Programing Languages: Structures and Techniques, MIT Press, 1992.

Haack S.
Deviant Logic, Cambridge University Press, 1974.

Haack S.
Philosophy of Logics, Cambridge University Press, 1978.

Haynes C.
"Logic Continuations", *Journal of Logic Programming* 4, 1987.

Helman P. & Veroff R.
Walls and Mirrors, Addison-Wesley, 2005.

Hendrix G.
"Encoding Knowledge in Partitioned Networks" in *Associative Networks*, ed. N. Findler, Academic Press 1979.

Henglein F.
"Global tagging optimisation by type inference" in ACM Conference on LISP and Functional Programming, 1992.

Henkin L.
"Systems, Formal and Models of", in Edwards P. (chief editor), *The Encyclopaedia of Philosophy*, MacMillan and Free Press, 1967.

Henson M.C.
Elements of Functional Languages, Blackwell, 1987.

Hewitt C.E.
"PLANNER: A Language for Proving Theorems in Robots", *IJCAI* 1969.

Hindley J.R. and Seldin J.P
Introduction to Combinators and Lambda Calculus,. Cambridge University Press, 1986.

Hodges W.
Logic, Pelican, 1977.

Hogger C.J.
Introduction to Logic Programming, London, Academic Press, 1984.

Hogger C.J.
Essentials of Logic Programming, Oxford, Clarendon, 1990.

Holmes B.J.
Introductory Pascal, DP Publications, 1993.

Hughes G. E. and Cresswell M.J.
An Introduction to Modal Logic, Methuen, 1968.

Hughes G. E. and Cresswell M.J.
A Companion to Modal Logic, Methuen, 1984.

Hughes G.E. and Cresswell M.J.,
A New Introduction to Modal Logic, Routledge, 1996

Hughes J.
"Why Functional Programming Matters", in Turner D.A. (ed.), *Research Topics in Functional Programming*, Addison-Wesley, 1990.

Ito T. and Halstead R.H.
Parallel Lisp: Languages and Systems, LNCS 441, Springer-Verlag, 1989.

Jackson P.
Introduction to Expert Systems, International Computer Science Series, 1999.

Jones N.D., Sestoft P. and Sondergaard H.
"An Experiment in Partial Evaluation: The Generation of a Compiler Generator", in Jouannaud 1985.

Jorrand P.
"Term Rewriting as a Basis for the Design of a Functional and Parallel Programming Language", in W.Bibel and Jorrand P. (ed.) 1986.

Jouannaud J.P.
Rewriting Techniques and Applications, LNCS, vol. 202, Springer-Verlag 1985.

Kac M. and Ulam S.
Mathematics and Logic, Pelican, 1971.

Keene S.E.
Object-Oriented Programming in Common Lisp: A Programmer's Guide to CLOS, Addison-Wesley, 1989.

Kernighan B.W. and Plauger P. J.
"Ratfor – a Preprocessor for a Rational Fortran", *Software, Practice and Experience*, 1975.

Kleene S.C.
Introduction to Metamathematics, North Holland, 1952.

Knight K.
"Unification: a multidisciplinary survey", in *ACM Computing Surveys*, 1989.

Knuth D.E. and Bendix P.B.
"Simple Word Problems in Universal Algebras", in Leech (ed.), *Computational Problems in Abstract Algebras*, Pergamon Press, 1970.

Knuth D.E.
The Art of Computer Programming, Sorting and Searching, Addison-Wesley, Reading, Massachussetts, 1998

Kounalis E. and Rusinowitch M.
"Mechanising Inductive Reasoning", Bulletin of the European Association for Theoretical Computer Science.

Kowalski R.
Logic for Problem Solving, North Holland, 1979.

Kripke S.
"Identity and Necessity", in Munitz M. (ed.), *Identity and Individuation*, New York 1971.

Lajos G.
"Language Directed Programming in Meta-Lisp", *First European Conference on Practical Applications of Lisp*, 1990.

Landin P.
"The Mechanical Evaluation Of Expressions", *Computer Journal*, 6, 1964.

Lemmon E. J.
Beginning Logic, Hackett Publishing Co., 1978.

Lenat D. B. and Guha R. V.
"The Evolution of CYCL, the CYC Representation Language", *SIGART Bulletin*, 1991.

Linsky L. (ed.)
Reference and Modality , Oxford University Press, 1975.

Liu Y. and Staples J.
"btC: an Extension of C with Backtracking", *Proceedings of the Sixth International Conference on Symbolic and Logical Computing, Dakota State University*, 1993.

Lam C.W.H.
"How Reliable is a Computer Based Proof?" *Mathematical Intelligencer* 12, 1,1990.

Lipson J.D.
Elements of Algebra and Algebraic Computing, Benjamin Cummings, 1984.

Lloyd J.
Foundations of Logic Programming, Springer-Verlag, 1990.

Lopes R.H.C.
"Inductive Generalisation of Proof Search Strategies from Examples", Ph.D. thesis, School of Computer Studies, University of Leeds, 1998.

Loveland D. W. (ed)
Automatic Theorem Proving: After 25 years, American Mathematical Society, 1984.

Maier D. and Warren D.S.
Computing with Logic, Benjamin/Cummings, 1988.

Martelli A. and Montenari U.
"Unification in Linear Time and Space", Internal Report B76-16, Insituto di Elaborazione di Informatione, Pisa, Italy, 1973.

McCarthy J.
"Recursive Functions, Symbolic Expressions and their Computation by Machine", *Comm. of the ACM*, 1960.

McCarthy, J.
"History of Lisp". *ACM Sigplan Not.* 13,8 (Aug. 1978), 217-223.

McCarthy J.
"Circumscription: a form of non-monotonic reasoning", *Artificial Intelligence* 13, 1980.

McDermott D. and Doyle J.
"Non-monotonic logic", *Artificial Intelligence* 13, 1980.

McDermott D.
"A Critique of Pure Reason", *Computational Intelligence 3*, 1987.

Mendelson E.
Introduction to Mathematical Logic, Chapman and Hall, 2009.

Minsky M.
"A Framework for Representing Knowledge", in Winston P. (ed.), *The Psychology of Computer Vision*, McGraw-Hill, 1975.

Murch R. and Johnson T.
Intelligent Software Agents, Prentice Hall, 1998.

Nipkow T., Paulson L. and Wendel M.
Isabelle/HOL: A Proof Assistant for Higher-Order Logic, Springer, 2002.

O'Donnell M.J.
Equational Logic as a Programming Language, MIT Press, 1985.

Ousterhout, John K.; Jones, Ken
Tcl and the Tk Toolkit (2nd ed.). Addison Wesley, (2006).

Paulson L.
ML for the Working Programmer, Cambridge University Press 1996.

Paulson L.
Logic and Computation: Interactive Proof with Cambridge LC, CUP, 1990.

Peirce B.
Types and Programming Languages, MIT Press, 2002.

Pettorossi A.
"A Powerful Strategy for Deriving Efficient Programs by Transformation" *ACM Symposium on LISP and Functional Programming*, 1984.

Peyton-Jones S. and Lester D.
Implementing Functional Languages, Prentice-Hall, 1987.

Plaisted D.
"Equational Reasoning and Term Rewriting Systems" in Gabbay, Hogger and Robinson, vol. 1, 1993.

Post E.
"Formal Reductions of the General Combinatorial Decision Problem", American Journal of Mathematics, vol. 65, 1943.

Quillian M.R.
"Semantic Memory", in Minsky M. (ed.), *Semantic Information Processing*, MIT Press, 1968.

Reeves S. and Clarke M.
Logic in Computer Science, Prentice-Hall, 1990.

Reiter R.
"A Logic for Default Reasoning", *Artificial Intelligence* 13, 1980.

Reppy J.H.
Concurrent Programming in ML, Cambridge University Press, 2007

Robinson J.
"A Machine-Oriented Logic Based on the Resolution Principle", *Journal of the ACM*, 1965

Robinson J.A. and Sibert E.E.
"Logic Programming in Lisp", research report, School of Computer and Information Science, Syracuse University, New York, 1980.

Russell S. and Norvig P.
Artificial Intelligence: a modern approach, Prentice Hall Series in Artificial Intelligence, first edition 1995, second edition 2002.

Schwartz J.T., Dewar R.B.K., Dubinsky, E., and Schonberg, E
Programming with Sets: an introduction to SETL, Springer-Verlag, 1986.

Shrobe H.
"Symbolic Computing Architectures", *Exploring Artificial Intelligence*, ed. Shrobe and AAAI, Morgan Kaufmann, 1988.

Simon H.
Models of my Life, New York, Basic Books, 1991.

Sitaram D.
"Handling Control",   Proceedings of the SIGPLAN Conference on Programming
Language Design and Implementation, 1993.

Slater R.
Portraits in Silicon, MIT Press, 1989.

Sloman A.
"POPLOG: a multi-purpose multi-language program development environment", *Artificial Intelligence - Industrial and Commercial Applications.   First International Conference*. 1985

Smullyan R.
First Order Logic, Springer-Verlag, 1968.

Smullyan R.
Theory of Formal Systems, Princeton University Press, 1960.

Steele G.
Common Lisp: the Language, Digital Press, 1990.

Sterling L. and Shapiro E.
The Art of Prolog, MIT Press, 1994.

Stickel M.E.
"A PROLOG Technology Theorem-Prover" in *New Generation Computing 2*, 1984.

Stickel M.E.
"A Prolog Technology Theorem Prover: Implementation by an extended Prolog Compiler",
CADE 8, LNCS vol 230, Springer-Verlag, 1986.

Stickel M.E.
"An Introduction to Automated Deduction" in W. Bibel and P. Jorrand (ed.), 1986.

Sussman G. J. and Steele G. L., Jr.
"Scheme: An Interpreter for Extended Lambda Calculus" *AI Memos* (MIT AI Lab), 1975.

Tarver M.
"Towards a Unified Theorem Proving Language", M.Sc. thesis, *University of Leeds, School of Computer Studies*, 1989.

Tarver M.
"The World's Smallest Compiler-Compiler", *European Conference on Practical Applications of Lisp*, 1990.

Tarver M.
"A Rationalisation of Lisp", *University of Leeds, School of Computer Studies Report 90.19*, 1990.

Tarver M.
"An Algorithm for Inducing Tactics from Proofs", *University of Leeds, School of Computer Studies Internal Report,* 1992.

Tarver M.
"A Language for Implementing Arbitrary Logics", *IJCAI*, 1993.

Tarver M.
"Representing the Types of Polyadic Lisp Functions", in *International Lisp Conference* 2002.

Tarver M.
Logic, Proof and Computation, 2nd edition FastPrint, 2014.

Tecuci G.
Building Intelligent Agents, Academic Press, 1998.

Thompson S.
Miranda: the Craft of Functional Programming (second Edition), Addison-Wesley, 1995.

Thompson S.
Haskell: the Craft of Functional Programming (second Edition), Addison-Wesley, 1999.

Thompson S.
Type Theory and Functional Programming, Addison-Wesley 1991.

Thompson S.
Haskell: the Craft of Functional Programming (second Edition), Addison-Wesley, 1999.

Torkel F.
Logic programming and the intuitionistic sequent calculus. SICS Research Report, 1988.

Turner D. A.
SASL Language Manual, University of St Andrews Dept. of Computer Science Report, 1976.

Turner D. A.
"A New Implementation Technique for Applicative Languages", in *Software Practice and Experience*, 1979.

Turner D. A.
"Recursion Equations as a Programming Language", in Darlington, Henderson and Turner, 1982.

Turner D. A.
"An Overview of Miranda" in Turner (ed.) 1990.

Turner D. A. (ed.)
Research Topics in Functional Programming, Addison-Wesley, 1990.

Walther C.
"Many-sorted unification", *Journal of the ACM*, 1988.

Wand M.
"Continuation Based Program Transformation Strategies", *Journal of the ACM*, 27, 1980.
Warren D. "An Abstract Prolog Instruction Set", Technical Note 309, SRI International, Menlo Park, 1983.

Wikstrom A.
Functional Programming Using Standard ML, Prentice-Hall, 1987.

Winograd T.
"Understanding Natural Language", *Cognitive Psychology* 1972.

Wright A. and Cartwright R.
"A practical soft type system for Scheme", *1994 ACM Conference on LISP and Functional Programming*, 1994.

Index of System Functions Used in this Book

Index

A

B

C

D

E

S

T